How to
CHEAT
at
EVERYTHING

How to
CHEAT
at
EVERYTHING

*A Con Man Reveals
the Secrets of the Esoteric Trade
of Cheating, Scams, and Hustles*

SIMON LOVELL

RUNNING PRESS
PHILADELPHIA • LONDON

Copyright © 1996, 2003 by Ed Rosenthal and Steve Kubby

First published by Thunder's Mouth Press in 1996

Library of Congress Cataloging-in-Publication Data is available

ISBN-13: 978-1-56025-973-2

Book design by Simon M. Sullivan

This book may be ordered by mail from the publisher.
Please include $2.50 for postage and handling.
But try your bookstore first!

Hachette Book Group
1290 Avenue of the Americas
New York, NY, 10104

Contents

Bar Bets

Some Bigger Hustles

Unfairgrounds And Crooked Carnivals

More Street Cons and Others

Cheating At Cards

Cheating With Dice

Sneaky Ways To Beat The System!

Acknowledgments

WHEN YOU ATTEMPT A PROJECT OF THIS SIZE YOU NEED LOTS OF HELP AND I'VE been lucky enough to have some of the best. In no particular order big thanks are due to the following splendid folk . . .

Andrew J. Pinard for coming up with the idea of using sequential art to illustrate the book, convincing Louis to pay for it, and getting Alan Wassilak to put his talented pen on the drawing board (not to mention Andrew's superb work at putting all the writing and photographs together in a readable form)!

Carl Mercurio for taking on the monumental task of editing and proofreading the manuscript.

Bruce Walstead for his technical advice and notes in the carnival section.

Todd Robbins and Wesley James for additional material and front words.

Alan Wassilak for his fabulous graphic vignettes!

Tom Gilbert, Carl Mercurio, Todd Robbins and Steve Lerner for additional photographs.

Michael, Jamy and all the gang at Monday Night Magic for continued support and encouragement.

Izzy and Ida, the greatest and kindest landlords in the universe!

Pia and Walter, whose friendship keeps me sane (well as sane as I ever get!).

Louis Falanga and the gang at L&L Publishing for constantly allowing me to break deadlines!

And finally, a big thank you to all the shadier characters I've met over the years who have been kind enough to share some, if not all, of their work with me. You know who you are!!

"Life is only a game of poker, played well or ill
Some hold four aces, some draw or fill
Some make a bluff and oft get there
While others ante and never hold a pair"

———•———

The suicide note of San Francisco gambler Pat Hogan,
written, somewhat poignantly, upon an ace of hearts.

Foreword
Wesley James

WHEN I FIRST MET SIMON LOVELL, SOME TWELVE YEARS AGO BY MY TALLY, I knew of him only by his reputation, only as a fellow who performed a novel yet deceptive Second Deal. Our first meeting came at the annual gathering of a by-invitation-only group of the world's best sleight-of-hand performers. I had no notion of his membership in the zany fringe of the British comedy community. I also had no inkling of his affinity or affection for the secret and guarded world of the con man. To this day, Simon remains a curious balance of droll free-form poet, benevolent lunatic, serious practitioner of the craft of sleight-of-hand and devoted student of the short con. These divergent elements of his ranging interest became evident, however, almost from the first. I learned during the first days of our acquaintance that he had assembled much of the information that is a part of this volume. I learned also that he is quick with a glib, if non sequitur, rejoinder and affable in most any situation. This, combined with his passion for the afore-mentioned subjects, in which we share devotion, has been the cornerstone of our novel relationship. We often laugh at how others misunderstand the way we interact. Our animated discussions seem to persuade others we are on the verge of fisticuffs yet there has always been a shared joy in the fervor of our exchanges. The passion that has fueled our friendly disputes also drove this work. I have looked forward with whetted anticipation to the day this collection would become available. Today is the day and the fruit is tasty.

Any work, whatever its genre or perspective, can only be fairly judged by the goals it sets for itself. It is grossly unfair to judge a wine as flawed because it makes a poor beer. Simon has set himself a herculean task in crafting this volume. Presenting so much information of such diverse and arcane nature in a form that is both readable and accessible is no mean feat. The task is all the more challenging because it demands, as prerequisite, that one have accumulated and assembled the knowledge in the first place. Most prior works of this broad type have been somewhat academic in tone, more tutorial than entertainment, more preparatory than protective but always with a sense of distance. Those who have undertaken such quasi-educational compilations have endeavored to remain removed from the fray, judging from a preachy perch. Mr. Lovell has set about to present more of the mind-set of the immoral denizens who persuade themselves they are merely amoral. This outlook is difficult to embrace for those who do not share it yet, in its way, appealing for the color and edge such a life view spawns. Dostoevsky and Runyon might smile for, to the degree it succeeds, this work allows the reader to invade the mind of the impure of heart without becoming impure.

Simon's task was to balance these disparate elements in this one rather-sizable volume. While each reader will perforce judge their experience of the work for him/herself, there are criteria one can apply in determining his achievement: Do you come away from reading this work with a wide range of knowledge you did not have prior? Failing that, do you find it a more complete assemblage of such arcane material than you have found elsewhere? Do you find Freddy, the protagonist of this spicy yarn, colorful, despite his meager morals? Does Freddy help hold the information together, putting a human face on what could be a dry compilation of data? Finally, will you find yourself referring to this work whenever you cross paths with some hustle, scam or con that threatens your bankroll, hopefully before forking over your money?

I suspect the answer to most of the above questions will, for many, be a resounding, "Yes!" A few will find issues raised herein propound a moral quagmire; few cons prove effective on the completely honorable. Still, there is no culpability in being a con's target. Without offering the cheat any absolution, one does share complicity in being a con's victim. Remember that this book is not a primer for the cheat-in-training but an advisory for the would-be victim. If you come away wiser, cannier and just a bit more suspicious of any deal that looks too good, this book will have served its purpose. Thank Freddy the Fox and Simon Lovell, your guides on the road to enlightened skepticism. Mr. Lovell will have achieved his goal and you, good reader, will be amply rewarded for having enlisted this recording of his lifetime of experiences.

June 30, 2002

Read This, Bugger!

Todd Robbins

OKAY, IF YOU ARE AT THIS MOMENT STANDING IN A STORE BROWSING THROUGH this book to see if it is something you should buy, then close it right now, go to a salesperson and buy it. Don't read any more, BUY IT NOW! I mean, if I know enough about you that I know you are reading this, then I know enough about you to know what you need. BUY THE BOOK NOW!

Okay, so I'm going to assume you have bought this book and you are sitting at home reading it. This is good. You need this book. You are an inquisitive person and that is good. You have an independent mind. You are someone that looks at all sides of a thing before making up your mind. You have a better than average education, but school was not a complete experience for you. I will go so far as to say that what you have learned in life you have really taught yourself. It is clear that you are the kind of person that will continue to keep an open mind and learn all throughout your life. You have a strong sense of curiosity.* This is a good thing, but it can also get you into trouble. This book will help avoid some of that trouble.

You see, there is a lovely group of people out there that are interested in you. What they do is known by many names . . . cons, scams, cheats, flim flam, grift, advantage play and other glorious euphonisms. The only reason they are interested in you is because you have money. And since you are an inquisitive person, they will play upon this and entice you to become interested in what they have to offer. If they get you to become more interested in what they have to offer than you are interested in your money then they

---

*The preceding sentences are an example of cold reading technique used by Gypsy fortune tellers and TV hotline psychics. They will lay on the flattering generalities to soften you up, and soon you will start to believe that there is something legit about it all. That's when they will hit you up for big bucks to remove a curse, make contact with some dead relative, do an in depth reading, past life regressions, psychic development classes or other crap. The origins of this scam go back before recorded time and it's embarrassing how well it still works today.

will get your money. And after it is all over, you will find that what they got you to be interested in is really not that interesting after all.

This book will help keep that from happening. In these pages, you will find a wondrous array of scenarios and techniques specifically designed to separate the inquisitive from their hard earned money. Read about them, remember them and walk the other way if you should see them coming down the pike in your direction.

In the years that I have been in this business we call Show, I've had the opportunity to rub up against some of the folks that make a living by employing these various scenarios and techniques. Fortunately, the contact I have made with them has been purely social. They have looked upon me kindly since I am a magician.

In a way, we are distant members of the same family. We both use deception to pay the rent. Since I am kin but not competition, and they are like the craftsmen that takes pride in their work and enjoys talking about it with someone that can appreciate their handy work, these folks have told me about a number of the things they have done. And the things they have done (and will do again, I have no doubt) will be found in the following pages.

Simon Lovell has spent more time with these shady beings and has gone much deeper into their world than I have. When Simon talks about the subject of deceit, I listen, for I know there is the ring of truth to what he puts forth.

And that is why I am writing this. He has put down so much of what he knows about the topic in the chapters ahead. It is the real thing, for he has only chronicled that which he has encountered. I heartily encourage you to read and heed the lessons he lays out before you.

But two warnings must be made before you go further. Only a fool would read this book and try to pull off any of the ruses that you are about to read. I'm not going to waste time writing about the dire consequences of that course of action. I don't think you are that stupid, so that's all the warning needed in this area.

What concerns me is that you might read this book and think you know enough to beat the cheat at his own game. This is an idea that can only be classified as bad. Let's say, for instance that you find the winning card in a "game" of Three Card Monte. You quickly pick up the money and go on your way. You see, the problem is that you think the game is over, but to the person you are playing against, you have just upped the stakes. This person will get their money back and probably take all of yours in the process. It will not be surprising if they find your body in a dark alleyway, pockets empty and the words, "A little knowledge is a dangerous thing" carved into your lifeless flesh.

So do yourself a favor. Read the book and learn what to avoid. And as your absorb this tome, you will also be getting a graduate course in human behavior and psychology. Plus, you'll find it entertaining how devilishly clever the workings of this malevolent material can be. So, you see, this book will amaze and amuse. It's what an inquisitive person like you needs.

Introduction

THIS IS A BOOK ABOUT CHEATING.

Not the cheating you see in Western films or read about in James Bond novels. This is a book about *real* cheating.

Most people assume that cheats and con men are relatively rare animals that they are unlikely to ever meet. They argue that even if they did meet one the con would be so obvious that they would never fall for it. Card players, for example, will say that they only play with friends on a Friday night and, as such, are safe. "*Friends don't cheat friends*," they will say. "*Anyway the stakes are low, who would bother!*"

Hopefully this book may help to change such idiotic attitudes. The cheat is a common animal (*Cheatus Commonus*) who infests life at every level. Not only are you quite likely to meet one during your lifetime, but may well already have done so without realizing it.

Within the pages of this book you'll see the techniques of a top-notch cheat and hustler known to his associates as *Freddy the Fox*. The methods are real and are described *exactly* as they are being used today. I know they work. I've used some of them myself!

Professional cheats may specialize in learning just one or two tough moves to take your money. The rash amateur will try anything. Some techniques take just minutes to learn while others can take years of dedicated practice. You will see them all here. You will also learn how odds can be calculated and, more importantly, twisted. There's a visit to a traveling carnival that will open your eyes wide. There are con games that will curl your toes.

Some will sound like fiction.

They are *all* real.

It could be argued that, by exposing the methods of the cheats, I am encouraging others to learn and copy them. That is a possibility but I think it's unlikely. Cheats are not made, they are born. The slight disadvantage of someone picking up these techniques is far outweighed by the protection such exposure will give to the ordinary man or woman who, after careful reading, will have a fighting chance of knowing how to avoid being taken.

Many cheating methods are as ingenious as they are criminal. Some require tremendous skill. Still others need an enormous understanding of human psychology.

You will see them *all*!

You'll learn how a cheat is put into operation. Not just the moment of the cheat but the set up, the talk and the final sting. You'll learn *everything* you need to know.

Cheats like Freddy may not be too happy about seeing this book in print but, then again, they'll probably just argue that, *"Even a person with knowledge can be conned or cheated by an expert."* I suspect they may be right. Just knowing about cheating is not enough. You have to be on your guard at *all* times. A cheat may be a stranger but may also be your best friend.

Strangely, the safest games to play in are those where top notch gamblers play for big money. They play in an atmosphere of icy distrust of each other. They all know a great deal about cheating and, for them, there are no friends at the table. It's all about money. The game is *business*! With their knowledge and constant attention to what is going on a cheat would need steel balls to ply his trade. It's been done but only by a handful of the best of the best. At the other end of the scale, in the real world, the infestation becomes thicker and you need to develop the keen eyes of the pro. You don't have to play in a big money game to gain the same attitude as those players. Whether it's for thousands of dollars or just a few cents, you can learn to *think* like a pro.

Learn to spot the build up to a con or hustle and be aware that anybody, any time, could be trying to make a mug out of you.

Don't think it can't happen to you.

Just assume that it *will* at some time.

A Quick Note

ALTHOUGH THE CHEATS AND HUSTLERS REFERRED TO HERE ARE PRIMARILY described as being of the male gender it should be noted that there are plenty of female cheats around. Yes, my friends, the fairer and gentler sex can be equally as devious as the men who haunt the shady world you are about to enter!

So, if you ever lose a bundle of money to a pretty lady, don't say you weren't warned!

Freddy The Fox

BIG FREDDY THE FOX IS THE SORT OF MAN WHO WOULD NOT ONLY SELL HIS mother for a profit but probably already has. If he has then it's also very likely that he stole her back to re-sell her again at a later date.

The Fox is a professional gambler. Unlike most gamblers he never loses, not *ever*! You see, just between the Fox and us, he has a little advantage over other players. He cheats.

Over the last twenty years or so the Fox and I have become pretty close friends. So close that twice he has almost told me his real name and, on one very memorable occasion, almost let me beat him in a game of pool. I have watched him hustle bar bets for a beer, play darts for five hundred dollars a game and calmly pick up the keys to a sports car in lieu of cash in a poker game. He is so persuasive that, every now and then, I am tempted to take on one of his little bets. I have never beaten him.

Just lately though a change has come over the Fox. Maybe he's seen the light, maybe the whiskey has finally got to him or, and much more likely in the opinion of the few who know him well, maybe he's constructing one last great con to convince God that his soul is being cleansed and that, when he finally pops his clogs, he should be allowed into that great casino in the sky. Whatever the reason, the Fox wants to come clean. He wants you, the mug suckers and marks of the world, to know how it's all done.

"Winning isn't everything," says Freddy, *"But it beats the crap out of losing."* Freddy has seen so many people lose, mostly to him, over the years that he seems to be getting a little bored with it all. He wants to take on a whole new role in life and, amazing though it seems to his friends, play the good guy. He seems to have decided that the best way to do this is to become the self-elected champion of the common man. He wants to change you from a wimp into a Rambo. He wants you to be so armed with knowledge that you'll never get hustled again. Well that's what Freddy says. Personally I go for the last great con theory. I suspect that the less than

humble fee he suggested for his experiences may also have something to do with it.

Whatever, the new Freddy is a lovable rogue; but the story he tells is real. Cheating is a multi-million dollar a year industry. It goes on everywhere. Don't think it can't happen to you because that's when it is often most likely to! The pros will tell you that, *even armed with knowledge*, you can be hustled. Hopefully though, if you learn your lessons well, their job will be that much harder. In much the same way that a car alarm won't stop your car from being stolen, it will at least put off all but the most determined of crooks. Actually, Freddy tells a wonderful tale of a guy having the alarm itself stolen from his car, but that's for another time.

It is not the Fox's objective to turn out a whole new breed of hustlers. Knowing and doing are two completely different things. Should you decide to fill up a silver hip flask and don a gray Fedora hat, it's more than likely that you'll come a cropper. People like Freddy aren't made, they are born.

But for every Freddy there are hundreds of part time cheats who are out to get your money. The friendly game around a kitchen table, the local pool hall, even the upper class Bridge club have all been infiltrated by cheats on the take. Hell, you aren't even safe, as you'll learn, just walking down the street on a Sunday afternoon going home from church! It's a fair guess to say that, worldwide, the number of cheats of one sort or another probably runs into the millions. Sitting down with strangers can be dangerous, sitting down with friends can be deadly.

With Freddy's knowledge you'll be able to spot most of the cheat's moves. You'll learn what to do *when* (not *if*) it happens to you. Freddy gives advice on how to play like pro, how to *talk* like a pro (one sentence for example that could stop you from being cheated at any carnival!), how to spot a hustle. In other words, he'll turn you into *fast company*.

Talking the language is as simple as turning to the back of this book where you'll find a comprehensive guide to both old and new Cheatspeak. It may shock you to discover just how many words there are to describe you, the mug! The rest of your honors degree course lies ahead. Study hard. It could save you a great deal of money.

It must be stressed though that Freddy hasn't given you this knowledge to encourage you to cheat. Don't be tempted. It's a tough world out there and walking on crutches is no fun.

But Freddy does want to see you have some fun. An occasional fun swindle, for low stakes, is allowable. Your friends will find them most entertaining and you, as a fun person who knows a trick or two, may get some decent party invites on the back of your new found notoriety. But, be warned, when stakes get high so do tempers. You might take the money but, if you do so, you'll probably lose all of your friends. Use Freddy's knowledge carefully. First to protect yourself and second to enrich your life with some fun.

Freddy has spent a great deal of the last five years with me working to create this book. As he has explained the bets to me and why I could never win I have been constantly amazed that sane and rational people would ever fall for them.

I've even managed to keep a straight face as I've handed over the money.

Starting with bar bets and working through street hustles to big time card and dice hustling, it is astonishing to see the psychology and ingenuity of cheating techniques. As Freddy puts it, *"If money is involved, it's a sure bet that cheating not only could occur, but probably already has."*

Sit back and relax. Prepare yourself for a roller coaster ride alongside one of the most knowledgeable men in the business. Freddy has lighted up one of his favorite cigars and is ready to hold court.

Freddy the Fox is seventy-three years old and likes cats, whiskey and high stake poker games. He currently lives in New York City with his cat, Boris, and his Ferret, Armageddon.

"If you ever play five aces, you'll soon be playing a harp."

———◆———

unknown gambler

How to

CHEAT

at

EVERYTHING

SAY, BARKEEP, WHAT'S THAT LITTLE "SHRINE" ON YOUR SHELF?

OH, THIS DOOHICKEY? IT WAS *HERE* WHEN I BOUGHT THE PLACE A FEW MONTHS BACK!

LEMME SHOW YA...

THE $600 CIGARETTE

SEEMS A BIT WRINKLED, BUT HARDLY SPECIAL! *"THE SIX HUNDRED DOLLAR CIG,"* HUH? IS THERE A *STORY* BEHIND THIS?

IS THERE? IT'S A *LOCAL LEGEND!* Y'SEE...

CONCEPT: A.J.P. SCRIPT/ART: Alw

"THE COFFIN NAIL CONTORTIONIST"

ABOUT TWO YEARS AGO, I'M TOLD, THIS *STRANGER* SHOWS UP: A NATTY DRESSER, KIND OF A SHOPWORN PAN, BUT WITH A CHEROOT-CHEWIN' *GRIN* THAT'D MELT ARMOR PLATE OFF A BATTLESHIP! HE HOBNOBS WITH THE REGULARS— CARRIES ON LIKE A HARMLESS GLADHANDER!

"OUTA NOWHERE, HE BUMS A BUTT AN' CLAIMS...."

THERE MIGHT BE A WAY TO *TIE THIS IN A KNOT* WITHOUT TEARIN' THE PAPER THE TINIEST BIT!

NOT A CHANCE!

NO WAY! GUY'S DREAMIN'!!

A FIN SEZ IT'S A *CROCK!*

"SOON, ALMOST *EVERYONE'S* FLASHIN' THEIR CASH FOR SOME *EASY ACTION!* ALMOST *RELUCTANTLY,* THE STRANGER ACCEPTS THE CHALLENGE!"

"WELL, THE STORY GOES THAT THE STRANGER MAKES *GOOD* AND I DON'T MEAN MAYBE!"

GASP! HE *DID* IT!

A TIGHT LITTLE KNOT, *NEAT* AS YOU PLEASE!

IT *HASTA* BE TORN *SOME-WHERES!*

YEAH! MAKE 'IM *UNTIE* IT AN' SHOW US IT'S *OKAY!*

HE STRAIGHTENS IT OUT AGAIN AND HERE IT IS: THE VERY SAME *INTACT* "COFFIN NAIL," JUST AS HE *LEFT* IT ON THE BAR! POCKETS *SIX HUNDRED BUCKS* AND FADES FOREVER, NEVER TO BE SEEN AGAIN!

SO I'VE BEEN *TOLD*... BUT NO ONE'S TOLD ME HOW HE *DID* THE *DEED!* SOMETIMES I THINK THE WHOLE YARN IS SOME-ONE'S *BOOZE-BRAINED DELUSION!*

IT IS HARD TO SWALLOW...

BUT Y'KNOW, THERE *MIGHT* BE A WAY... LET ME THINK....

Bar Bets

As Freddy so rightly points out, there really is only one kind of bar bet when he's playing: a losing one for the mug.

But, within the esoteric world of the hustler, there are actually three kinds of bar bets. The first kind is the *Proposition Bet*. These are where the hustler bets you that he can do something which seems to be completely impossible, such as tying a cigarette into a knot without tearing it or damaging it in any way.

The second type is known as *Odds Bets*. These are gambles where the mug may occasionally win, but the odds are so heavily stacked against him that he is most unlikely to do so over a period of time. For instance, do you know how many people you need in a room for it to be a 50-50 chance that two will have the same birthday? And if you do (unlikely), have you any idea how many you need to make the odds 4-1 in your favor?

The third kind of bet is the one most favored by the neighborhood hustler. These are known as *NAP Bets*. Nap does not refer to the popular card game of Napoleon. Instead, it is an acronym for *Not A Prayer*. Whatever the game, however much it seems to be in your favor, you have absolutely no chance of even sniffing a win. They are also known as *Miracle Money* bets because only a saint (with an extremely high I.Q.) might stand a chance! Games such as Nim (where the last player to pick up a match from a pile wins) fall into this category.

Freddy the Fox is, as you've probably already guessed, a master of all three types of bets. Let's take each in order to start your ride through the world of easy money. Easy money, that is, for the hustler. Without the knowledge you are about to read you wouldn't have a hope of holding onto enough cash to pay for a bus ride home!

PROP BETS

The proposition bet, or *prop*, can be a sneaky way to earn a few beers from your friends at the local bar. At the high end of the market, legendary gamblers such as Titanic Thompson made fortunes from them. Let me give you an example.

The Fox and I are sitting in a coffee shop on McDougal St. in New York City. It's known to some of the boys around there as The Office. I'm happily sipping at my second cup of coffee when I notice that, just for once, the Fox has gone pretty quiet. He picks up my cigarette packet and removes one. He eyes it carefully, turning it over and over in his hands.

"*What's up?*" I ask.

"*Shhh!*" is his only reply.

I remove a cigarette myself and start to study it to try to see just what the hell he is trying to find.

"*Maybe, just maybe,*" the Fox muses quietly.

"*Maybe what?*"

"*Well, I heard about a guy once who reckoned that he could tie a cigarette into a knot without tearing any of the paper. I think I might have worked out how he did it.*"

Now I am no expert on paper but it seems obvious to me that this would be an impossible feat. I try it with the cigarette I am holding and wreck it. Just to be on the safe side I try another with predictable results. I realize that I am being hooked in and start to think about trick ways it could be done.

Myth? Myth? Hey buddy, you ought to do something about that lisp!

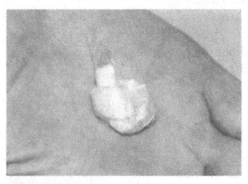

Not a myth.

My main theory revolves around something being knotted about the cigarette. Then the cigarette would have been tied *into* a knot. That has to be it! I keep a straight face and allow the Fox to reel me in. For once I'm ahead of him.

"*It's totally impossible,*" I say, setting myself up.

The Fox smiles. He thinks he has me hooked but I'm about to wipe that grin from his face. He suggests a small wager on the outcome of the event. I agree but add my killer rider. The cigarette itself must be knotted. The smile doesn't fade. For good luck I add that he must use one of my cigarettes, it must be dry when he does it, and it must be smokable afterwards. The tiniest tear loses him the bet. I am slightly shaken when he accepts all of this without turning a hair. I take this as bare faced nerve and recover my confidence. In my mind I am already spending the ten dollars we have bet. And, I'll have beaten the Fox!

It takes him around forty five seconds to win the ten dollars.

The Fox carefully removes the cellophane wrapper from the cigarette packet and flattens it out. Then he tightly rolls the cigarette into the cellophane making sure it ends up completely within the wrapper. He then ties the cigarette into a knot and even has the audacity to ask me if I want to pull the knot tighter. Carefully he undoes the knot and unrolls the packet. Lying before me on the table is, although a bit twisted, a totally untorn and smokable cigarette.

This little tale illustrates two points. First, the bet itself. Many prop bets rely on a specialized or obscure piece of knowledge. In this case knowing that a tightly wrapped cigarette can actually be tied into a knot without tearing it. Second, it shows how Freddy (in his role as the prop man) sets up the bet. There's little point in just saying, "*I'll betcha.*" The system known as *hook, line and sink* is much more subtle than that.

> *The Hook*—The Fox creates an interest before the bet is suggested by quietly studying the cigarette and getting me to wonder what the hell is going on.
>
> *The Line*—The Fox muses as to whether or not a cigarette can be tied into a knot. He hints that he *might* have found a way. He allows me time to realize (in my own mind anyway) that it is impossible and must be a trick. He let me sell the idea of a wager to myself! When he suggests a bet I am ready to bite his hand off provided he can meet my completely irrelevant conditions.
>
> *The Sink*—The Fox does the impossible and picks up the money.

Many prop bets appear to be so outrageously impossible that the mug will often suggest the wager himself. The prop man may, at this point, argue that he doesn't want to gamble on it, he was just wondering if it were possible or not. Unless you are a close blood relative (and then only if he's in a good mood) it's a running certainty that he will allow you to talk him into money changing hands.

As with the cigarette bet the best prop bets are those which seem to be completely improvised. If it appears that the bet is made up as you go along then so much the better.

Here are eleven more of Freddy's rather large collection of small time moneymakers.

1. Match Tossing

Get a book of matches and remove one match. Make a mark on one side with a pen (Freddy likes to draw a little arrow pointing towards the head of the match). Now toss the match up the air a few times letting it fall onto the bar or table surface. Keep doing it until somebody asks you what you are doing. Explain that you are just playing a little gambling game with yourself. You are betting that the marked side will land up and are keeping score of how well you are doing. Somewhat predictably, you add, you are just about breaking even. It won't take long for your imaginary game to become a real one with small stakes being bet on the outcome. It's all down to luck but at least you'll win as often as you lose. This is all part of the hook.

When the time is ripe for the kill offer a slightly different bet. Your mug can have both sides of the match and you'll only win if the match lands on its edge! In return for giving them such a huge advantage you will, of course, want better odds (say 10-1) if your bet wins. This is, in case you haven't noticed, the line. After they've played with the match for a while you shouldn't have any problem getting a wager down. They'll think you've just had one drink too many and are being a bit silly.

When the bets have been placed pick up the match and, just before you toss it up, bend it with your thumb in the middle. This makes the match a 'V' shape and, as such, it can only land on its edge!

Freddy suggests that you could win at every stage of the game by switching in a match marked on both sides at the start of the game. Even he admits that this may be gilding the lily just a tad too much!

2. Giddy Heights

This is one of Freddy's big money spinners. Even when you know the answer it just looks totally impossible.

Put a beer glass (or coffee cup, etc.) onto a table and start musing about which would be the longer distance, the circumference of the rim of the glass or the height of the glass from top to table. Most people with even a glimmer of mathematical knowledge will guess the circumference. This is the hook. Now put a packet of cigarettes under the glass and ask the question again. The height this time includes the cigarette packet. Most people will think that the distances are pretty close at this stage. You may even help them along by suggesting it.

Now comes the line. Add another cigarette packet. Most will argue that the height is now the greater distance. You say that you think the circumference is still bigger and let a friendly argument begin. Eventually, one side will offer to bet on it.

Giddy Heights..

Add another cigarette packet and offer to double the bet. As if insane, add a fourth packet and offer to double the bet again! Let them put any limitations they like on the bet. No measuring with elastic, no squashing of the packets, no sneaky tricks, and they are allowed to do the measuring! Get the bet as high as you can and then measure the distances with a shoelace.

You may be staggered to discover that the circumference of an English Pint Glass is longer than the distance from top down to table *even* when the glass is on top of four cigarette packets. Actually, if the truth be known, you can add another couple of packets. Some glasses can be taken to nearly twice their original height! Freddy knows just how much can be put under *any* glass or cup you can imagine and has never failed to take a small fortune on this little puppy. He claims his 'research' into circumference/height ratios has paid for several cars and very expensive holidays. I believe him.

3. The Swallow

Here the bet is that somebody can't do everything that you do for the next ninety seconds. Let them add all the 'useful' limitations. This bet will include no contortions or specialist athletic movements (*"Ah Candy, Candy. What a gal,"* muses the Fox as I write this. I didn't ask.) Assure them that all your actions will be those that can be done by a completely normal person. This is a great hook, and you should have no trouble raising a *poke* (bet) on this one. Put two matches on the bar, one for you and one for them. Now reel them in as you do the following.

Turn your match end for end. They do the same.
Take a drink noisily from your glass. They do the same.
Turn your match again. They follow along.
Raise your glass to your lips. They do so as well.
Spit the drink you sneakily held in your mouth back into your glass.
Because they swallowed theirs they will be unable to complete this simple action. You walk off with the cash!

Because all attention is on the match the drink is a secondary thought. Actually, Freddy often does this bet on people who know the secret. Suicidal? No! He has an *extra* finish. When he does the spit back he keeps some in his mouth. The sucker repeats the spit, laughs and reaches for the money. That's when Freddy spits a *second* mouthful back into the glass. As he is so fond of saying, *"Remember, I taught you everything you know. But not everything I know!"*

4. Matchbox Teaser

Sometimes Freddy's prop bets don't make huge amounts of money, but they are great fun to do. Despite the low *apron* (win) on this bet, it's one that gives Freddy a lot of laughs. Try it and see why.

Have a matchbox with a one dollar bill folded up inside. Make sure that the one spot can be seen. Ask to borrow a dollar bill and fold it up. Put it into the matchbox and, without making it obvious, let them see the dollar already in there. It is critical to the hook that they see the bill but 'know' that you haven't noticed them doing so.

The hook and line come in one. Say jokingly, *"Of course only a fool would pay a dollar fifty for what's in this box right now!"*

He thinks he's got you. He knows that there are two dollars in that box and that you don't know that he knows. Forgetting that a little knowledge can be a dangerous thing he offers, with a rush of blood to the head blocking out logical thinking, to buy the box.

You stumble and stammer a little but he will insist. Eventually give in and sell them the box.

It could take you quite a time to explain how this gives you a fifty-cent profit. You see, one of the dollars he just bought was his own. For more on this 'buy back your own money' stuff see *Jam Auctions* later in this book where the principle becomes an art form.

Freddy has been known to do this with fifty-dollar bills in a cheap wallet thus netting twenty-five dollars (he charges seventy-five dollars for the wallet) each time he does it. This approach is not recommended to the faint hearted.

5. *Dominoes Dosh*

Where dominoes are played for money (and before you ask, yes this is another game I've never seen the Fox lose at) Freddy has a delightful end of the night bet. He gets one of the players to shuffle up all of the dominoes and form them into a line as if a game were being played. As the player does this Freddy writes two numbers down on his cigarette packet. When asked what he is doing he makes the claim that he has worked out the entire chain that will be made and has written down the two numbers that will be at the ends.

This ludicrous claim is met with disdain and, more often than not, an offer of a bet that he is wrong from one of the players. Like a lamb to the slaughter they go as Freddy takes the wager. He wins. He may, if in a 'generous' mood offer to double or nothing on the bet to give them a chance to get their money back. They can play this little game all night with the only result being that Freddy may need a truck to carry away the money.

The secret, and it's little known even amongst experienced domino players, is that a full set of dominoes will form a circle. All Freddy has to do is steal a domino (not a double) from the set and write down those two numbers. If he steals a three-five for example he writes down three and five.

It takes a tiny amount of nerve to replace this domino and steal another as the tiles are being mixed up to repeat the bet. The cheat is well hidden here as everybody assumes that Freddy is using remarkable mathematical skill. As Freddy often says, "*Don't assume too much.*"

6. *Coin in the Glass*

The hardest part of this bet is setting it up! You need pretty steady hands so it's not for the nervous hustler.

Put a glass onto the bar. On top of the mouth of the glass place a beer coaster. Now comes the hard bit. Balance a cigarette on top of the coaster and on top of the cigarette balance a small coin. If Freddy has had a whiskey too many he'll often roll up a dollar bill into a tube and balance a quarter atop that. It easier to do but, in his eyes, is less artistic. Using the cigarette it's easier if the tipped end is down on the coaster. Anyway, taking time with the set up is all part of the hook.

Ask them if they think it's possible to get the coin into the glass without touching anything at all. Claim that you can do this seemingly impossible feat. Let them add all the usual riders such as not banging the bar, getting anybody else to help and no jumping up and down or related jiggery-pokery. Let *them* suggest a bet on it.

When the money is down kneel down on the floor and blow sharply upwards on the underside of the beer coaster. It will flip upwards and away from the glass taking the cigarette (or rolled up bill) with it. Thanks to inertia the coin will stay right where it is for a split second before dropping down into the glass like a little homing pigeon returning to roost.

Coin in the Glass.

7. Burnt Fingers

Light a match and hold it upside down so that the flame bends up towards your fingers. As soon as you feel heat drop it into an ashtray. Repeat until somebody asks what you are doing. Reply that you once saw a guy hold a lit match upside down for forty-five seconds without getting burnt.

Let them work out the impossibility of this statement. Your ongoing attempts will help them realize that it can't be done. They may even offer to bet that it can't be done (with the usual riders of no gloves, etc.)

When you want to win light the match and hold it upside down. Slowly move your hand from side to side. Not only does this make the match burn slower but also rather neatly keeps the flame away from your skin. With practice you can extend the time to a minute with no fear of burns.

Freddy often uses this little bet to lead into Nim (of which more later) where he'll go for the serious money.

8. Six Glass Scam

This is a cute little bet which should win you a few drinks for your trouble. Place six shot glasses in a line along the bar. Fill the first three with whiskey or beer and leave the last three empty. The bet is to get the glasses alternated—beer, empty, beer, empty, beer, empty—with the minimum amount of glasses moved. Allow a discussion and several test runs to take place.

Then drop your hook. Claim to be able to do it by moving only one glass. That's right you are only going to touch one glass! Try it yourself to see how impossible (ish) this is.

To perform this neat trick pick up the center of the three filled glasses. Pour its contents into the center of the three empty glasses and replace your now empty glass where it started. You only touched one glass and nobody said the contents had to stay in the same glasses! As Freddy often says, "*Nothing is impossible if you cheat!*"

9. Egg Balancing

Gamblers, it has been said, will bet upon anything. At the local Deli Freddy takes advantage of this using the following bet to get his bill covered. Typically he also has *outs* (different methods) just in case somebody has read of an older method.

The bet is to balance a fresh egg on its end without it falling over. The traditional and reasonably well known way of doing this is to wet one end of the egg and stick some grains of salt to it. The salt allows the egg to be balanced and is easily secretly wiped away afterwards.

Should one of the inevitable riders be that no salt is allowed Freddy uses the following, very little known, technique. He shakes the egg violently which will break the yolk inside. Then he holds the egg upright and allows the yolk (heavier than the white) to settle. With care the egg can now be balanced on its end with the yolk (like a Weeble toy) keeping it up.

On one memorable occasion Freddy just smashed the end of the egg onto the bar, breaking it in the process. The bulk of the shell stood up! Freddy pointed out that nobody had said the egg had to stay in one piece. You really have to be careful when setting the riders!

10. The Lit Cig Prop

Freddy for fun, and perhaps a small remuneration, will offer to demonstrate that he can light a cigarette, take four full drags on it, knock off the ash and still leave the cigarette *exactly* the same length it started.

The secret is as simple as the bet. He doesn't light the cigarette at the end. He lights it in the middle!

11. The Triple Turn

This is one of the great old bar bets. A classic if you will!

Freddy puts three whiskey tumblers in a row. Two are base up and one is mouth up. Freddy offers the following bet. You have turn two glasses at once. You're to do that three times. You have to end with all three glasses mouth up.

Freddy can do it every time but for some mysterious reason you will be unable to duplicate his actions. It may cost you quite a few dollar bills before you start to catch on!

Here's how Freddy does it. The three glasses are set in a line with the end ones mouth down and the center one mouth up. First he turns an end glass and the middle glass. Then he turns both end glasses. Then he turns the two mouth down glasses (one at the end and one in the center) mouth up to complete the bet. He does this very swiftly to convince you that it's the turns that win the bet.

The actual reason you can't do it is simple lack of observation. Not the moves but the start position. Freddy sets the tumblers for you with the middle one face down and the two end ones mouth up. With straight-sided shot glasses or tumblers this looks the same but the best you can do is finish with all three mouth down!

Freddy rarely lets honesty get in the way of winning, and he'll do whatever it takes to pick up the money. This bet (and several others) can be seen on *The Party Animal* video tape from *L&L Publishing*.

Freddy, as you can imagine, has a huge collection of prop bets. If one doesn't get the mugs biting he'll move onto another one. One thing is for sure. The moment you show any interest, it's going to cost you money.

I once asked Freddy, from a safe distance, if he'd ever lost a bet himself. He admitted that he once lost money on a prop bet!

He'd been playing poker with a genial old man in Manchester in the venerable lands of Great Britain. The old man had lost money, and Freddy was a happy camper. Then the old man offered a bet. He bet Freddy that he could bite his own right eye. Freddy was fascinated, the poke was small enough to cover the cost of learning the bet and so he accepted. The old man removed his glass eye and bit it. Laughs were heard around the bar; it was one of the old boy's favorite tricks. Then came the line. He offered a big bet that he could bite his other eye. Freddy was so grossed out by the glass eye bit that he'd lost cognitive thought. He fell into the required track of thought by assuming that, since the guy had been playing poker all night, he couldn't possibly have two glass eyes. After some considerable thought Freddy took the bet.

The old guy removed his false teeth and bit his right eye. Freddy puts that story forward as an example of the phrase, *"You never stop learning."*

Perhaps the finest bar bet I've ever seen was shown to me by Todd Robbins (known, for some inexplicable reason, as Reno to Freddy). We were all sitting round a restaurant table and Todd put a small box on his plate. Inside the box, he told us, was something unique. It had never been seen by any human being before and, after one showing, would never be seen again. He offered us all the opportunity to be the only people in history to see this incredible item for a mere five dollars each.

How could we turn him down?

He opened the box and removed an unshelled peanut. He broke open the husk and showed us the nut. *"This has never been seen before,"* he said quite truthfully. Then he chewed and swallowed the nut before saying, *"And it will never be seen again!"*

Much laughter followed amidst general agreement that, that was easily a great five dollar value!

CHANCES AND ODDS

Before we enter the heady world of odds it may be useful to take a brief overview in what they actually are. Few people outside the gambling world (and a surprising number within it) actually know the difference between odds and chance.

Chance is something the mug believes in with a passion. Although he doesn't understand exactly what it is he has some vague idea that it has something to do with things happening over a period of time. The belief in lady luck has lost more than a few fortunes over the years. The poor lottery player who says, "*Well somebody has to win, it may as well be me!*" is a good example of this often misled fervor.

Odds are the exact probability that one event or another will happen. Or, to put it another way, the exact ratio between what will be paid against what will be bet. Knowledge and understanding of this ratio is critical to winning. It is Odds 101 to know that there is only a theory of probability (chance) but a definite law of averages (odds).

Let me give you an example. If I toss a coin into the air it can land heads or tails. Assuming a perfectly balanced coin and no cheating the chance of a head coming up after a toss is 50-50. The odds are 1 in 2.

Or, to put it another way, if you have a BLT Sandwich once a week the chance of you having a BLT on any given day is 1 in 7. The odds are 6-1 against.

Chance often translates to luck to the mug. They act is if chance had an intelligence all of its own. Their theory states that a run of bad luck must surely be followed by a run of good luck, the, so-called, lucky streak.

If I toss a coin one hundred times and it comes down heads a hundred times I could get a string of people willing to bet stupid money that the next toss will produce a tail. The chance they will argue is high in their favor. The odds dictate that it is still a 1 in 2 shot!

If you think that sounds silly then you should talk to the large number of gamblers whose entire Roulette system consists of waiting for red to come up six times in a row and then backing black to come up. They will argue (presumably on the assumption that the ball can 'remember' where it last fell) that it is more likely to do so. They forget that probability theory is calculated over an infinite number of runs and it is exactly this sort of thinking that makes them poor in very short order.

Casino owners love these kinds of systems. Don't be a mug. Forget chance and learn the odds.

Skilled knowledge of twisting the odds are what makes the following bar bets so strong. If you fail to learn the simple math involved you'll forever be stuck with the rest of the sheep and, as Freddy says, "*Ripe for a little shearing!*"

Odd Odds

Even if you can't work out odds very well at least you are slightly ahead of the game by knowing the difference between them and lady luck. By twisting or concealing the odds on a bet, the hustler can make a small fortune simply by winning more often than he loses.

A simple example. A coin is tossed into the air to fall either heads or tails (with a 1 in 2 chance of either result). If I offered you a bet where every time a head came down I would pay you a dollar but that every time a tail came down you would pay me three dollars it should be obvious that, if you foolishly took this bet, you'd go broke pretty quickly. Simply by twisting the odds (rather too openly here) I've given lady luck a big kick where it hurts the most. The problem with this bet as written is that it is obviously stupid. However, by subtly twisting odds, people like Freddy have turned odds bets into an art form. Even if you don't understand some of the calculations given here you only have to try the bets with a pile of play money to see how math suddenly becomes a lot less boring when it turns into a money-making machine!

1. The Seven Card Hustle

Freddy will take five red cards and two black cards from a pack. He will ask you to shuffle them and then, without looking at the faces, lay them out in a row along the bar. He'll bet you that you can't turn over three red cards.

Kindly man that he is, he'll even explain how the bet is in your favor. The first draw is 5 to 2 (five red cards and two black cards) in your favor. The second draw is 4 to 2 (or 2 to 1 if you like) because there will be four red cards and two black cards left. The last draw is *still* in your favor by 3 to 2 (three reds and two blacks). The game seems heavily in your favor, but Freddy, for reasons you can't see, is willing to offer you even money that you can't do it! Should you take the bet?

No way!

He's only given you the odds on a perfect winning draw while, rather forgetfully, leaving out all the other possibilities. The real odds (including all the losing draws) add up to a whacking 5 to 2 against you!

After you've felt enough pain of losing Freddy may turn the bet around. *He'll* try to pick out three red cards in a row. What a guy! Your pain will increase exponentially as he does it over and over again. Perhaps he also forgot to mention to you that he's secretly marked the backs of the two black cards making them easy to avoid?

2. The Nine Card Hustle

This is Freddy's follow up bet if the victim has any more money to lose after the first one has lost interest.

He takes two more red cards from the deck and adds them to the seven already in play. In his most genial way he explains that there are now seven red cards and only two black cards. You just can't lose! He'll ask you to shuffle up the cards and lay them out in a three by three square. He'll bet you even

Your worst layout of the Nine-Card Hustle.

money that you can't pick out a straight line (horizontal, vertical or diagonal) of three red cards. The odds seem to be staggeringly in your favor, what should you do?

You want my advice?

Run like hell!

The bet has subtly changed. You are no longer picking three cards at random but three cards in a line. There are only eight lines available (three horizontal, three vertical and two diagonal). If both black cards lay side by side in a corner then it's an even money bet. In this position there are four winning lines and four losing lines. That's the good news. Unfortunately this is the best break you can hope for. If one black card is at a corner and the other is in the center then there are only two winning lines against six losing lines. All other layouts leave five losing lines to three winning ones. To make it even worse there are only twelve ways your fifty-fifty bet can happen but a total of twenty-two, count em and weep, ways (four of the six to two and eighteen of the five to three) that the odds will be well against you.

Still want to take the bet?

3. Elusive Queens

Freddy removes two kings, two queens and two jacks from a deck of cards. Once more he'll ask you to shuffle them and to draw two cards. He'll bet you even money that one of them is a queen. Although the odds seem in your favor they are actually 3-2 against you. Not much but enough to sweeten you up for a bigger bet.

After you've lost a few times (and, because of the odds, you'll lose more than you win over a period of time) you may start to get the idea that it's easier than you thought to pick the queens. That's when Freddy pounces and offers you 10 to 1 that you can't pick both queens.

A good bet?

Only if you like bucking odds of 15 to 1 against. This is just like the obvious coin tossing bet we described at the start of these prop bets but just more cunningly concealed. Are you starting to get the idea now?

4. Birthday Boys and Girls

This is one of Freddy's favorite bets. I know because when he took me for fifty dollars with it he laughed so hard I thought his sides would split.

We were standing in a bar enjoying a drink when Freddy asked me my birthday. I told him and was 'amazed' to discover that his birthday was the same as mine. An astonishing coincidence! Astute readers will have already seen the hook sinking in here.

Freddy then offered to bet me that another two people in the room would share a birthday. He even offered me 3 to 2 on my money. At a rough guess there were around thirty-four or so people in the bar. I took the bet. I assumed, before I learned odds properly, that with around thirty people in the room and three hundred and sixty five days to share out the odds had to be about 12 to 1 in my favor! Boy was I wrong!

You see I wasn't betting that two people would share a specific birthday but just that two would share *any* birthday. The odds calculation becomes progressive with each new person tightening in the figures sharply. It may surprise you to know that the odds become even money with just twenty-two people. With thirty-four people in the room Freddy had a huge 4 to 1 edge!

5. Tossing Coins

We've already seen from a naive example how tossing coins could be twisted into an odds bet. Here's how Freddy works a scam using just the very same odds!

Freddy explains that the chance of a head or tail coming down after a coin is tossed are fifty-fifty (even money).

He then asks you how many heads are likely to turn up if a coin is tossed ten times. If you answer five (I did) you are well on the way to accepting a bet on it (I did) and losing your money (I did several times).

Freddy will even offer you 2 to 1 on your money that you cannot toss a coin ten times and get five heads and five tails.

Sure five heads and five tails will turn up more frequently than any other *single* combination (one head, nine tails for example) but the *sum* of all the other possibilities is much greater than the single five heads, five tails combination.

True odds are 5 to 2 in Freddy's favor.

6. Aces Wild

Have you ever played Poker Dice? These are just like normal dice except that instead of spots they have card faces upon them, from nine to ace. They are very popular in bar games until Freddy pulls this little number.

He'll tell you that aces are wild (they can stand for any value), and you are to roll them out (there are five dice in a set). Every time you roll a pair Freddy will pay you, every time you roll three of a kind you pay Freddy. Of course everybody knows it's harder to roll three of a kind but Friendly Freddy will offer you even money on the bet.

A set of poker dice.

Take the bet and you may as well just hand Freddy your wallet. With aces wild it's easier to roll three of a kind! Freddy has odds of 3 to 1 working in his favor!

7. Money Madness

Freddy asks you to remove a bill from your wallet and to screw it up without looking at it. He offers you even money that you can't guess three out of the eight digits that make up the serial number of the bill. You must guess three with no misses. This would seem to be in your favor as you only have to pick three from eight! But don't forget that lots of serial numbers have repeat figures (such as C10026202D, for example, which is a number, a great one for this bet, on a dollar bill taken at random from my wallet). And don't forget those zeros! Here are the true odds for you.

All numbers different—a mere 2.15 to 1 in Freddy's favor
One duplicate figure—3.42 to 1 for Freddy
Two duplicate figures—6 to 1 for Freddy
Three duplicate figure—12 to 1 for Freddy
Getting good isn't it? Well, for Freddy anyway!
Four duplicate figures—30—1 for Freddy
Five duplicate figures—120 to 1 for Freddy

Getting the idea?

Freddy often does this bet with his own money. He'll screw up a five dollar bill and offer the bet. If you take it you'll be highly pleased when you win. The bet is repeated with another five dollar bill and you'll win again. If you could only walk away right now, but the bet seems so easy!

Freddy only has a fifty dollar bill left. It would be a shame to quit while you were ahead wouldn't it? This poor old chap has had one drink too many and is giving away money isn't he? It's a great bet for you, isn't it? Your first guess is wrong! Freddy offers you double or nothing that you still can't do it. You already know that one of your first numbers was wrong so this time it's a cinch, isn't it? You lose again and are suddenly ninety dollars out of pocket. I guess Freddy just got a lucky break huh?

You see Freddy has a fifty dollar bill with the number 88888558 on it. I pointed out to him that this meant he couldn't lose. "*Really?*" he said, "*And I just thought that it was a lucky note!*"

8. Three Lucky Piles

Freddy gets somebody to shuffle a deck of cards and to cut it into three piles. He offers to bet even money that a court card will turn up on top of one of the piles. The logical mug will work out that Freddy has twelve winning cards (four jacks, four queens and four kings) against forty losing cards. He figures that the odds must be about four to one against Freddy on a pile. So, in his mind (and Freddy may help him along by explaining all this) Freddy would need four piles to make it an even bet. With three piles it's in the mugs favor. Right?

Wrong!

This bet has cost people who should know better considerable sums of money. We'll be looking at some of the math in detail later on but here's a quick preview of why hustlers carry calculating machines with them. To understand this bet you must first realize that you are effectively picking three cards at random from a deck so you need to know how many three card combinations there are in a deck. It takes Freddy about three seconds to give the answer 22,100. Now you need to know how many of those three card groupings have a court card in them. Freddy tells me it's 12,220 before I finish typing the words! That leaves the mug with only 9,880 (I did the math then using only a calculator to help me!) winning combinations. If you translate this down to odds you'll find that the bet is just around 5 to 4 in Freddy's favor. In the long run that means you'll win around eleven cents for every dollar bet. That's a higher percentage than a casino works on and look at the carpets they put down!

Odds can seem to be very complicated and frightening to the normal person. But here's an easy rule from Freddy for you to remember. "*If somebody is explaining odds to you and trying to get you to lay a bet you can be sure that their odds are wrong!*"

Right Odds

If you are offered a proposition bet of any sort it really does pay to be able to at least have a good idea of how to work out the correct odds on the bet. That way you'll be able to recognize the rare occasion when you might actually be getting a fair shake.

Working out complex odds can be a nightmare for even a competent mathematician. Working out simple ones can be easier if you follow logical steps and refuse to be frightened by figures.

First remember that odds represent a ratio between how often a single event will occur against a total number of possible outcomes. So a coin tossed in the air can come down heads or tails. The total number of events is two (heads or tails). If you bet on heads your odds are 1 in 2.

Another example would be rolling a single die. There are six numbers on the die so there are six possible outcomes. If you bet on number six the odds of it coming up are 1 in 6 or, to put it another way, 5 to 1 against. If somebody offers to pay you 3 to 1 every time a six appears then they are hustling you. They should be paying you 5 to 1 to make the bet fair. See? It can be easier than you think!

Okay, let's complicate it slightly. Can you work out the correct odds on two sixes being thrown with a pair of dice?

Well, first you need to know the total number of possible outcomes. There are six faces on each die so the total number of ways they can land is thirty-six (six multiplied by six). There is only one way to roll a double six so your true odds are 1 in 36 or 35 to 1 against. Understand this and you are well on your way to being a hustle-buster!

Let's test the brain cells a little. Once again we'll throw two dice. This time try to work out the odds on a total of seven turning up before a total of twelve.

It sounds hard but it's easy to work out if you follow simple steps. The total number of all possible outcomes is thirty-six again. Now work out how many ways you can get a total of seven. Here are the combinations—one/six, six/one, five/two, two/five, four/three, three/four. So there are six ways to throw seven with two dice. There is only one way to throw twelve (two sixes) so the odds are 6 to 1 on that a seven will be rolled first. Or, if you like, 6 to 1 against a twelve being thrown first!

So if somebody offers you 4 to 1 on throwing a twelve before a seven they are hustling you and will take your money over a run as sure as odds are odds!

Notice that when working out your combinations you must take *all* outcomes into account. Five/two is not the same as two/five!

Now let's look at a few examples where the odds just are not as they appear. They've been magnificently twisted by a hustler like Freddy.

First let's look at that Three Little Piles game in closer detail so you can see how the figures were arrived at. When somebody cuts three piles they are, in effect, randomly picking three cards from the deck. So first we need to know how many three card groupings (the total number of all possible outcomes) there are in a deck. The odds on picking any one card are fifty-two divided by one (the total number of possible events divided by the single event). The odds on any other card turning up next are fifty one (we've already removed one card so the total number of all events has fallen) divided by two (we now have two single events). The odds on any third card turning up are fifty divided three. If we put this all together we get . . .

$$\frac{52 \times 51 \times 50}{1 \times 2 \times 3}$$

. . . which will give us the total number of three card groupings in a deck of cards! This comes out, as mentioned before, to 22,100. Now, stick with me because our next calculation will be very similar. We need to know how many of those groups will win for us and how many will lose. If we take out the court cards from a deck (our winning cards) we are left with forty cards. These forty, our losing cards, can make up how many combinations? Working out how many three card groupings there are in forty cards is a very similar calculation. It looks like this . . .

. . . and gives you an answer of 9,880. So, and here's the rub my little number crunchers, out of 22,100 total possible outcomes only 9,880 will lose for us. More importantly, that means that 12,220 will win for us! That's odds of 5 to 4 in our favor!

These simple formulas can be used to calculate all sorts of fun little bets from a winning poker draw to just how good your chances in a raffle are. Read the above again and try to understand it. Unlike a great many school math classes this is one that can absolutely relate to how much money stays in your wallet!

Let's use the same kind of math to show you how Birthday Boys and Girls works out.

The odds that a person will have the same birthday as himself are one hundred percent (a true NAP bet if you will!). The odds that somebody standing next to you has the same birthday as you are 364 divided by 365 (the total number of possible events into the losing events). The odds that a third person will share a birthday with you or your new found friend are, therefore . . .

$$\frac{365}{365} \times \frac{364}{365} \times \frac{363}{365} \quad \text{or} \quad \frac{365\times364\times363}{365\times365\times365}$$

This is just the same kind of calculation we used when working out our card groupings (trust me). Okay, let's give your calculator a bit of a work out. Carry on the above calculation in the following manner . . .

$$\frac{365}{365} \times \frac{364}{365} \times \frac{363}{365} \times \frac{362}{365} \times \frac{361}{365} \times \frac{360}{365} \times \frac{359}{365} \times \frac{358}{365} \times \frac{357}{365} \times \frac{356}{365} \cdots \text{etc.}$$

Stop doing the math when your total is just about 0.5. You'll find that this happens between the twenty-second and twenty-third calculation. This teeny number is telling you that the event will happen 0.5 out of 1 times. In other words it will happen half the time. In other words, to rub it in, it's a fifty-fifty bet!

If your calculator hasn't blown up yet carry on to thirty-four calculations (that's thirty-four people when doing the bet) and your fraction will show the odds to be approaching 4 to 1 in your favor.

It is the wording on the bet that is very important once the math is understood. You are betting that any two people will share *any* birthday. Don't offer to bet that two people share a specific birthday such as April the first. Although to the neophyte the bet may seem the same the odds against this happening are . . .

$$\frac{364}{365} \times \frac{364}{365} \times \frac{364}{365} \times \frac{364}{365} \times \frac{364}{365} \times \frac{364}{365} \times \frac{364}{365} \cdots \text{etc.}$$

Keep multiplying that nightmare out and you'll discover that you need 253 calculations (or people) before it becomes a fifty-fifty bet. With only thirty people in a room the odds would be around 8 to 1 against. However, this is the way Freddy gets you to think about the odds when laying the bet!

I used to wonder why Freddy carried an expensive calculator with him. Now I know better.

Twisting odds is one of the hustler's favorite pastimes. Here's a few more you may see around. See if you can work out the correct odds. I'll give you the answers afterwards.

1. Three Little Buttons

Freddy shows you three buttons which are painted red on one side and white on the other. He explains that if he tosses the buttons into the air there are four ways they can fall. All red showing, all white showing, two reds and a white or two whites and a red. He offers you the following bet. If all three come up the same color he'll give you two dollars. If a combination comes up you pay him a dollar. He is apparently offering you 2 to 1 on a fifty-fifty bet! Should you take the bet and, if not, why not?

2. Three Little Buttons Again

Freddy shows three buttons again. This time one is white both sides, one is red both sides and one is red one side and white the other. He asks you to mix them up behind your back and to bring one button forward and lay it on the bar. Let's assume it shows a red face. Freddy offers the following bet: "*It's obvious that this isn't the button which is white both sides so it must be one of the other two. It's either the button that it red both sides or the red/white button. That makes the color of the other side a fifty-fifty bet. Hey, but I'm feeling lucky today so I'll bet a dollar against seventy-five cents that the other side is red!*" Once more Freddy seems to be offering good odds for you on a fifty-fifty bet, but is he?

3. Under and Over Seven

Here's a clue on the following bet. It has been called one of the biggest sucker bets of all time.

A dice game is suggested and Freddy unrolls a piece of felt upon which is printed the following . . .

Under 7	7	Over 7
pays even	pays 4 to 1	pays even

You put your money down on any one of the spaces and roll two dice. If you bet on 'under seven' and throw 2, 3, 4, 5 or 6 Freddy will pay you even money. If you bet on 'over seven' and throw 8, 9, 10, 11 or 12 you'll also be paid even money. Betting on, and getting, a seven will earn you 4 to 1 on your money. Work out the odds and see if you want a flutter!

Now, and it may be said somewhat reluctantly, Freddy gives the correct odds.

1. Three Little Buttons

This does sound like a fifty-fifty bet but it isn't. It's a good example of working out *all* the combinations that go towards making up the total number of possible events. There are only two ways the spectator can win (three red or three white) but there are *six* ways the buttons can land in a combination of reds and whites! These are shown below for you in case you can't work it out for yourself.

So the real odds are 6 to 2 (or 3 to 1) against you. Freddy offering you 2 to 1 is hardly generous, more downright dirty!

2. Three Little Buttons Again

Again this sounds just like a fifty-fifty bet but it isn't!

If you lay out a button red side up it is not a fifty-fifty bet that the other side is red. You see here there are three possible events not two. In one event the other side is white but the other two events say that red is on the other side. Why? Because the red button could be brought out with *either* red side showing! You really do have to be pretty careful when working out *all* possible outcomes!

So here Freddy wins two out of three bets over a run. That's a dollar fifty (twice seventy-five cents) for every dollar paid out. Nice work if you can get it!

All he has to do when a button is laid out is bet that the other side will be the same color as the face showing.

3. Under and Over Seven

This one should not have caused you too much trouble as every pay out is wrong! The true odds on throwing under seven are 7 to 5 against. The same for throwing over seven. You are only being paid even money on a five dollar bet when you should actually be getting seven dollars!

The odds on a seven being thrown are 6 in 36 (1 in 6 or 5 to 1 against you). The operator is only offering you 4 to 1 on a 5 to 1 chance!

Some really low-down types label the center box as 'Four for One'. This means that for your one dollar bet, if you throw a seven, you get four dollars in return. This equates to a miserable 3 to 1 payout on a 5 to 1 shot!

Well gang you hopefully have a rough idea of how to look at odds and, far more importantly, how a hustler can use them to empty your wallet.

Even if you found the math a little hard to follow I hope you see that the odds are high that the hustler will *never* offer you an even break on a bet.

If it's any consolation a great many professional gamblers have lost hundreds of thousands of dollars on bets just like the ones you've been learning about. Freddy says that it's one of life's great pleasures to beat somebody who really should know better.

THE BIG FREEZE OUT

However much the odds are in Freddy's favor there is, of course, still the chance that the mug could win. Even a hundred to one shot comes up once in a while!

So how do hustlers like Freddy guarantee a pay out on an odds proposition?

They use a technique called the *Freeze Out*.

A Freeze Out is a bet where two players agree a total sum to be gambled over a series of events. Freddy won't offer you a single bet on a proposition. What he will do is offer you the proposition at a dollar a bet and the game will end when one player is twenty-five dollars ahead.

This gives the odds time to grind their little mathematical teeth into your money. The longer the run, the less your chances become.

If *either* player wants to stop at any time then he must pay the *full* amount of the bet to the other. The longest Freeze Outs between professionals have been known to last three days!

The proposition hustler will always seem to be a pleasant easy-going character. He'll often appear, perhaps as though he's had a drink or two too many, to be a little confused. He'll often seem to have made up these silly bets on the spur of the moment just to pass the time.

It is also worth noting that a good prop man will often make in excess of two hundred thousand dollars a year.

Next time somebody offers you a little wager *just to pass the time* you could be well on your way to contributing to that income.

NAP BETS

We now come to the third kind of bar hustle. NAP is an acronym for 'Not A Prayer'. These are either games of pure skill or employ absolute trickery. No luck is involved at all. Freddy and others have made fortunes from these bets. You're about to see why.

It was a dark winter's night and Freddy and I were sitting in the back room of a bar in Hartford, CT. I had the honor of being Freddy's driver that night and so was free to just sit and watch the action. The game was Seven Card Stud Poker. Freddy was playing (and I assumed cheating) superbly. He was on a roll and, if he carried on like this, we were going to need a car with a bigger trunk to carry the money home. Then, during a game break, he suggested a fun little game with matches just to break the monotony a little. The pile of matches on the table won him over a thousand dollars. The game was NIM.

In its simplest form the game looks innocent enough. Twenty matches are dropped onto the table and each player, in turn, can pick up one, two or three matches. The loser is the person who picks up the last match.

The secret of NIM is to hit key numbers. In other words to leave a *known* number of matches on the table to guarantee a win.

Freddy needs to hit one of the following numbers 5, 9, 13 or 17 in the pile to win. Once he hits one of the key numbers he simply thinks of the matches as being in groups of four. So once he's hit 17 (for example) and the victim takes, say, two matches then Freddy will also take two matches to make up a group of four and hit the next key number of 13 matches left. Once there are only 5 matches left and it's the victims turn to take it's easy to see that the victim can't win whatever he does.

That's all well and good if Freddy has first go. In a twenty match game he just takes three matches to hit the high key number of 17. But what if the victim goes first, takes three and hits the key number. Freddy could be playing against a guy with knowledge. Well, first Freddy, on his next go, will remove only one match. This gives him a better chance of hitting a key number next time around. But it's still not a one hundred percent (NAP) at this point. So just how does Freddy win *every* time, even against people who know something about the game?

It's so devious that I'm surprised the Fox can sleep at night. He waits until his opponent hits a key number then Freddy removes one match. Well, that's what they see. What they don't see is the match hidden in his hand which he secretly adds to the pile thus giving him the key number! He's taken a match and added a match effectively leaving the pile the same!

The infamous gambler Nick the Greek is reputed to have made nearly a quarter of a million dollars using this exact NIM ploy!

As Freddy says, *"The mug doesn't look too close when he's excited about winning."*

Among big time money players NIM is played with an unknown number of matches. A pile is just heaped on the table. Each player can remove from one to six matches with the loser being, once more, the one forced to take the last match. Although it sounds more complicated the system for winning is just the same.

Once the pile gets to a reasonable size the cheat will quickly count the matches. Freddy can count matches faster than dollar bills and, trust me, that's fast! He divides the result by seven and any odd matches left over are his next take. From then on, so long as he leaves his mug with a multiple of seven (7, 14, 21, 28, 35 etc.), he must win. If the total divides exactly by seven he takes just one match. Then, unless his mug takes six matches, he can hit a key number next time. Oh, and he can always add a match if he needs to!

Once he hits a winning position he can always hit his key numbers by noting how many matches the mug takes and then taking enough to make up a group of seven. Easy huh?

Once there are seven matches remaining the cheat must win because the opponent can't take more than six matches.

A lot of NIM men seem to nervously shuffle the matches around as they make their next choice. While they are playing with the matches they are making their count. Since they often use a pen or pencil to push the matches around these guys are known as *Pencil Pushers*.

There are numerous variations of NIM all of which Freddy is an expert at. In one version (often used as a follow up to the above) the last player to pick up a match *wins* the game. The secret (with twenty matches), as you may have guessed, is to hit different key numbers. Here the keys would be 16, 12, 8 and 4 and, again, you just can't lose.

My good friend Wesley James, the underground card and gambling expert did a pre-read on the book and added the following NIM stuff!

> *While you are essentially correct in your Nim explanation, the method for developing the keys is more formulaic than you state, though your examples are correct. You use specific examples but the general mathematical theory states that the keys are multiples of the maximum single-play removable number plus one. When playing with the cheat going first, the initial number of counters is largely irrelevant, provided he knows the keys and the mark does not. If the mark is allowed to go first, the initial number of counters should be odd. This avoids the need for the cheat to use the fake-take ploy that Nick the Greek employed. That's the reason the best known version of the game is played with 31 counters, it allows that the mark can go first. With that in mind, if the initial number is odd and the cheat must go first he removes two, retaining the odd count. He holds the matches he has removed in his hands. Unless the mark always removes two, he must at some point make the count even. At that point, the cheat removes one and hits a key. If the cheat suspects that the mark has happened upon the scam, he then uses the fake-take ploy to keep from losing that game and squirrels any further play. This is easy since he has been holding the matches he has removed in his hand. Strictly speaking, what you write is correct, merely not comprehensive.*

Wesley also told me of his days as a NIM player where he would often use a bowl of bar nuts for the game. If there was an even number of nuts in the bowl he would simply eat one to guarantee starting with an odd number!

Now that's sneaky!

NIM is played with matches, coins, beer coasters, playing cards, in fact just about anything that can be laid out in a pile on a table. Freddy's advice on this game is sound, *"Don't play the game if it even minutely resembles the above!"* Although one of the oldest of all gambling games (dating back to ancient Egypt) NIM is still good in loose company for a quick money raiser.

But while NIM has become known in fast company (with the exception of Freddy's little palming trick) another NAP bet known as the *Game of 31*

Simon and Wesley James play the infamous game of 31!

hasn't. It is one of the most devious and nasty little bar swindles of them all. It is a game where you can *teach* the mug the secret of winning and yet still take their money!

Actually this should really be called "NANAP" (Nearly A NAP) because it is possible to lose at the game. However this is so unlikely and rare that Freddy and his ilk count this firmly in the NAP category.

J.H. Green, a reformed gambler, wrote a book in 1850 entitled *One Hundred Gambler Tricks With Cards*. I know because I've just read a copy lent to me by Freddy. Here's what dear old J.H. has to say about the game, *"A trick often introduced by sporting men for the purpose of deceiving and making money by it. It is called 'Thirty One'. I caution all not to play or bet with a man who introduces it: for, most probably, if he does not propose betting on it at first, he will after he gets you interested, and pretend to teach you all the secrets of it, so that you can play it with him; and perhaps he will let you beat him if you should play in fun; but if you bet, he will surely beat you."* Dubious grammar aside, J.H. is giving fine advice. Freddy is just glad that not too many people ever got to read or take notice of that advice!

Here then is the deceptively simple game of 31. Let Freddy take you through it in detail. Once you know the real work I'm sure you'll never be tempted to play it.

Freddy removes all the aces, twos, threes, fours, fives and sixes from a deck of cards. He places them in six separate piles as below.

ACES   TWOS   THREES   FOURS   FIVES   SIXES

Freddy then hooks the mug into a little game of chance (hollow laugh) and explains that each player will draw a card in turn. The players draw alternately keeping a running total of the pips of the cards (so if the first three cards drawn were an ace, six and four, the running total would be eleven).

The player who draws and reaches thirty-one, *or as close as possible without exceeding it*, wins. If a player is compelled to go over thirty-one on his draw he loses. Either player may take the first card. Sounds simple doesn't it? It is simple provided you don't mind losing money all night long.

Once you have lost a few times Freddy will help you out. He'll kindly explain that the game is a game of key numbers. He'll tell you that these key numbers are 3, 10, 17 and 24. He'll do 'everything' he can so that you understand the key number theory. But, infuriatingly, when you try to use his advice you'll find that there are not enough cards in certain piles to make up key numbers, the cards required to reach thirty one will have run out, bottom line; you lose again. You may think that, your failure was just an odd coincidence and play again. You could try all night and all you'll see is a master hustler walking off with your money.

Until now that is.

Now Freddy is going to tell it all. Not just the key numbers but the whole hog. It may read a little complex at first but try it with cards in front of you. With a little practice you may soon be able to give the hustler a run for his money.

1. Basic Principles

Try to make one of the four key numbers: 3, 10, 17 or 24.

When you explain to the mug about these key numbers let him use them *but* use up four of a kind by the time he reaches 24. He then scores a number with which to make 31, but there are no cards left meaning he will lose the game. This means he will lose if he is at 10 with two of a kind gone; at 17 with three of a kind gone; or at 24 with four of a kind gone! This is the little bit of critical information you don't tell them! Don't worry if you don't see why this works. Freddy is going to give you some examples in a moment.

An ace, 2 or 5 lead inevitably (if you know what you are doing) wins. A 3, 4 or 6 inevitably loses (or at least gives the hustler some work).

2. The Winning Leads

If Freddy has first take (the lead) he pulls a five. He automatically wins if the mug plays an ace, 2, 3, 4 or 6 because he can hit a key number on the next draw. If the mug replies with a five Freddy takes a two letting the mug hit the key number of 17 *but* with three of a kind gone (three fives)! The last option would look like this . . .

Freddy	5		2		2		2
Mug		5		5		5	
Score	5	10	12	17	19	24	26

The mug can't use a five to make 31 because they've all gone. The closest he can get is to play a four to make thirty and Freddy wins with an ace!

Leading an ace or two does make winning a little harder but even Freddy likes to give himself a challenge sometimes! Let's look at Freddy taking an ace first just for his own amusement. If the mug replies with a 3, 4, 5 or 6 Freddy automatically wins because he will hit a key number on his next play. If the mug replies with a 2, he replies as follows (allowing the mug to hit the key numbers).

Freddy	A		6		6		6		6
Mug		2		A		A		A	
Score	1	3	9	10	16	17	23	24	30

Freddy wins because there are no more aces left to make up 31!

If the mug replied to Freddy's ace lead with another ace then Freddy can run out four of a kind in the following ways.

Freddy	A		6		6		6		6
Mug		A		2		A		A	
Score	1	2	8	10	16	17	23	24	30

Freddy	A		6		6		6		6
Mug		A		A		A		2	
Score	1	2	8	9	15	16	22	24	30

Leading with a two is a bit more work for Freddy. Freddy automatically wins if the mug plays a three or five because he will hit a key number on the next play (don't forget Freddy is also watching for four of a kind running out *against* him!). If the mug plays anything else then Freddy will let them hit key numbers but run out four of a kind as shown below.

Mug replies with an ace:

Freddy	2		6		6		6		6
Mug		A		A		A		A	
Score	2	3	9	10	16	17	23	24	30

Mug replies with a two:

Freddy	2		4		4		5		5
Mug		2		2		3		2	
Score	2	4	8	10	14	17	22	24	29

Mug replies with a four:

Freddy	2		2		4		5		5

Mug	4		2		3		2	
Score	2	6	8	10	14	17	22	24	29

Mug replies with a six:

Freddy	2		A		6		6		6
Mug		6		A		A		A	
Score	2	8	9	10	16	17	23	24	30

Of course these aren't all the plays possible but you should be getting the idea that by hitting key numbers *or* by running four of a kind it is possible for Freddy to win the game every single time he has the lead against a mug regardless of whichever card he decides to take! But what if it's the mug's turn to lead?

3. Winning Returns

If the mug leads with a 3, 4 or 6 they instantly lose in the following ways.

Mug leads a four:

Mug	4	
Freddy	6	
Score	4	10	Freddy hits a key number

Mug leads a six:

Mug	6	
Freddy	4	
Score	6	10	Freddy hits the key number again!

Mug leads with a three:

Mug	3		3		3		3	
Freddy		4		4		4		4
Score	3	7	10	14	17	21	24	28

No 3's left to make 31!

As you can see the game actually becomes *easier* for the hustler after he's explained about the key numbers!

4. Harder Returns

If a mug leads with an A, 2 or 5 Freddy won't panic. Unless he has come up against another 31 expert (as likely as running into a blind nun in a brothel) then all will be well. Freddy says that the odds on him accidentally meeting another 31 expert are about the same as those on me beating him at the game. I have *never* beaten him at this game.

Against a strong lead Freddy will always try to run out four of a kind on the key numbers. He claims that, after a while, the plays become automatic and, to be sure, I've never seen him so much as pause on a play. Here are Freddy's replies to my A, 2 and 5 openings during a teaching session.

Me	A		A		A		A	
Freddy		2		5		6		6
Score	1	3	4	9	10	16	17	23

Now I can't make the last key number of 24 because all the aces are gone . . . damn it!

Me	2		2		2		2	
Freddy		A		3		5		5
Score	2	3	5	8	10	15	17	22

Even playing around in the middle (Freddy says he was getting bored) Freddy makes sure that I can't hit the last key number because, this time, all the two's are gone . . . double damn it!

Me	5		5		5	
Freddy		5		4		2
Score	5	10	15	19	24	26

I was so amazed that I'd spooked Freddy into giving away the last key number that I forget to remember that the fives were going. Now I can't make 31 again . . . triple damn it!

I have still never beaten him at the game. In fact I have never seen Freddy lose at the game unless he's playing for fun and trying to hook another player into a money game. He says, "*It's taken me years to get good at this game. Unless you've put some serious time into it as well, you don't have a chance.*"

Stay away from this game or anything that even remotely resembles it. There is even a version with a die which, while looking different, is exactly the same game. You'll see it explained later on in this tome!

As you can see by NIM and 31, hustlers like Freddy will train hard on games to take your money. That's their job.

However, not all NAP bets are as difficult to learn as 31. Some require only a bold nerve and a larcenous heart to pull off a score. You'll see, from the following examples, that they often move more into the area of a con game of which you'll learn a great more as Freddy's un-nerving look at life carries on.

Freddy and a fellow hustler (Freddy usually works with a guy called Sam, nicknamed The Stoat because of his thin body) will often pull the *Odd Man*

Out ploy to raise some money. Here's how it works.

You (the mug) are standing drinking in a bar and get into conversation with Freddy and Sam. After a few drinks Freddy suggests a little game to decide who is going to pay for the next round of drinks. The Stoat agrees and, not wishing to embarrass your new-found friends, you agree to join in as well. Freddy explains that you will each toss a coin into the air and let it fall. The odd man pays (so if two heads and a tail come up the guy who threw the tail will pay). If all the coins fall the same the bet is void and you toss again. Simple huh?

You could play this game till the second coming of a deity of your choice and still never win. The reason? Well, Freddy and Sam are both using *Double Headed Coins* (coins with a head on each side). Their two coins must *always* match. Over a run they will switch back and forth between double headed and double tailed coins so that it doesn't become too obvious. Every time you throw a coin that doesn't match theirs you lose. The *best* you can do is match theirs and call the bet void.

Playing the game this way is relatively harmless. The most you can lose is a few rounds of drinks. But, the same game played differently can be used to make a much larger score as follows.

You are drinking with Freddy, a new-found friend, at the bar. You are getting along well, laughing at his endless stream of jokes and tricks, when a drunk wanders into the bar. He tries to muscle in on your conversation, offers to buy drinks and, spotting a few of Freddy's tricks on the bar, announces that tricks are stupid, he's a great gambler, a cheat, a winner. He flashes a huge *wedge* of money that he's won earlier today on the horses. He throws some money down on the bar for drinks and goes off to the toilet.

"*What an ass,*" says Freddy, "*Do you fancy taking some of that money from him?*" If you agree you are in big trouble. But, you will, Freddy is persuasive like that. Freddy explains that he'll suggest a bet of matching up coins. The three of you will toss coins in the air and the man who gets the odd coin will win. He explains that every time he calls heads you call tails and vise-versa. That way, one of you *has* to match the drunk and the other will win. After he's gone, you can split the money. You don't like the drunk, he's been pushy and obnoxious, sure you'd like to see him taught a lesson. Unless you are the Good Samaritan himself it's a dollar to a small flea that you'll agree to play along.

Back comes the drunk who, after a few more drinks, agrees to play along. Stakes get higher and higher but you don't panic because you are winning all the money along with Freddy. You may even feel a bit thrilled at cheating an admitted cheat. Eventually the drunk has lost his cash and doesn't want to play any more. You are keen to split the spoils (oddly Freddy is holding all the cash here) but the drunk just won't go. Freddy announces he has to leave and you follow him outside to split the money. Suddenly the drunk comes out as well and, seeing you both with the money, accuses you of cheating him. You try to pacify him. You are probably also getting rather worried that the drunk will call the police as he is threatening to. A bit of simple revenge is turning into something that could prove very embarrassing to you. "*We'll walk off in different directions*," says Freddy. "*I won that money fair and square, I was just offering my friend here some cab fare home, I'll do the same for you if you like!*" The drunk gets quieter, and Freddy whispers to you that he'll meet you back here in half an hour to split the cash. You are so relieved that the trouble has passed that you agree.

Half an hour later you return to the bar. Pull up a stool and get comfortable, you're going to be waiting a very long time. That's the last you'll ever see of Freddy or the drunk (superbly played by The Stoat).

This game is known as *The Smack* (from the sound of a coin hitting a bar) and is often worked at tourist resorts, bars and hotels where there is a quick turn-around of people. Watch out for anybody offering to split an easy money bet with you. While you are waiting for your split, they'll be spending your money elsewhere. And, think about it, who are you going to complain to? Are you really going to go to the police to report that you had your money stolen, "*as you were trying to con another man out of his!*"

Freddy has a number of ways he'll use a double headed or tailed coin. One of his most unusual NAP bets with one is a little number he refers to as the *Half NAP*. You see here although Freddy doesn't always win, he can never lose!

For a bet, say a meal tab, he will toss a coin into the air and invite you to call heads or tails while it is spinning. If you call correctly you win, if not, you lose. Freddy says that the coin will be allowed to fall freely to the floor so that no sleight-of-hand can be used.

Freddy tosses a double headed coin and, if you call tails, he lets it fall to the floor making you a loser.

If you call heads he snatches the coin out of the air and says, "*Just kidding, I wanted to see if you were a gambling kind of guy!*" He then moves on to another game.

Freddy wins the bet fifty percent of the time, but he can't lose the bet! Don't be fooled by its simplicity. Gamblers have been known to bet thousands of dollars on the toss of a coin. Imagine picking up fifty percent of that over a run of time!

For small change Freddy often poses little trivia questions, not any questions of course but ones that you might think you know the answer to but don't. Here's a selection of his trivia winners.

Who was the first American in Space?
    Over three quarters of the population rush to answer John Glenn but it's actually Alan Shepard. Glenn was the first American to orbit the earth and was the third American in space (Guss Grissom was the second by the way).
Who was the first President of America?
    Bit of a sneaky one here. John Hancock was the first president of the Continental Congress and thus is the answer to the question as posed here!
What's the longest race in the British horse racing Flat Season?

Another sneaky one racing fans. The answer is the Grand National. Even though it is a jump race, it's run in the Flat Season!

I've never seen Freddy lose at Trivial Pursuit either!

One of Freddy's favorite after dinner stories (and he has plenty to keep the boys entertained) concerns one of the most ingenious NAP bets of all time. Read and learn from the following proposition reputed to have been put to Willie Moretti by Benjamin 'Bugsy' Siegel, the famous prohibition racketeer and one of the founding fathers of Las Vegas as it is today. The proposition is said to have taken place in a hotel room at the Flamingo Hotel, Nevada in 1947.

Bugsy laid out two sugar cubes and a matchbox. He explained to Willie that inside the matchbox was a live fly. The bet was for each man to pick a lump of sugar and the first cube the fly landed on, after being released from the box, would be the winner. Willie figured that even Bugsy couldn't have a trained fly and agreed to the bet. Five minutes, and five thousand dollars later, the fly was sitting on Bugsy's sugar lump.

Willie offered to double or quits the bet. He even chose Bugsy's sugar cube. He thought it was possible that somehow his cube had been tampered with somehow. Once more he lost the bet. He cut out of the game ten thousand dollars the poorer. The truth was, however, that he could have played the game until the fly died and still never won. Think about it. He could choose either cube yet Bugsy was guaranteed to win! Can you work out the gaff?

Willie was close when he considered that his cube had been tampered with. Actually *both* cubes had been gaffed up. Each had a spot of DDT on one side. Whichever cube Willie picked was manipulated by Bugsy to be DDT side up while his was positioned DDT side down. Willie had 'Not A Prayer' that the fly would land on his cube.

This bet has become so famous that it was featured, and can be seen, in the 1954 French film *The Sheep has Five Legs*.

Finally here's a NAP bet you can try, for laughs only, on your friends and family. Have your mug shuffle a deck of cards and place them face down on the table. Tell them that the two of you will take turns turning over cards. The first one to turn over a picture card loses. This looks like a fifty-fifty bet, either of you could turn one over, but you can win every time.

Whenever you take a card peek at it before you turn it over. Don't hide this, in fact make it quite obvious. If it's not a picture card, turn it over.

Carry on with the game. If the mug turns over a picture card next, you win. But what if they don't? Worse still, what if you peek a picture card before they get one?

If you peek a picture card simply place it face down onto the pile and peek the next card—If this is a picture card place it face down on top of the first. Keep doing this until you reach a non picture card and flip it face up.

The mug, a bit disconcerted by this, will reach for the other face down card/s and flip them over. He can claim you cheated all he wants but you still win the bet.

You see, he turned them face up, not you!

Be prepared to run at this point!

I learned this last little number from, who else, Freddy. You should be glad you got here for free. It cost me ten dollars.

If you've read through this chapter carefully you'll have noted overlaps between NAP bets, prop bets and odds bets. You'll also see as you carry on how some also overlap into what can be considered con games. I really must stress that we've only touched the tip of the iceberg here. Space simply doesn't allow for the hundreds upon hundreds of bets of this nature that abound everywhere. But, by seeing some of them, you have hopefully learned that the sucker is never offered a good deal on his or her money in these situations.

So you have under your belt a few ingenious and downright sneaky bar bets and hustles. You don't, I must stress again, have *every* one that could be offered. So, if in doubt, follow Freddy's top eight tips to hold onto your money.

1. *Never* bet on anything that looks impossible to do.
2. *Never* believe any odds that are explained to you in a betting situation. Carry a calculator with you and work them out properly. If you can't do the math then don't take the bet.
3. *Do* watch out for bet variations. Hustlers spend sleepless nights trying to think up new twists to conceal old principles.
4. *Never* accept a Freeze Out type of bet. Offer to bet just once (giving you at least a chance) and watch the hustler run.
5. *Never* get chatting about odds and gambling. You may be getting hooked in. Once you realize what is happening it may be too late. For the same reason never take a few tries on a bet for free, *just for fun.*
6. *Never, never, never* tell a gambler that you know about cheating techniques. It's 20–1 he'll use your knowledge against you. Professional prop men take great pleasure out of beating professional gamblers out of money on impossible bets. What chance have you got?
7. *Never* get carried away by the heat of the moment. You may think the gambler, a little drunk, has offered a bet the wrong way round. You may think that he is just a kindly old guy having some fun. And surely a little old lady couldn't be a cheat? Listen very carefully to what is being offered and turn it down. Freddy describes cheats as having, *"The faces of angels, the hands of gods and the hearts of sewer rats."*
8. *Don't* point out loudly to all and sundry that the bet being offered is a mug's one. Pro hustlers often carry baseball bats along with their dice and cards. Just refuse the bet and leave quietly.

Do you get the idea?

These bets are for idiots only.

Some Bigger Hustles

FREDDY THE FOX USES THE TYPE OF BETS YOU'VE READ ABOUT SO FAR TO WIN SOME quick, easy money. Sometimes he wins a lot, sometimes not so much. It all depends on how much you are willing to bet.

They are the kind of bets you can play with friends using matches or pennies to bet with.

Bigger hustles are designed simply to take money, a lot of it, in the most despicable manner. Counted amongst these would be *The Drunken Paw, Three Card Monte,* variations of the *Walnuts and Pea* (commonly seen nowadays with three matchbox covers and a rolled piece of paper), *The Tat* and the *Crossed Deck.* To ensure your money stays in the hustler's pocket he may use the *Tear Up* to guarantee it.

You don't know them? Don't worry you soon will. You're not going to be taken by these guys and others like them; least ways not after Freddy has explained them all to you.

Read on, the roller coaster ride hasn't hit the first big drop yet!

"You don't play the game, you play the man."

———◆———

advice for gambling games
very applicable to con games

The Drunken Paw

Y OU'RE ENJOYING A DRINK AT YOUR FAVORITE BAR, PERHAPS TRYING TO TALK
that attractive bar lady into a dinner date when the joint shuts up for the
night. As ever she is turning you down but, what the hell, it's a pleasant
evening and you are feeling no pain from three or four Martinis whisking
around your system.

All that is about to change. As the opening for the television show *Sting-
ray* used to say, *"Anything can happen in the next half hour!"*

Into the bar rolls the worst kind of drunk. Loud, obnoxious and just this
side of being thrown out straight away. Everybody takes an instant dislik-
ing to him. Nobody wants to talk to him and all are relieved when he picks
on you.

"Hi yer mate!" he says, far too loudly, in your ear as he lurches against
you, *"Lemmie buy you a drink. Ho! Bar lady, a drink for my pal!"* Politely you
refuse the drink and turn away, but this man does not give up.

"Aw, come on matey," he continues, *"I know I've had a few but...,"* he looks
around and whispers, *"I've been really lucky today! C'mon just have one little
drink with me to celebrate, eh? I've got money, look!"* He opens his wallet right
under your nose. It's stuffed with money.

Much as you may try to ignore him, the drunk, as all drunks do, insists on
telling you the full story. In between mouthfuls of drink and the occasional
burp, he tells you, and anybody else who will listen, about how he's just won
big in a game of Poker. He throws a deck of cards triumphantly onto the bar
top. *"Even took their damned cards off em!"* he shouts, almost falling over in
the process.

"Tell you what," he says, *"I'll play you for a drink buddy. Come on, I just
can't lose today. Waddya say huh? Just one hand for fun!"* The last thing in
the world you want to do is to play cards with this lout but before you can
object he's shuffled the cards (dropping some in the process on the floor)
and dealt out two hands of five cards each.

He picks up your cards and pokes you with them. *"Come on,"* he jibes, *"Are you a man or what?"* You try to remain calm. The idiot has flashed the faces of your cards at you. By 'monumental luck' it consists of four kings and an odd card. Now you start to get interested in a bet, and not just for a pint.

He picks up his cards and takes a quick look. He then reaches for his wallet. As he removes the wallet he makes another 'mistake'. You can see his cards. His hand consists of three jacks and two odd cards. You might suspect a hustle is in operation but obviously this madman has messed it up. Now you can show him up for what he is and take his money in the process! You've got the winning hand!

"Wanna real bet sonny?" he goads, throwing a hundred dollars onto the bar, *"Or are you just too frightened to play the big winner?"* With growing anger you cover the bet.

Mistake number one.

"How many cards you wanna draw kiddo?" he asks. Suddenly you realize that you are playing Draw Poker which entitles the players to change some of their cards. You stand pat (no change) thinking, quite logically, that the best hand he can hope for is to change the two odd cards and pull a Boat (a Full House consisting of three of a kind and a pair) or, at very best, the extra jack to make up four of a kind. Whatever, you'll still have the winning hand. You decide to stay in the game and really teach him a lesson.

Mistake number two.

He changes two cards confirming your theory. *"HA!"* he cries, looking at his hand, *"I'm the luckiest S.O.B. this side of Venus! I told ya I just couldn't lose! It's gonna cost you five hundred to see this little puppy!"* He throws down another four hundred dollars on top of the one hundred already in place. You assume he's drawn the fourth jack and decide to cover the bet. You may even have to borrow money from your pals in the bar (or visit the ATM) but you really want to beat this guy and see him shamed.

Mistake number three.

You throw down your four kings, laugh heartily and reach for the money.

Mistake number four.

The drunk stops you and throws down his hand. A very sad moment for you. He didn't change the two odd cards. He changed two of the jacks and drew two cards to make his hand a Straight Flush (five cards in a run, all the same suit). A Straight Flush, in case you hadn't already guessed, wipes out four kings.

While you are too stunned to move the drunk grabs the money and runs for the door. You recover just in time to see the drunks wallet fall to the floor as he exits. Rather than chase him you stop to pick up the wallet. At least you'll get your money back and have the last laugh on him.

Mistake number five.

The wallet isn't the same one he showed you. It's stuffed with newspaper to delay you long enough for the 'drunk' to make a quick hop into his car outside. By the time you discover the wallet switch and get through the door you may just be in time to wave goodbye as he drives off.

HOW THE PAW WORKS

This little game, perhaps above all others, demonstrates to perfection a W.C. Fields observation that says, *"You can't cheat an honest man."* It is an essential ingredient of most con games that the man who is being swindled believes that he has an unfair advantage.

If you had been an honorable sort you would never have taken advantage of a poor drunk who flashed his cards at you, however obnoxious the drunk was. But you did, and you paid the price for your larceny.

The actual mechanics of the game are very easy. The cheat has all the cards he needs pre-stacked on top of the deck. The order, from the top down, is as follows . . .

K, 7D, K, 9D, K, JD, K, JC, A, JS, 10D, 8D

It is an easy matter for him, as you'll see in later chapters on card handling, to shuffle the cards leaving his simple stack on top of the deck. He doesn't even have to false shuffle well! There's no pressure, no careful watching eyes, on the old drunk shuffling the deck. When he deals them out you will get four kings and an ace. He will receive the 7D, 9D, JD, JC and JS.

When he flashes his cards the jacks draw your attention. You pay little or no attention to the two 'odd' cards. When he changes his cards he throws in the JC and JS to draw the 8D and 10D from the deck to complete the Straight Flush.

The wallet drop is a standard ploy for this type of game. The wallet, duplicate to the one you saw full of money, is a delaying tactic to give him extra get-away time. All of his money by the way will be *Snide* or counterfeit just in case he gets into real trouble during the bet.

Finally, and perhaps most obviously, is that the drunk was not a drunk at all. It was Freddy the Fox displaying more acting talent than many a film star. His whole act is designed to make you dislike him, designed to make you want to beat him. You get carried away with the moment and, by the time you get an inkling that all is not as it should be, it's way too late.

THE DOUBLE PAW

Occasionally the Drunken Paw is worked as a *twofer* or by two hustlers working together. A man arrives at the bar and gets friendly with all present. The drunk arrives later and latches onto this likeable fellow. When the cards are dealt, our friendly chap will draw others into the game and ask their advice. If he needs to borrow money to back up his bet, his new found friends will lend it to him. After all, it will all be repaid with interest as soon as the hand is won! Nothing like the lure of easy money to turn an honest man into a *Shylock* or money lender.

When the final *sting* has happened and the drunk has left, the first man will stay behind to *cool the marks*. He'll explain that he's lost all his money and he's as sick about it as they are. He may shed a few tears as he begs his pals not to call the police, he doesn't want his wife to know he was conned. His new pals feel sorry for him. They may even feel guilty as it was they who advised him to bet! The first man will do anything he can to *buy time* for the 'drunk' to get away and for tempers to quieten down. It's quite common for the mugs to feel so sorry for the nice guy that they buy him a few drinks and give him some cab fare home!

Later the two will meet to split the money. The first man is known as the *inside man* while the drunk, in cheat's parlance, is known as the *outside man*. Both are outstanding actors with nerves of steel. The Double Paw is very common in holiday resort towns where a good team may hit three or four bars a night.

The Paw has variations for just about every bar game under the sun. One very famous variation on a Pool Table known as *Young Man, Old Man* was featured in the Paul Newman and Tom Cruise movie *The Color of Money*. It's worth renting the movie just to see this Paw in action.

Whatever the game. Be very wary of offers from drunks that look too good to be true.

BEATING THE PAW

The only chance, should you stupidly decide to play, is to play erratically. Don't stand pat on your four kings. Keep three kings and change two cards. This gives you a fighting chance of destroying his stack and therefore his advantage.

Of course, if he is a competent *Cellar Man* (Bottom Dealer) he'll just give you two from the bottom of the deck and you are really screwed. An experienced player will also increase the stack by adding the last jack under the 8D. Then *even* if you draw two cards he can draw one to give him four jacks against your three kings!

So, how to beat the Paw?

You just can't hope to do so. Instead learn to recognize the set up. Whatever the game they all carry the same traits. Drunken guy, messing up bet, offers to play, you need to bet. Just refuse the bet. It's better to be called a coward and a fool than it is to look like one. If the drunk protests too much reach for the phone to call the police, tell the drunk the local cops can sort this out for you. You'll see a great magic trick known as the vanishing drunk at this point. He'd rather leave and go off to find an easier *touch* than you!

Hopefully nobody will call you sucker on this one!

The Tear Up

LET'S GET ONE THING OUT OF THE WAY BEFORE WE TROMP ANY FURTHER INTO the bigger money bets. Freddy likes to play for cash and lots of it. But what if you don't have the cash? In these days of ATM machines on every street corner it's much easier for you get hold of the green stuff, but would Freddy ever take a check? After all, especially in big cities, people don't like having large amounts of cash on them for fear of being mugged.

Checks are all well and good if the Fox is playing with people he knows. Yes, he does play cards with people he knows well. He doesn't cheat them, it's just his recreation time where he actually gets to play for the love of the game. He'll always take a *marker* (an IOU) or a check from these people. He knows where they live!

But if he's playing a con game away from home on a stranger does he really want a check? He doesn't if there is any other option because the mark, after some thinking time, might start to realize they'd been conned and cancel the check with his bank. Freddy is unlikely to turn up to complain even if he could track down the mark again.

But, it would also be rather churlish to turn down the offer of a check at the point of the *sting*. It could arouse suspicion to do so. So, at times like this, Freddy will use one of the most insidious little tricks in the hustlers pocket book. It's known in the trade as the *tear up*.

Don't be fooled by its simplicity. It works.

Let's say that you've been playing Poker with Freddy. It's towards the end of the night and, just for once, you've been dealt a good hand. So good in fact that you think it's the winning hand. Undeterred by your strong play Freddy puts a big bet into the pot.

You don't have the cash to cover it, no *markers* are allowed, so you ask if you can throw in a check to cover the considerable difference. Freddy agrees and may even magnanimously lend you a pen with which to write it. You throw in the check to call Freddy and the hands are turned. Horrors, you lose!

Freddy picks up the pot and stashes it away in his wallet. Suddenly he has second thoughts.

"*You've been a real good sport,*" he says as he looks at your crestfallen face. "*That last hand was killer bad luck my friend. Tell you what, forget about the check!*" He takes your check from the wallet and tears it into tiny pieces before throwing it away. "*Let's just call it quits on the cash you lost!*"

You leave thinking what a great guy he is.

Until you get your next bank statement.

The check you thought you saw being ripped up has been cashed through your account. There is no come back. Are you going to complain to the police? Even if they could find Freddy all he will say is that you lost the bet and must have been mistaken about him tearing up the check. "*Who in their right mind would do that?*" he will argue!

The tear up gave Freddy time to cash the check without any fear of you canceling it!

HOW THE TEAR UP WORKS

Freddy collects checks like some small boys collect stamps. Within his wallet he has ten or twelve different types. Whatever your check looks like it's a safe bet that he has at least one that is similar.

All have writing on them in purple ball point. When you write your check he lends you a purple ball point with which to do so.

After he has won the pot (of which much more later!) he will pop the money and check into his wallet. Then, appearing to have second thoughts, he will look as though he's taking your check from the wallet.

What he *actually* does is remove a check *similar* to yours. You see a check, catch a glimpse of purple ink and see it shredded. You are so relieved by this gesture that you don't look too hard at the piece of paper being destroyed. You are far too busy thanking Freddy!

The real check lies safely in Freddy's wallet to be cashed the next day.

If there is any suspicion that you've been conned *always* cancel a check, even if you have seen it torn up right in front of your eyes!

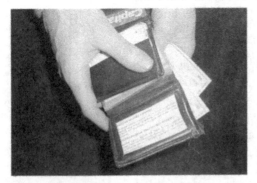

The Tear Up.

Another amusing piece of cheat trivia came from a dinner with Wesley James when he said this was very commonly done on board cruise ships. The check would be torn up and tossed overboard so that nobody (unless crazy enough to jump after it) would be able to confirm it was the same check!

ADD-ON

Freddy, if feeling particularly larcenous (about 98 % of his waking time), may well tear up the check and

How to Cheat at Everything

accept another check for half of the amount owed. After all, he can't very well just cancel out the whole bet but he doesn't want to break your bank, he'll explain. You'll love your next bank statement even more when you see that he's cashed both checks.

You have to realize that people like Freddy don't care about you at all. They only care about the money. The sooner you realize this simple fact, the better off you will be.

PERCENTAGE CALL

I asked Freddy if any checks had ever been canceled on him anyway. "*Sure,*" he replied, "*One or two over the years but that's just a teeny viable loss. After all it's not just about winning, it's about winning and keeping the money. This ploy has let me keep a great deal more than I would have otherwise. Anyway, the add-ons make up for the canceled ones!*"

So, bear in mind, as we sally forth into some more hustles, that the tear up is always there lurking and ready to be used!

The Crossed Deck

At the very start of this book you were warned not to try to emulate the scams of people like Freddy the Fox. If you do so there's a real danger of you really coming a cropper. The Crossed Deck scam is a perfect illustration how, if you are drawn into Freddy's world as a hustler, the fall can be a painfully expensive one.

This is a con designed specifically to be used on the person who knows that they are not a skilled con artist but who would just love to have that 'edge', that danger, that profit in their lives for once! It is often worked on small time and amateur cheats by the professionals. It is so versatile that it is almost impossible to spot until it's too late. As you can imagine, with such advantages, it's a favorite with the big boys!

It follows a classic hook, line and sinker technique so we'll take it in those stages during the following example. Let's go back to a bar again where you are enjoying a quiet beer. The stage is set, the overture is over and the curtains have opened.

A gentleman enters stage left.

THE HOOK

The bar is quiet and, as often happens in drinking establishments, you get chatting with the gent. He is a charming man and soon you are swapping anecdotes and jokes.

After a few more drinks Freddy (yes it's him) tells you he is an amateur magician. He pulls out a deck of cards and gets you to take one. The card is shuffled back into the deck and somehow, you're not sure how, he finds it. He proceeds to dazzle you with a number of tricks. Even after a few beers you can see that he is pretty damn good at this stuff.

As all folk do, you ask him how he does that stuff. Could he maybe teach you a trick or two to show your pals? Freddy is a little reticent so you let the subject drop.

A few more beers go by, and Freddy is getting a little tipsy.

"*Hell,*" he says, "*I've got to tell somebody. You're a good mate, do you mind?*"

Notice how alcohol, the universal friendship maker, has played a role again already!

The tale starts to slowly unfold. You listen, first with interest, then with fascination.

Freddy isn't an amateur magician. He's a cheat. He was even considering setting you up to take a few bucks but he likes you and just couldn't bring himself to do it. You've heard about men like Freddy, maybe even seen them in films like *The Sting* (itself a great example of a Cross in action by the way!), but this is the first time you've ever met one. This man *actually* cheats at cards for a living!

He picks up the deck again and this time they come to life in his hands. His tricks may have been good but this is something else. Even after all the drinks his hands move with a fluid ease. He shuffles and deals two hands of Poker. You didn't see a thing but Freddy has four aces. You shuffle and deal and, once more, Freddy gets four aces. He shows you the rudiments of card Stacking and Palming (which you'll see later *without* being drawn into a con!) and your estimation of him rises even further. The skill level required is phenomenal.

Freddy even explains to you how this all works in a real game. He tells you that he has a partner to whom he deals the good cards. There is no pressure on him as the dealer because he'll lose the hand. His partner picks up the money and they split it afterwards. You are getting an insider's look at an esoteric world that normally hides behind closed doors. This is an amazing guy!

THE LINE

Freddy then explains why he's a bit morose tonight. It appears that his idiot partner has been arrested doing a little *B and E* (Breaking and Entering). He'd been short on his stake for the game and now the fool is in prison awaiting trial. Freddy has lost his partner.

"*But surely you can just get another one!*" you exclaim.

You learn from Freddy that it just doesn't work like that. The partner has to be just the right sort of person. One who won't panic under pressure. A man who'll know when to bet and not get carried away. A man who can be trusted implicitly; after all he'll walk away with a huge stash of money, and Freddy needs to know that he won't just vanish with it. The partner must look like a normal guy looking for a game, even better if he looks like a bit of an inexperienced player with a few bucks too many to lose. "*A good partner,*" he sadly explains, "*Is very difficult to find. I mean, it's not like I can advertise, can I!*"

You may suggest what follows. Perhaps Freddy does. After a few more beers it gets difficult to remember.

But you end up at a small Poker game to see if you've got what it takes.

Freddy has bankrolled you (given you some money) and you are working with him. He's taught you the signaling system so that you know just when to bet. You follow his signs, win a few hands and, afterwards, meet up for a few beers to split the cash.

Your take comes to over two hundred dollars. Easy money! "*Chicken feed!*" says Freddy. Lady luck has shined on him tonight. He's found a perfect new partner and, not a moment too soon. There's a big game in town the very next day! You start to think of all your bills disappearing in a puff of smoke. You are hot for what follows.

"*It's a big game,*" explains Freddy, "*A five thousand sit down.*" He explains to you that this means that you need five thousand dollars to buy the chips for the game. They'll want to see the money up front or you don't get to play. He has the money for himself but hasn't got enough to bankroll you. Is there any chance you could raise the money?

It's a once in a lifetime experience to get in on a world of easy money. Miss out and he may never give you another chance. Like so many who've fallen for get-rich-quick pyramid schemes you decide you'll raise that money somehow!

The next night you have the money. You may have emptied your savings or sold your car but what the hell. Freddy has assured you that the take could easily be ten thousand each. You'll double your money at the very least! You force yourself to remain calm as Freddy explains the plan.

"*Play along and lose a few hands. Let them gain confidence in you. I want you to appear to be a real mug. Then, later on, when the game is running hot and I'm dealing, I'll throw you the hand. You'll get the signal, go for it! Then act like you just got the luckiest hand of your life and get out of the game. Say you gotta phone your wife or something and just get out. They'll think you are a jerk but who cares! I'll see you back here for the split. Don't think about not showing up.*"

Freddy may even give you an extra few hundred dollars he's *managed* to raise during the day to make sure you have enough for the kill. You head is spinning with thoughts of easy money. It's all happening so quickly but isn't that what success in life is all about? See the chance and grab for it!

THE GAME

The seedy, smoky atmosphere of the game is a whole new world to you. Hardened gamblers, chewing heavily on cigars, sit hunched over their cards. You're glad you are in Freddy's company. You're going show these guys a thing or two. You order a whiskey and soda to calm your nerves and sit in on the game. Freddy has made it very clear to you that you must not, under any circumstances, show that you know him. You throw down your money to buy the gambling chips with a casual aplomb you imagine a pro may use. Enjoy this moment. It's the last time you'll ever see that money.

The game proceeds. You lose a few hands, maybe even win the odd small one or two. You are staying pretty even money-wise but tension is growing. Time is getting short. When is Freddy going to pull the big one? You take a slug of your whiskey. At least the girl serving drinks isn't slow!

You pick up a hand. At last! It contains three kings. You casually look to Freddy who, although looking away and ordering a drink, is giving a signal with his fingers. You start to bet. You pull the last king. It's big money time. Obviously, Freddy has somehow given some of the other players good, but lesser, hands as well. They are staying with you and the pot is growing to a monumental size. As far as you are concerned, the more the merrier.

You push the bet, just as Freddy has taught you to. The whole poke goes in. The pot in total stands at around twenty three thousand dollars by your rough calculation. Only one man is left and, seeing you are out of money, he rather reluctantly calls your bet.

You flip your four kings and reach for the pot.

THE SINKER AND COOL OUT

The other man turns over a low Straight Flush. "*Tough break kid,*" he rasps as he takes the money. For the first time you notice that Freddy looks as mad as a man can be without actually exploding. He storms away from the table and goes outside. A little unsure of what to do, you follow him.

As soon as you are outside he turns on you.

"*You dumb @$#,*" he exclaims, "*What the #$% @ were you doing betting on that #@$%ing hand! I told you only to bet when I was dealing, you $%^&#$#%@ing @#$hole!*" In the shock of it all you now can't remember just who did deal those cards.

"*You even lost my #$%@ing money as well,*" rages Freddy, "*Perfect @#$%ing partner! Get outta my sight. Jesus, what the @#$% was I thinking using a rube like you!*"

You plead that you lost your money too. You may even beg him for another chance. But Freddy, in a rampaging temper, stomps away. You decide to talk to him next time you see him at the bar when he's had a chance to cool down. The sinking feeling that you've just blown five thousand dollars of your own money may also be starting to settle upon you. You feel like a complete idiot at having thrown away such a great chance.

You'll never see Freddy again if you are lucky.

HOW THE CROSSED DECK WORKS

Anybody who has ever gambled, and most people have at some time or another, has fantasized about a sure fire bet. A one hundred percent winning certainty. Freddy is offering the mug just that very opportunity.

The mug's greed is Freddy's biggest weapon.

The money you won on the first night is all *snide* (forged). There's no way Freddy will let you walk away with the real stuff. The few hundred extra dollars he gives you for the big night is forged as is all the money at the game, except for yours.

The game is a *Hot Seat* table. That means that all the players are in on the scam.

The one truth Freddy told you is that he is a master card mechanic. Late in the game Freddy will *Iron Man* (switch) the deck after a shuffle for one that has been pre-set to deal out the required hands. He hands the deck to the man next to him who deals. While all this is happening the others will be neatly distracting you so, afterwards, it's hard to say just what did happen.

You've seen the rest. You lose.

Don't think that the money here is exaggerated. Often the Cross will be pulled for a great deal more. Freddy is an expert at summing up just how much cash you can raise if given a good hook. He always goes for the full amount! In some cases the Cross has literally been pulled for hundreds of thousands of dollars.

The moment of the sting is timed to perfection. After all, Freddy and his boys have had a great deal of experience in setting up other victims. He knows just how to brush you off afterwards. Sometimes with temper, sometimes with compassion. If you are really unlucky he'll even give you another go to prove your worth in another game.

Your biggest problem, apart from getting hooked in the first place, is that you have absolutely no come back. Do you really think it would be a good idea to go to the police and try to explain that you were a cheat's partner who screwed up! As you'll see a lot of con games go unreported simply because the mugs would rather write off the money than look stupid in a court of law.

VARIATIONS ON THE CROSSED DECK

Sometimes marked cards will be part of the ploy. You'll be taught the secret marks but on the night, for some reason or another, you'll get them wrong.

Sometimes it may be a dice game. Freddy will show you how he can switch in gaffed dice. Surprise, surprise when you bet at just the wrong time.

Often you may be part of a con that just falls apart. It may not even seem to be your fault but your money will disappear just the same. An 'armed robbery' mid game is more common than you may imagine. Guys bust in, fire a shot or two (blanks) into the ceiling, grab the money and leave. Bummer huh? And just when you were on the verge of making your big time cheating break.

A great example of a Cross being taken to the absolute limit can be seen in David Mamet's wonderful film *House of Games* which features Ricky Jay.

Here a lady is slowly lured into a team play, through several smaller cons, into a huge pay-off. The accuracy is quite chilling. It is well worth watching to learn more about the Cross and about con artists and hustlers in general.

AVOIDING THE CROSS

This is tricky as the Cross can turn up in a million and one disguises. Following these simple rules should help you avoid most of them though.

1. Be *very* wary of a man who tells you he is a cheat especially after short acquaintance. The only time a cheat will do this is when they are setting up some kind of con.
2. Be *extra* wary if he suggests that you put some of your money into a bankroll.
3. Remember that your greed is the hustler's greatest weapon. It may look like easy money but nothing in life is free.
4. Ask yourself why a man with such skill and knowledge has to ask you to be a partner. That's a rhetorical question by the way as, if you do ask, the hustler will give you a million and one very plausible reasons! Surely this man would have, despite his protests otherwise, a network of underworld contacts he could pull from?
5. Turn down the proposition however good it looks.

THE NATURAL HABITAT OF THE CROSSED DECK

The real answer to this really is almost anywhere. However the Cross is most often seen at holiday resorts. People arrive, with spending money, every week or so before returning home. There's a relaxed atmosphere, lots of drinking and a general innocence that seems to descend upon people on holiday. A cheat's Disneyland if you like.

Reading a scam like the Cross in cold print is quite different to being exposed to it in action. You may think it seems obvious that it must be a hustle. 20/20 hindsight is a wonderful thing.

What the printed word can't convey is the cheat's consummate understanding of human nature. His experience of psychology, his superb and convincing acting, his entire *sell*. Oh, and of course, his absolutely chilling lack of regard for the mug and what may happen to them afterwards.

If you are convinced that you can't be conned there are con men who'll tell you that you are already half way towards being so. Let's be careful out there chaps!

The Tat

THIS IS AN OLD-TIME HUSTLE WHICH IS MAKING A COMEBACK IN A BIG, BIG WAY. It is now very common at business conventions and seminars which are often run at large hotels. The business men will have had a few drinks and be in a jolly mood. After all, they've had a long day of meetings and lectures and are ready for some fun. The hotel bar is a good start.

All we need now is Freddy (complete with name tag—don't ask) and the scene is set.

The boys from YEY Electronics are onto their third round of drinks. They may have decided to play a game of Spoof (a coin game you'll learn about later) to see who buys the next round of drinks. They merrily play a game or two and fling down a few more drinks. Whatever is happening, the drinks are flowing. Freddy enters the bar and, seeing he's one of their own (the name tag remember?), they invite him over. If a game is being played he joins in after the rules are explained to him. If not he buys some drinks anyway. After all, it's play time for the company boys now!

The drinks continue to flow. Isn't it amazing how many hustles seem to happen when you are impaired somehow?

It is around this time that one of the YEY boys will find a die on the floor. Perhaps it's been dropped from one of the hotel games but, whatever, it won't take long for a game to be invented. Freddy may even help shape the rules. They'll roll the die and the guy who rolls the lowest number buys the drinks. Much merriment ensues as the evening wanders ever forward.

Freddy then says that he once saw a game where a dice (he will use common terminology here as there's no point in giving away *any* indication that he may know what he's talking about) was put into a paper cup. You put your hand over the mouth of the cup and shook it up. You looked into the cup and made a note of the number showing on top. You repeated it three times to get a total. The guy with the highest total won the game! He adds that he was told that using the cup made cheating impossible, or something like that anyway.

It doesn't take long to find a paper cup in a hotel. Nor does it take long for somebody to suggest playing for money instead of drinks. It may even be Freddy.

As with all drunken bar games the betting escalates as the guys play the ever popular 'My dick is bigger than your dick' tactics on each other. These high-powered business men are showing off to all and sundry just how rich they are by upping the bet stupidly. There'll be much taunting going on if a guy turns down a bet.

Suddenly the time is ripe. There's a *lot* of money on the next round and it's time for the kill. Freddy, amidst much cheering, not only covers the bet but ups it even further. To save face his challengers cover the stake.

A hush settles as an up and coming whiz kid scores and looks good with a total of fourteen. There's only genial Freddy between him and the money. Freddy's first shake shows a six. His second a five. Some of the lower, already eliminated, scorers are cheering Freddy on.

He shakes the cup for the third time and raises his hand. A five shows giving Freddy a total of sixteen.

He picks up the money with a shaking hand. Despite protests he insists that the betting is getting just a little too rough for him and he's going to go off to bed. He leaves to some jeers and cries of, "*We'll getcha tomorrow night, you lucky SOB!*"

The boys carry on playing, unaware that they've just been taken by a master hustler and that they will never see Freddy again.

HOW THE TAT WORKS

When pulling any company scam Freddy always has a name tag (false name of course). Getting it is as simple as stealing it from the registration desk or *dipping* (pickpocketing) one from a person and changing the name. That person just assumes they've lost their tag and gets another. If you don't think Freddy could take a tag unnoticed just trust me. By simply brushing by you he'd have time to imperceptibly take your wallet as well. At a Trade Show, Freddy may just use a generic company tag.

The die the YEY guy found had not been dropped by accident. If he'd been just a little more sober he may have wondered just what a die was doing on a bar floor in the first place. After a few drinks Freddy's explanation that it must have fallen from a game set seemed quite plausible. It was just a lucky break to add some fun to the night.

The die had actually been dropped by Freddy sometime during the chatting and drinking. Contrary to what you may be imagining this die is completely normal.

The one in Freddy's pocket, however, is not normal. It is designed with only sixes and fives on its six sides (three of each). This *gaff* would be transparent if the die were rolled on a bar. But, looking into a paper cup means that only the top face of the die can be seen! The side faces are hidden by the wall of the cup.

*A Tat die—
note the extra six!*

At the point of the kill all Freddy has to do is switch the die into the game on his turn. Against hardened gamblers this would be an *under the gun* (tough) move. Against a group of playful drunks it is child's play. He simply holds the fake die in his left hand. With his right hand he picks up the real die. He pretends to put the die into his left hand but just holds back the die with his right thumb. He then drops the fake die into the cup. A very simple switch that is done in an instant.

Three shakes later he's a big winner. All eyes are on the money and the loser so switching back the real die is, again, child's play. You'll learn a great deal more about dice switching in later chapters here. After the switch the gaff goes into Freddy's pocket with the money.

He leaves the ordinary one behind. After all, he's got a few hundred more in the trunk of his car.

If nobody spots the die on the floor Freddy will ignore it. He won't point it out himself as that would put far too much attention on him. He may, however, wrangle the conversation round to another hustle. As he says, "*If you throw enough mud at a wall, some of it is going to stick.*"

A variation on this particular scam (using a magnetic die) can be seen in the movie *The Grifters* starring John Cusack. "*He does it pretty well,*" was Freddy's comment after watching the film.

THE OBVIOUS QUESTION

But what if one of the mugs throws fives and sixes as well? It's back to the odds folks!

The odds on shaking a five or six are 2 in 6. To do it three times on the run brings up odds of . . .

Work this out on your calculator and you'll get the figure 0.037. Divide 1 by 0.037 to get 27.02. So, the odds on another player shaking three times and getting fives or sixes is one chance in twenty-seven or 26-1 against. Even Freddy will take those odds!

So why doesn't he just use a die with sixes on all the faces? Then his challengers would have to throw three sixes (215-1 against) just to tie his score. Freddy says that this would put way too much heat on him. He'd rather risk the occasional loss than risk exposure. If he loses he can always return another time to take another shot at it and, with the odds so favorable for him, that's something he's happy to do. As he's very fond of saying, "*You can only kill a sheep for meat once but you can shear it for wool once a year*"

The Watch Fob Off

THIS CON EXPLOITS, AS SO MANY DO, ONE OF MANKIND'S OLDEST TRAITS. Greed.

If everybody were totally honest it is likely that a great many con men would go out of business by the end of the week. So many cons work by seeming to offer an unfair advantage to the mug before they are taken for their money. Read the following carefully and learn from an expert at work.

THE SCENARIO—ACT ONE

It is a reasonably busy night at the local watering hole. A man goes to the toilet. Upon his return he has a puzzled look upon his face. It appears that he has found a watch. It looks to him as though it's a pretty expensive one. He asks around if anybody has lost a watch or not. You would notice, if you were watching closely enough, that he doesn't ask any of the bar staff. A truly dishonest man may try to claim the watch is his but since he can't describe the inscribing on the back his claim is soon dismissed. The watch owner is nowhere to be found.

The watch finder goes outside to see if he can find the owner in the street or anywhere near by.

THE SCENARIO—ACT TWO

Meanwhile, almost with perfect timing, another, rather flustered looking gentleman enters the bar. You recognize him as a man who had been at the bar earlier and who you'd been happy to see leave. He had been boasting loudly about his fabulous lifestyle and about how much money he made in the city. He'd rubbed his wealth into everybody's faces. Nobody had liked him.

He calls a bartender over and *by accident* you overhear the rather annoyed conversation.

It appears that the man has lost a watch, an expensive one. He tells the bartender that it is worth over two thousand dollars. The money, of course, is not important but it has great sentimental value. The bartender, of course, not having heard the earlier announcement of the find has no idea of the situation but promises to ask around. The man is in a hurry to leave to get to an important meeting but promises to return. In the meantime he leaves a business card with a contact number on it should anything turn up. He also promises a substantial reward to the finder. He sighs deeply then leaves the bar.

THE SCENARIO—ACT THREE

The watch finder enters the bar again and sits down next you. He orders a drink. *"Must be my lucky day,"* he says as he eyes up the watch. *"Nobody seems to know whose this is, so I guess it's finders keepers! Man, I'll bet this little puppy is worth a couple of hundred dollars at least!"*

You enviously agree. The man offers to buy you a drink to celebrate his find. As he does so he feels inside his jacket pocket. He can't believe it, he's lost his wallet!

It won't take him long to try to sell you the watch. He needs money to get home. Since he figures the watch is worth a couple of hundred dollars he'll take a hundred and fifty. He needs the money. He needs it so badly that he may even let you beat him down to hundred and twenty-five.

What do you care. You are buying a two thousand dollar watch. Even turning it in for the reward (something you are unlikely to do) would turn you a tidy profit!

The deal is done and so are you. Finis.

THE SCAM

Actually, if you've read even this far in the book the scam should be obvious to you. You have been an unwitting member of a small troupe acting out a time honored playlet.

The watch you've bought is worth around five dollars. You will never see either of the men again. The business card given to the bartender is a fake.

What's more interesting is *why* the con works. It shows the psychology of a con in all its glory. The watch-loser is a man who had everybody hating him. He has boasted about all the money he has. He has bragged about his position in life. You certainly disliked him and almost certainly felt some jealousy toward him. You may also have thought, along the way, that it was a good thing that he was losing just for once.

Had he been a charming old man the thought of stealing from him would probably not have entered your mind. But, you figure, this arrogant guy has everything. If he can't look after it then that's just his hard luck.

On the other hand the finder of the watch is a good enough guy. He may be a little scruffily dressed, maybe you think he deserves a break. When he loses his wallet you feel a little sorry. But not sorry enough to give him the real value of the watch. After all, if somebody is going to be a winner here, it's going to be you! Hey, he only wants a hundred and fifty bucks. That's obviously a tidy sum of money to him and you, being the good guy, can help him out and turn a profit in the process. How much better does life get?

It's all about playing the man, not playing the game. Cons don't work from their mechanics. They work because they control your thoughts and actions. Great con men play mugs like string puppets. It's all over before you think about it starting.

Frightening, huh?

VARIATIONS

If you don't have the cash with you the seller will be happy to go with you to the local ATM machine.

Sometimes the scam is worked without the lost wallet ploy. The seller will just offer the item to you for cash. You can be sure that he will have *peeked your poke* and know just how much cash you are likely to want to spend.

The Scam may also be worked on the street. It doesn't have to be a watch, it may be a ring, a pendant or a necklace. It may be *anything* that looks as though it has some value.

Everybody knows the thrill of finding something on the street even if it's just a coin. Imagine the thrill of finding something really valuable looking but getting beaten to it. Next time somebody picks up a watch you've just spotted on a street corner beware. This is precisely the start of the psychological factors that begin a *Fob Off*.

This scam has even been worked with animals! A person may have with them a pet, a cat or dog perhaps. They continually grumble about having got the thing as a present from a long gone lover or friend. Maybe they inherited it from a relative or parent. However they got it doesn't matter, they just wish that they could get rid of it. They leave for a few moments asking you to watch it for just a few moments. Somebody comes in and 'mistaking' the animal for yours praises this most rare breed. "*Good grief, they may say, I wish I had the three thousand dollars needed to get one of those beauties. I don't suppose you'd take two thousand for it? Think about it, I'll get cash!*" They rush off before you can say a word. The owner returns and immediately starts grumbling about the wretched animal again. It won't take long before you are manipulated into trying to buy it to turn a quick profit. The owner may hate the animal but he wants five hundred dollars for it. Torn between paying the money and the thought of a swift fifteen hundred dollar profit the pressure is on. The other person could return at any moment and your chance will be lost. The *Fob Off* is once more in full swing. If you fall for it the best you can hope for is that the animal they picked up for free at a shelter is friendly. You're going to have it for a long time!

Next time somebody finds something and offers it to you at a ridiculously low price keep your wallet in your pocket.

You may just be turning down the bargain of a lifetime. Freddy will offer you 100-1 that you are not.

"Only a sucker expects something for nothing."

————•————

Freddy the Fox

How to Cheat at Everything

The Lucky Penny

T HIS IS A SMALL OLD-TIME SWINDLE THAT HAS BEEN WORKED THOUSANDS OF TIMES over the years. It is still being worked today. I once had the dubious pleasure of standing in for Freddy's normal partner (Sam) and so have seen this in action very close up indeed.

Freddy and Sam use it to raise their drinking money for an evening. Their idea of drinking money is at least a couple of hundred dollars.

Worked a few times it can also stake a small poker game.

Freddy and Sam are holding court in a bar or pool hall. The conversation is light and pleasant. Drinks, as usual, are flowing and everybody is having a grand old time. It is at times like this that gentlemen are apt to play practical jokes upon each other. Freddy is going to do just that.

With expensive results.

Sam gets up from his seat and decides that it's time for him to go. He bids all good night and leaves. On the chair where he has been sitting is an odd shaped little purse. When this is pointed out, Freddy says that Sam must have dropped it. *"There's nothing in it but for an old 1946 penny,"* he says, *"Sam's had that penny for years. He says that it brings him luck."*

You may suggest what follows. Maybe it's Freddy.

Somebody will suggest playing a joke on Sam. *"Let's hide his lucky penny,"* they say. *"Take it out of the purse,"* they say. *"See him panic when he finds that it's gone missing,"* they say. On such childish pranks men have built after-dinner speaking careers, and so the penny is removed and the purse replaced on the chair.

Sam rushes, breathless, back into the bar. He runs straight over to his chair and, upon finding the purse, breathes a deep sigh of relief.

"You must have a lot of money in there," somebody says waggishly, *"to be so bloody worried about such a battered old purse."* Everybody stifles their giggles. *"There's nothing in it but an old penny,"* replies Sam, *"Sounds stupid, I know, but I think of it as a kind of lucky charm."*

"*You mean you ran all the way back here for a penny!*" somebody else exclaims. "*Sam, you are finally losing it!*" The giggles are getting harder to control.

"*Not just any penny,*" says Sam getting annoyed. "*My lucky 1945 penny!*"

"*It's a 1946 penny,*" says Freddy. "*You showed it to me once.*"

"*1945,*" shouts Sam. "*I should know!*"

Like a lot of practical jokes played in drinking situations this one is rapidly turning into an argument. Tempers are being lost. That's when your sense tends to get lost as well. The shouting gets higher and higher in volume.

"*You haven't got a 1945 in that purse,*" yells Freddy.

"*Oh yeah, wanna bet?*" Sam screams back.

There, it's been said. Money has been mentioned.

Suddenly it all becomes rather interesting. Since there is no penny in the purse Freddy *has* to win.

"*I'm saying there's a 1945 in that purse,*" rages Sam, "*And I've got,*" he checks his wallet and throws a pile of bills down onto the table, "*Three hundred and fifty dollars that say I'm right!*"

Freddy protests that this is all getting a little out of control but Sam just shouts, "*Either put up or shut up!*"

Now you haven't known Freddy very long. You may, in fact, have only met him and Sam that afternoon when they joined your group at the club. But you know they are good friends. You know that, under normal circumstances, a friend would never take advantage of a friend. But, these aren't normal circumstances, tempers are high and honor is at stake.

Freddy removes his wallet and counts out his money. He only has a hundred and fifty dollars.

"*Wanna help me take this sucker?*" he asks the group. "*He's so drunk he can't even remember the date on his damned coin.*"

"*Yeah, come on @$$holes,*" yells Sam. "*Stick your money down with the loser here. It'll be nice to wipe those stupid grins off your stupid faces. You're all losers!*"

Sam is out of control and is really getting irritating to all now. You see an easy way to double your money quickly and shut him up at the same time. You cover the rest of the bet.

You are asked to open the purse. With a big grin you do so.

Out drops a penny. The date on it is 1945.

Sam quickly gathers up the money and, after a final abusive burst, leaves the bar in a huff.

"*Don't look at me,*" says Freddy, "*I lost big time as well. I don't know how he did it but I'm going after that little bugger!*"

It all happens so quickly that it seems like a blur. If you gather your senses fast enough and follow Freddy you may just be in time to see his car disappearing down the road.

With Sam at the wheel.

THE SCAM

In its simplest form there are simply two pennies in the purse. Although you don't quite remember who removed the first penny, I'll tell you it was Freddy.

Sometimes a purse with a hidden compartment is used. Sometimes Sam will use simple sleight-of-hand to add the penny or even switch purses at some point in the argument.

It's not the penny but the wonderful set-up that is so important. The joke, the following argument, the bruised egos and the inevitable bet.

Notice especially how your attention was confused by the bet being about the *date* on the coin. Sam isn't betting that his coin is in the purse, he's betting about the year it was minted! It was your mind that talked you into taking the bet because there 'isn't' a coin in the purse. You think that it doesn't matter about the date, you *have* to win because the coin is gone.

"*Quite delightful,*" muses Freddy and, yet again, I'm forced to agree.

SAM'S MAGIC TRICK VARIATION

Freddy and Sam will occasionally work a variation of the 'joke leads to bruised egos leads to big bet' system. This one involves Sam and his supposed ability as an amateur magician.

During a conversation Sam decides to do some card tricks. He is undeterred by the fact that nobody else is interested in them. They just want to chat and drink.

He brings out his deck of cards and clumsily shuffles them after removing the two black aces. He then asks Freddy to cut the deck into two piles. With a sigh Freddy does so. Sam asks Freddy to help with his new miracle. Reluctantly he agrees provided that Sam doesn't go on all night with his *boring* entertainment.

Sam puts one of the aces face down on top of one of the piles. He places the other ace on top of it. Finally he puts the remaining cards on top of all, burying the aces in the deck. Sam asks Freddy to give the deck a couple of straight cuts. He then claims that the aces will still be together. Since this is self-evident to all but the most idiotic of card handlers the group jeer this pathetic trick. Sam ignores them and starts taking cards from the bottom of the deck turning them face up as he does so. When a black ace shows he stops and says, "*I could even bet you that the next card is a black ace! Good trick, huh?*" He shows that the next card is, as expected, the other ace. Ignoring the jeers Sam says, "*It works every time, I'll show you again!*"

Sam is starting to get irritating.

Nobody wants to watch the whole charade again but Sam starts with cutting the deck into two piles. He places the first ace on top of a pile as before. He turns away for just a second to order a drink or, perhaps, to draw somebody else over to look at the trick. As he turns away Freddy winks at the others and puts a few cards from the second pile on top of the ace.

Sam turns back and drops the second ace into place followed by the rest of the pack. The watchers are now interested in seeing the result of Sam looking stupid. Freddy split the aces and now the irritating amateur magician is going to come a cropper! Sam lets Freddy, who seems barely able to control his laughter, cut the pack a couple of times.

Once more he starts taking cards from the bottom of the pack, turning them face up as he does so.

The first black ace appears and Sam says, "*You've all watched closer this time, anybody want to bet on my magic trick now? I'll bet that the next card is a black ace!*" Sam seems a little surprised when everybody wants to take the bet. He is most amused when quite a pile of money is thrown on to the table top. Luckily he has quite a lot of money with him and so is able to cover the bet.

You can't wait to see his face when he turns that next card!

The next card is turned. It is the second black ace. "*You guys are nuts!*" says Sam, "*I told you it works every time!*"

The best you can do is give him credit for being a better magician than you first thought. Even Freddy is shaking his head with disbelief!

HOW?

Freddy, by the way, is shaking his head in disbelief that anybody would fall for this. But they do, over and over again.

Once again it's not the tiny amount of sleight-of-hand required (we'll look at that in a moment) but the build up to it.

Sam has bored everybody with his trick then irritated all by insisting on repeating it. He is pompous about how great a trick it is and won't listen to anybody arguing otherwise. So, when Freddy splits up the aces, it's seen as an amusing way of bringing Sam down a peg or two. By the time it has escalated to a real bet, it's too late for anybody to pull out.

Sam, after shuffling the deck peeked the top card of the deck. Let's say it was the four of clubs. He cuts the pack in two and puts the first ace on top of the four of clubs. Freddy, as Sam turns away, puts about six cards from the second pile on top of the ace. Sam turns back and adds the second ace before putting the rest of the cards on top. Everybody watching knows that the aces are split by some cards. What they don't know is that Sam also knows this. Plus he has an additional piece of critical information. He knows the card directly under the first ace.

It is little known to laymen that not only will a series of straight cuts not split up a pair of cards (except to put one on top and one on the bottom) but that the order of the deck will not be disturbed with regard to the cards positions in relation to each other. All cuts do is change where the order starts and finishes. Freddy cuts the deck twice to avoid splitting the aces, one on top and one on the bottom. His cutting ensures that the little group stays near the center of the deck.

Sam then pulls cards from the bottom of the deck turning them face up as he does so. As soon as he sees the four of clubs he pulls back on the bottom card (the first ace) with his fingers. Magicians call this 'move' *The Glide*. Sam now starts pulling the *second* card from the bottom each time keeping the first ace in place on the bottom.

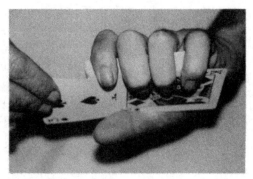

The Glide.

Sam waits for the *second* ace to show then squares up the cards. He can now conclude the bet successfully.

As a money-maker he's right. It *is* a pretty good trick!

THE LATE TURN

Sam or Freddy can use another old magic trick as a one-man variation of the above ploy. Here's how.

Freddy shuffles the cards and gets you to take one. He boasts that he is brilliant with cards and can beat anybody with his skill.

He gets you to return your card and then to give the deck a number of straight cuts. He then starts to turn cards over one at a time from the top of the pack and onto the bar. You might be amused when he goes right past your card.

Suddenly he stops and says, "*The next card I turn over will be your card!*" You might point out that you don't think it will. Whatever, Freddy offers to bet you that he's right.

You can't help it. It's an easy twenty bucks. You take the bet.

Freddy reaches into the dealt pile and turns your chosen card face down. He didn't say which way he was going to turn over the next card! It's not his fault that you assumed he was going to turn the next card of the deck face up!

HOW?

Once again Freddy *hooks* you superbly. After his boasting you'd like to see him fail. When it looks like he might you are more than willing to put up a little wager. It's just icing on the cake for you!

The sleight-of-hand required is an old, very simple, magician's trick. Freddy has prior knowledge of the bottom card of the pack. You replace your card and cut the deck several times. This places your card directly under Freddy's known card.

He turns up cards looking for the original bottom card of the deck. As soon as he sees it he knows that the next card is yours. He could just stop there and prove that he is a capable amateur magician. Instead he goes past your card and deals another six or seven. He then offers his bet.

And another sucker is born.

Small bet? Sure, but as Freddy says, *"Every win is a win and pretty soon they start to add up. Would you turn down free money?"*

There are thousands of variations on the *let's get one over on the wise guy* or *let's play a joke on so-and-so* routine. All will seem to offer you easy money by giving you a sure-fire advantage during a confrontation of some kind. Your safest bet is to refuse to have anything to do with a wager, however good it looks, between two strangers. Refuse a wager where another man seems to have gone sadly wrong.

Sure-fire winners are like Unicorns. Nice to dream about, but they don't exist.

Spoof

SPOOF IS A VERY POPULAR BAR GAME IN EUROPE. IT IS ALSO RAPIDLY BECOMING popular worldwide. It doesn't take much searching to find a game on any given night of the week.

The game is a simple one. Players take three coins behind their back. They then bring forward a closed fist. In their fist they may have placed a total of none, one, two or three coins. Each player in turn tries to guess the combined total of all the coins held by the players. You can't say a total that has already been called.

The player who guesses the total correctly drops out of the game and then the game carries on. First call goes in rotation around the players. The last man in the game pays for the drinks for the group. If nobody calls a correct total then the game is void and played again.

Spoof is not just played for drinks. It is often played for big money.

A POPULAR MISCONCEPTION

Many people assume that Spoof is a game of luck. Play against Freddy for a while and you'll soon discover that you are losing far more often than chance should suggest.

Spoof is a game that combines skill and strategy.

Freddy doesn't cheat at Spoof but his knowledge of the mathematics and tactics of the game give him such an edge over an unskilled player (that's you) that he may as well be.

Stay close. Freddy is going to turn you into an expert Spoof player. He can't guarantee that you'll never lose. But he will guarantee that you'll win a lot more often than you lose!

PLAYING STRATEGY

Let's start off with the simplest of all games, a two-player game. It is worth noting right from the start that lying is allowed in most Spoof games. You could be holding three coins and yet still call an impossible total of zero just to put your opponent off his stride.

Each of the two players can hold none, one, two or three coins. In order to win the man with the first call must guess the total of the coins held by his opponent. Since his opponent has four options the first player has a one in four chance of doing so.

So, in a two-handed game, with first call, your chance of guessing the total correctly is one in four. The player with second call can, however, use the information given by your call to infer, rather than guess, a total.

Freddy's Rule Number One—Always try to get second call in a two-handed game.

A first call of, "*None*," tells the second player that (lying aside) his opponent is holding no coins. If the opponent opens with a call of, "*Six*," then (once again with lying aside) he is holding three coins. In either of these two cases the first caller has a one in four chance of winning the game by calling the correct total. But, since he will miss three out of four times, the second player will win, or void, the game three games out of four!

Freddy's Rule Number Two—Never call six or none with first call in a two-handed game *unless* you are lying.

Freddy's Rule Number Three—With second call in a two-handed game never hold none or three coins.

A first call of one, two, three, four or five is less informative to the second player.

If the first call is, "*One*," then the player is probably holding one coin or none. A call of, "*Five*," means that the player will probably be holding two or three coins. A first call of, "*Four*," means he is holding one, two or three coins. A call of, "*Two*," means that they are probably holding none, one or two coins.

The odds, though lessened, still favor the second caller. For a call of one or five the first caller has a one in four chance of guessing correctly. The second player has a fifty-fifty chance of guessing correctly (as, assuming no lying, he limits his choices to the smart ones) and an even chance of voiding the game.

With a call of two or four the first player, once more, has a one in four chance of guessing correctly while the second player has four chances out of seven thanks to, once more, limiting his choices to the smart ones. That's odds of 4 to 3 in his favor.

How to Cheat at Everything

Are you starting to get the idea that there may be more to this game than meets the eye?

Freddy's Rule Number Four—From a mathematical standpoint your best first call in a two handed game is three. This is because a call of three reveals nothing about your hand. You could be holding nothing or anything.

However, an expert like Freddy will rarely use an opening call of three. Why? He will have studied you for playing faults, that's why! Many players tend to stick to the same number of coins throughout a game. Freddy will have noticed this and will exploit the information accordingly. Some players, trying to be sneaky, will alternate between none held and three held. Don't think you are fooling Freddy.

Freddy's Rule Number Five—Mathematics are sometimes less important than observation of another caller's poor psychological play.

Freddy's Rule Number Six—Vary the coins in your hand constantly. Don't follow any pattern. Don't let anybody get an idea that you are following some kind of system or pattern.

An expert player with first call in a two-handed game, knowing just how much the odds are against them, will lie to nullify the second call advantage. He may hold two coins but call a total of none. You assume they are holding no coins and call your total accordingly. At the very least they have no idea how many coins you are holding!

Freddy's Rule Number Seven—Lying at the two-handed stage is a powerful weapon if you are forced to call first.

SPOOF WITH THREE PLAYERS

Although it's a little more complicated the last caller still has a mathematical advantage over the others.

The first caller knows that the other two players can, between them, hold between none to six coins. There are various ways each total can be made up. The combinations can be summed up as follows.

> None or six—One way for each total
> One or Five—Two ways for each total
> Three—Four ways
> Two or Four—Three ways for each total

In other words those two players are holding between them one of sixteen combinations. Since three is mathematically the most common total, the first player's best bet is to add three to the total he is holding and make that his call.

Freddy's Rule Number Eight—With first call in a three-handed game add three to the number you hold and make that your call.

With second call in a three-handed game reverse the above strategy to discover how many coins the first player has. If he has called six you subtract three to leave three. It is a mathematically sound judgment call that the first player is holding three coins. You know from our study of a two-handed game that you have a one in four chance of guessing the coins in the last callers hand. Make that guess and add the total you have deduced for the first player to your own coins and make at least a well-reasoned call.

Freddy's Rule Number Nine—If you have to guess at least make it an intelligent one!

If your well-reasoned total has already been called by player one your best strategy is to go one higher (if you are holding two or three coins) or one lower (if you are holding none or one coin). Don't call further than one away from the first player's call unless you are *really* sure (having watched the other callers playing flaws). If you do a wider call without thought you may be giving away too much information about your total to player three.

For example, the first player calls one and you, as second player, call five. This is a dead give-away that you are probably holding three coins. Player one is almost certainly holding no coins at all. Do you want to place a bet on who's going to win this round? Freddy's guess is already on player three by the way! He thinks it's a pretty good call, and I agree with him!

Freddy's Rule Number Ten—Keep your call close to already stated calls *unless* you are absolutely certain.

The third player has the advantage of hearing the two calls before him. If the second player calls lower than the first player the third player can assume that they are holding either one coin or an empty hand. If the second player calls higher than the first player it can be assumed that they are holding two or three coins.

With three experts playing the game the first caller has a one in four chance of winning the game (see rule number eight). The second player has also got a one in four chance of winning, by having a good call on player one but having to guess at player three's total. The third player has a one in three chance of winning by using strategic calculations on the totals of player one and two. The remaining totals will result in void games.

Freddy's Rule Number Eleven—Last call is still the best in a three-handed game.

MULTI-PLAYER SPOOF

You are either now a little boggled with figures or, after careful reading, are turning into a mean two or three player Spoof opponent. But most Spoof games start with five, six, seven or more players. I've seen one that started with forty-two players! What's your best strategy in these situations?

Obviously the last call advantage starts to wane as more players are added to the pot. The more players there are in the game, the greater the chance of the correct total being called before the last caller gets a chance. Even the totals either side will almost certainly have been called already!

Freddy's Rule Number Twelve—Avoid last call if there are more than three players.

Your best strategy with a larger number of players is to work the averages. Since each player can have none, one, two or three coins then the *average* number of coins held by each player over a period of games will be one and a half.

Assume, amusingly, that every player has one and a half coins. In an eight-handed game that means the other players are (mathematically speaking) holding ten and a half coins (seven times one and a half). Round the total up or down according to the number of coins you are holding. If you are holding no coins your call should be ten. If you are holding one coin your call should be eleven (ten and half plus your one rounded down). If you are holding two coins you would call thirteen (ten and a half plus two rounded up) and if you are holding three coins you would accordingly call fourteen. You might not win but at least you'll be using the averages to give an intelligent call.

Freddy's Rule Number Thirteen—With more than three players call as close to the smart average as you possibly can.

Obviously, if you don't have first call, take careful note of the calls before you to make your guess even smarter. If player two calls a very low total it is safe to assume that they are holding no coins at all. Reduce your average total by one and a half (the number of coins the averages would say they should be holding) accordingly.

Freddy's Rule Number Fourteen—Always listen to the calls before you. They can help you adjust your average guess to be closer to the exact total.

If your call is wrong you'll be in the game with one less player. If you are still in the game when it gets down to three players at the very least you are back on very familiar ground.

A Sample Game

Let's take a look at Freddy playing in a real game of four-handed Spoof that I recorded at the Village Tavern. Here's how it went.

Four players were in the game. Freddy, with bad luck, had last call. He was holding three coins and calculated the total to be eight (his three coins plus three times one and a half rounded up).

The first caller took eight, the second nine and the third seven. This left Freddy a call of six or ten, neither of which was a likely winner, and he took ten simply because of the high number he was holding. Eight proved to be the correct call and that player dropped out leaving Freddy with first call against two others.

Freddy held one coin and, using the mathematics of rule eight, knew that the best average call for the other two's total was three. His call was a calculated four (three plus his one). Player two called three. Freddy's guess looked a little weak as it was now likely that player two held no coins. Player three calculated that Freddy was probably holding one coin. He did this by reversing rule eight and taking three from Freddy's call. He also calculated that, thanks to the low call, player two had either no coins or, at most, one coin. He decided that it was more likely that player two was holding no coins. Player three was holding one coin and so made a superbly calculated call of two. He was right. It was a great call. He had intelligently worked out the best total and dropped out of the game.

Now it was down to a two-hander between Freddy and player two. Freddy, calm as ever, had the critical second call. He admitted afterward that it had also become rather apparent that player two always seemed to either have three coins or no coins in their hand.

The game was set. Player two called six. Freddy was holding two coins so player two *couldn't* win the game. The worst that could happen would be a void game. All Freddy had to do was decide if player two was lying. Had he been playing a double bluff by letting it be seen that he always had none or three? Was he, right there and then, trying to psyche Freddy into believing that he had three in his hand to force a void game and then give himself the second call in another game?

Freddy decided that he was and called two. The opponents face dropped, and Freddy knew that he'd made the right choice. The opponent was holding air and Freddy was out of the game leaving player two the big loser.

If you followed that all the way through you'll see that Spoof is not about guessing inanely. It's about guessing smartly!

CHEATING AT SPOOF

Unless it's a very loose game it's unlikely that anybody will attempt to use sleight-of-hand manipulation to adjust the score. If players routinely allow coins to be tipped from one hand to another to show the coins then it's possible, with palming, to hold back coins to adjust totals. Most games do not allow such chicanery. The fists are held out fingers up. When all calls have been made the hands are opened out flat and the total added.

If Freddy ever finds a game where hand to hand transfers are allowed or all the coins are poured into a pile to be counted he'll end the Spoof game as soon as possible and move into some *really* profitable money makers. As he puts it so bluntly, *"If they are that stupid it's up to me to bleed-em dry and make-em weep! After all, that's my job."*

But a far more common form of cheating at Spoof is both effective and almost undetectable. It is called *Collusion Play*. Yes folks, that's right, two players teaming up. They can have signals where they can tell each other just how many coins they are holding. The advantages this gives do not, I hope, have to be explained to you. Two against one can be devastating in action and, in the trade, is called *Toasting*. You'll see this technique later on when we discuss cheating at cards and other games. If you suspect that this is happening to you there is little else to do except drop out of the game.

It's unwise to play any money games with strangers. If a friend always seems to be the lucky winner you may want to reconsider playing with him as well. He may just be really lucky but why take the risk?

FREDDY'S LAST CALL ON SPOOF

Like many apparently simple games, there is a good deal more to Spoof than meets the untrained eye. A good Spoof player is not only pretty good at mathematics, he is also an excellent amateur psychologist.

It is worth noting that in some schools, lying is not allowed. In these games, the math really comes into its own and should be used accordingly. It's also wise to check the lying rule before starting out. You don't want to lose a game simply because you were unaware of local rules.

By following Freddy's rules you can't be sure to win all the time, but at least you won't lose, as so many do, through stupidity. Every call you make will be soundly based on math. Every chance you take will be soundly based on your observation of other players.

And hopefully, nobody will read your call with the certainty that you read theirs.

The Monte Man

ONTE OR THE THREE CARD TRICK MAY NOT BE THE OLDEST HUSTLER OF all. It may not be the biggest money making hustle of all. It is certainly not the most skillful hustle of all. It is, however, the one hustle that seems to have become synonymous with scam artists. It has been featured in numerous films and television shows. It has been exposed in books, newspapers and many times on television (including by myself on the network special *Beat the Cheat*). Everybody seems to know about the game and yet, for reasons that are inexplicable to Freddy and me, people still choose to bet, and lose, on the game in droves!

Freddy thinks that it may be for a number of reasons. First it looks so damned easy. All you have to do is pick one card out of three. The mug may argue that, even with just blind luck, they must be right now and then. They may work out the odds that the game is one chance in three or only two to one against. Of course why anybody would bet even money on a 2-1 against shot is also beyond Freddy and me! The second reason that people still bet on the game is that, although the game has been exposed many times, the people, including myself, did not give *all* of it away. Maybe they didn't know the subtle points, maybe (on television) there were time constraints or maybe they just wanted to keep some information to themselves.

Now Freddy is going to tell you everything he knows about the game. If, after reading about Freddy's considerable knowledge of the game, you are still tempted to have a go at finding that little lady, you may count yourself as being amongst life's lost causes. This really is the Grandfather of mug bets.

THE GAME

You've played the mug quite a few times so far so, for this chapter, Freddy is going to cut you a break. For this game, you can watch from the sidelines as he takes a score.

Comfy? Good, let the game begin!

Freddy is out on the street tossing three cards onto a newspaper which is sitting on an upturned box. A crowd has gathered around and a great deal of money is being bet on a little game. The game? Freddy is throwing two black tens and a red queen face down. All the crowd has to do is pick out the queen and they are winning. Freddy is looking pretty sick.

Into this scenario walks Albert Fisher. He's a tourist out buying presents for his family and friends at home. Unfortunately for him this means that he has a wallet full of money.

Albert watches for a while as Freddy keeps up a constant stream of patter.

"*Men, I have here three little cards, two black tens and the lovely queen of hearts. The idea is that, after I toss-em out and mix-em up all ya gotta do is find the queen. Lookie, lookie, lookie. Hey diddle, diddle, the queen's in the middle! Pick out the lady and you win, it's as simple as that friends. I'll throw them fast but if your eye is faster you'll take the money. I'll take bets of five, ten, twenty, fifty or a hundred that you can't follow her. Hey, if you don't speculate, how can you hope to accumulate? I'm a fair man, I won't take a bet from a hobo, a cripple or a pregnant woman. Anyone else feel free to join in. Lookie, lookie, lookie. Have your money in your hand or it's no bet my friend!*"

Albert watches as one of the crowd picks out the queen and wins fifty dollars. Albert is excited because he had followed the queen as well and had known exactly where it was. A man pulls Albert to one side and says, "*Sorry to bother you mate but could you lay down a bet for me? I've been winning too many times and he won't take my bets any more.*" He pushes a hundred dollars into Albert's hand and gently pushes him closer to the game. "*I'll whisper which one to bet on,*" says the guy. "*Get the money down quick! Now! Put it on the middle one!*" In a fluster Albert puts the hundred on the middle card. There is a roar of approval when the card is turned and Albert wins! Albert passes the money to the guy behind him but feels a bit sore. He hadn't needed the guy to whisper where the queen was. He'd followed it himself and that could have been *his* win! He decides to play a couple of games himself.

He's smart. He decides to start with a few small bets just to really get the hang of it. With a slightly trembling hand he puts down a twenty on the card of his choice. Immediately another man puts a fifty down on one of the other cards. Freddy brushes Albert's bet aside saying, "*Sorry sonny, one bet at a time only and I always take a man's bet over a baby's!*" as he does so. The other man loses. As Freddy picks up the cards Albert sees that he had been right. Damn it, now he's really sore at himself.

The cards are tossed again, and Albert slaps down a fifty onto his choice. The card is turned. Albert looks full into the face of a black ten and can't believe it.

The cards are tossed again. The Monte Man turns to make some change for one of the crowd. One of the crowd peeks at a card, and it's obvious he's found the queen. First because Albert had followed the cards really carefully this time, and second because the fellow in the crowd has a smile on his face that the Cheshire cat in Alice in Wonderland would be proud of. Freddy, his business done, turns back.

What follows next delights Albert.

Freddy must have seen the guy peek at the card. While the man is trying to borrow money from his friend to make a big bet, Freddy swiftly changes the position of the queen and the card next to it. Albert follows all of this. The guy puts down a big bet. The card is turned and he loses. The guy just can't believe it, he didn't see Freddy's extra little switch move. But Albert did. Freddy smiles at the guy and says, "*Thought you'd cheat an honest man did you my friend. Well let me tell ya, a cheat never prospers!*" He then announces, "*To show ya how honest I am, if anybody wants to bet a hundred I'll give-em a choice of the last two cards. It's a fifty-fifty shot my friends, a real honest man's bet!*" Albert practically throws a hundred dollars onto the card the guy originally peeked. The card is turned and, once more, Albert is staring at a black ten. "*Tough luck big guy,*" says Freddy as he picks up the money.

Freddy turns to get a cigarette. Another member of the crowd picks up the queen and puts a slight bend into a corner of it. He winks at Albert. Freddy turns and picks up the cards, his lighted cigarette dangling from his lips. He tosses out the cards with hardly a glance.

Albert can't believe that Freddy hasn't seen the bent corner. The man who bent the queen puts a hundred dollars on it and wins. He collects the money and walks away, yelling back to Freddy, "*Your hands are slowing up old man. You just ain't got it anymore!*"

Freddy throws the cards again. He *still* hasn't seen that bent corner. "*Last bet of the day,*" he announces, "*Time to win with a man's bet or walk away a sad and sorry loser!*"

A member of the crowd puts a hundred and fifty dollars down but on a *wrong* card! Albert can't believe it. That bent corner is sticking out like a sore thumb to him! He throws two hundred dollars, pretty much the last of his money, onto the bent cornered card, "*Now that's what I call a man's bet my friend,*" says Freddy.

He turns the card.

Somehow the bent corner has migrated onto a black ten. By the time the shock wears off, Albert realizes that the crowd has gone, vanished like a waft of smoke. Albert is broke and, like tens of thousands before him, walks away in a daze.

It isn't until he gets home that he discovers that his pocket has been picked as well and that his credit cards had better be cancelled real quick.

The Team

Albert and Freddy are just two members of an elaborate cast that go towards making up a Three Card Monte team. Their two roles are the only obvious ones. Freddy is the card man (known as a *Broad Tosser*) and Albert, playing his role to perfection, is the mug.

The other members are as follows.

1. The Wall man

The Wall man or, more commonly, men are, apparently, innocent bystanders. Actually their sole job is to watch for the police. Three Card Monte is an illegal game. Should the police be spotted you'll hear a cry of, "*Slide!*" and never did a magician do such a vanishing act. The game will disappear faster than you can say, "*Huh?*"

2. The Dip

Another member of the crowd is the Dip or pickpocket. His job is obvious. Even if you don't bet on the game, he'll make sure you pay just for the pleasure of watching.

3. The Hook

Often a Monte team will employ a charming and attractive young lady to *hook* guys into the game. She will encourage you to play and perhaps just 'put down a ten for me hun.' It is also one of her jobs to *Peek the Poke* of the mug. In other words she will get a look into your wallet as you remove some money and estimate how much you can lose. These sweet, charming, young ladies can often estimate a stack of bills to within a dollar at twenty paces.

Some teams will use a man to steer the sucker into the game. They will often claim to have inside knowledge of the works of the game and will encourage the mug to watch them win. After a while the mug is encouraged to join in. These helpful fellows are referred to as *Ropers*. At truck stops, one of the more common places to catch the game these days, the *Roper* will often pretend to be a fellow driver.

4. The Shills

The Shills have nearly as important a job as the Broad Tosser himself. While Freddy manipulates the cards they manipulate the crowd. The guy who got Albert to lay a bet for him right at the start was a Shill. All the winners in the game were Shills. The Shills also manipulate, with dynamic choreography, the peeking and bent corner ploys. A Shill is quite easy to spot. He's the *only* one who ever wins money. If the team does not have a *Hook* (girl) one of the Shills will also take on the job of *Peeking the Poke*. It is interesting to note that, because Freddy is so good at the sleight-of-hand involved, the Shills doing the betting can get lost. For this reason the queen is often secretly marked to allow them to find it every time.

5. The Heavy

This is the muscle end of the game. If you *beef* too loudly or do anything to mess up the flow of the play you are liable to meet this guy very quickly. Forget your ability to wrestle and box in college. Forget your occasional bar room brawl. These guys are professionals who hurt people for a living. In the trade they are often called *Freddy* which is short for *Fourteen Week Freddy*. That's because fourteen weeks is a pretty good estimate of how long you'll stay in the hospital should you ever meet one.

In fact, in a game, you may be the only person involved in it that isn't a member of the team!

The Basic Sleight-Of-Hand

Freddy's sleight-of-hand ability is central to the whole scam.

The Hype.

The throw at speed—note the blurring!

The main move of the Monte man is called the *Hype* or, by the young kids today, the *Slide*. Now if you ever hear a kid say to another, *"Man, you got a fly slide,"* you'll be able to translate that to meaning that the kid is good at *Tossing the Broads* or at the sleight-of-hand required for the game!

To throw the cards the Monte man takes two into his left hand and one in the right. The cards are held with the thumb at the rear and the fingers at the front narrow end.

The *straight* toss is to throw the bottom card (queen) of the two in the left hand, followed by the single in the right hand, followed by the remaining card in the left. These three tosses meld into one smooth action.

The Hype looks identical to the straight toss. When the Monte man wishes to confuse the issue he will first throw the *upper* card of the left hand ones. Trust me when I say that it looks *identical* to the straight toss. These guys practice for countless hours to make it so.

The secret switch occurs *before* the cards hit the playing surface! However well you follow the cards being moved around you are following the *wrong* card!

By combining the Hype with several straight tosses at speed it can get very confusing even for Freddy. Even he can lose the queen! As we've mentioned, the queen is marked to avoid any money losing errors (for the team) happening should the queen get lost.

Opening Gambit

Albert was forced closer to the game to lay a bet for another player. As soon as he was close enough to play a couple of Shills would have moved in behind him to make it harder for him to walk away. Since he was playing with the team's money he was watching a straight game. He won but had to give the money away to the guy who had asked him to bet. This made him thirsty to try a bet of his own. The only time you'll ever pick up money at the game is if you are laying a bet for somebody else. They will *never* let you win a couple of bets with your own money whatever others may tell you.

Now that the mug was in place the scam proper could begin. Albert watched another straight toss and made his bet (which was on the queen). A Shill immediately placed a higher bet on one of the other cards. Albert now was not only convinced that he knew the game but also knew that he had to bet high enough not to have his bet stolen away from him. He encouraged himself to bet higher!

The Double Bet Ploy And Other Sneaky Malarkey

This Double Bet is also used should the mug *accidentally* bet on the queen at the wrong time. As you can see the moment real money goes on the queen, a Shill puts a higher bet on a losing card leaving the mug out in the cold.

If the mug starts to *beef* then Freddy will call all bets null and void for that toss. He picks up the cards and throws them out again before the mug has a chance to continue arguing. This technique, once again, infuriates the mug into betting higher next time around.

Let's look at a couple of other 'correct bet' ploys Freddy and his team will use to ensure that the mug *never* gets the winning card *even* if they've got a large bet sitting right on top of it.

The Monte man has tossed the cards, and the mug has got a large bet on the queen. The Double Bet ploy has been used so it's time for more fun. A Shill, pretending to be drunk or distracted by something stumbles and knocks against the orange box. Cards and money go flying. Due to the 'accident' all bets on that toss are void.

Alternately, the Monte man or one of his Shills will signal to a Wall man who will suddenly call, "*Slide!*" The cards are scattered and the team heads away. By the time the 'false' alarm is discovered the mug has no chance of getting his bet back on. Actually he should be pretty happy if he even gets his original money back. Those teams can vanish *really* fast!

Magicians sometimes tell you that the Monte man can use a switch to change one card for another. They call this move the *Mexican Turnover*. The switch move got its name from the fact that Monte got its name from the legitimate game of Mexican Monte (also known as Spanish Monte). The two games are completely unrelated but the Monte men called their game so to give it a certain legitimacy by its implied association. Many of their moves, real or otherwise, are called the 'Mexican _____' for just this historic reason. The use of the switch move in a real game is a subject of controversy amongst cheat experts. Some will claim it is never used, others may say that it is used in various off-beat ways such as switching in a winning card to let a shill pick up money, for example. Still others will quote variations on the switch. I have seen the switch used by magicians. I have never seen it used in a real game of Three Card Monte, and I've watched a *lot* of games. Freddy says he's never seen it either but muses, philosophically, *"That doesn't mean somebody, somewhere isn't doing something like it"*

What is important to fix in your mind, however, is not the use or none use of certain moves. Just fix into your mind that, once your money is out, you will *never* be allowed to win money on the queen.

BACK TO THE GAME

So Albert lost his first fifty dollars thanks to the Hype. He simply followed the wrong card and swiftly, before anybody could beat him to it, put his money down.

But how did he lose the second time around? He'd seen the man peek the queen and followed its position exactly.

Albert fell for a superbly choreographed playlet. The man in the crowd (a Shill) *acted* as though he'd seen the queen. Actually, he'd peeked at a losing ten. The playlet was designed to make Albert believe he just couldn't lose. Once more he just followed the wrong card!

Finally the team, going for the throat, pulled the Bent Corner ploy. This play, in various forms, has been around almost as long as Monte itself. It relies on Freddy's supreme sleight-of-hand ability.

All the players in the scene are, as we've seen, in the team. The corner of the queen is bent and the cards are tossed. The Shill wins. Notice how this absolutely cements into Albert's mind that the card with the bent corner is the queen. He's seen it bent, he's seen the cards tossed, he's seen the bet laid and the queen, still with the bent corner, turned face up. Finally, this has to be payback time. He may consider that the reason Freddy hasn't noticed the bend is because of the cigarette and its ensuing smoke. He may not care. He *knows* that if he can get a bet down fast enough he'll be a winner.

Freddy picks up the cards and, under cover of the back of his hands, his fingers take out the bend in the queen. As he throws out the cards he will, with blurring speed, place a new bend into a losing ten. Don't think you'll spot him doing it. It's a move he's practiced a million times.

The cards in Monte, as you can see from the accompanying photographs, always have a sharp longitudinal bend in them. This gives them a little 'pup tent' like shape. Apparently this makes them easier to pick up. That may well be the case, but it also gives more *shade* or cover for moves like the Bent Corner.

How to Cheat at Everything

The person who bets on the wrong card is actually a Shill placing a large bet on the real queen. Not only does this make sure that Albert has to lay a larger bet, but also effectively takes the queen out of play.

Albert has been cleaned out in around five minutes. Nice work if you can get it. Note how Albert is forced to bet swiftly and impulsively with little time for thought. Confusion abounds as the bets get higher and higher. It's like riding a roller coaster. Once you are on it, it's real difficult to get off while it's still moving.

Secretly bending a corner.

The Bent Corner, known as *Putting in the Lug,* has several variations. Sometimes the Shill will mark the queen with a pencil mark. Freddy can easily rub this away. He will add a pencil mark to a losing ten using a small piece of pencil lead jammed under his thumb nail.

Other times the Shill will rub a little cigarette ash on the queen. Once more this is easily rubbed away to be replaced on a ten.

Whatever the ruse a simple rule applies: the easier it looks to find the queen the less likely it is that the card actually is the queen.

So now you know how Albert got cleaned. Let's take a look at a few other ploys the teams use in their quest for easy money.

More Sneaky Ploys

To encourage a *Deadhead* (a mug who just won't get his money out) Freddy will throw an easy straight toss. He'll draw the guy in by offering a free go at the game. "*Come on my friend,*" he'll say, "*which one would ya say it is? A free go to let me see how good your eyes are!*" They pick the queen and Freddy says, "*Whew, you're fast. I thought I had ya there. Man, am I glad you didn't have any money down!*" What would you like to bet that this guy is already reaching for his money? Just remember Freddy's golden rule, well worth repeating, "*Once your money is out you have absolutely no chance of seeing the queen even if you bet on it!*"

Another ploy is called in the trade *Earnest Money*. This ploy takes money from a man who didn't even know he was betting! Once more Freddy offers a free play. He tosses the cards and asks the mug where the money card is. When the mug points to the card Freddy tells him it's the winner and starts to hand over fifty dollars. "*Wait a minute,*" he says, "*You'll take my fifty for a win but I never saw the fifty you'd give me if you lost!*" He pulls back the fifty for a moment but keeps it, enticingly, in view. Freddy explains he just wants to see if the mug had got the money to pay if he lost. A Shill helps along by saying, "*Just show him your fifty and you'll get the money. You've got him beat!*" They thought it was a free play but, what the hell, if they're going to get fifty bucks for just showing fifty bucks then they'll show it! With a rush of adrenalin they show the money. Freddy grabs the money and adds it to his. *"Turn the card,"* he says. The mug turns a losing card. Freddy may act a little surprised or apologetic. He will not, however, give them back their money. After all they lost the bet.

If a guy is with his wife or girlfriend the team will try to split them up quickly. Nothing like a lady nagging to put a guy off making a bet or two is their theory. They'll hustle about between the pair in such a way that the guy ends up at the front and the girl ends up at the back of the crowd. One of the Shills will be entertaining the lady with stories about the area and its sights, leaving the guy free to lay a few bets without worry. If she gets bored and starts to protest, a very large gentleman may just whisper, *"Don't worry, he's just having some fun. He'll just be a moment or two."*

Although not strictly a ploy upon the mugs it should be pointed out that the Monte man is constantly talking and, in doing so, is issuing orders to his team. This is often in the strange language of the hustler. Other times I've heard them give orders in direct English. The mug was too caught up in the game to notice.

The Monte man may use an outright con to try to raise a lower bet to a higher one. The mug throws twenty down on a card. Immediately a Shill throws forty down onto another card. The Monte man hustles them into a higher bet by breaking the rules. *"I saw you go down first my friend,"* he'll say, *"but you know I gotta take the higher bet. Tell ya what I'll do. You want to up the bet, and I'll letcha keep that card!"* The shill may protest a little but he'll soon agree that it's only fair. You may just decide to up your bet. In fact, if you're convinced you've got the queen, especially right after being beaten by a bigger bet on a previous toss, it's odds on that you will. You might win. Yeah, and pigs might fly.

A TIDY SUM OF MONEY

If you haven't already got the idea that this is a game of fast easy money and lots of it let me give you a brief tale from George Devol. George, a famous Monte man himself, writes about Canada Bill in his book *Forty Years a Gambler on the Mississippi.* Canada Bill, whose specialty was beating preachers and priests, was said to have offered Union Pacific $25,000 a year to allow him to work the trains, *"without molestation, a condition of the offer being that he would not attempt to victimize any class of passengers except preachers."* Not a small sum of money considering the book was published in 1926! If he was prepared to pay that much just how much do you suppose he knew he could take in?

Arrest seems of very little concern to the teams working the streets today. As with Hookers the fines are hardly a deterrent. Once arrested they pay the fine and are back out working within hours. The whole scam has been well organized in large cities. Get to an area early enough and you'll see a van dropping off teams at intervals. Later at night the teams, often young kids between the ages of 15 and 20, will all be picked up by the same van. These teams are paid a daily wage and, each day, deliver their take to the organizer of it all. The kids running the games will have adapted the talk of the game to suit the street style of the day. One day it may Hip-Hop, another it will be a Rap chat. It's still the same game.

A SUMMARY OF MONTE

It doesn't matter what it is called. Cherchez la Femme, the Three Card Trick, Monte, Bonneteau (the French version also called Little Cap because of the bend in the cards) or Broads, it's all the same game. Freddy says that whenever you see three little cards being tossed onto a newspaper you should always bear in mind the following points before reaching for your money.

1. Whenever you see anybody win at Monte it will be a Shill. It's a myth to believe that they'll let you win a couple of games to hook you in. Anybody who tells you they've won at the game has either been a Shill or is a liar. You will *never* be allowed to place a winning bet and get the money.
2. The easier the game looks (peeked card, bent corner, etc.) the more you are being suckered.
3. There is no such thing as an honest game of Monte.

Nobody, repeat *nobody,* beats the game of Monte. It is a testament to greed and stupidity that the Three Card Trick has remained almost unchanged since it's birth in the mid 1800's. There always seems to be a long line of mugs who are willing to fall for its patter line and easy money appeal. Hopefully, you won't be counted amongst them.

When spotted the team will split up so quickly that they are very difficult to catch. By the time you've reported the crime to a policeman they will have vanished. However, one of my police pals, Mario, had a fairly unique system for catching the Broad Tosser even if the rest of the team escaped. He'd put a long coat over his uniform and get on a bus. As the bus came up to the game Mario would get the driver to quickly stop and open the door. He'd then pounce out and grab the Broad Tosser. *"The bus drivers used to love to help out,"* he says, *"I guess it added a little excitement to their days!"*

A QUICK BIT OF HISTORY FOR THE BUFFS!

Three Card Monte was given its name to associate it with the game of Spanish Monte (also called Montebank). Although this is mentioned in other books of this nature the original game isn't explained.

THE "THREE-CARD MONTE"—A SCENE ON CONEY ISLAND.—[SKETCHED BY STANLEY FOX.]

The legal game originated in Spain and was very popular in the mid to late 1800's in the Western Territories thanks to a strong Mexican influence in those areas. It is, by many, considered to be the precursor to the game of Faro and certainly both games contain very similar elements of play.

From a forty card deck (the Spanish Deck) the dealer would set out *Layouts*. The remainder of the deck would be turned face up to expose the bottom card which was called the *gate*. If the *gate* matched a card in the *Layout* the bets on that card were paid off. In some games there were additional bets available such as matching the suit or value of the *gate* card.

The odds heavily favored the dealer and the game finally fell by the wayside. The term *Mountebank* has become associated with a swindler or fraud because it was considered such a poor game for the bettor.

However poor its odds it still offered the player a better chance than the game of Three Card Monte, which took its name from the original game!

Perhaps the most famous Broad Tosser of them all was Canada Bill Jones, who is mentioned earlier in this chapter. He was born in a tent to a gypsy family in Yorkshire, England but, as a young man, emigrated to Canada. After learning the game of Monte from another legendary cheat, Dick Cady, he left for America and spent his life winning and losing several fortunes as a man of the road. He always won at Monte but, tragically, was a compulsive poker and euchre player of little skill. Although famed as the greatest Monte man of them all he is even more famous for a statement made after he'd lost all of his money in a crooked poker game. *"Didn't you know the game was crooked?"* his friend asked. *"Sure,"* replied Bill, *"but it was the only game in town!"* Bill died penniless in Reading, Pennsylvania, in 1880 and his funeral costs were paid for by a group of gamblers.

*"I got into my three card monte gyp because
I loved to kid, and because I loved to trim suckers."*

Frank Tarbeaux

Three Shells

ALTHOUGH THIS LITTLE SCAM DISAPPEARED FOR QUITE A TIME IT HAS, LIKE THE proverbial bad penny, turned up again and is making a comeback a fallen film star would be proud of. It's one of the oldest swindles of them all. Some claim that it dates back to Ancient Egypt but that now seems unlikely. Still, it's old!

Long used by magicians for entertainment purposes, a description of the Three Shell Game can be found in a very early conjuring catalogue published by W.H.M. Cranbrook. In those days the game was called the *Thimble and Pea*. In essence three thimbles were shown along with a small piece of rubber shaped like a pea. The player, after a mix around, had to guess which thimble the pea was under. In street parlance a man working the game today is still often called a *Thimble Rigger*.

The origin of the game is pretty ancient and it would seem to be quite closely related to one of the oldest magic effects of all, the *Cups and Balls*. In that effect (still used by many magicians today) balls jump, multiply and grow in size under three cups. It has been called a yard stick for sleight-of-hand ability. The Thimble Rigger isn't interested in entertainment possibilities. He's only interested in making sure that the pea isn't under the cup (or cover) that you are betting on.

The game was very popular on American Carnivals being played with three half walnut shells and the little rubber pea, and this is often the form you'll see a magician entertaining with today. Of course, if you are really unlucky, you might find yourself watching the game at the hands of a hustler.

Although the game had all but vanished for quite a while, such a good little con couldn't slumber for long. Today it is back with a vengeance and can be seen taking money at holiday resorts worldwide. It is especially common in Mediterranean countries where it is of played with matchbox drawers and a rolled up piece of paper. In New York City, at the time of writing, you can see the game on Jamaica Avenue in Queens, where it's played with three bottle caps and a piece of sponge.

If you've ever bet and lost at this game console yourself with the fact that you are only one of millions to do so.

THE GAME

Like the Three Card Trick this is a street game. Walking along the road you may just see Freddy standing behind an orange box upon which are three matchbox covers.

Stay around and you'll see him place a rolled up piece of paper under one of the covers then mix the covers around. He'll invite a member of the crowd (read *team*) to try to guess which cover the paper is under. One of the crowd members (read *Shill*) will place a bet and win. You may think that you (read *mug*) can win as well. You join the game.

Ten minutes later you are broke. That little ball of paper suddenly became very elusive indeed!

The Work

There is no chance of picking the draw the paper ball is under because when you make your bet it isn't there! All the drawers are empty. After your bet has been placed the ball will be re-introduced under a losing cover. Here's how.

In the process of shifting the drawers around the one containing the paper ball is pushed forward about two inches. As he does this Freddy lifts the back edge of the box very slightly. The ball of paper, nipped between the back edge of the box and the traditionally rough working surface (newspaper, coarse cloth or wooden box), is squeezed out. It arrives between Freddy's thumb and second finger which lightly pinch it. All of this happens under cover of Freddy's hands. Because you are looking at the back of his hands you can't see it *even* if you know what's going on!

Freddy's hands move back (with the hidden paper ball) and he offers the chance to bet on any of the covers.

Your bet is accepted and your chosen cover turned.

No ball of paper.

Freddy will then re-introduce the ball of paper in the following manner. Once your cover is chosen Freddy pulls back the other two drawers to 'get them out of the way'. In a reverse of the take he will release the ball of paper from between his finger and thumb allowing it to travel back under a losing cover.

He can then, after you've lost your bet, show that

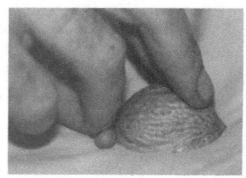
An open view of the pea coming out from under the shell.

the ball was under one of the covers all along. You just missed which one it was!

The Team And Variations

As with Three Card Monte the team is all present and correct. They will hustle and chat you along into making bets. It's worth repeating that you may well be the only non-team member in the game.

The three matchbox covers and ball of paper are the most common props in use today. Only a real mug hustler would try to take you using the magician's kit of three walnut shells (often plastic) and a rubber pea. But you may also see the game being played with three beer caps or three hollowed out corks and a ball of paper. Sometimes the head of a match is used instead of a pea.

Whatever the form, it is worth asking yourself why you should bet on something that a magician can use as a trick. If a conjurer can make the ball jump from cover to cover (cups in their case) then why couldn't a gambler do the same?

In Freddy's library is a rare little book by J.H. Green called *One Hundred Gambler Tricks with Cards*. You might recognize the title from the description of the game of 31 earlier on. In the book J.H. also describes the techniques of one of the most famous Thimble Riggers of the day, Dr. Bennett. Here's an extract which gives a great example of early Double Bluff techniques in action.

> *Now, in the moving of the little paper ball, we thought we had discovered the cause of the doctor's misfortunes, for becoming a little unrolled, a portion of the paper which it was made of, stuck out from under the thimbles. This our Connecticut friend (the mug of this particular tale) plainly saw, and we presumed the doctor, through old age (now about seventy), had his sight so impaired as not to be able to see it, and could not, therefore, play the game with his usual adroitness. But the tale was soon told. Our Yankee friend proposed to double the bet 'having the thing dead'. The doctor, impatient of repeated losses, told him to make it hundreds instead of tens. This was done, and our friend bet three hundred dollars against one hundred. Just here I thought it was a shame to take advantage of a professional gambler's blindness, for the location of the ball was evident.*

The mug lifted the thimble and, surprise, the ball wasn't there. The mug, as mugs so often do, had let greed and larceny rule his head only to pay the price of doing so.

Be sure to re-read the Monte man chapter. The team ploys and money grabbing techniques are also used, with minor adaptions, in this hustle.

At the end of the 1800's one of the best known shell men in the country was Jim Miner also known as Umbrella Jim. He used to introduce his game with a wonderful little song, thankfully recorded in *Gambling and Gambling Devices* by John Phillip Quinn (a reformed gambler), which went as follows:

> *A little fun, just now and then*
> *Is relished by the best of men.*
> *If you have nerve, you may have plenty;*
> *Five, draws you ten, and ten draws twenty.*
> *Attention giv'n, I'll show to you,*
> *How umbrellas hides the peek-a-boo.*
> *Select your shell, the one you choose;*
> *If right, you win, if not, you lose;*
> *The game itself is lots of fun,*
> *Jim's chances though, are two to one;*
> *And I tell you that your chance is slim*
> *To win a prize from 'Umbrella Jim'!*

How amusing that during his opening 'sell' on the game he seems to be warning the player not to have any expectations of winning!

Freddy has one last piece of advice for you if you are ever tempted to pick an object from underneath one of three covers or one card out of three, "*Don't bother. Just give the operator your wallet instead. It'll save you some time.*"

Gee Gees And Woof Woofs

THERE IS LITTLE DOUBT THAT ONE OF THE MOST POPULAR FORMS OF GAMBLING in the world relies on trying to guess which one of a number of horses or dogs will win in a race! A good race is very exciting to watch, and there's always that chance of a long shot coming in to pay big dividends on a bet. Freddy enjoys a day out at the races as much as the next man.

There are lots of ways to lay a bet. You can do so quite legally at the *OTB* (Off Track Betting) or, in Europe, a Turf Accountants shop. You can bet at the track. You can also bet illegally. We aren't too concerned with laying of bets here. You see Freddy doesn't study the horses or dogs too much.

He studies people.

Now he's going to point out a few people and facts that could save you being taken for a sucker.

CHARACTERS AT THE TRACK

The first hustler you are likely to meet at the track, after the valet parker (don't get me started on that!), is a guy called, among other things, the *Tout*. This character comes in various breeds. Watch out for all of them. The first is the *knowledge man* who, for a small premium of course, will sell you a race card marked up with likely winners. Before falling for his chat line, which usually revolves around being banned from betting because of excessive winning, ask yourself why he sells these cards for a flat fee rather than a percentage of any winnings. Ask yourself why he just doesn't get somebody else to put his great bets on for him! Of course he's just spent the previous day marking up cards with horses picked pretty much at random. He'll vary the cards so that, by blind luck, some of them will win, most won't. You can get the same odds by throwing darts at a race card while wearing a blind-fold. Of course, since some of the horses win, he'll be running around bragging to everybody about picking yet another winner. It is, of course, pretty easy to pick the winner when you have effectively picked every horse in the race! Should you have been lucky enough to get a card with a few winners on it you'll be looking to buy another card from the same guy next time round. As you'll see, this 'cover all the horses' by *spreading the money* scam is run in various ways.

Inside, normally near the bar, you'll meet the *Form Man*. He will be making copious notes in a pad, will have an armful of reference books of facts and figures, and will appear to be winning pretty well. The money he is making generally comes from selling dubious tips along with some *kick back* money from a bookie ("*Ya don't want to bet at the window, Charlie will give ya an extra point or two on the odds*") he sends his little lambs to.

A favorite of Freddy's is the old *Story Man*. He'll be one of the aged race track 'characters' who everybody seems to know. He's full of great tales covering his lifetime of coming to the track and will, of course, have a *Hot Tip* for that day's races. For a drink or two he'll share a few more tales and the tip with you. The Story Guy is one of the best values you can get at the track. The price is reasonable and the entertainment factor high. This is one guy we'll advise you to fall for. For once, it's often worth the investment in amusement!

The *Percentage Tout* is a guy who *spreads the money* a little more scientifically than the first guy we met. He will sell a winner to all and sundry. What he actually does, for a small fee, is tip the first horse in the race to several people, the second horse to several more, the third to a few more until he has covered most, if not all, of the horses. He may even give these tips away and ask for a percentage, say 10 %, of the winnings. This magnificently cunning system allows him to bet on every single horse in the race without risking a single penny.

SPREADING THE MONEY

An up-to-date version of the *Percentage Scam* is the telephone tip line (also becoming quite prevalent on the Internet). You phone a premium phone line where you will, after a somewhat lengthy and expensive chat, be given a tip. Callers are automatically rotated through every horse in the race so that in a five horse race, for example, twenty percent of callers will win. The winners, of course, will soon be calling in for another tip! Actually, and somewhat sad to say, often losers may call again choosing to grasp at any straw they can! It must be stressed that not all call lines are guilty of this rather insidious practice!

Yet another version of the *Percentage Scam* is a postal club. Yes sports fans, you too could be a member of a *Hot Tip Club*! Members receive their information for free but must sign a legally binding contract to bet a certain amount of money on each tip. This is normally between twenty and fifty dollars depending both on the odds and on the club. A percentage of that bet, should the animal win, is due, at *Payout Odds*, to the club. So if your horse or dog wins at four to one and your club expects you to bet fifty dollars, twenty of which is their *Seed Money*, you'll owe the club eighty dollars. Once again, by rotating the animals among the members the club can, effectively, place a large stake on every horse in a race without risking a single penny of its own money. Again it must be stressed that not all tipping clubs do this. A great many are run by honest individuals who by studying racing form will really try to give you a winner as they see the race. *"They really do it the hard way,"* is Freddy's comment on them.

NIFTY TOYS

Another form of tipping device you can buy is a little hand-held computer that looks a little like a Palm Pilot. You enter in the horse or dog names, their form (from the track program), the weather conditions, ground conditions and so on. The program will then whizz along and pick a winner for you. It may also, of course, pick a loser. No guarantees are given that you'll even get more winners than losers! Freddy suggests that these devices are simply an expensive version of covering your eyes and sticking a pin into a list of animal's names. I tend to agree with him as none of the manufacturers or sellers of these devices has advertised retiring to a life of luxury, paid for by winnings at the track, just yet!

You would think that such operations would quickly go out business as the majority of the tips, by the nature of the hustle, will lose. It's sad that tipsters of any sort will rarely run out of idiotic customers who are ever chasing the elusive big win. This stays true even when they lose time after time after time. John Scarne, a well known magician and gambling advisor in the 1940s and 1950s, used to tell a wonderful tale about two touts meeting at the course. One said, *"I've got a great client who is richer than I can imagine. He's betting a hundred dollars on each horse I give him! But so far I've given him seven losers in a row, what should I do now?"* The second tout thought for a moment before replying, *"Give him up, he's bad luck!"*

HOOVERS

Actually, as we drift back to the course, it must be said that picking a winning horse or dog is no guarantee of some gamblers getting their money! You might be amazed at the number of fun gamblers who don't understand the mechanics of the bet they have made! For fun, perhaps after a drink or two, they'll try a more exotic bet such as a *Round Robin* in England or, perhaps, a *Tri-Fecta* in America. Often, with multiple selections, they'll fail to know if it's a winning ticket or not! There are truly naive *punters* who will bet on a horse or dog *each way* (or to *place*) and assume that the bet is a losing one if the animal wins! It sounds outrageously stupid but they'll throw a winning ticket away! You can laugh and say that such a thing could never happen. Don't check with me, check with another race track character called the *Hoover*. He's a guy who wanders around picking up discarded tickets and often pays for his day out by doing so. If you are going to make a bet at least make sure you understand just what you are betting on. Another time to watch for a *Hoover* is right after a race finishes. The losers often throw their tickets away in disgust the moment an animal's nose crosses the line. But what if there is a Steward's Enquiry or photo-finish called on the race? Suddenly those discarded tickets could be winning ones and you stumble around to pick up your ticket. You may get it, but only if you get there before our pal the *Hoover*!

THE TIC-TAC MAN

At an English race track a fascinating guy to watch out for is a *Tic-Tac* man. At the race track a line of legal bookies will be spread out down the track. Obviously they need to be aware of what odds are being offered by everybody else. They also want to know what odds the *Tote* or betting windows are offering. In these days of cellular information the *Tic-Tac* man is sadly disappearing but he can still be seen. He's the guy who uses a series of signals to tell his employer just how the odds are running. If he extends his two first fingers and points them at each other, then moves them up and down he is signaling odds of even money. A hand stretched out covering his nose means odds of two to one. Three to one is signaled with a hand beneath his chin. For four to one he will wag his hand from side to side at waist level. Touching his right shoulder indicates five to one. Moving his hand between his right shoulder and the top of his head signals odds of six to one. It's like a specialized sign language unique to the race tracks! A few others would be his right hand touching his left shoulder (seven to four), his hands cupped over each other at waist level (five to four) and touching the fingertips of both hands to their respective shoulders (nine to two). So if you see a guy making movements like these you are not witnessing somebody having a fit, you are watching a skilled *Tic-Tac* man in action! Of course these guys are not hustlers (though their employers may well be) but at least having knowledge of them will impress your friends!

FREDDY AND THE MINX MAKE MONEY

Now let's take a look at one of Freddy's favorite little race track hustles which he'll use to pay for a nice day out at the races. It does not require him to pick any winning horses, study any form, place any obscure bets or have any form of inside knowledge. He doesn't need to mark up or sell any race cards. All Freddy has to do is pick a group of mugs. Something he is truly an expert at.

Freddy teams up with a female, in his case it's normally an older woman who goes by the nickname, the *Minx*. Together they look like a pleasant older married couple out for a day of fun. They go into the bar and order a couple of drinks. They are talking just loudly enough so that people around them can hear some of what is being said. They don't catch everything but it's something about a tip he's bought and her thinking that they shouldn't bet everything on it. After a few more words Freddy holds up his hands, turns and walks out of the bar.

The Minx nervously talks to some of the guys around her. She tells them that her husband paid fifty dollars for a tip on a hot horse and has gone off to bet on it. Some of the guys, wary of tipsters, may grimace slightly at this news especially when she tells them he wants to put quite a chunk of their savings on the horse. They may even buy her another drink to calm her nerves before she goes to the window to watch the race. As the horses cross the line she jumps up and down, yelling, *"We won! We won!"* She may even spill her drink but nobody minds. They are kinda happy to see a winner, especially this sweet lady. Freddy returns and shows her a pile of money. He whispers to her, loud enough for others to hear, that they've just made seven hundred and fifty dollars.

Freddy makes a phone call and nods a few times. After he's hung up his cellular phone he tells her that there is a tip for the third race but the guy wants a hundred dollars for it. Should he take it? he asks her. She's a little nervous about it but reluctantly agrees telling Freddy that they'll try it just one more time. Freddy disappears again leaving his wife with a little fun money. She has another couple of drinks, is getting a little tipsy and flirting with her new found friends. They find her quite delightful. They may also be hoping that she'll give away a little information they can use.

Freddy returns after the third race with a big smile on his face. He gives her a huge hug and informs her that they are now fifteen hundred dollars ahead of the game!

His cell phone rings and Freddy answers it. He is obviously arguing heavily with somebody at the other end. Finally he shouts, *"I'll get back to you!"* and turns off the phone. He explains to his 'wife' (and to half the bar who are trying to listen in by now) that the guy has a very hot tip for the last race. The odds will pay great money but he wants a thousand dollars for the tip. He knows what they've won so far and knows what they could make. He considers the tip a bargain at that price but Freddy isn't so sure. The Minx, playing the tipsy, elated wife to perfection tries to argue him into it. *"You said we should stop after the last one!"* argues Freddy. *"But sweety, we won, we won twice! Think how much more we could win!"* she argues back. *"I'll offer him two hundred but that's it,"* growls Freddy reaching for his phone. The phone conversation obviously does not go well and Freddy informs her that they are going to leave while they are nicely ahead.

In retrospect it can all get a little fuzzy about how the idea of a syndicate arises. If Freddy puts in a couple of hundred and eight others put in a hundred each he could buy the tip and they could all profit nicely. "*Hey,*" they'll say, "*Think how happy your wife will be!*" The Minx helps them talk Freddy into the idea. It doesn't take them long and, with money in hand, he goes off to get the name of the horse. The Minx stays behind with her friends. He returns and shares the number with the syndicate who all go off to bet. Freddy doesn't run off with the money. "*Too tacky,*" he says. No, he prefers the finesse of being with the group and watching the race run.

If the horse wins everybody is delighted and it's champagne all round. I say *if* because there are no real tips. The money Freddy has been flashing around is *cabbage* (forged). The last great tip was a long shot Freddy picked at random. If the horse loses nobody blames the couple. After all, they lost everything as well. It wasn't their idea to form a syndicate, nobody forced anybody to put their money in. They just have to settle for the fact that it was a bad tip, this stuff happens. They'll all commiserate each other with a few drinks before heading their separate ways.

With Freddy and the Minx eight hundred dollars richer.

Can't happen, you cry? This con is as common today as when it was first used years ago. It works for a number of reasons not the least of which is Freddy and the Minx giving Oscar level acting performances. Another reason it works is the sheep-like stupidity that can take over the most logical of people who are trying to pick a winner. If somebody wins then *everybody* wants to know what they are going to bet on in the next race *especially* if they seem to have some form of inside information. Freddy and the Minx set a perfect stage for the punters to come flocking with money in hand.

Freddy claims that, more than once, a syndicate member has followed him out afterwards and, being convinced that Freddy had been given two out of three winners, offered to buy the name and number of the tipster. Two out of three is a great deal! Freddy has, as you can imagine, been happy to sell the guy a name and number. Often this number may 'accidentally' be the Stoat's number (remember him from Freddy's betting scams?). "*It's nice to keep a friend in the family,*" says Freddy.

PUTTING THE FIX IN

Well so far we haven't even looked at the animals themselves. People tend to believe that, in these days of random drug testing, races just can't be fixed. There are also people who believe that Elvis is alive and well on the planet Mars! For animal lovers sake we'll just take a quick glimpse into the world of *putting the fix in*. I'll certainly try to avoid any of the very cruel ways this can be done and stick to some of the rather clever ways it can be done.

I once spent quite a time in the company of a gentleman called *Blackie*. He got this nickname after he painted a tan dog with black paint to get better odds on it. You see the tan dog was a well known winner, but, after the paint job and a change of name, it was just another dog! In those days before lip tattoo's for animal registry became the norm he may well have gotten away with this extraordinary ploy but for one thing. The paint didn't dry too well and, in the winner's circle, he gave the dog a big hug and a pat. I think you can imagine the rest! He didn't walk for the exit, he ran! This is an extreme example of trying to disguise an animal but, at lesser levels, it is very common. An episode of the George Peppard television series *Banachek* (about an insurance detective) featured the disguising of a race horse very accurately indeed and, should you catch it, is well worth a watch.

I met Blackie on the island of Jersey where I was working for the summer and he told me many a lurid tale of his days of *putting the fix in*. He told me that dogs (greyhound races were his specialty) are rarely drugged these days. Random dope testing has made it very difficult, though by no means impossible, to get away with. But there are lots of other ways a good dog can be held up allowing a long shot a better chance than they should have of winning the race.

One way he could guarantee giving a dog a slow start was to stuff two tiny pieces of cotton wool right down inside the dogs ears. It's easy to see how this can pass a cursory vets examination but what good does it do? Well, greyhounds are taught to listen for the hare or lure coming around the track. As it gets nearer and nearer the dogs get ready to run. Our poor little fellow can't hear the hare! The first he knows of the race starting, thanks to his temporary deafness, is when the gate opens and he sees the other dogs rushing out. This simple disadvantage can easily cost him the race.

Another use can be made of cotton wool in a very cunning manner. Most dogs are either *inside* or *outside* runners. That is, they will either drift into the center of the track or out to the edge when running. A good dog is, of course, trained to use their particular quirk to advantage in a race. The fixer will place tiny balls of cotton wool between the toes of the dog to exaggerate or lessen the dogs natural drift, For example, a dog that naturally runs inwards could have cotton wool balls placed between the toes of his front left leg. This will cause him to drift outwards during the race. He'll tread more carefully on this foot because the slightly splayed toes cause it to feel uncomfortable. It will certainly slow him down considerably.

A different way to give a dog a slow start is to leave his (or her!) claws slightly long. When the gate opens the dog will scrabble a little on the hard floor of the box making a slower start than normal.

A small piece of fluffy grass or fur inserted in the rear end of a dog can make it feel uncomfortable and so cause it to run erratically.

A good dog can also be made to look bad. No, I'm not talking about painting it but about making a fit and healthy dog look like it couldn't make the run never mind win the race! This is done to keep the odds high on the dog. Nobody wants to put money on the animal except the cheats! The secret? They feed the dog up on hard boiled eggs. It makes the animal look fat and unfit but doesn't affect its speed at all.

There are, as Blackie will assure you should you ever find him, a hundred and one ways to fix horses and dogs. I don't think we need to explain *acid ears, tail tots, sniffers, fliers* or *passports*. It's enough for you to know that animals can be fixed.

Perhaps the funniest tale Blackie told me concerned a race where they had decided to dope the dogs, slowing their run, to let a long shot win. They had decided to wait until the last possible moment before giving the dogs the drugs just in case there was a drug test called. They bribed a dog handler who was to load the dogs into the boxes to give each dog a quarter of a strong sleeping pill just before putting them in their boxes. A lot of money was going down and the handler was warned of the consequences should he not get his job right. He must have been just a little too frightened about the consequences. Instead of giving the dogs a quarter of a pill he gave each animal a whole pill. The hare went around and the gates opened. One dog, the long shot, ran after the hare leaving the other five sound asleep in their boxes! Blackie used to roar with laughter every time he told this tale!

At the horse track Blackie suggests that it is much easier to *put the fix in* on the jockey. A horse race can easily be thrown by the man or woman on the back of the horse. Bribery or fear can be very enticing factors for them. A lot of money may convince a jockey to race just *hands and heels* rather than going all out. Fear of retribution to themselves or their families may cause a jockey to take serious risks to avoid winning. On the island of Jersey I went to local track meets with Blackie. He once warned me against betting on a favorite and to take a long shot instead. Coming into the last corner the favorite was ahead but, as the horses turned the corner, the jockey on the favorite didn't so much fall off his horse as hurl himself from the horse. Blackie, roaring with laughter as usual, explained that the jockey had wanted to make it obvious to his temporary employers that he was really doing his job and throwing the race!

A final lesson from Blackie was how they laid the bet to keep the odds they wanted. A single player going to a bookie or window to lay a huge bet could adversely affect the odds and reduce their payout. Instead three or four of them would simultaneously approach different bookies or windows and lay smaller bets. This stopped the animal being *bet off the board*. A huge bet could have been refused. Several smaller bets are much more unlikely to be turned down *especially* if laid at the same time in different places. The money is on before anybody really realizes just how much has actually been bet. Blackie called this system of placing the money *Betting across the board*.

SUMMING UP

Bear in mind that most of the scams and hustles you've read here are pretty much interchangeable between the dog and horse track. Some are animal specific (cotton between dog's toes) but most are not. At the track it is most unwise to assume that everything is fair!

For a wonderful and entertaining look at a race track based scam, and other hustles, watch the film *The Sting*. Although a comedy movie, the hustle is based on fact. The *Cross* is used here to make a killing on a rich sucker. Within the story the sucker is convinced that the team can get the results of a race prior to the OTB betting window being shut (don't worry the film tells you how!). For the sting he bets the wrong way and loses a fortune. You can laugh at the movie but you can also rest assured that this complicated con has been used in real life.

Are you getting the idea? Even if everything were straight at the various tracks the odds will grind you down eventually. With everything from touts to jockeys being paid to take a fall (and a *lot* in between) it's hardly a winning proposition for you. But a day out at the races can be fun if you follow a few simple rules.

1. Decide before leaving home how much you can afford to bet. Add the price of your day out (food, drink and travel) and take *only* that amount of money with you. Leave *all* credit cards, check books, ATM Cards and further cash behind.
2. Bet only cash. Don't raise your bets to chase losses and, should you win a nice big bet, don't raise your bets to play like a big time gambler on a roll.
3. Ignore touts. Picking names because they amuse you, are the same as a pet tortoise you once owned or because you just stuck a pin in it are just as reliable as methods or systems and probably a whole lot more fun.
4. Don't think that you have a system or can pick a winner by your superior knowledge of a form book. When you pick a winner, it's good luck. You can beat *a race* but inevitably, if you go wild, *the races* will beat you!

Keep these simple rules in mind and you can have a great day out. A small wager or two makes watching the *Sport of Kings* very exciting indeed. However small your bet you can still cheer your jockey or dog along. If you win you can cheer, if you lose you can groan! Hey, it's fun! It could actually be some of the most fun you can have gambling with just a few dollars. So long as you keep your head clear and your eyes peeled for Freddy and his ilk! And while you are keeping those eyes peeled do avoid the Three Card and Shell men. The race track is one of their favorite hunting grounds!

"Horse sense is what keeps horses from betting on what people will do."

Damon Runyon

"Only a madmen or a drunk would bet seriously on horses."

Nick the Greek

How to Cheat at Everything

"The race track is the only place where the windows clean the people."

———•———

unknown

"I bet on a horse at twenty to one. It crossed the line at quarter to five."

———•———

Tommy Cooper

Unless you are very careful a fun day out at the race track can rapidly turn into a very dodgy business at the best of times. Meet Freddy and it can be suicidal!

HOOF NOTE

Nick the Greek (Nicholas Andrea Dandolos), despite his above quote or perhaps because of it, was once said to have parlayed a few thousand dollars into over a million during a drunken betting spree at the horse track. He later claimed that it was the only time he ever bet serious money on the horses and refused to do so ever again. He said that a man could only be that lucky once in his life!

Unfairgrounds And Crooked Carnivals

IF A TOURIST RESORT IS THE CHEAT'S DISNEYLAND THEN A FAIRGROUND OR CARNIval can only be described as his heaven.

An area tightly packed with people all out to have as much fun as possible. They have pockets full of money that they are happy to spend. Young men will have girlfriends they might want to impress. Older guys may have families with young children. They want the kids to have a memorable time so will do their best to win them a big cuddly toy. Single men may have a stomach full of beer and be out on the prowl for a girl or two they can chat up.

Freddy describes it as *"Heaven as it would be run by devils."*

It will sound harsh but your chances of getting an even break at the fairground or carnival are about the same as your chances of picking up the queen in a game of Monte.

A walk around the area with Freddy (who spent much of his youth working these scams) is a real eye opener. I was also very fortunate in getting top bunko investigator, Bruce Walstad, to take a look over this section of the book. His additional notes and comments are a confirmation that not only do these cheats exist but that they are rife. My thanks to Bruce for providing both his valuable time and knowledge to make this section as accurate as possible.

Ready?

Let's go, but stay close.

You know that tilt-a-whirl down on the south beach drag
I got on it last night and my shirt got caught
And they kept me spinnin'
I didn't think I'd ever get off

Excerpted lyrics to "4th July, Asbury Park (Sandy)"
Bruce Springsteen's album *The Wild The Innocent & The E Street Shuffle*

Hanky Panks

*H*anky Panks, as they are known in the trade, come in many shapes and sizes. Despite Freddy's warnings about getting an even break, these games are generally run quite fairly. Of course that doesn't mean you are getting an even break!

The *gaff* or cheat in this type of game is in the value of the prizes offered against the amount spent. Here are some common examples for you to watch out for.

FOUR BIG CARDS

You'll see several large boards arranged in a circular fashion around the center of a stall. On each board are four large (jumbo) playing cards arranged in a square formation. Every other spare piece of space in the stall is taken up with cuddly toys of all shapes and sizes. This large and colorful display which lures you to the stall is called *The Flash*.

For just a dollar you get three darts to throw at a set of cards. To win all you have to do is to hit three separate cards.

Sounds easy?

It is!

When you hit the cards (which, unless you are severely impaired somehow, should take no more than a couple of attempts) you will be congratulated and given a token that entitles you to any one of the smallest fluffy toys. These toys cost the operator about twenty cents each.

You could take the little toy or try again to get another token. Two tokens (minimum cost to you, two dollars) gets you a bigger fluffy toy. Cost to the operator may be around thirty-five cents.

Three tokens (minimum cost to you, three dollars) will get you an even bigger toy which has cost the operator around forty cents.

The operator can, of course, claim this is just a profit margin. *"Nice margin,"* comments Freddy.

All the Hanky Panks work on this 'pay more, get less' system. Here's a few more.

DARTBOARD CHAMPS

One of the most common types of all the Hanky Panks revolves around the game of darts. Hanky Pank prizes and a subtle *gaff* can empty your pockets very quickly indeed.

I'm sure you've seen these games. A stall full of dartboards and for just a dollar you can get to throw three darts at one of the boards. To win all you have to do is score under ten with three darts. In some variations you have to score higher than ten. The way the games are laid out make it look very easy to win but it's wise to carefully read the full game rules first.

Often doubles or trebles do not count at all. They can sometimes make your entire score null and void. Some boards are missing the double and treble sections altogether!

Then, on further reading, you discover that you must score under (or over) with each separate dart.

To make it even harder each dart must score in a different number. Two darts hitting the same number will null and void your bet.

Add the fact that you'll be throwing darts from an unstandard distance of around five feet (dart games are played from around seven and a half feet) and at a board that is so weathered a chisel might have trouble sticking into it and you're starting to get the idea that a fluffy toy, worth about a third of what you are paying to play, just isn't worth the effort.

In his extensive collection Bruce Walstad has a set of darts that have both damaged flights and lead weights in the shaft! As he puts it, *"With one or two of these in a set given to you it really screws you up!"*

You might also want to check out

Typical Hanky panks—note how little air is in the balloons!

How to Cheat at Everything

just how blunt the points on the darts are. The blunt points can be especially irritating when you are trying to pop a number of under-inflated balloons to win a Gonk.

THE HORSE RACE

A version of The Horse Race.

"A winner every time!" calls Freddy to the crowd, *"Roll up, roll up! We just need to fill three more seats before we begin the next race! Remember folks, there's a winner every time!"*

This is the Horse Race. It is any type of game where a number of players compete against each other for a prize. Eight or ten players sit down and for a dollar each get to have a go at moving a horse along a track by throwing balls into holes, blow up a balloon by firing a water gun into a slot or, perhaps, race a car around a track by pulling on a lever.

The winner collects a prize. It'll be worth, if the winner is very lucky, about fifty cents. The rest of the money goes straight into the operator's pocket.

Sure there is a winner every time. But remember, because the game doesn't start till the seats are all but full, there will also be seven to nine losers each game!

CHICKIN' LICKIN'

These are mechanical games you'll see spread around. Traditionally they will consist of a large model of a clucking chicken surrounded by plastic eggs. For fifty cents the chicken, with a large cluck, will deliver a plastic egg to you.

Inside the egg is a Hanky Pank worth around five cents.

The lure? Well, some of the eggs, a notice assures you, are really quite valuable. Perhaps some will have watches or money (ranging from one to ten dollars) inside. You can even see some of those prizes in clear eggs near the top of the pile. You may get quite carried away trying to get one of those lucky eggs. It might take quite a time before you work out that the chicken delivers eggs at the bottom of the pile and that it could take quite a time for the big winning eggs to work their way down.

Needless to say, to keep those big paying eggs in good clear view Freddy will top up the egg pile each night.

On the billion to one or so shot that you get one of these eggs you'll not be desperately happy. What looked like a twenty dollar bill is actually a coupon for you to get some free tries at other games. What looked like a nice watch is actually worth around a dollar.

Hanky Panks come in all shapes and sizes. Some will even offer a prize if you lose! It may only be a balloon or some such (costing the operator around one cent) but at least, as Freddy says, *"It's better than nothing."* Hanky Panks are among the very few games where, for a small fee, you can actually walk away with a prize without busting your wallet.

Arcades From Hell

I T IS A FAIR BET THAT, WHILE WANDERING AROUND OUR LITTLE LAND OF TAINTED fun, you've taken a stroll through one of the tents full of arcade style machines. Freddy loves these operations since they make money for him with practically little or no effort on his behalf at all. "*Real easy money,*" he smiles.

Luckily for you Slots are not allowed in many places. Freddy seems to have no idea why this should be so. "*Just harmless fun,*" he claims. They are, however, very common on European fairgrounds. And just about every pub you enter in England will have two or three of the machines. So don't think you won't run into them at some time or another!

FRUIT MACHINES

Any small bar or club owner will tell you that a couple of Slot Machines (often called *Fruits* in the trade) will give enough profit to often cover the cost of running the place.

Freddy will tell you the same. He should know. He owns several in the town where his mother lived just outside London, UK.

A casino manager will inform you, if he's in a good mood, that slots are easily the biggest money maker he has. Their profit often outstrips all the other games put together.

A fairground or carnival arcade will be packed with them.

Players may argue that they get a great deal of fun watching the wheels spin around as they hope for a large pay out. They will tell you all sorts of ways to know which machine is hot and ready to give up a jackpot. They'll show you books of highly complicated playing systems they've learned by route. It is worth noting that, despite these 'Can't lose' systems, there is no such animal as a professional slot player.

People who enjoy playing these machines all day would probably also argue that throwing their money down a sewer drain would not be fun. Yet, with just a little eye candy popped on top, that's exactly what they are doing.

Fruits are *big* money makers for an operator.

Invented by Charles Fey of the U.S. in 1895 these machines offer stupendous odds against the player.

The player could argue that these machines are wonderful. After all they pay out ninety five percent! A more logical person could argue that this actually means that the machine is *taking* five percent. These percentages are also not quite as fair as they appear. The figures are worked out by a very complex system which, surely by chance, is very favorable to the owner and not to the player. But, assuming that the machine, as many do, advertises a ninety percent pay out. What does that actually mean to a player?

To put a coin, or coins, into a machine and spin the wheels takes around four seconds. This means that, for a single coin per play, the machine is capable of taking nine hundred coins an hour. With a ninety percent payout that means that, on average, the machine will hold back ninety coins (or ten percent) for the operator. At just a quarter a go the machine is making the operator, on average, around twenty dollars an hour! And that's if the machine is playing fair! A fairground or carnival machine may well have had its payout reduced to almost zero despite what it says on the machine. "*Hey, we're always moving them around,*" Freddy may whine. "*It's not my fault the payout slot got twisted up. It musta just fallen or something.*"

The original slots, because of the arm that had to be pulled to spin the wheels, swiftly became known as *One Armed Bandits*. They are still known by this name. In casinos you'll often see little old ladies wearing leather gloves on their 'pulling' hand to protect their skin. Even with electronic starts the machines still often have the handles that gave them their name. People seem to like the thrill of pulling a handle rather than pushing a button. Go figure. Amazingly you'll hear people say, "*Let's go play the one armed bandits!*" Even Freddy shakes his head in disbelief.

On a straight machine the odds against hitting the jackpot (not just a tiny pay out) are minimal at best. With three wheels of twenty symbols each the odds of lining up three particular symbols are 1 in 20x20x20. That's 1 in 8000 or 7999-1 against! Since these odds are rather greedy, even by Freddy's standards, the jackpot symbol is repeated several times on the first two wheels to increase the players chances and thus keep them interested.

There is no system to beat the machines. In these electronic days the payouts are truly random. Watching for a machine that hasn't paid out for a while and going in for the kill is about as sensible as waiting for red to come up ten times in a row before betting on black at the roulette table.

Freddy sets his machines at the fairground or carnival arcade to pay what he considers a reasonable return. He lets them pay out a bit. After all, most winners just carry on playing and re-invest their winnings anyway.

Playing slots in a casino is your choice. Playing in Freddy's arcade is just stupid.

ARCADE MACHINES

The day Space Invaders (an early video game) was released by the Nintendo Corporation of Japan, Freddy practically whooped with joy and considered becoming a Buddhist. I asked why and with considerable foresight he said, "*Think how much those machines will be worth when the kids get a little tired of them.*"

He was right. The moment a new game came out the older ones could be picked up for a song. These days a game over a year old seems to be almost antique. Freddy buys year-old machines.

He puts them into his arcade. People seem rather drawn to them in a nostalgic manner. "*I used to knock up a killer score on these! Man, I haven't seen this little puppy in ages!*" Of course, for the pleasure of playing the game to relive old times, they'll have to invest a dollar as against the twenty five or fifty cents it used to cost them but, what the hell, it's fun. They just love standing at those machines zapping aliens or blowing up monsters. Freddy loves watching them. As far as he's concerned it's the perfect scheme. He doesn't even have to provide the lure of a payout!

Old players like re-living the experience and new players like to try out the old machines. The new players invest even more money as they learn the various levels of the machines and nobody likes to be beaten. They keep on going till they hit that final screen! Freddy also has the advantage that his machines are constantly traveling and, therefore, constantly finding new players.

When the machines break or become too well known to turn a good profit he just ditches them and buys new ones. The cost, compared to the income, is peanuts.

PENNY FALLS

Inflation has turned this, more commonly, into Quarter Falls, but the game remains the same.

A pile of quarters lie on a number of moving metal shelves. The shelves move constantly backward and forward.

You can drop a quarter into one of a number of slots and it will fall down to rest on the upper shelf. If it lands in the right place it may well push some quarters from the upper shelf to the lower shelf. They may, in turn, push some quarters into the pay out slot giving you a win. If no quarters appear in the pay out bin you can, of course, always try again.

Quarter Falls. Sure, I was tempted, but not that much!

On some machines if you do have some quarters pushed into the pay out chute there is the added hazard of a *house chute* where some of those coins are taken back by the machine. This can be up to 80 % of the coins so 'some' can mean a big problem for the player! The house chutes are set at the side of the machine. In the center of the machine inside the front is a 'V' shaped piece of plastic. The plastic shape pushes the coins to the side allowing a lot of them to fall into the house chutes at the side. A small lip running along the front of the machine, about one eighth of an inch high, also helps move the coins towards the sides rather than into the payout slots. The player doesn't see the lip or the plastic shape because they are covered with coins above them. The result of this set up is that a lot of the coins get shunted to the sides to fall into the house chutes while only the top layers of coins make it into the player's winning chute.

All Freddy has to do is employ somebody to make change all day long.

Sometimes you'll see prizes such as watches or rings resting on top of the coins. If you should win one you can rest assured that you'll have paid for it at least five times over. *"Hey, make that ten times over,"* Freddy has just shouted. *"I need to turn a profit you know!"* These heavy prize objects also tend to press weight onto the coins to stop them from moving forward as fast as they should.

In the interests of research I stood and watched this game being played at a local fairground when I was living in England. The date, around 1988. The machine was taking fifty pence pieces. The coins were going in, by my count, at roughly ten a minute. The largest pay out I saw over the course of several hours was around five pounds, most of which was immediately re-invested.

It's a mug's game. One gambling writer once said that he had been amused to hear the operator of such a game whistling the tune *Pennies from Heaven*. Amusing if it's not your money I guess.

No gaffs are required in the machines. The way the shelves work will rake the money in easily. It takes a *lot* of coins before they are squashed up enough to drop into that pay out chute. Your only consolation is, I guess, that you've at least lost your cash fairly, even if you did do it by being pretty stupid.

My good friend Todd Robbins (the Coney Island Wonder Worker) has seen some set-ups that don't pay out the coins. Instead they pay out in tokens which can be exchanged for cheap prizes from a booth. I think, and Freddy agrees, that this is just plain greedy and these machines should be avoided at all costs unless you want to go bankrupt very quickly indeed!

In some jurisdictions these machines are considered to be akin to Slot Machines and, as such, are considered gambling. Even the FBI has taken an interest in these devilish contraptions and, within his collection, Bruce Walstad has an article from the FBI Law Enforcement Bulletin entitled *Penny Falls, Friend or Foe.*

GRABBERS

This machine has a pile of prizes of varying attraction inside a clear plastic case. For a few coins you get to try to control a grabbing claw to snatch a prize and drop it down a chute. For such a simple looking thing it is infuriatingly difficult to grab anything, never mind get it in the chute. No gaff is required, it's just too damned difficult to win at. *"It's pretty good at grabbing money though,"* comments Freddy who owns three or four of these machines.

PENNY PITCHES

You'll often see this little money maker just inside the entrance to the arcade or right by it. The investment set-up is very low and the rewards are very high indeed.

This is what you'll see.

A large painted board decorated with circles or small squares lies flat inside a stall. Within each circle is either a number or a blank space. Leading from your side of the stall to the edge of the board are lots of thin upright chutes.

The game? You roll a quarter down the chute and onto the board. If it comes to rest completely within a circle or square on the board, and that circle or square has a number in it, then you win that many quarters in return. If it lands completely in a blank area you may win a balloon or tiny furry toy.

It is highly addictive and even appears to have some element of skill to it.

There is no element of skill.

Even with the luck of a God it is incredibly hard to roll a coin so that it comes to rest completely inside a circle or square that is *just* big enough to surround it.

While at the fairground in England on my research trip I watched one of these games for a considerable period of time. Over the time I counted around seven hundred ten pence pieces rolled for a total pay out that added up to seven pounds. Most of that payout was re-invested by the happy little players.

Of course I have to say that the arcades, with the possible exception of slot machine payouts, are not truly hustles in the real sense of the word. Nobody is actually conning you into losing your money. You may even have some fun as you lose it. But, it must also be stressed that, nobody is going out of their way to point out that the games are far harder to win at than they appear.

It is a gray area I guess. But even in gray areas the money still seems to end up in Freddy's pocket.

Down And Dirty

WELL YOU MAY NOT HAVE WON MUCH ON OUR TRIP THROUGH THE CARNIVAL or fairground but you also haven't lost much either. You may even have actually enjoyed playing a few of your old video game faves and be wondering what all the fuss is about.

Your wallet has stayed pretty much intact and you may even be carrying a few furry toys to give to your kids.

That's all about to change.

We're going to tread forth into the nastier rip-off areas of the fun palace, where it stops being a gray area. Every game, every piece of 'fun', from now on is designed to do just one thing and that's to separate you from your money swiftly and efficiently.

Don't worry, we'll take it nice and slow so don't get too worried too quickly.

SHYS

You've all seen coconut shys. I'm pretty sure you may have even tried, with little success, to knock one of those little puppies off its stand. Freddy has no need for a gaff here to take your money. The cost of a coconut is less than the cost of your go anyway. Take six or seven shots at knocking one of them off (as many do) and you've given the operator a tidy profit.

The coconut shy is little more than a Hanky Pank. The nuts aren't given away every time though. In fact, because they are pushed into mounds of sand to keep them upright, they are much tougher to knock off than you might at first think.

But there are other kinds of shy stands!

Six Little Bottles

Six wooden bottles or cans are arranged in a 3-2-1 pyramid on a shelf. You buy three balls and all you have to do to win a prize is knock the six objects from the shelf. It looks really easy when the operator demonstrates it for you.

Sadly it isn't when you try. Three of the bottles are very light and three are very heavy. If the three light objects are at the bottom of the pyramid then a reasonably skilled throw can knock them all down.

If the three heavy objects are at the bottom and spaced well apart then a professional pitcher from a major league baseball team doesn't stand a chance!

So the game can be set up to be possible to beat or impossible to beat. Games that can be set both ways are called *Two Way Joints* by Freddy and his pals.

Three Little Bottles

A variation on the above looks even simpler. One bottle is balanced on top of two others in a tiny pyramid. The idea is the same. You purchase one ball and have to knock the three bottles down. The operator can demonstrate just how easy this is to do, but you can play all day and fail until you run out of money.

Freddy can gaff the game in a number of ways. If the bottom two bottles are set up evenly, side by side facing the player, they can be knocked over. Just by setting one of the bottom bottles a little forward of the other makes the game next to impossible to beat since the forward bottle will absorb all the balls energy and deflect it away from the rearward bottle.

Heavy bottles (often filled with lead) are also used in this variation. Using one weighted bottle, the game can be set to go both ways. With the weighted bottle on top the game can be beaten. If it's on the bottom you've got no chance. Some of the bottles in Freddy's collection weigh over ten pounds and the balls he hands out are pretty light! In Bruce Walstad's collection is an innocent looking set of three bottles. The set weighs in at thirty pounds with one bottle topping the scales at seventeen and a half pounds!

A nice tale revolves around this very game. So the story goes, a carnival was playing in San Francisco when a huge earthquake shook the

Three little bottles.

Another version using ten cans.

city. Tents fell, the river flooded, buildings collapsed and people ran screaming everywhere. When it was all over the carnival had been completely
destroyed.

Except for one thing.

The one thing left standing was a simple wooden shelf.

And standing on it was a little pyramid made up of three bottles.

The Cat Rack

This little number is also known as a *Punk Rack*. Here Freddy shows you a
shelf upon which is a line of stuffed dolls. In the trade these dolls are called
cats or *punks*. Your mission, should you decide to invest your money and
take it, is to knock three dolls from the shelf with three balls.

The game is gaffed in a number of ways. First the dolls, should you get a
close look at one (unlikely), are a lot more fur than substance. They really
have a much smaller area to hit than you may think. Especially when you
are throwing pretty light balls at them. You have to hit them very accurately
to even hope to move them. They also tend to be heavier at their base and so
have a tendency to act like the well known toy, Weebles. They wobble but
they don't fall down.

Freddy can also stop them falling from the shelf (a requisite of winning)
in a number of ways. He can wedge the bases of the dolls into slots in the
front of the shelf. He can stand to one side and pull the back wall of the tent
in a little to leave less room for the dolls to fall through. Don't bother checking, you won't see him do it! He also has a cunning set up where he can pull
a string and extend a second shelf out behind the first. When this extra shelf
is hidden away he can demonstrate how easy it is to knock the dolls from
the shelf. When the extra shelf is extended your chances of doing so dimin-
ish to exactly zero. Finally the pretty colored front piece on the shelf does
double work of both making the stand look nice and flashy as well as cutting down the target area just a little more!

THE STRING GAME

Freddy stands in front of a stall full of prizes. A string travels from each prize
(ranging from televisions to small furry toys) down to his hand. For a dollar
you get to take a string. Whatever is on the other end of your string is yours
to keep!

Lucky you. You win another cuddly toy.

This is nothing more than a neatly concealed Hanky Pank store. The
strings from the big prizes do go to Freddy's hand but they don't come out of
the other side of his fist. The big prize strings have either been cut shorter
than the rest or have had the strings turned around in his hand. The strings

you get to pick from are all connected to the little prizes.

Should somebody *raise a beef* Freddy can easily show that big money prizes are 'available' by tracing the strings back to his hand.

Perhaps one piece of good news is that Bruce Walstad was happy to report that this game is now very rare, and he hadn't seen one around in quite a while. That doesn't mean that it won't make a come back though! Like bad pennies these games can often pop up when you least expect them.

The Raffle Variation

A similar game is played with raffle tickets. Freddy stands in front a big display of prizes each of which carries a number. He holds a basket full of little raffle tickets which are a dollar each. You conclude that Freddy *can't* be cheating because the tickets are sealed into little folders. You need to tear them open to see if you've won or not.

Freddy once calculated the odds on this particular game at around six million to one against the player. Even *if* a big prize goes, the only two people who know about it are Freddy and the winner. You don't want to carry your big prize around all night so Freddy gives you a receipt and offers to look after it for you until the end of the evening. If you don't want him to do this he'll tell you that you'll have to wait until then for it anyway as to get at it means dismantling half the stand.

Now he'll carry on selling tickets as if all the prizes are still available. The final take easily covers any accidental winners.

Freddy asked me not to mention that it is possible to buy the raffle ticket folders in numbered batches. He said that this could mean that an unscrupulous operator could make sure that there were *never* any winning tickets!

Surely not?

GUNS AND OTHER WEAPONS OF WAR

The ultimate manly games! What could be better than winning a prize for your girl by showing what a great shot you are with an air rifle or bow and arrow? Freddy loves people who are great shots coming to his stands.

He knows that they've probably never practiced trying to hit an undersized target with a cheap weak bow and a slightly bent arrow with a blunt point.

Knowing that a crack shot likes a challenge of their skill he'll kindly provide them with an underpowered air rifle which, if aimed correctly, is sighted about eight inches off true. "*It let's them test their skill,*" Freddy claims.

It'll take you quite a few goes to win a prize token. That's when you need to ask yourself if you really need another fluffy toy to add to your ever-growing collection.

BUCKETS AND BALLS

You see Freddy standing behind a wide stall. At the back are lots of wooden buckets angled towards the playing area. Freddy is casually tossing balls into the buckets and most of them are staying inside.

"*You look like a man with a good eye,*" he says. You realize he's talking to you. "*Come on, it's easy my friend. You get all three balls in a bucket you win a star prize. Get one or two in and you'll win a cuddly toy. Hey, even if you miss them all I'll still give you something! I can't be any fairer than that can I? Just a dollar for three balls and a chance to be a big winner!*"

The star prizes look pretty good. Portable radios, CD players, electric blankets and more. You watch Freddy almost casually throwing the balls into the buckets and keeping them in. You decide to risk a dollar or two.

Good luck, you'll need it!

The angle the bucket is tilted forward looks as though it is to help you. It isn't. From your throwing line you'll need to toss a ball pretty hard to reach a bucket. Thanks to their extra bouncy nature the balls will bounce out around nine hundred and ninety nine times out of a thousand.

Buckets and Balls.

Freddy can do it every time because not only is he throwing from a closer distance but he's also throwing from an angle so he can hit the side of the bucket giving him a better chance of keeping the ball in. Of course the fact that the balls he throws may be a lot less bouncy than the balls he gives you may be a factor as well!

If he is using baskets made of wooden slats (Bushel Baskets) Freddy can also make the throw easier by leaving a ball in the basket. This deadens the bounce of further balls being tossed in, acting, if you like, as a damper. Your ball hits the ball in the basket and this takes all the bounce from it. When you take a toss to try to win he reaches in and, as if tidying up, removes the damper ball. Bruce Walstad picks this little puppy from the litter as being, "*A very bad game*"

Freddy can make the game even harder to win at, if that's possible, by using a *backboard* or *jam*. Using a secret, foot operated, lever Freddy can lift into a place a hard wood board against the back of the bucket stand. The board, pressing against the base of the buckets, takes out any 'give' the buckets may have that could kill a bounce. The ball hits the base and bounces hard, right out of the bucket. By using the *jam* Freddy can turn his game into a *two-way store*. If the *jam* is out of play and he hands out slightly softer balls the game, although tough, is a genuine game of skill. Freddy won't offer such great prizes but you do have a chance. He tends to set the game this way when there is a chance that any *heat* (law enforcement) may be around. On the last night of the visit he'll put in the *jam* and really go for the throat. Thankfully the use of such backboards is becoming rarer these days.

The Upright Bucket Store

Some variations of the Bucket Store do not angle the buckets at all. But they tend to use narrow headed buckets or, more commonly, milk cans. The balls you'll be given will be soft, bouncy and quite large.

Your chances of getting one in are marginal at best. The *only* toss that stands a chance is one where the ball is thrown directly over an opening to fall in without touching the sides of the neck of the can. The low roof of the stall makes such a toss virtually impossible. Add to the low roof the plethora of prizes hanging down from it and you can see just how hard such a toss would be.

Another variation involves tossing ping pong balls into jam or preserve jars. Get one in and you'll win the goldfish swimming merrily away in the jar. Not only are ping pong balls *very* bouncy but the jars are made of hard glass. Still want to take a shot? You'll also see this set up with small circular goldfish bowls. The neck of the bowl isn't much bigger than that of a jar and the toss is just as tough.

And do you really need a pet goldfish?

Flukey Ball

With this variation you have to toss a ball against a target mounted on a stand. Your ball has to bounce off the target and land in a bucket or laundry basket set below it. Freddy can run this as a *two-way store* not by gaffing the target but by gaffing the balls thrown at it. Though all the balls look the same he actually has two types. Some are pretty dead, having been filled with cotton. Using these balls, and a good eye, a player (or Freddy) can hit the bucket. The other balls just bounce away and are next to impossible to get in the bucket. Guess which balls Freddy normally gives you? Bruce Walstad points out that the balls are often taped up to conceal the cuts in the balls where the cotton has been inserted. Black tape is wrapped around the ball over the cut.

If the target is mounted on an easel Freddy can also change the odds on success simply by positioning the target differently. The more the target is over the bucket the less chance the player has of winning. By moving the target back the game becomes easier. This variation of the game is also called *Bank-A-Ball*. Here the balls are ungimmicked but the game is set up so that, because of various factors (the angle of the easel, the weight of the ball, the position of the basket and the throwing distance), it is impossible to get a ball to stay in.

The only way a player can get a ball into the basket (without cheating) is to hit the rim of the basket. You've probably already guessed that Freddy has a little sign up that reads 'No Rim Shots'!

The operator can get a ball in by cheating. While he demonstrates the shot he focuses your attention on the ball being thrown. This misdirects you away from the fact that, using his body, he his bending in the rope foul line so that his throw is from an 'illegal' distance. Should you try this cunning ploy you can bet that he's going to be watching for it.

Often there are ten or twenty dollar bills in the baskets. These are lures, little green sirens if you will, to encourage you to play. Your chances of seeing a single bill leave a bucket to be handed out as a prize is exactly zero.

With astonishing luck you may, after investing ten dollars or so, walk away with a cuddly toy worth around a dollar from a Bucket Store. *"It warms my heart to see the ladies and kids smile when they get the toy,"* muses Freddy. Not to mention warms his wallet.

If you don't get a ball in at least you'll get a penny balloon. Don't feel bad. Look closely and you'll see a lot of other people with balloons just like yours.

Hoops—note the sloping face of the blocks in the upper photograph.

HOOP LA LARCENY

Another common sight on the fairground or at the carnival are the games that offer you three hoops (commonly made of wood or plastic) for a dollar. To win a prize all you have to do is toss one of your hoops over a wooden block upon which is resting a prize.

Freddy offers you the following bet. Stand and watch at one of these stalls for an hour. He says that if you ever see anybody win a large prize he'll pay you fifty dollars. He thinks his money is safe, and I agree.

Hoop La has more twists, turns and variations than a good prop bet. A general rule of thumb is that, the bigger the prizes, the less chance you have of winning.

Even the *straight* rules are against you!

The Rules

1. No leaning over the prizes.
2. The hoop must come to rest flat on the surface around the block upon which the prize rests.

Simple and fair? Sure. But now you try putting a four inch square block of wood with a watch on top of it on a table in your kitchen. Now try throwing a five inch hoop over it.

Not easy is it?

You see, to get the hoop over the block it must fall down directly from above. An angled throw is doomed to failure. When you get pretty good at tossing your five inch hoop over the four inch square block don't go rushing to the nearest hoop joint.

Freddy would *never* give you a five inch hoop to toss at a four inch block!

HOOP LA GAFFS

Even though it's next to impossible to win the game fairly Freddy likes to take away any nagging doubt he might have that a lucky toss could nab a big prize. *"Stress is bad for me,"* he says. He can gaff the game in a number of ways.

The Velvet Touch

Freddy shows you that the hoops can fit over the blocks upon which some very nice looking prizes are laying. *"Only a criminal or a con man,"* he will tell you, *"would use a hoop that couldn't go over a winning block!"*

Yet you can throw hoops all night and not win. Why? The blocks are covered in expensive, velvet looking cloth. You may think this is an effort to give the stall some class. It isn't. The velvet covering the blocks has the nap of the cloth pointing up. The hoop can be forced down over the block against the give of the nap. But it is too light to fall around the block by itself. Even a perfect throw will bounce away from the nap.

Sometimes the cloth covering is concealing more than just a simple block of wood. Underneath its innocent look are three blocks of wood one on top of each other making up the shape of a single block. When these blocks are all in perfect alignment the hoop can pass over them. If, however, the center block is pushed to one side a little (the give in the cloth allows this) a hoop can't pass over it fully. Another losing throw for you!

A Cute Angle

Here the tops of Freddy's tall blocks of wood have been cut at the top to angle the prize more towards the player. It makes those expensive looking watches and bracelets look even more enticing! It also makes winning them totally impossible.

The top of the slanted area is bigger than the hoops Freddy is using. Freddy can show that the hoop fits over the block by swinging it over the rear high edge of the cut and letting it fall. The player tossing the hoop can only hit the front of the slanted area and so must fail every time. When the hoop strikes the front of the block its far edge can't clear the top high edge. If the hoop hits the high edge first it can't slide down around the block because the prize stops it.

The only throw that could stand a chance is one thrown from the rear of the block. You may think that throwing a hoop across the stall at a block on the far side (facing away from you) you could have a chance.

Nice thought but no cigar.

It will either be against the rules or the stall will be partitioned up to stop you doing so.

Often an operator will have small prizes on low blocks at the front of the stall and the larger, more expensive, prizes in the middle on taller blocks. Even the little prizes are tough to hoop. The big ones are impossible.

"*And they have the nerve to call it a game,*" says Freddy.

SWINGING TIMES

Behind this stall Freddy demonstrates one of the carnivals oldest games of 'skill'.

A five inch bowling ball hangs on the end of a chain or rope beside a skittle or bowling pin standing on the counter.

The game is to swing the ball past the skittle and knock it down with the ball on the return swing. The only rule is that you have to release the ball before it passes the skittle.

Freddy can casually demonstrate the game over and over again. A few practice goes may convince you that it's a pretty easy proposition. Sure you might need to add a little spin or something but it is advertised as a game of skill!

The moment your money comes out the game suddenly becomes impossible to beat!

The gaff is not in the ball but in the positioning of the skittle. A small nail projecting from the counter serves as a guide to position the skittle. It fits into a hole in the base of the skittle.

What may not be apparent to you is that the hole is slightly off center. It's not off by much so don't feel too bad about not spotting it.

If the bulk of the skittle is set to the left then a well executed and practiced swing (Freddy has one) can *just* clip the skittle on its return swing.

If the bulk of the skittle is set dead center then the outward swing of the ball must be slightly wider to miss it. The greater arc this produces means that, even with a perfect swing, the ball must miss on the return. Only when the skittle is slightly offset can a winning swing be made.

Other Ways to Fix the Swing

The hole may not be drilled off center but may just be oversized. "*Wear and tear,*" may be Freddy's claim but it also means that the skittle can be positioned accordingly.

Some operators have a red circle on the counter to position the skittle. In this variation the skittle will have had its base cut at a very slight angle so it can be set leaning either to the left or right. The lean doesn't have to be much so you won't see it with the naked eye unless you look really closely and that kind of looking is discouraged.

The simplest gaff is to place the skittle between two pieces of wood nailed into a right angle on the counter. If the skittle is placed dead center in the guide it is impossible for the mug to win. If it is placed just off center and not quite perfectly into place then the skittle can be knocked over. The superb psychological ploy at play here is that the mug can be allowed to position the skittle themselves! By playing fair and positioning the skittle correctly they put *themselves* into a *losing* position!

The game is under Freddy's control at all times. He can let you win a few practice swings or he can make sure you lose all night.

POOL HUSTLES

A pool ball is resting in the center of a painted circle on a baize-covered board. On top of the pool ball rests a coin or coins. All you have to do, to win a prize, is hit a ball up the board and strike the object ball in such a manner that the coin ends up outside the circle.

You might be a great pool hustler but you aren't going to beat inertia. Hit the ball softly and the coin will fall gently off the object ball to land in the circle. Hit the ball hard and the object ball will shoot out from under the coin letting it fall, once more, into the circle. The only freak shot that stands a chance is if the coin drops onto the cue ball to bounce off it and out of the circle. "*That's the skill shot!*" claims Freddy. I've watched this game a lot and never seen it. Freddy, after some coaxing, admits he's never seen it either.

If the coin is positioned perfectly centrally on the object ball it is safe to say that, despite the possibility of the freak shot, the game is impossible to beat.

But Freddy can show you that he can do it. He sets the coin a little off center so that it has a slight tilt. He may also use a tiny piece of wax to make the coin sticky. Then he can knock that coin out of the circle!

Tee-Ball.

Want to try and knock the bottles over? Tee-Ball comes in all shapes and sizes..

Crazy Golf or Tee-Ball

This is a neat little money maker for Freddy. It has been adapted from an old Pool Hall betcha. A golf tee is stood up on the table and then surrounded by three pool balls in a triangle. Your job is to hit a cue ball up the board and knock the golf tee over. It's not difficult, it's impossible.

It all depends on exactly where the tee is placed. Three balls are formed into a triangle around the tee pointing towards the player. If the tee is towards the rear of the space in the middle of the balls it is impossible to knock it over. The impact of the cue ball channels the force of the shot *around* the tee. If the tee is right behind the front ball Freddy can make the shot to demonstrate just how easy the game is.

It is important for Freddy that the balls are touching square against each other (if there is any space between the balls the shot becomes possible) and so you'll notice, if you watch closely, that he often wipes his thumb over them before placing them down. The wiping transfers a little dampness from his thumb to the balls making it easier to ensure contact between them.

Wouldn't an angle shot stand a chance? Well on most games of this type there are no rails or cushions to play an angle shot to. The ball just disappears into a channel. If the board does have rails you can bet your wallet that an angle shot will be against the rules.

SPOT THE SPOT

Freddy shows you five plastic or tin discs three inches or so in diameter. On his counter is a larger, white, spot about five inches in diameter. He shows you that the red discs can cover the white spot completely. He does this by dropping the discs one at a time from a height of about six inches above the spot. "*It takes a knack,*" he confides, "*But if I can do it, you can too!*"

You could try all day.

An old gaffed version of the game, rarely seen today, consisted of having the white spot painted onto a canvas covering. The cloth could be stretched a little by the operators thumb to make the spot a little oval in shape. The discs, even if carefully placed, couldn't cover the expanded circle.

The reason this isn't bothered with today is that the game really is just so difficult that it doesn't need to be gaffed. There is only one way those red discs can cover the white spot. If *any* disc is off, even by a fraction, the game becomes impossible. Freddy will provide helpful suggestions but your chances of success, while dropping the discs six inches, are about the same as those of an eighteen handicap golfer winning the Masters while playing with only a putter!

Freddy can demonstrate it because he practices a lot. Oh yes, and because the discs he uses to demonstrate with are slightly larger than the ones he gives you. "*Well, my eyesight's getting a little dodgy these days,*" is his excuse for this ruse. But you can bet he won't point the size difference out to you. He may also use just one gaffed disc to make his throw easier. This disc will be slightly egg shaped. You won't be able to tell unless you get a chance to compare it with a perfectly circular disc. You have a better chance of beating the game than being allowed to do this. Bruce

Spot the Spot.

Walstad has also seen a bold technique called *Shading*. Here the discs are too small to cover the spot but the operator can toss them down, dropping the last disc to the back right of the spot, and block the players view with his right hand held out over game palm down with fingers spread out. This is a bold maneuver but nobody ever accused these game operators of being less than bold!

Bruce has also seen game boards that are two sided. On one side the spot is small enough to be covered by the discs but on the other it is too large. This would mean that sometimes the operator could be running a fair, but very difficult, game while at others he could be running a crooked game.

During a game Freddy may even drop the first two or three discs for you.

If you stick with the game long enough he may very kindly position the discs so that the white spot is covered. He'll lift up one disc and all you have to do to win is drop that one disc back into place. Shame his thumb 'accidentally' moved one of the others as he picked up the disc. Sadly that makes your job impossible.

HAMMER HEAD

This game is commonly seen at Rodeos and animal shows. Freddy loves it. It makes big, strong men look small and that makes his day!

It all looks so deceptively simple. Freddy has a large lump of wood set between two trestles. Into the wood he is tapping one and a half inch nails. He leaves just over an inch of each nail showing.

All you have to do, to win, is to drive the nail completely into the wood block with one blow of the hammer. Freddy isn't that big of a guy yet he can do it every time. The big guy flexes his muscles, pays his dollar and gets ready to collect his prize. His girlfriend waits close by.

She could have a long wait.

Freddy will offer all sorts of advice on why the big guy can't seem to do it. He'll tell them it's not just strength, there's a knack to it. He'll demonstrate it a few more times and give 'valuable' hints at the knack.

But as long as money is at stake the big guy will never manage it.

You see the little apron Freddy keeps his nails in has two pockets. In one side are the normal nails with which the feat is possible. In the other side are nails with blunted points. They look the same but just can't be driven in with a single blow. They will bend under the force of it. The harder they are hit the more they will bend.

Freddy can let you win if he lets you use one of his nails. He can also guarantee that you'll lose.

Freddy says he once saw an infuriated carpenter lose over three hundred dollars on the game trying to prove how strong he was to his wife. "*She wasn't very happy,*" noted Freddy.

CLOTHES PEGS AND PING PONG BALLS

Freddy has a long string full of clothes pegs strung across his stall. He'll happily show you just how each peg has a number on it. The numbers point away from the players. He'll also show you a list where certain numbers relate to certain prizes on the stall. Some of the prizes are really rather good look-

Pick a duck, any duck, but don't expect a big winning number on it. A variation of the Peg Game.

ing, others are just, you've guessed it, more cuddly toys.

He'll even show you that the big winners are on the line then he'll mix the pegs up. For a dollar you get to throw a hoop at the line. If you manage to hoop a single peg then you win the prize allocated to the number on the peg.

The game would be hard enough if it were played straight. Freddy doesn't play it straight.

The digits on the peg are stenciled one above the other. Players assume that this is because the peg is narrow. All the big winning prizes consist of three digits *but* start with low digits (113, 127 or 104 for example). What you might also notice if you were allowed to examine the pegs closely is that there will be a slight gap between the second and third digits on the big winning pegs.

When you ring a single peg, a pretty hard act in and of itself, Freddy will quickly, and I mean *quickly*, peek the number on the peg. This fast look earns this genre of game the name of a *Peek Joint*.

If it is a big winner he will cover the bottom digit with his thumb making, as if by magic, a high winning number into a low, consolation prize, two-digit number. 127 suddenly becomes 12 for example.

The four foot distance between you and Freddy combined with the speed he shows and replaces the peg makes this ruse impossible to catch. The moment he has replaced the peg Freddy will start mixing them up again as if for another go.

If you *beef* he will simply claim that he can't remember where your peg has gone. If you argue he will stand his ground until you get too fed up to be bothered (see *The Blow Off*).

This same thumb cover ruse is used with ping pong balls in a bingo machine. You pay your dollar to get the first ball up the tube. Freddy's athletic thumb makes sure you miss out on the CD player and earn a cuddly toy. Before you can ask to look more closely at the ball it is back in among all the others.

BASKETBALL

All you have to do here is toss two basketballs, one after the other, into a hoop. Remembering your high scoring days from high school you know you have to have a better than even chance at beating this game!

Of course at high school you played with a regulation sized hoop at a regulation height. The hoop probably wasn't loose on the backboard and, it's a safe bet, that the ball you played with wasn't over-inflated to make it more bouncy.

Ah well.

A LITTLE BIT OF HISTORY—WHEELS OF FORTUNE

Although much less common these days *Wheel Joints* can still be found. All are basically the same. A large arrow on a spindle clicks around a board to come to rest in one of a number of spaces set around its circular path. You also see these games in casinos where they are often called the *Wheel of Fortune*.

There is little need to gaff the wheel. The odds are so high in Freddy's favor that he feels that the extra expense of installing the gaff would not be worth it.

On Freddy's layout there are one hundred spaces around the wheel. Eighty of them will give you a cuddly toy or consolation prize. Ten of them will give you nothing. Five of them give you a free go. Three of them have payouts of ten dollars, one has a payout of twenty dollars and one has a payout of fifty dollars. Work out the odds for yourself. Your best win is fifty dollars (fifty to one) on a one hundred to one shot. Oh, and although not strictly gaffed, I have noticed that the big pay out spaces look, on close inspection, a little smaller than the others on Freddy's wheel. *"Really?"* he says, *"I'll check them out later."*

Gaffed Wheels

Some operators are just so greedy that they can't resist gaffing up the wheels or, as they put it, *putting in the G.*

On most wheels the spinning arrow is stopped by a plastic tape clicking between nail heads that separate the sections. Other wheels have the nails in the wheel itself which spins. A long plastic clicker at the top gradually slows and stops the wheel. The easiest gaff is, of course, to have the losing sections slightly wider than the winning sections.

The spindle upon which the arrow spins can be controlled by a concealed brake. Such wheels are called *Creepers* because the operator lets it get down to a very slow speed before gently applying the brake. This makes the increased slowing action much harder to detect.

In some cases the posts the arrow clicks against are made of flat wire twisted into fancy spirals. The posts alternate so that an inwards twist on one post alternates with an outward twist on the next. The clicker is long enough to reach the inward twists but not quite long enough to reach the outward twists. The clicker can be made to miss every other post or, more commonly, just a few of the posts. Some boards have been made where, using a hidden gaff the operator can lift the spindle slightly so that the clicker will now hit the twists it missed the first time and miss the twists that it hit! Using this extreme gaff up the operator can eliminate either half of the board at any one time.

Gaffed wheels are extremely rare but it is wise to be aware of them. There are still suppliers who can sell them to you, fully gaffed and ready to go, if you know who to contact of course. If they are for sale it means they are being used somewhere!

THE STALLS IN GENERAL

There are lots of games that just can't be beaten. You've seen quite a few examples in this chapter. Notice how most of them are *two-way joints* so that the game can be demonstrated to be beatable but then is impossible.

All of the stalls will have a big *Flash*. This is a big display of very expensive looking prizes to attract players. Sometimes some of the big items are just part of a display and are not actually up as prizes. "*If people think they are some of the prizes, that's not my fault.*" comments Freddy.

The games all fall into the category of unbeatable unless you have the luck of a God. Such games are called *Flat Joints*. Where the game appears to be one where skill may be involved are also called *Alibi Joints*. They are so called because the operator will always have a long string of excuses as to why you just can't seem to win.

Is your head spinning just a little?

Okay, let's make it real easy for you with a very simple rule of thumb.

The more expensive looking the prizes are and the older the operator is, the less likely it is that you'll win. It is more likely that the operator will eventually have to replace his prizes due to them getting out of style or, in the case of blankets and coats, rotting away from old age, than it is he'll ever have to give them to a winner.

Got it?

Good.

Shorting The Change

FREDDY WOULD LIKE TO POINT OUT, WITH NO SMALL DEGREE OF LOYALTY TO HIS fairground and carnival chums, that you are liable to be *short changed* anywhere. Especially when he's around.

But since short changing occurs at fairgrounds and carnivals with alarming regularity, it seems just as well to cover it here.

THE PALM

You give Freddy a five dollar bill. He counts your change out onto his left hand. Turning his hand he dumps the change into your waiting hand. You put your change in your pocket and play the game.

You've just been short changed.

While Freddy dumped the coins into your hand he held back one or two by palming them. If you had seen his hand palm up you'd have seen the coins sticking, like limpets, to his hand. A good worker can hold coins back with controlled pressure from the muscles in their hand. Indeed, magicians use this very technique to conceal small objects in their hands during a sleight-of-hand performance.

A man with sweaty or unsuitable hands can smear his palm with cheap glue to get it sticky. There are even specialist creams available if

With Jamy Ian Swiss and Carol in front of the Cyclone at Coney Island— the scene of the great short change!

How to Cheat at Everything

you know where to shop. This same cream is often used by card cheats when *check copping,* of which more later!

The moment you put your money away Freddy is in the clear. Even if you check it later and discover the fraud he'll just claim that you must have dropped a coin or two, or lost it elsewhere.

Always check your change *before* putting it in your pocket.

A few coins may not seem like much but, over a day, it can soon add up.

DOUBLE PRICE TICKETS

Your girlfriend wants to ride on the Ghost Train. You're not so keen but, with a sigh, you agree.

The tickets are fifty cents each, and you hand Freddy a ten dollar bill.

He takes the bill and says, "*Two tickets, a dollar.*"

He counts dollar bills into your hand, continuing, "*Two, three, four, five, six, seven, eight, nine . . .*"

He puts your two tickets on top and finishes by saying, "*And the tickets make ten. Enjoy the ride folks! Right on there into the car!*"

Let's hope it's a good ride because you've just paid for your tickets twice. Freddy counted them both at the start and end of the count! Should you point this out to him he'll just say, "*Sorry sir, my mistake!*" and hand you a dollar bill. For everyone that catches the ruse there are a lot that don't.

THE LEAVE

The game operator will count out your change and put it down on the counter. If you pick it up he'll say nothing. He'll also say nothing if you don't pick it up. You'd be surprised how often people, caught up in the excitement, will just forget!

Take it or Leave it

A more sophisticated version of the leave happens when a ride operator is giving change from a booth. He pushes your change towards you but leaves some of it back towards the rear of the counter. The counters tend to be quite high so that money, often concealed by the posts that surround the window, is tough to see.

If you count your change and find it short he'll just point out the extra pile of money you've left behind. You don't suspect him of cheating, after all it looks like it was your fault.

Of course, if you don't check your change, then it is your fault. Some more money has gone into the operator's pocket.

My good friends, Todd Robbins, magician Jamy Ian Swiss, his lovely young lady Carol and me went for a day out at Coney Island. Jamy and Carol decided to ride the world famous Cyclone roller coaster. Todd and I, our stomachs full of Nathan's hotdogs we wanted to keep in place, decided to watch. When they returned we started to walk down the road. Suddenly Carol yelped, *"Wait a minute I gave the man at the booth a twenty!"*

Jamy went rushing back and there, right in the corner of the booth, was Carol's extra change. *"I kept it there for ya."* the guy smiled, *"I guessed you'd be back!"* In the company of three seasoned cheat experts Carol had nearly been short changed by the good old Take it or Leave it!

There was much laughter and more than a little teasing for some considerable time afterwards! What was, perhaps, most amusing of all was Todd, a Coney Island alumnus, whispering to me, *"He's well known for that you know!"* I am smiling broadly as I type this and can only hope Carol forgives me for putting the story in print!

CHAT CHANGE

Silly you, you are addicted to a dime machine in Freddy's arcade. Even sillier of you to give him a five dollar bill for change. You are probably silly enough, in fact, to fall for Freddy's fast line of chat. He is, after all, an expert *talker*.

He takes the five dollar bill and counts dimes into your hands in groups of three followed by a single coin. As he counts the coins he says, *"One, two, three, one dollar."* Each count is three coins and, as he says, *"one dollar,"* he's dropping the single coin.

His full chat will go like this, *"One, two, three, one dollar, one, two, three, two dollars, one two, three,* four, *and, one, two, three four makes five!"*

Read the chat at speed. Then read it more slowly. Notice how Freddy leaves the change for a dollar out completely! If you notice this ruse and start to protest Freddy will already be picking up more dimes. *"Hold onto your socks,"* he'll say, *"I can only hold so many of them at once you know!"* You'll probably apologize to him for being suspicious.

Of course, if you just walk away, he won't call you back. He doesn't consider that part of his job description.

CASH RIDES

In my dubious youth I spent a couple of summers working on a traveling fairground in England. It was an education to say the least!

These days a lot of rides work on a token system. You buy a token, put it in your Bumper Car and away you go. But a lot of traveling shows still use the cash system. People come to your car, get your money and, if it's needed, return your change.

It would, at first sight, seem to be a very tough job for the collectors to remember which cars have given which money. People assume that that's the reason that mistakes occur. Perhaps they didn't get the change or the change is brought to them after the ride has started. Nothing could be further from the truth. Bumper cars, for example, are brightly colored. Look closely and you'll see that the cars are in groups of four. Four red, four green, four yellow and so on. Each collector is in charge of one color. He collects from his four cars and makes any needed change to his four cars. This can easily be achieved before the ride starts. The reason that it often isn't is because you are going to get short changed.

The simplest method is simply not to give the change back at all. The money is often collected on the Bumper Cars by the guy jumping onto the back of your car and reaching over your shoulder. At best you get a minimal look at him. At the end of the ride you realize that he didn't bring you back fifty cents owed to you in change. It will cost you time and effort to even find the man who took your money and even more time and effort to convince anybody that you are due money. Are you really going to fight for fifty cents when you have a whining girlfriend or a couple of kids screaming that they want to try out another ride? Multiply that fifty cents by thirty or so times a night and it's a nice little earner for the money collector.

Since most of the rides involve spinning or crashing around it is also very common for items (such as cash and even wallets) to fall unnoticed into the car. When the guys, at the end of the night, say, "*I'm just going to clean my cars*," they are not talking about washing them. They check under the seats and in the wells of the cars. A profitable little game. I'll never forget one night when I was working the Bumper Cars or *Dodgems* as they are called in the UK. George, who'd been with the ride for years, was going over his cars and let out a yelp. He held up a very nice looking wallet. "*Celebration time lads!*" he yelled. Upon opening the wallet he found a library card and two bus tickets. I couldn't resist asking him if he was going to celebrate in the fiction or none fiction section of the library. For some reason he didn't find that too amusing.

On the Bumper Cars a wonderful technique known as the *Tip and Tilt* takes short changing almost into an art form. The mug hands over a large note, say a ten spot, for a one dollar ride. The collector will get the change of nine dollars as six ones and three dollars in change. He'll pocket a couple of the ones as his commission. Then he'll wait for the ride to start. You find yourself turning into the long straight when he hops onto the back of your car. As always, he steadies himself by holding onto the long pole that connects your car to the electrified ceiling. Just as you approach the next turn he will bend the pole a little towards the center of the track. This makes your car start to turn sharply inward. You adjust and your car will shudder and perhaps hit the outside rails of the track. He stumbles and drops your change into your lap. "*Be careful mate!*" he'll yell as he hops off the car. You, as most do, try to concentrate on steering around the corner while grabbing your money and shoving it into your pocket. The moment you do this the cheat is safe! Unless you stop the car, something you are most unlikely to do, and check the change right there and then, there is nothing you can do. If you complain after the ride he's more than likely to say something like, "*First you nearly ****ing kill me and now you're calling me a ****ing cheat! Get outta my face!*" Actually it may have cost you more than they pocketed. Some of that change that fell into your lap has probably fallen through the seat or onto the floor of the car to be 'cleaned up' later.

Other rides like the *Waltzer* or *Tilt-A-Whirl* collect so much money flying from pockets and under the seats that a good night is often had by all, except the mugs, on the proceeds.

Since metal flies more much easily than paper your change will often be given in coins. Not only does this make it more difficult to notice if it is short but also means that some more of it may end up in the seats.

FREDDY'S QUICK TIPS

Take change with you to a fairground or carnival and pay the correct money every time you can.

If you have to ask for change *always* check it *before* putting it in your pocket.

The Flat Count

or

Double Up

O KAY, I GUESS YOU'VE GOT THE IDEA THAT NOT ALL THE GAMES ARE QUITE AS *on the level* as they may have appeared. But you still haven't lost too heavily, a dollar here, a dollar there, and you've had a bit of fun along the way.

It's time to introduce you to a technique where those dollars can swiftly turn into tens and potentially into hundreds. It's a little number Freddy calls the *Flat Count*.

You walk by Freddy's stall and he calls you over. You go over to see what he has to offer. This is your first mistake.

It won't be your last.

"Come on in my friend," he entices, *"Let me show you just how easy this little game is. Maybe you can win your girl a nice prize or two. All ya gotta do is swing the ball and knock the skittle over on the way back. Sure, it takes a knack but you look like you've got a good bowler's arm. Why dontcha give it a try?"*

You take a free go and can see that the game looks pretty fair. You might even succeed in knocking the skittle over.

"A natural," exclaims Freddy. *"All you gotta do to win a big prize is knock the pin over ten times for a dollar! I'll even give you a credit for your practice try, can't get any fairer than that!"* Freddy produces ten discs from his pocket. He places them on the counter and slides one over to you.

The prizes look expensive so you ask if it's a dollar for every swing. *"Naw,"* says Freddy with horror, *"that would be too expensive! So long as the pin keeps falling down you keep going!"*

You pay your dollar thinking it must be worth a shot. You knock the pin down three times in a row but, just when you think it's a cake-walk, you miss on your fourth try. You start to turn away but Freddy pulls you back. *"I hate to see that mate. Look, I've had a good night, and I'd like to see you win. I'll let you carry on. You pay me a dollar to keep these points and a dollar for the new go. That means you'll be starting out with four points in the bank!"* You hand over another dollar but Freddy reminds you that, *"It's a dollar to keep these four points and a dollar for the go so you owe me two dollars. I may be in a kindly mood, but I gotta make a living here!"*

You may hesitate but Freddy reminds you that, so long as you keep knocking the pin over, you won't have to pay any more. The prizes do look good and you are practically half way toward winning one! You invest the two dollars.

You're soon happier because your next two goes are winners. Then you miss again. You've got six points and want to carry on. Of course it's going to cost you a dollar for the first four points, a dollar for the two new points and a dollar for your go. That's three dollars but, what the hell, you are over half way there.

Are you keeping a running total on this yet?

A few minutes later, even though it's costing you six dollars a play by now, you have nine discs in your pile. Just one disc to go!

You can only hope Freddy leaves you enough for cab fare home.

It has been estimated that the average player will try at least five and more commonly ten more times to get that last point. And all for yet another fluffy toy that Freddy gives you with a sympathetic line, *"I thought ya had me kid but I guess the old nerves set in. Ya sure ya don't want to give it just one last shot?"*

The Flat Count is a superb example of man management and positive re-inforcement in action. Freddy gets you addicted to the game. He lets you win enough to convince you that, if you keep your cool, you can do it. He'll offer advice and tips to you. Every time you miss he'll hint, to your frustration, that your nerves may be getting to you and advise you to relax on the game. You get to a point where you are going to win however long it takes to beat the stupid game. By the time those discs are at nine to one you'll be so hooked that only running out of money will tear you away.

Freddy has even been known to let people go home or to an ATM to get some more money to carry on playing (or should that be paying!).

The Flat Count can be worked with just about any of the games in the carnival. It is, in a slightly different form, called the *Ten Count,* the basis for taking huge sums of money at the game of *Razzle,* which we'll be looking at in just a moment.

Of course not every player goes for the count. Freddy doesn't need them to. He's quite happy raking in dollars until the ripe little mug walks by.

When it's all over, if the take is big, Freddy can disappear into the night faster than you can say, *"Excuse me officer, I think I've been cheated!"*

Anybody who knows the contempt with which fairground and carnival people regard ordinary people will be *very* wary of a man trying to help them beat the game!

The golden rule? *Never* play in a game where you have to keep paying to keep your points.

The Razzle Dazzle

IT HAD TO HAPPEN SOONER OR LATER. WE FINALLY ARRIVE AT A GROUP OF GAMES whose sole purpose is to take your money swiftly and in as large a take as possible.

The operators like Freddy love this game because there is no mechanical gaff for you to spot. That, and the fact that it takes more of your money faster than any other game on the lot.

The American press had a field day in 1957 when they reported that an American industrialist lost, are you sitting comfortably? $95,000 in a single session of this little game. The figure may well have been exaggerated but you get the idea!

A good Razzle man can easily, and I mean easily, make between one and two thousand dollars a day! His earnings will often be a great deal more!

The game comes in many forms. It could save you a great deal of money if you read this chapter very carefully indeed.

THE SIX BALL ROLL DOWN

This is one of the oldest variations on the game and is very common to this day.

Freddy is standing behind his stall waving three golf balls in each hand.

"Roll up, roll up!" he shouts, *"six balls for a dollar, win a radio, a CD Player, a toaster or any one of the fine prizes you see displayed here!"* You wander over. The first thing you notice, after the *Flash* display of prizes, is a big board that reads.

Numbers	6, 7, 8, 34, 35, 36	Wins a Star Prize!
Numbers	9, 10, 11, 31, 32, 33	Wins a huge cuddly toy!
Numbers	12, 13, 14, 28, 29, 30	Wins a consolation prize!

A standard Razzle set-up.

The Bonus Rules.

Then you look at the game itself. The playing surface is about two feet wide and about six feet long. The board is slanted so that a ball released at your end will roll down to the far end. At the far end of the board are thirty-six pockets arranged in a two foot square. Each pocket is marked with a number from one to six.

Freddy, should you choose to play, takes your dollar and you roll the balls down the slope. They come to rest, scattered about, in the pockets.

Freddy adds your total. What a shame. You just missed a Star Prize but have won a nice consolation prize.

It would seem impossible to have a gaff on the game. Freddy doesn't need one. Freddy uses odds and the occasional miscount to take your money. The miscount is important to note for it will be used extensively, and in a most unusual manner, in a big money Razzle game in a moment.

The Odds

On a Razzle board the total number of combinations that six balls can make will be around 1,950,000 (boards do vary slightly). The number of ways a big winning total of 6, 7, 8, 34, 35 or 36 could be obtained on the last board I looked carefully at was 596 ways. That's odds of just about 3,272 to 1 against the player! As you'll see, those odds, astonishing though it may seem, are quite generous by Razzle standards where some boards have gone as high as 30,000,000,000 to 1 (count those zeros again!) against the player winning in one go!

The Miscount

Freddy knows the *exact* total of your score *before* he starts to pick the balls up. He works this game all day and has become an expert at fast math. Sometimes he doesn't need an exact count to know that you have come up a loser. If there is a mixture of high and low scores on the pockets the balls are in then you *can't* be a winner. At least four balls must land in a '1' pocket to make a possible score of 6, 7 or 8 and at least four balls must land in a '6' pocket to make a score of 34, 35, or 36 possible.

Freddy knows instantly if you've beaten the massive odds working against you.

If you have managed to do so he will employ a fast miscount. He's real quick at math! He picks up two balls at a time, one in each hand, and calls the combined totals of both. When he repeats this three times at speed I would defy anybody to follow him closely enough to see the manipulation of the numbers. Want to *beef*? Freddy will tell you he counts these totals all day so he's fast. He's sorry you were a bit dumb at keeping up. Anyway, can you remember which pockets the balls were in?

Actually, as we move further into the insidious little world of Razzle you'll see that Freddy's miscounts are often made to *give* you points!

Variations on the Six Ball Roll Down

One variation on the game uses partitions instead of pockets. The end of the board is split into sections numbered one through six (not in order!). Also, along the board, there are lots of little posts to deflect your balls as they roll down. There does appear to be an element of skill but once more it's just a veneer. The odds and miscounts are just the same.

The Razzle system can also be used with a numbered board and darts. You throw six darts at a board covered with numbered squares. It looks like a game of skill but the miscount will take your money every time even if you are a red-hot darts player. If you try keeping a running score and argue that Freddy has the wrong total he'll tell you that he's never wrong. The darts are out of the board and you must have been mistaken. After all you're four feet away and those numbers are kinda small. If you persist he'll go straight into his *Blow Off* technique.

BIG MONEY RAZZLE

This is the big one boys and girls. Here Freddy combines all his skills with nifty psychology to take serious money.

Remember Albert Fisher, our pal who lost a lot of money at Monte? Watch him now at the fairground and learn from his mistakes.

Albert is walking through the fairground in a happy mood. He's carrying three cuddly toys for his kids and is feeling just peachy. His eyes are drawn to a stand displaying prizes which seem an awful lot better than the rest of the stalls. He decides to take a closer look. As he wanders closer he can't help but be impressed by the television sets, bottles of champagne with hundred

Razzle on the upright. A variation on a theme.

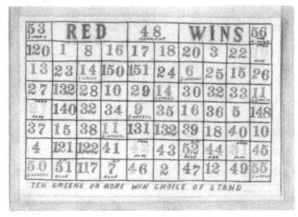

53	RED			48		WINS			56
120	1	8	16	17	18	20	3	22	
13	23	14	150	151	24	6	25	15	26
27	132	28	10	29	14	30	32	33	11
	140	32	34	9	35	16	36	5	148
37	15	38	11	131	132	39	18	40	10
4	121	122	41		43	52	44		45
50	51	117	7	46	2	47	12	49	55

TEN GREENS OR MORE WIN CHOICE OF STAND

Another version of the chart.

dollar bills taped to them, a nice stereo system and even a full computer system!

Freddy notices him and hands him a ticket. Albert looks at it and reads the legend *Good for one free play!* Albert thinks that's pretty good of Freddy and sits down to take his free go. Yes, you read that correctly. Freddy even provides nice little seats for his players!

In places where Razzle is frowned upon by the law (just about everywhere these days) these *freebie* play tickets are handed out on the street and are used to lure players to a game which is often hidden away in a portable shed or some such set away from the rest of the games and rides.

Albert, still a little cautious after his run-in with the Monte men, studies the game. Each prize has a luggage tag on it. On each tag is a two-digit number written in bright red ink.

Albert notices a board which says *One Dollar per Prize!* That seems fair. Even the low-end prizes look good compared to his cuddly toys.

Freddy comes over and says, *"Welcome along to the only game on the lot that'll give you a free game! It's a real simple game my friend. All you gotta do is roll these eight marbles onto the board in front of you. If you score the right numbers, you win the prize! Which prize do you want to go for? Any one you like!"*

Freddy hands Albert eight marbles in a cup. He looks down to the board on the counter before him. It has been drilled with a large number of holes (actually, although he doesn't count them I'll tell you that there are one hundred and twenty holes on Freddy's layout) all numbered from one to six. He decides that, since the go is free, he may as well give it a shot. He says he'll try for the computer system.

He's already half way to being hooked, drawn and quartered.

Albert rolls out his marbles and watches them settle into eight of the holes.

"Follow me quick," says Freddy. *"After ten years of doing this I just can't add up slowly!"* He lifts the marbles in groups from the board counting a running total rapidly as he does so. "Thirteen, twenty-three, thirty, thirty-six and the last two come to eight making a grand total of forty-four. *What does the chart say?"*

Albert, who thought he'd won a prize for that number, now notices a little chart beside his playing board.

It looks a bit like the table reproduced on the top of the next page.

This layout has been taken from a genuine Razzle set in my collection by the way. Now back to Albert.

Albert looks for forty-four on the chart and discovers that it scores five points!

"This is looking like your lucky day," says Freddy. *"All you need are five more points and you're a winner. The chart, as you can see has twenty-four winning,*

TEN POINTS OR MORE WIN!

18	42	38	15	19	41	37	14
H.P	1.5	H.P	1.5	H.P	1.5	H.P	1.5
8	20	45	36	13	21	46	35
10		5		5		8	
22	9	34	48	23	10	33	47
8		10		5		8	
11	24	44	32	12	25	43	31
5		5		5		5	
26	40	30	17	27	39	29	16
0.5		0.5		0.5		0.5	

28—ADD ON

scoring, numbers and only seventeen losers. That gives you odds of three to two for you getting a winning total!"

Albert nods sagely. He doesn't want this common fairground lout to know that he doesn't really understand odds. He just figures that he's got a free five point start so investing a dollar is well worth it. He pays up and rolls the marbles again.

If you are timid you might want to skip the next few pages. It's going to get kind-of ugly from now on. If you do decide to read on watch out for the Flat Count variation coming right up. In the form you are going to see it here, it's called the *Ten Count* or *Add-On*.

Freddy adds the total in a blur, "Seven, eight, twenty, thirty-one and ten makes forty-one."

Albert discovers that this scores one and a half points. *"Too bad,"* says Freddy. *"You need three and half more points but you could still win. For an additional dollar I'll let you keep your points and carry on. A dollar for your points, a dollar for another go. That's just two dollars my friend, and you only need three and a half points, you're over half way to the win!"*

Albert has just discovered, as you did in the Flat Count, that this means a further go will cost him two dollars. He argues to himself that it must be worth it. He's got six and a half points with two rolls. He only needs a total of ten for the big prize. He hands over his two dollars.

Albert rolls again and Freddy counts to announce a total of twenty-eight. This reads *Add On* upon the chart. Freddy explains that Albert can choose another prize to play for as well as the computer. When he gets his ten points he gets *both* prizes. *"A real lucky break fella,"* says Freddy looking a little worried. Albert points out a very nice bottle of champagne with a fistful of hundreds taped around it. He notices Freddy's worried look and starts to feel real good. He's hot, and he's ready to go for the kill!

Albert hands over his two dollars for another go. *"You still owe me a dollar,"* says Freddy pointing to the sign Albert read earlier. *"It's a dollar a prize!*

Still you only need three and half points my friend. You'd feel sick walking away right now wouldn't you?"

Albert is getting a little worried by the monetary increase but takes another go. He is considerably cheered by his total of fourteen which scores one and a half points. His total is now eight. With only two points to go he can't give up now!

His next total is eighteen which converts to H.P on the chart. H.P Freddy explains stands for house prize and hands Albert a cheap plaster statue. *"What a player,"* he exclaims, *"you're going to need a truck to get all your prizes home!"*

Albert then scores sixteen, followed by twenty eight (adding a microwave to his prize list), followed by forty, followed by eighteen (adding a cuddly toy to his statue), followed by twenty eight (adding a portable television to his prize list), followed by seventeen.

It's now costing him five dollars a throw but he's worked his way up to nine and a half points! He needs just one tiny half point to walk away with thousands of dollars in prizes.

You can hardly blame him for playing on.

And on.

And on.

Albert will never score that final half point. He will walk away broke wishing, as have so many before him, that he had just enough money for a few more goes to beat the game.

WHY CAN'T ALBERT WIN?

To understand just why Albert found it so easy to get up to nine and a half points yet failed miserably to go any further, we first have to look at the board itself.

Razzle boards vary from 72 holes to 143 holes in a board. A 120 hole board will be laid out as follows.

```
3 5 4 1 3 2 4 6 5 3 2 1 3 5 3
4 2 3 6 4 5 3 1 2 4 5 6 4 2 4
3 5 4 1 3 2 4 6 5 3 2 1 3 5 3
4 2 3 6 4 5 3 1 2 4 5 6 4 2 4
3 5 4 1 3 2 4 6 5 3 2 1 3 5 3
4 2 3 6 4 5 3 1 2 4 5 6 4 2 4
3 5 4 1 3 2 4 6 5 3 2 1 3 5 3
4 2 3 6 4 5 3 1 2 4 5 6 4 2 4
```

Notice that any number added to the number above or below it will give a total of seven. This makes Freddy's count very fast. For instance, if eight marbles fall into the box and end up in four pairs in vertical columns, Freddy knows instantly that the total must be twenty eight (four multiplied by seven).

Freddy will know your total before you've added the first two marbles together. He can easily, should he have to, turn a winning total into a losing one by employing a miscount. Notice that the board shown here has a lot more threes and fours than the other ones. A three miscalled as a four is much less likely to be spotted than a six being miscalled as a one; assuming you were even half capable of keeping up with Freddy.

Freddy is an expert at *cooling out* suspicious minds. He'll tell you that he just can't count slowly. He'll convince you that he's never wrong. He'll convince you, much to your cost, that he's an honest man. Anyway, why should you think he'd try to take points away from you. He's been giving you points all the way up till now. That big five point starting score wasn't just a lure to you, it's also a convincer that Freddy counts the marbles honestly.

Actually, Freddy is much more likely to miscount to get your score *up* and keep you interested.

For example, the chances of throwing twenty-eight (the infamous *Add On* number) are greater than all the other point values put together. If Freddy kept the game straight there's a pretty good chance that he could run out of prizes to add to your list before you gained any points at all!

Only very high and very low scores get the big point values. This is less obvious to a player than you may think because of the random layout of the conversion chart. The high percentage of threes and fours on the board make these very high and very low totals very difficult to score.

For example the points for scoring eight or forty eight are the same. Ten points, an instant winner! Don't try to work out the odds, Freddy will do it for you. With an *equal* distribution of numbers the odds of scoring eight or forty-eight with eight marbles are 1,679,615 to 1 against. On our sample board the odds, because of the high proportion of threes and fours, are even worse! The odds on twenty-eight being thrown are a mere 11 to 1 against.

Still think Freddy was a kind guy giving you that free go?

So when Freddy miscounts it's normally to put the total in your favor! That first five points you scored you got on a miscount to let you think the game was worth playing.

Remember that you'd only get suspicious of miscounting if you were losing. Nobody worries about a count that actually *gives* them points! The cheating happens in your favor!

The only time Freddy will miscount against you is if, by a freak chance, you actually score that extra half point.

To help get your score up Freddy may change his definition of H.P from House Prize to Half Point. He wants you to get close, but not actually achieve, the ten points required.

If you seem to be at all suspicious of Freddy's counting and his normal chat lines are not succeeding as well as he'd like then he may throw in a little extra convincer. He'll quickly count the first six marbles making his miscount among them. Then he'll get you to count the last two. His chat may

Razzle comes in many shapes and sizes!

sound like, "Twelve, eighteen, twenty, twenty-three and the last two are three which makes?" You can see the last two are correct and answer with, *"Twenty-eight."* Freddy says, *"Correct sir! Look it up on the chart, what does it say?"* Lucky you, it's an Add On. By getting you to help with the math and state the final total yourself he gets you to convince yourself that the total is correct. Afterwards you may even remember him letting you count all the marbles.

Read Albert's story again and see how Freddy slowly hooked him in. Freddy would have been a great musician. Just look at the way he plays Albert! Freddy gets Albert excited, convinced he can win, adds each little point or Add On prize at just the right moment, convinces Albert that he's worried about how well he's doing. Albert knows he can do it!

But he can't.

Remember it is next to impossible to score at Razzle. Remember that Freddy miscounts just to give you a score. He'll ride you like an expert horseman through a race to empty your wallet.

Don't ever play Razzle in any form. All of its family is evil. Whether you are throwing ping pong balls into numbered tins or rolling eight dice to score from their total. Some Razzle boards even have minus scores on them! The ignominy of it all. Roll a certain number and your score goes *down* by one point. Freddy times this roll to perfection making you even more determined to beat the game. You stand at nine points. Your next roll takes you back to eight points. Your very next roll scores one and a half points taking you to nine and a half. If only you hadn't lost that one point you'd be a winner! Of course you'll try another roll!

Sometimes you need to reach twenty points to win. You'll be amazed how easy it is to reach nineteen points!

So, what if you walk away after the free go and, with nerves of steel, leave those five points behind. Freddy doesn't care too much. Not too many people have that kind of nerve. Most will risk at least a dollar or two and Freddy is an expert at playing them along for maximum loss per person.

It has been calculated that with *no* cheating it would take just over 6000 rolls, on average, to score a winning total on a Razzle board. At a dollar a go that means you'd pay (with no Flat Counting or Add On increments) around $6000 for a CD Player. Now you know why Freddy can give away such great prizes. It's because he never gives them away.

Never play in a game that needs you to keep a running total to win a big prize.

Never play in a game where your score is converted to points on a conversion chart.

Always be suspicious of huge prizes that can be 'won' for a small investment.

Anything, and I mean *anything,* that looks even vaguely like the above game is to be avoided at all costs.

Razzle operators can get people so hooked into the game that, even when broke, the player will ask if they can go and get more money. Freddy will say, *"Sure, I'll give you twenty minutes then it's all null and void!"* The player will often actually *thank* Freddy for this chance!

Don't be one of those players!

The Blow Off

Y OU'RE CONVINCED YOU'VE BEEN CHEATED OR SHORT CHANGED.

You're going to stand there and shout until you get justice. This is bad for trade and Freddy wants to get rid of you quickly.

At a ride the other collectors will gather round and back up their own guy. Fairground and Carnival people really stick together. They'll convince you to get lost before your insults really offend them. If you are wise, you'll leave and very quickly.

But if Freddy is running a stand by himself he'll play it more softly at first. He'll use the *Blow Off*.

He'll start by gently explaining to you that he's sorry you didn't understand the rules properly. He'll tell you that you should have asked him to explain them to you. He will tell you that he is horrified that you think you've been cheated somehow. He is, he will claim, just an honest man like yourself trying to make a living. He will do just about everything except give you your money back.

You, following a long line of others, will just give up and walk away.

A small percentage though will stay and start to get more and more annoyed. Freddy's mood will change with astonishing speed. He'll look at you with steel cold eyes and harshly whisper, "*It aint worth talkin' to a **** like you. I've tried to be reasonable but now you can just go **** yourself.*" If you continue to argue Freddy will completely ignore you. "*Don't worry about him,*" he'll joke with new customers. "*Mommy wouldn't give him any more allowance to play with!*"

Most will just get fed up with trying. Bored, they will walk away. If you are one of the very few who just won't give up Freddy will invite you to go to the lot managers office to get this all sorted out.

The office is an area out of view near a noisy generator.

The sorting out is done with a steel tent peg.

No witnesses. Ouch!

I'm not kidding when I say just how loyal fairground and carnival people are to each other. It's like a little separate society that lives outside of the norm. I worked on a fairground for two short summers before moving on. Many years later I was a Special Guest performer at a large show in the Inn on the Park club on the Island of Jersey. After the show one evening a guy came over to me and said, *"So how you doin' Specs?"* It was the dodgem car owner I'd worked for years before! He told me his fair was in town, gave me a bundle of free passes and invited me and my pals for a great day out. And we did have a great day out! He'd organized a picnic for us, free rides and lots of surprises. Afterwards he put his arm around me and said, *"It's always nice to see one of our own doing well"* To him, I was still a member of their community even though we hadn't seen each other for years. It was a special moment for me.

But, it's a fair bet that you aren't a member of the family. If you have a complaint either go to a law enforcement officer or walk away. No amount of arguing with the stall or ride owner or worker is going to do you any good. At best it will waste your time and, at worst, you'll get hurt.

Is it worth it for a few dollars you shouldn't have been stupid enough to lose in the first place?

Freddy's Favorite Tent!

ACTUALLY FREDDY HAS QUITE A FEW FAVORITES MOST OF WHICH ARE RAPIDLY vanishing from traveling fairs and carnivals He tells great tales of the *Ten in One* shows where for just a few cents you'd get to see a magician, a sword swallower, the electric lady, the blade box and so much more. "*Easily the best bang for a buck on the lot,*" he reflects. The very last show of this type in the USA, and still running at the time of writing, is *Side Shows by the Sea Shore* down at Coney Island. The price of entrance is a dollar, and it's still the best value around.

Freddy also loves the side tents full of oddities. Sure the two-headed baby may not actually be alive, the three-legged cow may be a stuffed one and the promised flea circus may be mechanical but Freddy always considers the joke well worth it. He loves things like Professor Bobby Reynolds giant bat, *so big it could easily kill a horse!*

But he just *loves* to tell the tale of his very favorite tent of all.

Freddy was working a darts Hanky Pank in his youth and one day, when business was a little slow, he noticed one of the oddities tents. What made him notice the tent was the huge line of folks waiting to pay their dime and go inside. He then noticed women running screaming from the exit of the tent. Even grown men were coming out fast looking petrified. He considered this worthy of investigation and wandered over.

The boards on the tent read, '*Planet of the Ape People!*' '*Half men, half ape!*' '*Enter at your own risk*' and '*Do not feed!*'. To Freddy this seemed more than a little far-fetched but why were people running screaming from the exit?

He asked the owner if he could wander through. The owner warned him of the dangers then, with a wink, let Freddy inside the tent. Scattered about were three ragged cages. In each cage was a stuffed gorilla with a human mask rather crudely taped to it. Warning signs on the cages said '*Do not touch!*' It was, to say the least, pathetic. Very disappointed, Freddy headed for the exit.

Just as he reached the exit one of the 'stuffed' gorillas reached out and grabbed his arm. *"Got a banana?"* it asked. Freddy says, with a roar of laughter, that he nearly filled his trousers as he leapt through the exit flap. The owner, upon seeing him, apparently nearly fell over in hysterics as well. There's nothing like fooling one of your own. After the laughter calmed down he did, of course, warn Freddy not to *tip the work*. There was no way Freddy was going to do that. He used to love to send people to the tent only to see them hurtling through the exit flap!

My very good friend, Todd Robbins, The Coney Island Wonder Worker, *displaying the fine art of the* Front Talker *at the entrance of* Side Shows by the Seashore.

He considers this set up to be as near perfect as they can get. People go in and leave quickly, it has a fast turn around. People get a great scare and thus good value for their money. Best of all nobody wants to tell their friends what is in the tent! They want to see their friends get the same scare that they did. Finally, it is a very cheap set up. The two guys who ran the tent (one the outside *talker*, the other standing in the gorilla suit) cleaned up over the summer they spent with the fair, recalls Freddy.

"That's one great scam! I'm really jealous that I didn't think of it first," he muses.

Just remember though that there aren't many bargains like this at a fairground or carnival!

Freddy's Top Tips
For The Fairground

I<small>T CERTAINLY IS NOT</small> F<small>REDDY'S INTENTION TO STOP YOU FROM GOING TO A FAIR</small>-ground or carnival to have a good time. But, if you follow a few simple rules your chances of having a good time will be much improved.

Always count your change. Better still, take lots of change with you so that you can always give the exact money required.

Avoid any games where there is a score chart for converting scores into points.

Avoid any game where you have to pay more in order to keep playing or in order to hold a score.

Avoid games where the operator is offering fabulous prizes for a very low investment. Be *very* wary of free goes just to try it out or any advice given to try to help you win.

Don't play to try to work out the scam. It could cost you a fortune.

You are more likely to be heavily cheated on the last night of a fair's stay. The whole show will be moving the next day so there will be little chance for recourse. It's better to visit the fair or carnival early in its stay.

Prices for rides vary throughout the stay and, indeed, sometimes during a day. When the lot is busy the rides become more expensive and will get shorter in duration. When it is quieter the prices come down and the rides get longer to encourage you to stay. Try to visit the fair or carnival when it is quiet.

The safest games to play are those offering small prizes or games where you compete against other players. At least then you have a chance of getting something for your money.

Don't be tempted to use your newfound knowledge to go to a fair and loudly expose any scams to help others. It can get very ugly if you do so. If you suspect something is wrong, or consider that you have been cheated, go to a law enforcement officer.

Don't think that just because a game hasn't been mentioned here that it must be fine. It isn't possible in a book of this scope to cover everything. Of course not all games are illegal or gaffed. Some operators are proud that they run an honest game and can still make a living. There are others who are just as happy running a dishonest game and turning large profits!

Never play a game without understanding all the rules of the game.

Never play games that offer cash instead of prizes.

Carnivals are a huge money generating industry. In his law enforcement seminar *Carnivals and Carnival Game Fraud,* Bruce Walstad says that revenues generated from carnivals ranges between ten and fifteen *billion* dollars a year. That's quite a chunk of change! Follow these rules and, hopefully, a few less of those dollars will be yours!

Carnival and fairground people have a special language all of their own. The American *Carny Speak* is almost a pig Latin variant that is used to stop the rest of the normal world understanding a single word they are talking about. They take a word and between the first consonant and vowel will interject a sound a little like *e-az.* If the word starts with a vowel the *e-az* is put in front of the word. So 'Hello my friend' would become *Heazello my freaziend.* At speed it is really difficult to follow! This odd world also has its own special words and terms, some of which you've seen already and more of which you'll see in Freddy's Cheatspeak dictionary at the back of this book.

Perhaps the most famous of the words is *mark* meaning a mug.

The term *mark* is said to come directly from the carnival midway. After a bad run of luck the operator of a game would pat you on the back as he said, *"Bad luck pal!"*

As he patted your back he would leave a chalk mark on your clothing. That way *all* of his fellow operators would know that you were an easily taken mug. You were literally a marked man!

While you are learning a few words and phrases there's one that may get you out of a lot of trouble. A person who is *with it* is somebody who is either working for the carnival or is a visiting carny. They are somebody who is part of the esoteric little world of show people. If somebody is trying to hustle you into a game just quietly say, *"I'm with it."* They'll nod and walk away.

Enjoy the fair or carnival but do be careful. Even if the local police have had a look around don't take it for granted that everything will be run in a fair way. Most fairs and carnivals employ a very specialized character called the *patch.* His job is to distribute free tickets and, on occasion, cash payments to grease the wheels and give the fair or carnival a nice easy stay.

So enjoy the fair but do tread carefully.

It may look like a world of glittering lights and fun.

But not all that glitters is gold!

More Street Cons and Others

JUST BEFORE A BIG CARD OR DICE GAME FREDDY WILL OFTEN DISAPPEAR FOR A FEW days. When he returns he always seems to have a pocket or three stuffed full of cash.

It can often be as much as five thousand dollars. *"Just been out gettin' a grub stake,"* he comments.

It would seem fairly obvious that the money has been raised in a dubious manner, but how?

Freddy, as we have already seen, is a master psychologist and people person. You've already seen some of the stunts he can pull to raise cash. Of course you haven't seen all of his stunts! What follows is a collection of yet more of Freddy's money making schemes. He is, after all, a master con man with a huge repertoire!

Don't be fooled by the simplicity of what is to follow. All of them are in everyday use by the less honest members of our world.

Actually it's a fair bet that you've seen at least one of them in action!

All are proven money makers.

Simon shows Bill Wells his dice stacking bar bet (Son of Simon Says, *L&L Publishing*).

Jam Auctions

THE *Jam Auction* CAN BE SEEN EVERYWHERE. IT IS ESPECIALLY COMMON IN LARGE cities and cheaper holiday resorts. Take a walk along the streets of Blackpool in the United Kingdom and you'll see at least three or four of these auctions ready to take your money.

It is, as Freddy puts it, *"One of the slickest swindles of them all!"*

You are walking along a sea front promenade when you notice a large crowd gathered around an open shop front. Taking a moment to look inside you notice that the store area is also full of people, some of them holiday makers such as yourself.

At the far end of the shop, behind a large counter, stands Freddy. He is on a platform so you can clearly see him above the height of the crowd. Behind Freddy are shelves full of goods and products.

There are signs everywhere saying such things as *Clearance Stock Sale* and *Advertising Offer!*

Freddy, seeing that the store has filled nicely, changes from his *Roll Up* pitch (used to get people in) and goes into his *Sales Pitch*.

He holds up a nice looking watch.

He explains that these watches are excess stock. Normally they would retail at over twenty dollars but, to clear them out, today, and today only, they are going for just three dollars.

This looks like a nice cheap bargain. When Freddy asks who would like one, you put up your hand.

"It's not that I distrust you gentlemen," says Freddy, *"but I would like to see your money. There are ten watches only. The first ten customers with three dollars get the watches"*

Lucky you, you are one of the ten and you squeeze your way to the front with three dollars in hand. Freddy takes your money and puts a watch on top of it. You're pretty pleased because, just for once, it looks like you've got a bargain.

There are ten of you in a line.

"*Gentlemen, you've shown good faith in me,*" says Freddy, "*and I'd like to repay that trust. Let me make this an even bigger bargain for you! I'll tell you what I'm going to do. I'm not going to sell you this watch for three dollars! Since you are the first customers of the day, I'll practically give it away to you for two dollars! The company wants these watches to go to men who will appreciate them, show them to their friends, in other words, advertise them!*"

Freddy laughs and you laugh along with him. Not only are you getting a bargain but a mini cabaret as well.

"*All of you hold up a five dollar bill,*" says Freddy. One of the men in the line does so and, carried along, the rest, including you, follow suit. Freddy takes the first man's five spot in his left hand and picks up a watch and its three dollars in his right.

"*Here's the deal,*" he says, "*Five dollars takes the watch and the three singles. Three from five is two, it's breaking my heart. My saintly mother starving at home will never forgive me! But you get the watch for a mere two bucks!*" He winks to let you know he's having fun making the sale before continuing, "*This is a great deal made possible by the folks at _____ watches!*" He'll use a very well known watch company here to give the whole spiel a legitimacy.

He lays the watch and three dollars on top of the five spot and then offers the same deal down the line. If anybody turns it down Freddy shakes his head in disbelief. "*You don't want the deal! I'll just offer it to somebody else then. Who's the next lucky man in line!*" The man is quickly replaced with another.

Freddy kindly smiles at the men in the line. "*I just wanted to sort the real men out from the boys,*" he says. "*Men who would be proud to wear a watch like this! Men who the company will be proud to have wearing the watch! You've had the courage to put up your money, you are the kind of guys the company is looking for to help out with the big new advertising campaign!*"

You feel pretty proud of yourself.

Freddy picks up a watch along with its eight dollars. "*Here's the real deal my friends. I'm not selling this twenty dollar watch for three dollars, I'm not even selling it for two dollars. Look I'll add a dollar right here to the pile!*" He takes a single from his pocket and adds it to his handful. "*That's a twenty dollar watch and nine dollars in real money my friends. Give me a ten and take it away before I change my mind. You're getting a twenty dollar watch for just one dollar! It's killing me so make it quick, I can hardly stand the strain of practically giving these beauties away in the name of advertising!*"

The first man immediately puts up his money with a huge smile on his face. "*Thanks!*" he cries out and turns away as he admires the watch. All along the line people are offering money and you, considering this the bargain of your holiday, practically snatch it from his hands.

THE SCAM

First the watches are probably just about worth a dollar. They may even be stolen property.

One or two of the men in the line are shills. It is their job to lead the rest along. Human beings can be incredibly sheep-like at times. If you see two or three people doing something it assumes an air of respectability. You get carried along and do the same.

Freddy's chat puts you at ease. His glib remarks make you truly believe that you are getting the bargain of your holiday. When he adds his own money at the end you truly believe him when he tells you it's all part of a big advertising campaign for the watches and that you are just the kind of guy they are looking for. Hell, they are practically paying you to wear the watch!

Oh, and there's one other thing that, since you got a little carried away, you may not have noticed.

You are buying back your own money!

The three dollars he offers up with the watch are the three dollars you've already given him! The eight dollars he holds up the second time around are *your* eight dollars!

So for ten dollars you buy a watch worth a buck, get a dollar of Freddy's money (often a forgery if he's in a really larcenous mood) and buy back eight dollars of your own money.

That's a seven dollar or so profit to Freddy.

VARIATIONS AND THE ADD ON

The scam is often disguised by adding more goods as the deal goes on. You start off buying a watch but end up buying a box full of stuff. You drop out at any time and you lose the lot.

It all seems like such a bargain that you stay in.

So you end up with a pile of cheap or stolen items and your own money, bought at a price that gives Freddy and his cohorts a massive profit.

The open store is common on sea fronts and large city blocks but watch out for variations everywhere. Local fairgrounds or carnivals, tag sales, car boot sales, school and church fetes and even the local bar are all open territory. The next time you see a man with a suitcase full of gear that he wants to sell, beware. It may just be Freddy.

Don't think that you can't be fooled by this disarming swindle. A lot of very smart people before you have done so without ever realizing that they've been taken. Freddy is *really* good at convincing you that you are getting a great deal!

I hope that I don't need to add, but I will, it is not worth arguing with Freddy or, even worse, trying to wise up other suckers in the crowd. As you have learned, Freddy can have a nasty temper. Especially when he employs somebody else to fight his battles for him.

BLATANT BUT EFFECTIVE!

A cruder version of the Jam Auction is often to be found on the midway of state and county fairs in the USA.

The happy revelers are brought into a tent and told that, for giving up their valuable time, they will receive free items for a market research program. Each is given a pile of items consisting of things like pens, hats, brushes and so on. A 'spoof' auction is now run as each is asked to show money to the auctioneer for each item in turn. Any money collected is returned to the participants. As the auction goes on the amount of money requested gets higher and the number of participants decreases.

At the end of the auction there are just a few participants left. They are shown the very special item that has been reserved for people like them, people with the courage to get through all of the preamble! This special item will be quite an expensive sewing machine or food mixer. Just as before money is asked for and collected up exactly as has happened during the entire 'spoof' auction before. Each participant receives the item (worth a fraction of what they are being asked to put up) and are stunned to discover themselves being guided to the exit. They learn that the auction is over and that they've really bought the item! There won't be any money returned on this purchase!

BUYING A BRICK

Although not a Jam Auction this may be a good time to warn you about the practice of *selling bricks*.

Have you ever been stuck in traffic and seen a guy, carrying a box, walking through the cars? Have you ever seen him offer the contents of the box to somebody and walk away with cash? If you have then you've seen somebody buy a brick.

The box is one for a top of the line video camera. A cursory look inside the box lets you see the camera. Well, you see the plastic and polystyrene around a camera shape, but you can see the lens and a few controls visible through the holes the manufacturer strategically places in the packaging to entice you to buy it in its more normal habitat of a store.

The price the guy is offering it for is less than a third of the retail price. Obviously it's stolen but, what the hell, a bargain is a bargain isn't it?

If you buy it, you larcenous little devil, you deserve the punishment. You bought a lens and a few cheap controls positioned around a brick to give the package weight. This scam is also done with video machines, CD Players, televisions and, in fact, just about anything that comes in a box.

When he offers it to you, you have only a few moments to make up your mind. The traffic will be moving in just a second and you don't have time to examine the product. It's a *take it now or lose it forever* deal. Enough people take it to make this quite a profitable little trade when the con man has nothing else to do for fun.

This sordid little street hustle has its roots in the famous *Selling a Gold Brick* swindle. Charles 'Doc' Baggs is credited with the invention of a confidence game which involved selling a worthless lump of base metal as a gold brick during the days of the Wild West and the Gold Rush. Doc made enough money from this and his other less than honest games to live comfortably until his death in New York City in the 1930's. He became so well known in his heyday that he was often cited in the press. In fact when Oscar Wilde, famed for his "*Too, too divine,*" comment, visited Denver in 1882, the *Denver News* published a poem *Ode to Oscar* which included the following stanza,

> *If thou dost boast of being too, we will*
> *Produce Charles Baggs, M.D., who is as too*
> *As thou art, and a durned sight tooer.*

Yes, even the humblest of street cons can have an 'honorable' history!

But it still should be noted that if you are offered a box, however good it looks, don't buy it.

Not unless you have a rather odd hobby that consists of collecting bricks!

The Punchboard Con

I'M PRETTY SURE YOU'VE SEEN A PUNCHBOARD EVEN IF YOU DON'T RECOGNIZE ITS name.

A Punchboard is a thick piece of cardboard with around two hundred holes punched through it. In each hole is a small piece of rolled up paper. To play, you pay a fee (normally fifty cents or a dollar) and, in return, you get to push out one of those bits of paper with a metal prong. You unroll the paper and, if you are lucky, you win a prize. The prizes vary but on a dollar board with two hundred holes the top prize could be fifty dollars!

The profit, for the operator, is the difference between the total stakes required to clear the board and the total of the payouts. Punchboards are often used as charity fund raising devices.

What most people don't know is that, if you know where to shop, you can buy Punchboards along with a card showing you where all the prizes are situated! These special boards cost about four times as much as normal ones but their profit potential is much higher. Obviously if you punch out the big prizes yourself before putting the board on display your profit will be bigger. Of course that's illegal but it doesn't stop people from doing it.

Freddy has turned this small time scam into a monster.

He buys his boards in bulk. They cost him around ten to fifteen dollars each. He goes to a big city and sells them to clubs, bars and organizations for five dollars each. This is a good deal to the buyer because each board will give them a hundred dollar or more profit.

Freddy fails to mention, or indeed provide, the card showing the layout of prizes.

A week or so later the Stoat, or one of Freddy's other cohorts, will go to the same city. They'll wander around the establishments Freddy sold the boards to and play the game. Sam the Stoat loves to play Punchboard.

Especially if he knows where all the prizes are.

Follow him around and you'll never see anybody punch out so many big winners in so short a time.

Sam doesn't go berserk. He simply punches out a winner or two, finishes his drink and leaves. The owner of the board just thinks Sam is a lucky guy. He may even feel happy for him. After all Sam had been saying how worried about cash he was getting. The owner thinks it's nice that the sad guy won a buck or two to put a smile on his face. The owner doesn't feel too worried. After all, if he just fails to mention to future players that the big prize has gone, he can still get his profit from the board!

The owner is not alone. Sam hits just about every board that Freddy sold.

Sam, thanks to the maps of the prizes, knows exactly where to punch. This is a perfect example of an *inside* and *outside* man at work. Freddy sells the boards and leaves. Later, Sam enters the scene and picks up the money. There is nothing to catch!

Later, of course, they meet to split the money. A very profitable scheme indeed.

The reason Freddy sells the boards so cheaply is to get rid of as many of them as he can in as short a time as possible. He'd give them away if he had to.

He buys the boards, let's say, at fifteen dollars each. He sells them at five dollars. The top prize on the board, just for an example, is fifty dollars. If Sam just punches out the big winner, each board gives them a forty dollar profit between them.

Two Punchboards from my collection.

Freddy buys the boards in large quantities and will often work this scam with four hundred or more boards at a time.

Sitting comfortably?

That's a sixteen thousand dollar profit for little or no risk.

"*Not bad for a week's work,*" says Freddy.

Chain Letters That Pay!

Y<small>OU'VE ALMOST CERTAINLY SEEN A</small> C<small>HAIN</small> L<small>ETTER.</small> A<small>N ENVELOPE ARRIVES IN</small> your daily mail and you open it up.

The letter varies from chain to chain but all are pretty much the same in content. At least once in the letter a line will read, '*Good luck will come to those who keep the chain going but very bad luck will come to anybody who breaks the chain.*'

After the normal 'glowing' testimonials as to the effectiveness of the chain there will be a list of five names at the bottom complete with their addresses. You are instructed to send one dollar to the person at the top of the list. Then you are instructed to remove that name and add your name to the bottom of the list moving all the other names up one place. Finally you are asked to send this new letter to five of your friends.

The letter explains that if the chain remains unbroken, by the time your name reaches the top of the list, 3,125 people will be sending you a dollar! Not a bad return for a dollar and a small amount of your time!

The chain comes in many forms. You can even see it today on the Internet in various forms. The most popular Internet version involves selling reports by e-mail. We'll take a look at those in just a moment.

THE PROBLEM

The obvious big problem is that the chain, as described so far, despite grandiose claims ('*I made $50,000 in 90 days!*'), is rarely, if ever, completed. People throw away the letter, delete the e-mail or just don't bother to send the dollar. With just two or three breaks in the chain your profit is gone.

This is even more likely these days because, as so many of them turn up, people get irritated. In a typical week I will get ten to fifteen e-mails all pretty much offering the same 'Get Rich Quick' scheme of selling reports.

The chain letter is not a new idea. They started back in the Middle Ages when the peasants formed unwritten Good Luck Chains to protect themselves from demons, dragons and other mythical naughties. That's why, by the way, the modern chain letter still maintains the ideal that to break it is bad luck.

Unfortunately for you, far too many people do break the chain and stop it from being a good money maker.

FREDDY'S ANALYSIS

Freddy likes to look at any potential money maker. He looked at chain letters for quite a time before reaching the following conclusions.

Posting out just five letters is useless.

Assuming that the four people above you will carry the chain through is dodgy at best.

Only one or two people out of a hundred would be nuts enough to send money *even* if your name got to the top of the list. A fairly pathetic return.

The great majority of letters will be thrown away.

Even if it works there are at least two Federal offences being broken here. The Postal Service doesn't take too kindly to this sort of stuff.

FREDDY'S SOLUTIONS

Despite its obvious shortcomings Freddy thought that the idea of people just sending him money was a pretty good one. He decided that it just needed some fine tuning.

Freddy's Scam Part One

Freddy answered his above analysis in the following manner.

Why post five letters when you can post five hundred?

Why assume anything about the four people above you in the list? Why not just have four false names and four different post office box addresses or, better yet, four friends who'll collect mail for you at their addresses.

Unfortunately Freddy shelved the plan again after realizing that it still falls apart with the cost of the postage.

Freddy's Scam Part Two

After some more thought (*"I knew there had to be a way to make the damned thing turn something!"*) Freddy found a way to eliminate the postage charge.

He hired kids to deliver letters around housing suburbs and other dense areas of population.

He got the Minx to actually *sell* the letters. Her side goes a little as follows. She goes to a ladies group and explains that she is representing a charity to start a good luck (*spiritual* is a good buzz word at the time of writing) chain towards world peace. She'd like at least five people to help kick it off in this area. She has charity credentials (see the *Charity Raffle* for how to get these) and is a sweet, charming lady. Nobody would suspect her of being a rip-off artist. She shows the letter and explains the five name system. She has no trouble selling them. Some people buy them just to get rid of her! After all, you can only take so much chat about spiritual world peace and harmony of the cosmos in any one sitting. The Minx, on a good day, has been known to sell upwards of three hundred letters.

The Scam in Total

The Minx sells letters.

Freddy organizes hand delivered letters.

Freddy owns each and every one of the five names on the original letter. Any time somebody sends a dollar, it's going to him.

"Not bad," says Freddy, *"Even if I do say so myself!"*

CHAIN LETTERS TODAY

Freddy stopped using his scam a number of years ago. It was, as he put it, a little bit too much work to turn the money.

However, with the explosion of the Internet, a whole new form of the chain letter has arrived on the scene. I'm going to give you, word for word (only names, addresses and personal details have been blanked) one of the numerous e-mails I've received. But, before you read it, look back at the problems Freddy saw with the original letter scheme and see how this cunningly overcomes them all! Now, I'm not saying that this e-mail was sent with any intent to defraud but it is a fascinating read. It's quite long but it's worthy of your study.

> **Subject: Earn $50,000 in 90 Days!!**
> Please Do Not Delete This Message Until You Read It
>
> Dear Friend:
>
> Thank you for taking the time to read this. The message below explains a very simple program which can generate over $50,000 for you in a very short time, simply by sending out e-mails. Amazing, but tested and true. This is an opportunity for you to make a lot of money with very little effort! Once you decide to participate, your name will be at the bottom of this message and people from all over will be sending you $5 bills. $5 bills quickly add up

to thousands when you reach a large number of people! This may allow you to pay off some outstanding debts, plan for early retirement start, a savings account, or purchase something you and your family have wanted for a long time. This program allows each and all participants to "share the wealth" because by all participating, we're all making serious money!

Below is the message I received a few weeks ago. It contains testimonies from previous members who have had great success with this program. Those of us who are participating believe in this program enough to put our name and mailing address at the bottom of every message—that is part of being a participant and it helps others realize that average people are participating. I hope you find that you are interested in participating after you finish reading this message. Thank you for taking the time to read this!

The results have been truly remarkable. So many people are participating that those involved are doing much better than ever before. Since everybody makes more as more people join, it has been very exciting. You will understand once you try it yourself.

THE ENTIRE PLAN IS BELOW.

THIS IS A LEGITIMATE, LEGAL, MONEY MAKING OPPORTUNITY!!

It does NOT require you to come into contact with people or make or take any telephone calls.

<Long and astonishingly glowing reference deleted>

HERE'S HOW THIS AMAZING PROGRAM WILL MAKE YOU THOUSANDS OF DOLLARS$$$$! ! !

This is a perfectly legal money making business. As with all businesses, we build or business by recruiting new partners and selling our products. Every state in the USA allows you to recruit new business partners, and we sell and deliver a product for every dollar received. YOUR ORDERS COME BY MAIL AND ARE FILLED BY E-MAIL, so you are not involved in personal selling. This is the EASIEST plan anywhere!

The product is educational, informative and instructional material. Keys to the secrets of the magic of E-COMMERCE, the information highway, the wave of the future.

There are literally millions of e-mail addresses and 50 million people join the internet every month—you can reach many of these people with this simple program, and soon they will be sending you $5 bills.

Before you delete this program from your in-box as I almost did, take a little time to read it and really think about it. Figure out the worst possible response and you will still make money as I am doing now.

<Name deleted>

YOU CAN START TODAY—FOLLOW THESE EASY STEPS:

STEP #1. ORDER THE FOUR REPORTS

Order the four reports shown on the list below (you can't sell them if you don't order them). For each report send $5 CASH, to the name next to the number of the report you are ordering. Include your name, your mailing address, and of course your E-MAIL ADDRESS.

MAKE SURE YOUR RETURN ADDRESS IS ON YOUR ENVELOPE IN CASE OF ANY E-MAIL PROBLEMS! Within a few days you will receive, by e-mail, each of the four reports. Save them on your computer so you can send them to the 1000's of people who will order from you.

STEP #2. ADDING YOUR MAILING ADDRESS TO THIS LETTER

a. Look below for the listing of the four reports.

b. AFTER you've ordered the four reports, delete the name and address under REPORT #4. This person has made it through the cycle.

c. Move the name and address under REPORT #3 down to REPORT #4 (use copy/paste for accuracy)

d. Move the name and address under REPORT #2 down to REPORT #3 (use copy/paste for accuracy)

e. Move the name and address under REPORT #1 down to REPORT #2 (use copy/paste for accuracy)

f. Insert YOUR name/address in the REPORT #1 position. Please make sure you COPY ALL INFORMATION, every name and address, ACCURATELY! I recommend copying/pasting, NOT retyping the names and addresses.

STEP #3. Take this entire letter, including the modified list of names, and save it on your computer. Make NO changes to these instructions. Also do not reformat this letter in any way. The message looks best when its kept this way, at approximately 60 characters per line, or less.

THE ABSOLUTE BEST WAY TO PROMOTE THIS PROGRAM IS THROUGH BULK E-MAIL.

SENDING BULK E-MAIL: Let's say that you decide to start small, just to see how it goes, and we'll assume you and all those involved e-mail out only 2000 programs each. Let's also assume that the mailing receives a 0.5% response. The response could be much better. Also, many people will e-mail out hundreds of thousands of programs instead of 2000.

But, continuing this example, you send out 2000 programs. With a 0.5% response, that is 10 orders for REPORT #1. Those 10 people respond by sending out 2,000 programs each for a total of 20,000. Out of those 0.5% respond and order REPORT #2. These 100 people mail out 2000 programs each for a total of 200,000. The 0.5% response to that is 1000 for REPORT #3. These 1000 send out 2000 programs for a 2,000,000 total. The 0.5% response to that is 10,000 orders for REPORT #4. That's 10,000 $5 bills for you. CASH! Your total income in this example is $50+$500+$5000+$50,000 for a total of $55,550!

REMEMBER THIS IS ASSUMING 1,990 OUT OF THE 2000 PEOPLE YOU MAIL TO WILL DO ABSOLUTELY NOTHING. DARE TO THINK FOR A MOMENT WHAT WOULD HAPPEN IF EVERY-ONE, OR HALF, SENT OUT 100,000 PROGRAMS INSTEAD OF 2,000. Believe me, many of the people now involved in this program do just that!

Most people get maximum participants by sending out an absolute minimum of 100,000 to 300,000 messages. Many will continue to work this program, sending out programs WITH YOUR NAME ON THEM for months or years! THINK ABOUT THAT!

People are going to get e-mails about this plan from you or somebody else and many will want to work this plan—the question is—Don't you want your name to be on the e-mails they will send out?

GET STARTED TODAY: PLACE YOUR ORDER FOR THE FOUR REPORTS NOW . . .

Note: — ALWAYS SEND $5 CASH (U.S. CURRENCY) FOR EACH REPORT. CHECKS NOT ACCEPTED. Make sure the cash is wrapped in two sheets of paper. On one of those sheets of paper write:

(a) The number and name of the report you are ordering.

(b) Your e-mail address and

(c) Your name & postal address.

<Names of the four reports and ordering information deleted>

TIPS FOR SUCCESS

TREAT THIS AS A BUSINESS! Be prompt, professional and follow the directions accurately. Send for the four reports IMMEDIATELY so you will have them when the orders start coming in because: When you receive a $5 order, you MUST send out the requested report. It is required for this to be a legal business and they need the reports to send out their letters (with your name on them!)—ALWAYS PROVIDE SAME-DAY SERVICE ON THE ORDERS YOU RECEIVE—Be patient and persistent with this program—if you follow the instructions exactly, results WILL follow.

YOUR SUCCESS GUIDELINES

Follow these guidelines to guarantee your success: if you don't receive 20 orders for REPORT #1 within two weeks, continue sending e-mails until you do. Then, a couple of weeks later you should receive at least 100 orders for REPORT #2. If you don't continue sending e-mails until you do. Once you have received 100 or more orders for REPORT #2 YOU CAN RELAX because the system is already working for you and the cash will continue to roll in!

THIS IS IMPORTANT TO REMEMBER: Every time your name is moved down the list, you are placed in front of a different report. You can KEEP TRACK of your progress by watching which report is being ordered from you. To generate more income, simply send another batch of e-mails and start the whole process again! There is no limit to the income you will generate from this business!

Before you make the decision as to whether or not you will participate in this program, please answer one question:

ARE YOU HAPPY WITH YOUR PRESENT INCOME OR JOB?

If the answer is no, then please look at the following facts about this super simple program:

1. NO face to face selling, NO meetings, NO inventory! NO telephone skills, NO big cost to start! Nothing to learn, NO skills needed!

2. NO equipment to buy—you already have a computer and internet connection—so you have everything you need to fill orders.

3. You are selling a product that does NOT COST ANYTHING TO PRODUCE (e-mailing copies of the reports is FREE!)

4. ALL of your customers pay you in CASH!

YOU CAN RUN THIS PROGRAM AS A SUPPLEMENT TO YOUR CURRENT INCOME—YOU HAVE THE OPPORTUNITY TO MAKE MORE MONEY IN A SHORT TIME!

Thank you for your time and consideration. Have a nice day!

Whew! That's a lot of words to get through. The end piece amuses me most. After doing everything but actually sending you cash to convince you it works, it concludes with a very carefully worded caveat that you may make nothing at all. And, if you do make nothing, well, it's your fault! You just didn't work at it enough! A number of business agencies are mentioned with regards to just setting up a business of any kind. Their mention does seem to add a little more credence to the whole though in my opinion.

The teasers of what you can spend the money on are delightfully enticing. The math is most convincing until, of course, you recall the old adage that 'To assume, you make an ass out of you and me'. The simplicity is wonderful. An inventory free business!

It sounds like a dream. But some dreams can become nightmares!

Now this *may* be a legitimate business offer of a lifetime that I'm being foolish to ignore. But let's take a look at how Freddy's problems with chain letters are solved by modern technology and a devious mind.

Why send 500 letters when, for a small cost, you can send 15,000 e-mails? Or 15,000,000 for that matter? *If* you owned all four names that could generate quite a return for little investment. Even owning just one name could be pretty good. Especially when you consider that your initial investment is to order *all four* reports! No waiting till a name gets to the top of the list for these guys, *"Gimme five bucks now!"*

You are 'selling' a product by e-mail thus avoiding the legal problems of chain letters. Freddy points out that the names and addresses could also be combined into lists and sold off, for additional profit, to bulk mailing companies. The e-mails can also be sold to Internet companies.

A close look will show that, with the exception of not being promised bad luck should you break a chain, this is nothing more than a pyramid scheme of chain letters.

Legal? Despite its promises it isn't.

A money maker for the average Joe? Unlikely at best. I've asked around and have yet to meet anybody who has made a profit on such a scheme although I've spoken to several who say the profit over cost turnaround is just around the corner! I suspect that it'll be a bigger corner than they imagine.

Any letter sent to you promising riches if you'll just send out a few dollars should be ripped up and thrown away. Even when it is disguised in techno-babble from the Internet. The world is littered with people who have lost fortunes on chain and pyramid schemes. They are all so dubiously regarded that you'll note, throughout the e-mail above, its legality is stressed to the point of the lady protesting too much.

A few years ago I wrote in a column that the chain letter had fallen out of favor at that time because they'd become too well known to get a return for anybody, legally or not. I predicted that they'd probably make a come back in some form or another. I warned my readers to keep a watch out for them. I guess my prediction abilities are a little better than I first thought!

They just don't work. The *only* people who get returns on such schemes are people like Freddy who take them from shady to illegal in a heartbeat.

And Freddy has been pestering me to teach him about sending e-mails. *"I've got a few friends I'd like to get in touch with,"* he says.

Sparks Gives The Skinny On Techno Fraud

FREDDY IS THE FIRST TO ADMIT THAT HE DOESN'T KNOW *everything* ABOUT CHEATing. But, he knows people who are specialists in the areas he isn't so knowledgeable about. One such area, as we've just discovered, is the Internet. To date Freddy doesn't even know how to log on to the 'Net! But, one of his shady pals, known as *Sparks*, has been playing with computers from before home computers were even on the market. In the 70's he was learning languages like BASIC and FORTRAN and clipping out holes in little bits of cardboard to run his programs on main frames. He has kept up with technology and currently has a system that could, probably, easily run a small country.

I showed him the chain letter and his only comment was, *"Pretty typical."*

I asked him how wide fraud was on the Internet and his reply was to say, *"Rife. It's a whole new, wide-open field!"* He further explained how perfect the whole set up was for a con. *Any* kid with a computer can set up a scam. You don't need a lavish office, bar, betting shop or whatever set-up. All you need is a web page designer and some very rudimentary programming skills. It's very tough to do anything legally about any suspected fraud. Laws are being brought in by everybody but the laws vary from state to state and from country to country. Most are unenforceable across state lines or country borders! Any civil action can be incredibly expensive and, often, just isn't worth trying. Wide open only really begins to describe it!

Sadly, despite the great explosion of the technological age and the Internet, the main scams are really rather unimaginative. Most are based on schemes that have been run through mail order in magazines for years. Thankfully most are easy to spot and are as simple as a *delete* key away from removal from your life.

I asked Sparks about the top Internet scams and any advice he had with regard to them. Considering his part-time job, which is creating and running such scams, he was remarkably frank about the issue. I looked through my e-mail for a couple of days to see if I could find examples of any of his top scams. Astonishingly I found examples of them *all!* I've included with each one a sample from my own electronic trash bin. I'm not saying that the samples I've included are scams. But they do seem to fit the criteria for Sparks examples pretty darned well.

WORK AT HOME SCHEMES

Perhaps the most common of all these schemes promises you riches for stuffing envelopes at home. You may be promised as much as $3.00 for every envelope you stuff. If you've ever sent off for one of the start-up kits from a magazine ad (and the Internet ones are practically identical!) you'll already know that there is no real envelope stuffing involved at all. Instead, you are instructed to place ads instructing people to send $3.00 and a stamped, self addressed, envelope to you. You keep the three bucks and send the envelopes to the company. Don't be tempted, you won't make enough money to cover your registration fee never mind your advertising bill unless life has really dealt you an extraordinarily lucky hand. With the Internet versions you pay a registration fee (to show you are serious about these opportunities) and are then instructed to send out the envelope stuffing ad (via bulk e-mail) to others. If anybody you send the e-mail to signs up you are promised a fee for getting them to do so. You may or may not receive this fee. Sparks has yet to meet anybody who has even covered the cost of registration.

If you sign up for a *work at home* scheme like putting together toys or some such you will find that most, if not all, of your work is not up to the company's high standards. This means, of course, that they will refuse to pay you.

An example of one these *Hot* home-based businesses is as follows.

FOLLOW ME TO FINANCIAL FREEDOM!!
I am looking for people with good work ethic and extraordinary desire to earn at least $10,000 per month working from home.
NO SPECIAL SKILLS OR EXPERIENCE REQUIRED. We will give you all the training and personal support you will need to ensure your success!
This LEGITIMATE HOME-BASED INCOME OPPORTUNITY can put you back in control of your time, your finances, and your life!
If you've tried other opportunities in the past that have failed to live up to their promise THIS IS DIFFERENT THAN ANYTHING ELSE YOU'VE SEEN! THIS IS NOT A GET RICH QUICK SCHEME! YOUR FINANCIAL PAST DOES NOT HAVE TO BE YOUR FINANCIAL FUTURE! CALL ONLY IF YOU ARE SERIOUS!
<phone number deleted>

DON'T GO TO SLEEP WITHOUT HEARING OUR MESSAGE!
Please leave your name and number and the best time to call.
DO NOT RESPOND BY E-MAIL

CABLE DE-SCRAMBLER KITS

This scam offers kits or special inside information on how to get your cable or satellite TV for free. There are two rather obvious problems here. The first is simple, the kits and/or information simply don't work! The second, and rather more vital problem for you should you decide to go ahead anyway, is that, *if* the kit/information worked, it is illegal to steal service from a cable company. The cable companies have followed an ongoing campaign of very aggressively seeking out and prosecuting those who steal cable TV.

That doesn't stop e-mails like this from filling up my inbox.

OPEN EVERY CHANNEL ON YOUR SATELLITE OR CABLE SYSTEM REGARDLESS OF TYPE OR BRAND.

WHY WASTE $400-$600 $$$$$$$$ BUYING AN AFTER MARKET CARD WHEN THEY AREN'T GUARANTEED TO STAY UP!

YOU CAN PROGRAM YOUR CARD YOURSELF IN AS LITTLE AS 5-10 MINUTES.

YOU CAN OPEN EVERY CHANNEL ON YOUR CABLE BOX!

UNLOCK THE FULL POTENTIAL OF YOUR SATELLITE SYSTEM!

ALL SPOTS EVENTS

ALL PAY-PER-VIEWS

ALL PREMIUMS

ALL NBA

EVERY ADULT CHANNEL

EXTRA HIDDEN CHANNELS

100'S OF CHANNELS

EVERY CHANNEL IS UNLOCKED

VISIT OUR WEBSITE BELOW FOR MORE INFORMATION!

<web site deleted>

MAKING MONEY BY SENDING OUT BULK E-MAILS

These sweet people will offer you huge bulk e-mail lists (often with millions of addresses) along with some bulk mailing (spam) software. The lists are often next to useless being totally outdated, full of duplications and defunct addresses. The spam software is often of the lowest quality available. Of course it is unlikely that they'll claim anything other that their lists are brand new and that their software is of the highest quality! Some companies offer to do the bulk e-mailing for you at a fee. Sparks says, "*Anybody who falls for this idiocy needs their head examined. This is a BIG no, no!"*

Of course this won't stop the following, and a lot like it, arriving in my e-mail box to consider.

> 10 MILLION E-MAIL ADDRESSES FOR ONLY $99
>
> You want to make some money? We can put you in touch with over 10 million people at virtually no cost. Can you make one cent from each of these names? If you can you have a profit of over $250,000.
>
> That's right, we have 10 million fresh e-mail addresses that we will sell for only $99. These are all fresh addresses with no duplications. They are all sorted and ready to be mailed. This is the best deal anywhere today! Imagine selling a product for only $5 and getting only a 1/10% response. That's $1,350,000 in your pocket!
>
> Don't believe it? People are making that kind of money right now from doing the same thing, that is why you get so much e-mail from people selling your their product . . . . it works! We will even include, a FREE demo copy of the world's leading BULK MAILING SOFTWARE!
>
> These 10 million e-mail addresses and software are yours to keep, so you can use them over and over and they come on one CD!
>
> This offer is not for everyone.
>
> If you cannot see just how excellent the risk/reward ratio in this offer is then there is nothing we can do for you.
>
> To make money you must stop dreaming and TAKE ACTION.
>
> <ordering information deleted>

GUARANTEED LOANS, ETC.

This one has a lot of variants. Even Sparks finds it tough to keep up with them. Some offer loans, others offer easy terms on products. Still more will offer to consolidate your debts to save you money. They may offer home equity loans that don't require you to actually have any equity in your home, approved loans *regardless* of credit history, offshore credit cards *regardless* of credit history. Sometimes these offers will entice you further by offering to pay you to get others involved with these wonderful offers. None, to date, on our investigations, has panned out. Loans don't appear, loans are turned down unless incredibly stringent requirements are met, and promised, and paid for, credit cards do not appear. It is particularly sad that a scam like this feeds on the members of society with heavy debt who are least able to handle the loss. *"These guys are really pretty scuzzy,"* says Sparks who, although a part time Internet con man himself, finds this scheme, *"Tacky."*

A typical e-mail from my trash bin looks like this.

> GET OUT OF DEBT!!!
>
> THIS IS NOT A LOAN!!!
>
> YOU WILL NOT BE TURNED DOWN!!!
>
> $ARE you thinking about borrowing money to consolidate your bills?

$ARE you approaching or already past due on your credit cards?
$DO you usually only pay the minimum amount due on your credit cards?
$ARE your creditors harassing you over late payments?
$ARE family disputes over money a regular occurrence for you?
We can reduce your monthly payments by consolidating your unsecured debt . . .
*credit cards
*student loans
*department store cards
*collection accounts
*unsecured loans
*medical bills
Save 20$-60% by consolidating everything into one low monthly payment!
This is not a loan. How do we do it? We can reduce or eliminate the high interest you are currently paying. Let us help you . . . Help yourself!!!
For free information go to <web site deleted>

FREE VACATIONS

What a day! You receive an e-mail confirming that you have won a fantastic vacation. You may also have been *specially selected* to receive this holiday package. Reading the small print you may discover that only part of the package is free and that you are responsible for booking other parts of it such as the travel to and from the destination. Of course our friendly company will be happy to do that for you! If you take the vacation you could easily find that the luxury cruise ship is an old steamer from World War One or that the hotel has been described as 'Five Star' because that's how many of them you can see through the hole in the roof. Any requested upgrades are liable to be *very* expensive.

I do have to congratulate the sender of the following though. It is, at least, direct and to the point!

A free vacation awaits you
<web site deleted>

EASY MONEY

The senders of these schemes claim to have found *secret* flaws in the way the money market works. They offer to teach you how to make extraordinary profits by following their plan. There are lots of variations on these but all share the common trait of offering to make you rich with little or no effort required. Sparks puts it pretty well when he says, "*If you had a secret method of making money from flaws in the market would you tell anybody about it?*" Enough said, they don't work! The delightful movie *The Grifters* shows a sting involving this very type of scam. It's worth a watch if you can.

But the e-mails from these companies get ever longer.

Dear Friend:

If you have already responded to the following announcement a few days ago, that means your package is already on its way and it should be arriving soon! If you have not responded to this before, please pay attention to it now. This is very important!!!

!!

IMPORTANT ANNOUNCEMENT

IMPORTANT ANNOUNCEMENT

,,

Your Future May Depend On It!

!!

<testimonials deleted>

We are glad to announce that for the first time and for a very short period of time, <company name deleted>, will instruct a LIMITED number of people worldwide on 'HOW TO CONVERT $25 INTO ONE HUNDRED OF LEGAL CURRENCY'. We will transact the first conversion for you, after that you can easily and quickly do this on your own hundreds or even thousands of times every month. Take advantage of this "SECRET FLAW"!

****

It is even more explosive than we have yet disclosed. While currency does fluctuate daily, we can show you 'HOW TO CONVERT $99 INTO $588 AS MANY TIMES AS YOU WANT'. That means you will be able to EXCHANGE $99, AMERICAN LEGAL CURRENCY DOLLARS, FOR $580 OF THE SAME! You can do this as many times as you want, every day, every week, every month. All very LEGAL and effortlessly!

It takes only 5-10 minutes each time you do this. You can do this from home, office or even while travelling. All you need is access to a phone line and an address. Best of all you can do this from ANY CITY ON THIS EARTH!!!

Again, we must reiterate, anyone can do this and the source is never ending. For as long as the global financial community continues to use different currencies with varying exchange rates, the "SECRET FLAW" will exist.

>>>

As we said earlier we will do the first transaction for you and will show you exactly how to do this on your own, over and over again!

The amount of exchange you would do each time is entirely up to you. Working just 2 to 10 hours a week, you can soon join the list of Millionaires who do this on a daily basis many times a day. The transaction is so simple that even a high school kid can do it!

We at the <company name deleted> would like to see a uniform global currency backed by gold. But, until then, we will allow a LIMITED number of individuals worldwide to share in the UNLIMITED PROFITS provided for by worldwide differentials.

We do not expouse any political views nor will we ask you to do so. We can say however that our parent organization benefits greatly by the knowledge being shared, as we ourselves, along with YOU, benefit likewise. Your main concern surely will be, how will you benefit

As soon as you become a member, you will make transactions from your home, office, by telephone or through the mail. You can conduct these transactions even while travelling.

Don't believe us? Experience it for yourself!:

Unlike anything else, we will assure you the great financial freedom and you will add to our quickly growing base of supporters and join the list of MILLIONAIRES being created using this very "SECRET FLAW" in the world currency market.

****

DON'T ENVY US, JOIN US TODAY!!!!

There is a one time membership fee of only $195. BUT, if you join within the next ten days, you can join us for only the $25 administrative cost. Your important documents, instructions, contact names and addresses/names and all other pertinent information will be mailed to you immediately. So join us today!

(If you are replying after the 10 day period, you must pay $195 for membership. NO EXCEPTIONS, and no more e-mail inquiries please).

Upon becoming a member you promise to keep all the information CONFIDENTIAL!

<order form and glowing testimonials deleted>

CREDIT REPAIR SCAMS

These guys claim to be able to repair any bad credit you have. With the wave of a financial magic wand all negative information on your credit report will vanish leaving you free to apply and qualify for credit cards, loans and mortgages. The tiny problem? They can't deliver the promises they make. Their advice commonly consists of lying on loan and credit applications, misrepresenting your Social Security number and shadily acquiring an Employer Identification Number from the IRS using false pretenses. This advice is criminal. By following it you will be committing fraud and violating federal laws. *"Never, never, never mess with the IRS or the Feds,"* is Sparks advice. *"Don't ever fall for this scam!"*

Here's another business that seems to think that it is my friend!

Dear Friend,

Give yourself the ADVANTAGE of a new, legal, unblemished credit file in less than 30 days, allowing you to enjoy life more with EXCELLENT CREDIT!! Over the past ten years I have perfected a system called <name deleted> It's a guaranteed way for legally getting an excellent credit rating almost instantly. Here's how.

You will simply follow the simple program steps to quickly get a new, legal, unblemished credit file and establish excellent credit.

#1

Because no two people in the US have the same Social Security number banks and creditors access your credit file almost entirely by your SS#. You will not want to change your SS# because it is extremely difficult to do so and you need it for your employment, taxes and social security benefits. The FEDERAL PRIVACY ACT of 1974 clearly states that only the government and your employer can force you to use your SS#. Because of this law you are legally allowed to use another 9 digit number to use in place of your SS# on credit applications.

The first day you become our client you will receive your own number through the

Employer Identification Number Program. You will need us for this because 95% of all Employer Identification Numbers, although 9 digits, do not look anything like SS# numbers and cannot be used on credit applications. We will legally get you an Employer Identification Number that fits in the same range of SS# numbers in use today. Because the Federal laws do not require you to give your SS# to ANYBODY besides your employer and the government you can now LEGALLY use this number in place of your SS# on credit applications.

#2

No two people have the same mailing address, so you will need to obtain a new mailing address for use on your new credit file. A friend, relative or mailbox address in your area will be perfect.

#3

No two people with the same name have the same telephone numbers, so you will need a new telephone number for use on your credit file. A friend, relative, voice mail or pager will work perfectly.

#4

With your new SS#, new address and new telephone number we will open your credit file. It will now be totally impossible for any creditor to know anything about your past credit history.

#5

To guarantee that you will quickly qualify for credit again we will assist you by instantly adding positive information to your new file. This is an unknown way of adding real accounts to your new credit file to give you an EXCELLENT RATING in less than 30 days! As you know, the more positive information there is on your credit file the more money banks will lend you.

<glowing references deleted>

<ordering information deleted>

GREAT BUSINESS OPPORTUNITIES

These offers tell you about fabulous business opportunities that can make you a fortune with little, if any, investment and only a tiny amount of work required. Most are based upon illegal *pyramid* schemes or are loosely veiled Multi-Level Marketing schemes. They may sound great but your chances of picking a winner from the offers are less than that of winning the lottery, according to Sparks.

At least the sender of the following e-mail doesn't open with *dear friend*!

NOTHING LIKE THIS HAS EVER BEEN DONE BEFORE!

Proven, successful leaders will personally take you through every step of the way and teach you how you can build a substantial five figure MONTHLY income for informing people about a revolutionary new money saving, income generating service that EVERYBODY needs and hardly anybody knows about!

THE PERFECT BUSINESS HAS ARRIVED!

- Unique service, something almost everybody needs

- After someone sees what it is, they almost have to at least try it
- There is no risk of competition
- No RISK!
- No bosses, no collecting money, no inventory or products to buy
- Not a health or nutritional product or any kind of phone discount plan
- You will work directly with top earners to duplicate their success
- Some have made five figure ($$,$$$) monthly incomes in 6 to 12 months! (NO JOKE!) (You may do better or worse)
- AND BEST OF ALL! a WARM lead source you need to hear about to believe.

A very sellable product, a killer COMP plan and WARM leads, this has it ALL! If this has got you interested call us for more information!

<contact information deleted>

FREE PRODUCTS AND PROMOTIONS

These kindly companies offer such things as expensive computers or television satellite systems for free! But Sparks advises you to carefully read the e-mails and any contracts. To get the free stuff you may have to sign up with a club for a fee or order television channels through the company making the offer. They may ask you to get a number of friends involved before you get your free stuff, a very thinly disguised *pyramid*.

Ah well, I guess I won't be answering this e-mail then!

FREE SATELLITE TV SYSTEM

Watch over 500 channels of digital broadcast quality television on your own FREE satellite television system. These new digital satellite systems use the new 18" satellite dish antenna.

For a LIMITED TIME we'll give you this TOP OF THE LINE system for FREE!

We'll include FREE INSTALLATION!

All you have to do is call us to arrange delivery and order the channels you want to receive.

Don't miss this offer, it's only available while stocks last!

<telephone number deleted>

HEALTH AND DIET SCAMS

If you've ever read the tabloids you'll have seen adverts for 'miracle cures' and 'diets' that enable you to lose weight while maintaining your food intake and without any special exercises required. They promise that they are based on *secret* scientific breakthroughs, substances that actually destroy fat cells before they are absorbed by your body for example! Another advertisement may promise to cure hair loss or lack of sexual potency. They pretty much all share one thing in common. Even if you receive the 'stuff' they just don't

How to Cheat at Everything

work. These scams often include testimonials from *famous experts* you've never heard of and are most unlikely to be able to track down. Health and Diet scams are currently considered by many agencies to be the number one area of fraud on the web today.

I'm afraid I just couldn't resist sharing the following e-mail with you. Talk about really hitting a guy where it hurts!

> How would you like to know how to strengthen and enlarge your penis?
> Well we know how you can never become impotent and have a stronger large penis.
> Our system is doctor recommended.
> For more information just go to <web site, thankfully, deleted>

All of the sample e-mails are genuine. They look as though they've been written to back up Sparks observations but they are all real ones received by me! I'm not saying that they are not absolutely legitimate business opportunities or great offers. But Sparks says, *"Nothing is sure on the web—don't assume that anything is legitimate!"*

There are a few more examples to add to the above including, of course, chain letters which we covered in the previous chapter. Another big group of scams on the web at the time of writing are *investment opportunities* that promise outrageously high returns on any capital you invest. Many of them are illegal *Ponzi* schemes (named after the famed con man Charles Ponzi of New York City) in which early investors are paid with funds from later investors. This gives the early investors some faith in the system to invest more money and, when the *'use Peter to pay Paul'* system inevitably collapses, everybody but the owners of the scheme lose out big time. The promoters often promise to guarantee your investment which sounds nice. It won't protect you though because, by the time you try to collect on your guarantee, the promoters will be long gone.

Sparks also warned me about blatant theft on the web. If your company needs a search engine provider or web page designer there are companies who will take your money and never provide the work. It's very difficult and expensive to try to get your money back and this has cost companies hundreds of thousands of dollars. Sparks always tells his clients to avoid *online business* offers if possible. He also says to check references, ask for progress reports and, most importantly, to *never* pay up-front. It sounds incredible but it's true. They take the money and do nothing assuming that you won't go to the expense of litigation to get your money back!

The same is true of buying equipment on the web. Sparks says you should be *very* wary of low costs combined with a high pressure sales technique encouraging you to send money *now*! He also says it is very common for shady companies to get rid of damaged goods by selling them on the web and, later, claiming they were damaged in transit. Despite his huge computer system and knowledge of how it works, Sparks buys his goods the old fashioned way. From a store in the mall!

I had expected some new cons, something that exploited the freedom of the web, but no. All the cons are old ones just slightly re-written to exploit the mass mailing capability of e-mail. A sad but true example that, old as they are, people will still fall for them.

To check out Sparks and his list of top cons I also contacted the Consumers League. I wasn't surprised that they confirmed that Sparks was right on the money. According to them America's top five scams are: phony prize and free goods offers, bogus travel packages, fraudulent investments, work at home swindles and recovery room and medical scams. They also stressed that these are the top five of a *really* long list. Try a search on the web using the words *Internet Fraud* yourself. You may be stunned at the amount of information available to help you protect yourself!

Sparks' top tips to avoid getting ripped off on the web are as follows.

Never pay money to get money. If you are told a processing or membership fee is needed ask that it be deducted from the money due to you. The responses to this sensible suggestion can be *laugh out loud* funny as they try to explain how their system can't handle such requests.

Never use a credit card number to verify your ID, for an age verification or for any form of 'free' site which will 'only charge the card after the freebie period is up'. You can be certain that some kind of concealed fee will be charged to you. A business man in Washington had signed up for a porn site. His first month was free but he was asked for his credit card number to verify his age and to give him his password. The card, he was assured, would only be charged if he continued to use the site after the thirty day trial period. His final losses ended up at just a snatch over $120,000. To date he has been unable to recover one cent of the money. Credit cards were never meant to be used as ID cards and, as such, are useless. The companies asking for your number want to charge you somehow.

Never give out your password to anybody online. Scam artists will often pretend to be *Network Security People* or some such. Whoever they say they are *don't* give out your password.

Never, never, never buy anything from a bulk e-mailing (spam). Your chances of being scammed are astronomically high.

With regard to taking yourself off these spammers lists by using their e-mail systems Sparks advises you not to. "*Just delete the e-mails and let them keep coming,*" he says, "*Eventually they will think your e-mail is defunct and stop sending their particular stuff to you. If you reply to them, even to get off a list, they'll know your e-mail address is an active one, and you'll be on a ton of other lists before you know it!*"

To repeat Sparks' best advice. All your transactions are at your *own* risk. You can't rely on any law enforcement agencies to help you and any personal legal action can be prohibitively expensive. Nothing is sure—don't assume *anything* is legitimate! "*In fact,*" Sparks notes rather wisely, "*If you assume that everything is a scam you'll be much better off!*"

The web is an incredible thing. Just be really careful with it when it comes to anything that involves money or credit card numbers.

A FINAL SNEAKY WEB SCAM

One of my other shady pals is a porn king known as *The Raven*. He runs, as part of his business, a number of huge Internet sex sites. I asked him if there were any scams above and beyond the rather bland ones I had uncovered. He told me of one that, finally, was unique to the web itself. Its impact, until discovered, was huge and covered a whole number of site genres from porn to games. You were told that to watch a video or play a particular game demo you had to download a special video viewer. You did this and proceeded to happily watch your video or play your game. What the download had also done was, without your knowledge, change your dial in information from the usual local access code to an overseas international call routed through a telephone exchange owned by the scam company. From the moment your download was complete until the time you signed off for that session (not just the time of the movie or game but the entire web session you had from download to sign off) you were charged at an exorbitant international rate. This scam was discovered around June 2000 and, hopefully, discontinued. I'm sure it will pop up again some time or another. Spark's only comment on learning about this was, *"Man, I wish I'd thought of that, it's bloody brilliant!"* Both Raven and Sparks see this as just the start of a whole genre of scams that will take advantage of the electronic medium.

AN UPDATE – JUNE 2001

As this book wanders ever closer to being printed the latest reports on scams on the internet have been published. Holly Anderson of the National Consumers League says that, *"Con artists are smart. They read the papers and know what the latest fads are. As more and more consumers went on line, so did more and more con artists."*

On it's web site (www.fraud.org/internet/intset.htm) the National Consumers League says that the amount lost by customers filing with them alone was almost 3.9 million dollars in the year 2000. Clearly it's a fast growing haven for con artists!

Among the top ten scams that have appeared are the internet auction sites. A consumer will pay for an expensive product only to receive a less valuable version in return. They seem to be the lucky ones. Many others have reported getting nothing at all in return for their hard earned money! This is currently listed as the number one scam on the web and is responsible, at the time of writing, for over 78 % of the complaints to the National Consumer League!

Government agencies have stepped up efforts to help educate consumers and several new web sites have appeared. www.fraud.org/internet/inttip/ inttip.htm and the US. Federal Trade Commission's Top Ten Dot Cons (www.ftc.gov/dotcons) describe a whole variety of cons, scams and hustles being run right now!

If you have found yourself being taken advantage of there is finally a way to try to fight back. Both the National Consumers League and Federal Trade Commission's sites have forms you can use to file a complaint. Another complaint site is www.ifccfbi.gov. Your chances of getting money back are minimal at best but you may at least help to shut down a bad site.

Freddy often quotes an old line that is well worth remembering every time you read your 'junk' e-mail or decide to take advantage of a special offer. "*If it sounds too good to be true, it probably is too good to be true!*"

P.S. As this book gets ever closer to actually going to press, I have received multiple copies of an e-mail telling me that Bill Gates (one of the worlds richest men) will pay me around $250 for every time that I forward this mail to others. It seems he wants to give away some of his multi-billion dollar fortune to those of us (read the rest of the world) less fortunate than himself. Similar hoaxes involve a Nigerian man who wants to give you millions of dollars for helping him get his money out of his country. Let me quote from U.S. News (August 26th, 2002) which ran an issue dedicated to the Art of the Hoax.

Thomas Hayden writes:

> *For the record, Bill Gates will not give you a thousand dollars for testing an e-mail tracking application, and you shouldn't trust that dude in Nigeria who swears he needs your help to transfer millions out of the country.*

Alex Boese (who maintains the web site www.museumof hoaxes.com) adds in the same article, "*With e-mail anybody can potentially have access to millions of people. When that anybody turns out to be a hoaxer, the results can spread for years.*"

The Cost Of Love
On The Web

IT HAD TO HAPPEN EVENTUALLY I GUESS. AFTER ALL THE WORLD'S OLDEST PROfession is thought to be prostitution and so it was only a matter of time before women (or men pretending to be women) found a way to scam money from men in exchange for promises of love on the 'Net.

I'm not talking here about the pay-per-view sex sites or chat rooms. This is much more personal and conniving than that.

A friend of mine, who I'll refer to as BW to protect his anonymity, had placed an ad on a dating service on the web. He was genuinely interested in meeting a nice young lady to have a serious relationship with. At the age of forty he was thinking about marriage and children before he was too old.

He was delighted and interested by the following e-mail he received a few days after posting his ad.

> Hello,
>
> I've found your advertisement at <site deleted> and decided to write you. Your ad doesn't show you like a serious person. But I feel you are serious. I'm almost sure in that. And you are searching for a partner. I'm also looking for my second half. I didn't write you immediately after I've seen your ad because the problem is that I'm Ukrainian. And you are American. That is thousands kilometers between us. But I'm sure everything is possible in this life. And you never know before you try. That's why I decided to get a try. I'm 29. And you are a bit more. The age difference between us is perfect I guess. If you think that I'm wrong or even not polite, I'm sorry. Just do not reply to me. I'll understand. But if you believe in fate, and if you don't afraid of the difficulties and distances, and if you didn't found your special match yet, of course, let's try. May be? . . .
>
> <name deleted>

BW was intrigued by the e-mail with its rather endearing broken English. Yes, she was a long way off but stranger things have happened. He decided to reply.

Well Hi!

How are you? What a nice note. Thank you. You are correct in your thinking, I am looking for a partner—I'm surprised you didn't think my ad was serious though?? Anyway . . . so, a couple of questions come to mind . . . what do you do for a living? Any brothers or sisters? Where in the Ukraine do you live? Have you ever been to the US? Hey, just curious, what do you look like? Can you e-mail me a picture? Anyway, hope all is well and thanks again for your note.

BW

BW waited with bated breath for a reply. Could this be the start of a romance? He didn't have to wait long. The very next day he received the following reply.

Hi, dear BW,

Thank you very much for your reply. You want to know more about me. Well, I'm <name deleted> 29 years old. I'm a writer. I'm writing a fantastic stories. And this is not only my hobby. I've enter the University of Radio and Electronics and I'm working in the newspaper "Stars". I'm a private correspondent there. My society life is full enough but I can't say the same about my private life. I live alone in my own appartments in the centrum of my beautiful city Kharkov. My parents are farmers and they are living in the village 80km near my city. I like to visit them as often as I could. It's so nice to be at the real nature, to feel fresh air, to sweem in the lake and to walk in the forest. Ukrainian nature is too wonderful to be described with the words. But to feel it with all body and spirit it is nessersary to be together with some very close person. Two persons could feel together much more than one even very romantic . . . . Hope you'll understand me.

<name deleted>

He found the misspellings amusing and this young lady certainly seemed to be very romantic indeed. She included with this e-mail a picture showing a most attractive personage that piqued his interest. This was a lady he was getting more and more interested in. He wrote back to her.

Hi <name deleted>

I must apologize for my delayed response. First I was traveling in Lisbon and then to Madrid and then, last week, I went to Milwaukee, Wisconsin. Anyway, thanks so much for your response and the picture. I find it difficult to believe that a beautiful woman like you isn't married yet but . . . I guess you could say the same about me. My choices in the relationship area have not always been the best. So, I've never written to anyone from the Ukraine, what's it like where you live? Is it a big town or small like a village. I guess the closest I ever got was Leningrad (back in 1984) now called St. Petersburg. From my recollection, that was a big city. So, how is it you speak (and write English) so well? Let me say, I am very impressed. What is your normal day like? Do you have any brothers, sisters or animals? Anyway, I must run—I need to go to an appointment but I did want to at least say hi and return your note. I hope all is well,

BW

BW was already planning ahead and starting to consider a holiday overseas when he received his next e-mail. As you'll see it has a distinctly different tone to it than the earlier ones.

Hi dear,

Thanks for a letter with your concrete view to our relations. Should we decide that a bit later. We must decide now something less important but more current. The matter is that I'm not able to pay for the Internet in a moment. Can you do that for me? An Internet here in the Ukraine is cost $50 a month. Please send me the money via Western Money Transfer. You may get information about them at <web site deleted>. I've call them today and they told me that to send money you have to go to any of their offices. You have to know an exact name and address (as written in the passport) of the person you are sending money to. I'll remind you of my data <name and address deleted>. By chance it would be that guarantee I was waited for. I meen that if you are not going to pay for my Internet that is you are not serious to me. In this situation I must be happy that I understand it not too late. But if you serious, please send me in your next e-mail a transmission number from the Western Union. If you'll do that we will have a fast way (Internet) to discuss our future. Hope to hear from you.

<name deleted>

It was at this point that BW came to me and I, in turn, went to Sparks. *"This has been going on for quite a while now,"* he commented. *"She's probably got quite a few suckers already 'paying for her Internet' and is just looking to up her income. These girls commonly scour dating sites knowing that that is where they'll find the most desperate males. Once they have the men hooked with a nice chat line and a pretty picture they ask for the guy to pay for their Internet service. The guy, thinking he'll lose contact with this charming creature often pays up."* Sparks then smiled and added, *"You might not want to mention to your pal that a lot of these girls are women by picture only. The scam is often run by guys looking to make easy money!"*

The story does not have a happy ending. BW sent the following e-mail on my advice.

Dear <name deleted>

NO

BW

P.S. A friend of mine is a cheating expert and currently writing a book on Internet fraud and scams. I mentioned your e-mail to him and his reply was, "*This is one of the most common Internet frauds known today*" I'm forwarding your e-mails to him for his files. Unfortunately you didn't come up with an original enough scam so you probably won't make the book. Try better next time.

Not surprisingly he is still waiting for a return e-mail. I suspect he may have quite a wait.

Freddy found the whole tale most amusing indeed. *"I wonder if I'd make a good brunette?"* he asked me.

THE PRICE OF SEX ON THE STREET

I'm not talking about prostitution costs here but a much more amusing scam that was reported in the summer of 2002. It is almost certainly an urban myth but was far too amusing not to be included here! Hey, as William Randolph Hearst said, why let the facts get in the way of a good story! And you never know, stranger things have happened! It was said that men were being stopped in the streets of Bogotá, Columbia by glamorous women. The women offered the men a chance to lick their breasts for free. The men helped themselves to what was on offer, after all these were very attractive ladies! Later the men would wake up to find their watches, wallets and often their cars had gone. You see the ladies had dissolved powerful narcotic pills in water and rubbed it into their breasts. Licking the breasts caused the men to fall into a stupor! It was also reported that three women had been arrested. So if you are driving along in Bogotá and are stopped by a fantastic looking female remember that you normally have to have dinner and a few drinks before the lady will let you pounce!

The Charity Raffle

ANOTHER QUICK, NO RISK, MONEY MAKING SCHEME FOR FREDDY IS THE INSTANT charity raffle. Read on and you'll see just how heartless a man like him can be.

The scam is very common indeed in British seaside towns. If you look around though you can find it in just about any place where there are gatherings of people. Watch out for it because if you see it in action you may just be watching Freddy at work.

Freddy enters a bar carrying a large cuddly toy. He asks the bar owner if he can run a raffle in aid of a large charity or, perhaps, a local favorite fund raising organization. The charity he picks will always be a tear jerker such as a poor disabled child or women victims of abuse.

He shows the bar owner letters from charities thanking him for previous donations. The owner, should he care to can even phone in and check on the legality of these letters. *"Life has been kind to me,"* explains Freddy. *"This is just my little way of trying to give something back to it."*

The bar owner assumes that Freddy is just one of the large band of good-thinking people who have taken charity to their heart and who spend a good deal of time raising money for them.

Freddy has little trouble getting permission especially in a small neighborhood bar. The bar owner normally starts everything off by buying a few tickets himself and enticing others to do so as well.

Freddy sells his raffle tickets at a dollar for a little strip of five tickets. The winner gets the big cuddly toy and the money goes to the charity he assures them.

He sells a great many tickets and then makes the draw. The winner, to a huge round of applause is awarded the cuddly toy and Freddy, after thanking everybody for their generosity helping such a worthy cause, leaves the bar.

A while later Freddy sends a copy of a thank you letter from the charity to the bar so that their goodwill can be displayed.

Everybody feels great!

THE SCAM

Freddy does send donations to the charities. The letters are real.

But he doesn't send *all* the donations.

Here's a typical example.

Freddy buys a large cuddly toy. This costs him around three dollars for a *really* big one. He's kept up with old carnival supply contacts. He also buys a book or roll of raffle tickets.

He runs the raffle in the bar and, in a reasonably busy bar, will swiftly sell around fifty strips of tickets. In a very busy bar he can easily sell a couple of hundred dollars worth of tickets. Heck, some people just give him money for the charity and don't even take the tickets. They just want to help out they tell him. He thanks one and all who give him money.

After the draw he leaves the bar.

He deducts his expenses (around four dollars for the toy and the tickets) then sends a third of the remaining money to charity.

The rest goes right into his pocket.

The charity is happy to receive a donation and will send Freddy a nice letter to add to his collection. If the amount of the donation isn't mentioned he may send a copy of the letter to the bar.

The people in the bar are happy because they've donated money to a good cause. One of them even won a good prize to give to his wife or girlfriend!

Freddy is happy with his dubiously acquired profit. Even the Minx is happy as Freddy gives her some of the letters for when she goes out selling her spiritual good luck chain of harmony!

"*It's great,*" he says. "*Everybody is a winner in this one!*"

I really do wonder sometimes how this man sleeps at night.

Freddy works the scam three or four times a day for a week or so. With an average take, by his reckoning, of eighty dollars a bar that's over two thousand dollars for a week of doing 'good' deeds.

It's hard to believe that anybody could be quite that callous. Don't be fooled. Freddy is not a nice guy at all. There are no depths to which he will not sink in order to raise easy money. Quite simply, he does not care about anything or anybody other than himself.

He doesn't think that he's an evil man. He just thinks that you are a stupid one.

And he exploits that for his easy ride through life.

Free Meals
in Freddy's Youth

T HESE DAYS FREDDY ISN'T SHORT OF A DOLLAR OR TWO SO I WAS PUZZLED WHEN
I heard him and the Stoat laughing about beating a restaurant check.

"Why would you do that?" I asked. *"Even you pay your bills!"*

He replied that it was a once a year tradition to celebrate the old days when
he and Sam had had no money. They had still wanted to eat well and so had
come up with various schemes to beat a restaurant check. Each year they re-
ran one of them just for fun.

Ah well, each to their own.

Freddy and Sam were in a good mood, and so they took me over some of
the techniques they used.

TACKY METHODS

They had first looked at the methods already in existence. They'd heard of
people leaving sneakily and just running for it. They had met people who,
after excusing themselves, had crawled through toilet windows. They even
knew one who had broken his leg trying this stunt!

It all seemed a little too athletic, not to say inartistic, to them.

"If I'm going to do it, it has to have a sense of style," Freddy says.

They did consider carrying a cockroach or two so that, during dessert, they
could introduce them and, after claiming horror at seeing the beasts in the
pie, scam the meal for free after promising not to mention it. This idea was
shelved when neither of them wanted to carry the little beasts. It seems both
the Stoat and Freddy have a 'thing' about creepy-crawly stuff. *"Plus,"* added
Sam, *"who wants to spoil a good dessert?"*

They thought long and hard. They finally came up with the following
brazen solution.

TWIN CHECKS

They pick the eatery carefully. An upscale diner is perfect. They particularly look for an establishment where, after eating, you take your bill to a separate counter to pay. These counters are normally positioned right near the door, which is perfect for them.

They wait until the place is pretty busy and there are very few seats available.

Freddy enters first and sits down. He orders a large meal.

Sam enters and, after looking around, asks Freddy if he minds if he joins him at his table. *"Sure, no problem,"* says Freddy. Sam gets out some paperwork from his briefcase and starts making notes on it. *"Just a coffee,"* Sam says to the waiter. *"I'll make up my mind in a moment after I've looked this stuff over."*

The scene is set.

Freddy eats and Sam works. Sam, after a couple of cups of coffee looks at his watch and, deciding he doesn't have time to eat, calls for his check. As it happens Freddy calls for his at just about the same time.

The checks arrive and Sam, engrossed in his work for a moment, drops his check to the table. *"I'll kill that secretary,"* he moans loudly. *"She's got everything wrong!"*

Freddy leaves.

A few moments later Sam packs away his work and, after looking at his watch again, picks up his check. He glances at it and looks horrified. He calls the waiter over. *"I didn't have all this stuff,"* he explodes. *"I just had a couple of cups of coffee!"*

It appears that Freddy, long gone, had picked up the wrong check and, rather than rectify the situation, had just taken advantage of the accident at the cashier's desk.

What can the waiter do? Not much. He'll have to write Sam a new check for the two cups of coffee. Sam pays for the coffee and leaves.

Neither of them care much that the cost of the meal will probably be deducted from the waiter's wages. That's just life.

In a different diner the whole scene is replayed with Freddy and Sam changing roles. For the price of four cups of coffee they get two bumper meals.

"Now that has a certain panache," they agree.

IS THERE A DOCTOR IN THE HOUSE?

They also tried this little number when they wanted a rather more exciting and noisy exit.

Freddy and Sam would be eating at separate tables. Suddenly Sam would groan and fall face forwards into his dessert. Then with a serious of twitches he would crash to the floor.

"*Talk about overacting,*" laughs Freddy.

Freddy would immediately leap to his feet shouting, "*Stand back, I'm a doctor!*" He'd rush to Sam and, after a swift check would say, "*This man is having a massive heart attack! Help me get him to my car. He needs to get to a hospital now!*"

Exit Freddy and Sam.

Whoops, in all the excitement the checks were forgotten.

"*Now that one was fun,*" roars Sam.

I'm still waiting to find out if there is anything these guys won't cheat at.

Psychic Freddy

As I MENTIONED IN THE CHAIN LETTERS CHAPTER, FREDDY KNOWS NEXT TO nothing about computers. But, knowing nothing about a subject has never stopped him from trying to exploit it!

When home computers first came into vogue I had purchased a tiny, but at the time quite revolutionary, Sinclair ZX Spectrum. It's 48k memory and color graphics, displayed on a television screen, were incredible. Who cared that you loaded each program from a cassette tape that took four minutes to do the job?

I even played at putting together some programs myself. Using an adventure designer called *The Quill* I assembled three text adventures that took advantage of a hole in the market; there just weren't any X-Rated games around. The release of *Soho Sex Quest, Herpes or Bust* and *The Search for the Golden Scrotum* didn't set the industry on fire but they did make me a nice chunk of change. Even Freddy seemed pretty proud of me!

One day he turned up at my place and threw a cassette at me. *"Can you let me see what this does?"* he asked. I noted that it was a 'Print your own Horoscope' program and, rather than ask what he was thinking of, loaded it in.

It turned out to be a program you entered your name, date of birth and place of birth into. Then it would show a chart of your horoscope and a number of predictions about your future. It also gave a character reading of the kind of person you were. *"Perfect!"* said Freddy.

That little program which had cost him about ten dollars was about to make him a good pile of money.

Freddy doesn't believe in psychics but he knows that a great many people do. He has also noted that successful psychics don't have to do much except make people feel happy about themselves. That, combined with a little *Cold Reading*, can make a very nice living indeed. Freddy didn't want to become a psychic in real life but thought that a Mail-In Psychic might be fun to try out.

He asked me to come up with a name for the psychic. I have no idea why I said Daniel Jarmain but our psychic was born. Freddy took out ads in several papers reading:

> **Know Your Future!** *Don't be afraid of the unknown.*
> *Daniel Jarmain has helped thousands to make money or find love!*
> *Send your name, date and place of birth and receive a hand drawn*
> *horoscope, a full character reading and personal predictions*
> *for your future!*

The ad also mentioned the seven dollar fee. The audacity was amazing even by Freddy's standards. We were going to copy amateur readings from a simple computer program and sell them for a cost nearly equal to that of the entire program. Nobody would fall for it.

The post and the checks started to come in and Daniel's cottage industry was born.

The horoscopes, because of the computers limited memory, started to repeat. *"Don't worry about it,"* said Freddy. *"Just make some new crap up but make it happy crap!"*

Neither of us knew a thing but that didn't stop us. People started to send repeat orders just to see if their future was changing. Some ladies even offered quite enticing propositions to Daniel. We soon had quite a collection of letters saying that Daniel was the most accurate psychic they'd ever taken a reading from. Freddy soon added a little catalogue of Lucky Crystals and Amulets to go out with the readings. For twelve months it just grew and grew. I couldn't believe it. Freddy just smiled sagely.

Requests came in for Daniel to make personal appearances. That's when we both decided that it was time for Daniel to take a long spiritual retreat. It was growing large enough to a point where I thought law enforcement might like to take closer look at Daniel's business. He was becoming just a little too much like a local celebrity, and so Daniel vanished without a trace.

And yes, it really was that easy!

Freddy also took quite an interest in the 900 psychic lines a few years ago. With these you phone your own personal psychic and for $3.99 or so a minute can be given spiritual advice and incredible insights into your personal life.

Freddy, despite his claims, did not hand pick the psychics. In fact, he's never met any of the psychics who answer the phones. Freddy purchased four lines for around two hundred dollars. For the money he got the numbers that, if called, connected to an agency where nice ladies read from specialized scripts to give readings. Freddy has seen the scripts. *"Actually they are pretty good,"* he notes. Out of the $3.99 per minute the caller pays, Freddy receives around $1.40. The rest goes to the phone company and to the agency. All Freddy has to do is advertise his lines. He won't tell me how much money he makes from his Psychic Hot Line but he still owns it so I can only assume that it's doing just peachy for him!

He advertised it quite heavily in a Gay Magazine for a while seeing that market as being a good one. He talked the magazine owners into having a horoscope column beside his ad. Guess who got the job writing it? As a straight man who didn't believe in psychic phenomena in any form Freddy said he considered me over-qualified for the job of writing his column. He talked me into it and so Claude Starr 'Don't let your future get you twitchy' was born. Basically I looked at the horoscope column in several magazines and rewrote them in a very camp style. Freddy found them highly amusing. As with Daniel I soon had a nice pile of letters forwarded from the magazine telling me how wonderful and talented Claude was. After a year or so I stopped doing the column but am most amused to see that the magazine kept the name, and Claude still publishes a column weekly! So if you are gay and read Claude Starr's Horoscope Column you now know that you're not even reading the *real* fake Claude!

Most amusingly for Freddy one of Claude's bits actually read:

CANCER—Jun 21—Jul. 22
   Had one of those 'get rich quick' phone calls, lately, dear? Been tempted to pop some of your hard earned cash into a sure thing? Be very careful. It's time for you to concentrate on the main things in your life and not to spread yourself too thin financially!

"*Bit close to home isn't it?*" he smiled!

Freddy has, as he admits, just played with the whole psychic thing. It's more of a game for him. He has never been tempted to move into the lucrative world of Curse Removals where a 'psychic' will charge up to $14,000 to take a curse from a person. "*It just skirts a little too close to real jail time,*" he says. Note that it's not the theft and deception that bothers him, simply the higher risk of being caught!

To learn more about this whole world a flip through books like *The Psychic Mafia* by Lamarr Keene will be a big eye opener for you. It's a multi-million dollar a year industry with a sub-culture all of its own.

To any believers I'll honestly say that I can't prove that there is no such thing as psychic phenomena anywhere in the world. But I can show you proof that so much of it is fraud that when top psychic investigator and exposer of frauds, James Randi said that anybody using real psychic ability was doing it the hard way, you'll see what a smart statement he was making.

People have the freedom of choice to believe in whatever they like.

Just try not to make your beliefs expensive forays into stupidity.

"*I predict that whatever you say it'll still be a huge market,*" says Freddy. Sadly, that's one prediction I agree with.

Just for research purposes I sent off a stamped, self-addressed envelope and two dollars in stamps to an advert where a psychic promised me the secret of a happy, trouble-free, life. I received a photograph of an obscure statue and the offer of being able to hire, not buy, a statue to sit in my home. This statue ($30 for each three-month period I kept it) would change my life! "*It'll certainly change your bank account,*" Freddy pointed out. I chose to keep my life just as it was.

It appears that my name is now on a mailing list and I have, to date, received over two hundred packages. Some claim that I am cursed and that priests are praying for me right now. All I have to do is send $30 for them to say the final word of power or the demon will remain forever. Some claim that a satanic cult, for reasons presumably best known to themselves, have placed a curse on me. A group of angels are waiting to remove the curse. Why angels would need $60 to do this is a little beyond me but what do I know? I've been offered Golden Amulets, Neuro Linguistic Programs to bring me wealth, Secrets to the Holy Tabernacle and even an entire catalog (preferred status of course) of junk that will do everything from beat the tables at Vegas to get me out of any speeding fines to ten powerful items that used together will make my legal problems dissolve forever!

Do you want to be on this mailing list?

Some are amusing, some are simple begging letters and some are quite threatening. I can handle being told that Satan himself has targeted me and that unless I send $30 *right now* I could die a painful death. I wonder how many fragile or old people can't handle it and, in fear, send the money.

The only real curse in my life that I can see is being on that mailing list.

For the fake psychic, seers and fortune tellers there is one huge bonus. When exposed as frauds history has taught us that their followers quite simply don't believe it. Their desperate need for contact with an other world or spiritual plane completely outweighs their logical thinking. Some followers are so fragile or lonely that they'll believe in anything. And so the game continues. A week later the exposure is forgotten and the fake psychic carries on working just as before, often to the very *same* people as before. Astonishing but true. This sad example of human frailty is shown in the opera *The Medium* by Gian-Carlo Menotti. The fake medium, a Madame Flora, has an attack of good feeling and informs her sitters that all of her chicanery is a fraud.

> *Listen to me!*
> *There never was a seance!*
> *I cheated you!*
> *Do you understand?*
> *Cheated you, cheated you!*

Do her followers lynch her? Do they beat her? Do they tar and feather her before running her out of town? No. Her poor lost followers merely plead for her to continue.

> *Please let us have our seance,*

Madame Flora!
Just let us hear it once more,
Madame Flora!
This is the only joy we have in our lives,
Madame Flora!

Although this is from a work of fiction its basis is fact. So many frauds have been exposed over the years that it is, for a rational mind, amazing that the business continues to flourish and grow. The fact that it does so shows its appeal to the shadier characters you are reading about in this book.

The New York Police Department highlight fortune tellers in their publication *Scams, Stings and Con Games,* a booklet aimed at senior citizens. It points out that, *"Nobody has 'Magical Powers,"* and warns that, *"A Fortune Teller's 'work' is illegal."* In addition it warns people to keep an eye on their valuables. Under cover of a séance or reading the psychic, seer, or whatever they are calling themselves that week, will steal whatever they can get their hands on.

The psychic world is infested with some of the lowest cheats and hustlers that you can find anywhere.

Do yourself a favor and, for a better life, avoid them.

And that advice is free.

The Million Dollar Beggar

As you are swiftly discovering there really are no depths to which Freddy will not sink in order to raise his *poke*. If he is in dire need then he will actually *beg* for it!

Everybody has seen a beggar or panhandler on the street asking for a cigarette or a couple of dollars.

You may even have given one or two some change. Most people just walk right on by, shaking their head or holding up a hand to say no.

But most beggars aren't Freddy. When he begs he does so in style.

He says that his technique is perfect. He runs no risk and a much smaller chance of rejection. His sell plays superbly upon human nature. He says that it is genius in action.

Having studied it, I'll settle for *criminal* genius in action.

THE SCAM

You are walking along Broadway, in midtown New York City, when you see an older gentleman in some considerable distress. He is well dressed and looks very respectable.

You stop and ask him what is the matter.

He informs you that he was on his way to the train station. He is on his way to visit his sister in Hartford. As it was a nice day he had decided to save the cab fare and walk to the station. It was a big mistake. He's just been mugged and three boys have stolen his wallet.

He starts to cry.

You sit him down on a nearby step, your civic pride seething into rage.

You might suggest calling the police but the old man doesn't want to. It'll take time, he says. He doesn't want to fill in reports, he says. He just wants to get to his sister's, he says. He adds that she'll be so worried if he doesn't turn up. "*She's always telling me how dangerous the city is,*" he may add miserably.

He is very well dressed, probably a retired doctor or businessman perhaps. You feel very sorry for him.

"*Could I ask you a favor?*" he asks. "*I don't like to bother you, but you seem so kind. Could you help me to the station?*"

Of course you will. It's only a few blocks. How could you not help such a nice old fellow. You may even buy him a cup of coffee along the way to help calm him down. Funny how you've completely forgotten about the police by now. It must be the old boy's chatter and constant gratitude for your help.

Then this kindly fellow realizes that his train ticket was in his wallet.

It won't take long before you are offering to help. "*You've been so kind that I hate to ask any more of you,*" he says. "*But if you could lend me the money to buy a new ticket I'd be sure to get a check in the post to you as soon as I get to my sister's. I can even overnight it to you. I hate to ask but I was so looking forward to being with my family again. Her daughter has had a new baby you know.*" A few more tears creep down his cheek.

How are you going to turn him down? After all it's only sixty dollars or so and he's promised to send a check straight away. He takes a business card from his pocket and very carefully writes your name and address on the back of it. He even gives you one of his cards. "*If ever I can help you in return at some point please don't hesitate to call me,*" he says.

You bid each other farewell, he has to rush to get his train. "*Thank you so much,*" he says as he shakes your hand, "*You really have restored my faith in human nature. It's good to know that there are still kind folk around.*"

You leave the old man and walk away with quite a spring in your step. You feel really good about helping out a victim.

When the money doesn't arrive, at first you put it down to forgetfulness. Later, if you bother to check his card, you won't find a number on it that connects anywhere.

The old man was Freddy with a bit of gray in his hair. He doesn't, to the best of my knowledge anyway, have a sister in Hartford.

And he wasn't mugged.

You were.

Appearances can be very deceptive when Freddy is around. People have this ridiculous notion that con men look just like film gangsters. Sleazy, greasy, a cheroot dangling between their lips as they pull a Fedora low over their face. Nothing could be further from the truth.

Freddy will sometimes up the cost of the destination. He may also have the Minx along with him for the ride. Her hysteria is an added bonus, he says.

Cold hearted?

"*Nothing colder than an empty wallet,*" says Freddy.

Be very wary of plausible tales told in the street. Especially from total strangers. Freddy has played this game in various forms.

Sometimes he's the old man you've read about above.

Sometimes he's locked out of his house and the locksmith won't come without promise of payment. Unfortunately his cash and credit cards are inside. He asks you to stand surety for the cash and you agree. He is *very* persuasive. He calls the locksmith on his cell phone. Time passes. The locksmith is taking far longer than you thought so you leave him with the $50 and a promise that he'll send it straight on to you when his door is opened. The locksmith he calls is Sam. The door he's standing outside could be anybody's.

Freddy is an expert *soft touch* man and can run these scams four, five or more times a day. He has a fund of excuses for every occasion.

The tales may differ but the result is always the same.

You'll lose money if you are suckered into the game.

Hot Tips On Cold Cons

WHEN PEOPLE LIKE FREDDY *run a con* THEY ONLY HAVE A MINIMAL CHANCE of being caught for a number of reasons.

The victim, if they realize they've been conned, will be very reluctant to report it. Nearly all cons work by giving the mug an apparent advantage over the con man or over the situation. It's kind of embarrassing to tell the police that you tried to buy a five hundred dollar watch for sixty dollars only to find out it was worthless. It is insane to report to the police that you were part of a cheating team at a card game but messed up the cheat! The victim, often wisely, will decide to keep quiet and eat the loss.

Even if the victim reports the con it is unlikely that they'll be able to give enough information to give any trouble. Have you ever tried to describe an old man you helped out with travel money *two weeks* later? And do you really think the police will expend much time or effort trying to find him just so you might get sixty bucks back? If you push it you'll discover that it is very hard to give an accurate description of what happened. You only know one side of a complex event. It's like trying to describe a movie when you only have one of the actor's lines. Even if the police take it seriously, instead of trying to stifle giggles as is far more common, they know that Freddy and any team members may be anywhere by the time you report the incident.

If the con man is as good as Freddy the victim will, quite simply, not realize that they've been taken. They'll put the loss down to bad luck or any one of a number of excuses.

Your best bet is to, obviously, avoid being conned in the first place. By reading this book carefully you'll be armed with a lot of knowledge about cons but that's not enough. You have to fix two golden points into your mind.

1. A true con game is run by a person who will try to convince you to willingly hand over your money on a *sure-fire* venture of some kind or for some kind of service. The key word is *willingly*. Law enforcement can't do

too much if you willingly hand over your money however stupid you were. At this time of writing (July 2000) a huge expose is being made of Exorcisms for sale by a quasi cult religion here in New York City. Although most sensible people agree that this is a billion dollar a year con, little can be done because people are *willingly* handing over their money!

2. Many con games seem to give the victim (you) an unfair advantage and encourage him (you) to take advantage of it.

All cons regardless of their dressing rely on the same kind of build ups. Read them again and learn *how* and *why* people get hooked in. Never fail to underestimate the absolute coldness of a cheat's heart.

Revisit some of the work so far. Re-read such classics as the Crossed Deck and Three Card Monte.

Don't ever think you are too smart to fall for such tricks and schemes. The world is full of people just like you who have contributed to this multibillion dollar a year industry.

Be very wary of strangers especially if they seem to be offering business or *easy money* opportunities.

Learn to recognize the build up and its danger signs.

Then walk away.

However *sure fire* it looks.

Perhaps the best advice to avoid a lot of the cons is to never take advantage of somebody else's misfortune. Honesty is one of the con man's worst enemies. Greed is one of his greatest weapons.

If you think you've already been taken by a con some time then console yourself with the fact that your loss was probably not as bad as that of Andre Poisson. He was the French businessman to whom Count Victor Lustig, self-proclaimed king of the con men, *sold* the Eiffel Tower. Lustig never revealed how much he made from the sale but, as Poisson failed to report the con for fear of public humiliation, Lustig went back and sold it again to another businessman!

Even Freddy talks about Lustig with some degree of awe in his voice.

Well the time has come.

It's time to sit down and play some cards.

Ready?

IT WAS AN *ALL-NIGHTER* THAT LASTED FOR *DAYS!* OUR WORLD WAS THE TABLE TOP... OUR SUN WAS THE SINGLE LAMP OVERHEAD! -- I'D RECRUITED MY USUAL *CARD MOB!*

"*SAM THE STOAT* WAS MY *SIDEWALKER!* HIS HOLD-OUTS, OFFICE WORK, SPOOKING AND SUBWAY DEALS WERE A *SYMPHONY IN SUBTLETY.*"

"HE WAS BACKED UP BY *BLACKIE...* WHO TOOK A BREAK FROM THE TRACK TO *SHILL* FOR US."

"AS OUR *BANKROLLER,* THE *PRINTER* PLAYED IT SAFE! HIS *LETTUCE* WAS ON THE *LEVEL* AN' THE *SNIDE SAWBUCKS* STAYED HOME."

"*CANDY* STOCKED US WITH SNACKS AS SHE'D *HOVER* TO *COVER* OUR *ACTION* USING HER ATTRACTION AS *DISTRACTION!*"

"*MY MUSCLE MAN* WAS A GOON THEY CALL *THE DOCTOR...* YOU'LL SOON FIND OUT *WHY!*"

"*THE POT WAS BOILING OVER!* THE COWBOYS WERE CARELESSLY SURRENDERING THEIR STIPENDS, GIDDILY GALLUPING TO THEIR DOOM LIKE LEMMINGS OFF A CLIFF! THEY BARELY NEEDED *OUR* HELP TO KISS THEIR CASH GOOD-BYE!"

"*AND THEN IT HAPPENED!* THE *STOAT* HAD JUST WON THE POT AND ONE BINDLESTIFF GOT TOO BIG FOR HIS BRITCHES!"

HERE YA GO, PALLY! LADY LUCK'S ON *YOUR* SIDE!

"HIS MOVE WAS TOO SLOW AND THE COMPANY TOO FAST! THE *DOCTOR* DIAGNOSED A CHRONIC CASE O' *CHECK COPPING!*"

I SAW DAT!

"THE 'PATIENT' SUFFERED FROM TOO MUCH *AMATEUR* IN HIS BLOOD! IT REQUIRED A *MEDICAL EMERGENCY!*"

I C'N NEVER *FARO SHUFFLE* AGAIN!

WE HAD TO REMOVE AN *UGLY GROWTH* FROM THE GAME... *HIM!*

SCRIPT/ART: *ikw*

Cheating At Cards

After a journey through the bar, the street and the fairgrounds and carnivals we get to one of Freddy's main jobs. The shady world of the card table. Actually it's not always that shady. Cheats have been seen at the plushest Bridge clubs as well as the lowest dives. In fact Contract Bridge holds the dubious honor of being the game that has more cheating in it than any other! Cheats have infested every level of play from the friendly bar and Friday night games to the highest stake casino games.

They are everywhere. The one thing they all have in common is that they all do it for the same reason.

Money.

Freddy knows a great deal about cheating at cards. He should. It's been his life. Even he admits that he doesn't know it all but it's a fair bet that he knows more than you do! Now he's going to share all his knowledge with you. He reckons that your best protection against being hustled is to teach you enough about the moves so that, while you may not *see* the move in action, you have a fighting chance of knowing that *something* happened.

He'll teach you how to spot marked cards (more common than you could imagine), how the ruses and subterfuges are pulled, the mechanical aides a cheat may use, the unnatural or strange misdirections required for some scams, the secret language of the cheats and a great deal more.

Don't ever expect to catch an expert *second deal* or deck switch. But you should learn enough to know that it *may* have happened.

And that should be enough for you to get up and walk away from the game.

With some of your money left.

"Trust your friends but cut the cards."

———•———

old but very smart advice

Types Of Card Cheat

FREDDY IS A PROFESSIONAL CHEAT. AS I'VE SAID, THESE REAL HARDENED HUSTLERS are, thankfully for you, relatively rare. They normally only play for serious money. Unless you are a high-stake player it's unlikely that you'll run into Freddy at a poker table.

But cheating at cards does occur at all levels. Freddy splits cheats into three types.

THE AMATEUR CHEAT

This man really is a low-life. He lacks the digital expertise of a Freddy and is not prepared to put in the long hours of practice required to achieve it. But that doesn't stop him from fleecing his victims with blatant fraud and *fixed* cards.

His victims are normally his friends and acquaintances. In England you'll see him in the pub playing *Three Card Brag* or *Shoot Pontoon*. In America you'll see him in the Friday night poker game. He loves friendly 'get togethers'. The amateur cheat gets away with his unskilled work because nobody suspects him. He's just a *Lucky Jim* who happens to win more often than he loses.

Just because somebody is your friend doesn't mean that they may not try to cheat you.

THE SEMI PROFESSIONAL CHEAT OR HUSTLER

The semi professional cheat still hasn't learned the exquisite sleight-of-hand that Freddy can achieve but does use cheating to earn part of his living. He tends to be good at the games he plays and will use *paper* (marked cards) and other mechanical ruses to give himself a winning edge.

He often has a lot of fun bets to offer. You'll notice, for reasons that are apparent to you now, that he rarely loses at them. Unlike the amateur who sticks close to home, he will foist his bets upon anybody who is prepared to listen.

THE PROFESSIONAL CHEAT

The real professional cheat is a hard hearted and cold thinking human being. He earns his living purely from playing cards and *gambling*. He doesn't care who he busts out to keep up his lifestyle.

He practices for hours each day and, after many years of study, can do just about anything with a deck except make it sing (and I wouldn't take a bet against Freddy on that!). Although he tends to specialize in just one or two moves as his *big guns* he is often very proficient at most. This master of every angle is called a *mechanic*.

He will not only be superb at sleight-of-hand but will also know tons of bar bets and fun money propositions. He will be an expert con man who'll do anything to get the money.

The professional rarely stays in one place for long. He will make his kill then leave for pastures new.

The professional may also work with a team known as a *card mob*. It will consist of himself, a *bankroller* (who provides money to set up a score), a couple of shills (to steer likely victims into a game) and, maybe, a pretty girl. The girl will often be a hooker and she will 'distract' the victim in her own unique way to both cover moves in the game and to give the game partici-pants time to get away cleanly afterwards. The team will often have a *muscle man* to keep any arguments under control.

The professional cheat may also employ a local semi professional. The semi professional will know enough about the area to know where the real money is likely to be found and may well be able to provide an introduction to some games. If he sits in the game he can also provide valuable misdirection at critical moments. The semi professional has to be very careful if he's sitting in the game. If he isn't careful he could be being hooked with a *crossed deck* or similar ploy. There truly is no honor among thieves!

The cheat who plays in casino style games won't be covered in this book. They want the big casino take. Despite ever increasing security there are teams who are highly successful at this somewhat dangerous occupation and, as such, good *Crossroaders* are very highly regarded. Their work is, however, beyond the scope of this tome. For a look into their shady world a good in-troduction can be found in the various books on the subject available from the *Gamblers Book Club* (www.gamblersbookclub.com) in Las Vegas.

For now we'll just stick to the private games where you are more likely to find Freddy and his cohorts.

Hold on, the roller coaster ride is entering a really bumpy section!

Marked Cards

THE PROFESSIONAL WILL TRY TO AVOID USING MARKED CARDS OR, AS THEY ARE called in the trade, *paper*. The rationale behind this thinking is that the first thing an experienced gambler will check is the cards if he thinks cheating is going on. Since many experienced gamblers know how to check for marks the professional will do his utmost to make sure that there is no *work* for them to find. This doesn't mean that they never use them, they just prefer not to.

Another reason they prefer to avoid them is that, in large stake games, the deck is often changed. It could be changed once an hour or, as is very common in big money games, changed at the whim of the dealer who can call for new cards at any time. Unless the entire supply of cards has been marked (and, yes, it has been done) then the marked deck may only be in play for an hour or so. Hardly enough time to make the risk worthwhile *unless* the cheat is going for the kill with an *Iron Man,* of which more later.

The amateur cheat on the other hand uses marked cards very commonly. Often it's the first thing he thinks of. Even more often it is the only kind of cheating that he is aware of. He knows that marked cards are freely available at joke and novelty stores. If he can't find a commercially made deck it isn't too much work to mark up a deck or two himself. Nobody complains when he brings out his deck and offers a few hands of cards at the club. The other players are happy to join in for an hour or so fun. Nobody suspects their pal of cheating them! This has been confirmed to me by the large collection of marked cards I've picked up over the years from private games. On some, the marks are so amateurish that it is amazing to me that nobody else spotted them. This collection is mute testimony to the rule that if you aren't looking for something you are unlikely to find it.

Marked cards vary from the incredibly obvious (if you know what to look for) to the very sophisticated. The prices can vary from two dollars a deck to two thousand dollars a deck. The amateur is much more likely to be using one in the two to ten dollar range.

Shade work. Note the angel's wing. Markings are exagerrated.

Flash work.

Line work. Note the "belt" around the angel's waist.

Brace work.

Let Freddy guide you through a collection of different ways to mark up a deck.

MARKING METHODS

Shades

A tiny bit of the back design of the card is darkened, almost imperceptibly on a good deck, by using a solution of an aniline dye (obviously the same color as the back of the deck being marked!) diluted with alcohol. Another technique, using the same dye, is to shade the entire back of the card leaving only one tiny area unshaded. This type of shading is called *flash* work.

Blockouts

Part of the white part of the back design is filled in with a color matching the main design color of the card. This is, effectively, strong shade work.

Line Work

Thin lines are added into the design appearing to be part of it. These extra lines can be so subtle as to almost defy detection unless you really know how to check a deck. They can also be as obvious as the deck I picked up once in an English pub that had been crudely marked with a ball-point pen. Sometimes, instead of adding extra lines, an existing line will be thickened up. This type of line work is called *brace work* and, once more, can be very subtle or quite heavy.

Cutouts

Here the cards are marked in a completely opposite manner to blockout work. A small part of the design has been carefully scratched away to leave a small white area. These cards are also known, thanks to the white flecks that make up the marks, as *Dandruff.*

Border Work

Here the bordering edge of the design is thickened at various spots causing a readable bulge to appear.

How to Cheat at Everything

Sunning the Deck

The cheat will lay the high cards from the pack out in strong sunlight for a time. This gives the cards a very slight yellowish tinge. With practice these high cards can be spotted from the untinged low cards in a game situation.

Steaming the Deck

A primitive method to get a similar effect to the sunned deck is to run a low heat iron over the back of the high cards of a deck. This removes some of the glaze from the cards making them duller in appearance to the others. Once more they can be spotted in a game.

Cutout work. Note the large white space "cut out" of the curl above the angel's head.

Sorts

If the deck has an all over back design the cheat can assemble, from various decks, a pack where the high cards can be told from the low ones. The reason for this is that the pattern will vary slightly from deck to deck. Mixing high cards from one deck with lows from another creates a deck of *sorts*. Because of variations in color and design positioning *sorts* can also be made from bordered cards.

Border work.

High Line Work and Punching

The cheat marks the court cards in his deck using the back of an Exacto Knife blade or a dull blade. Each court card has a black line around the face design. The cheat will press the knife lightly along a short section of the line. Not enough to cut it, but enough to put a tiny ridge into the cardboard. The ridge cannot be seen but it can be felt from the back. This type of marking is very useful for games like Blackjack or the English variation, Pontoon. Not only do you know if your opponent has high cards but you know whether to *twist* (take a card) or not. In a game like Pontoon where the dealer chooses to take a card not regardless of the total showing this can give the dealer a big advantage. Simply by feeling with his thumb as he deals, the cheat knows the distribution of court cards in play.

A more sophisticated type of tactile work is known as *Punching the Deck*. Here a specialized tool is used to create tiny bumps on the back of the cards. The

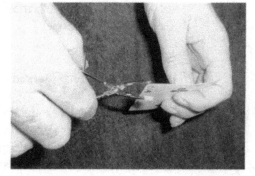

A Punch tool.

various positions of the bumps on a card mean that the entire deck can be marked for value and even, if required, suit. Just knowing the distribution of high and low cards can give a devastating advantage in a game. Knowing the values of all, or even some, of the cards is destruction for the mug.

Honest Marked Cards

Any pack that has been played with over a long period of time will have inevitable imperfections on some of the cards. Over the years Freddy has seen people playing with cards that were bent, stained with beer and, in some cases, even torn. It did not seem to be apparent to them that this would mean that a cheat could know the position of certain cards at any one time.

The cheat doesn't need to mark all the cards. Just knowing the position of a few gives him a huge advantage.

The cheat can also create an *honest* pack by purchasing several decks. Often design position and overall back color can be dramatically different between decks. Buy a dozen decks of Bicycle playing cards from a sale and compare them. You'll see what I mean. By mixing or *sorting* various packs the cheat can create a quite sophisticated *fair* marked deck.

Luminous Readers

These are pretty much a joke amongst the professionals. A red backed deck is marked with luminous red or green dye. Since the marks are invisible they tend to be huge. When viewed through a red filter the marks suddenly stand out like a sore thumb. Never play cards with anybody wearing red sun glasses, a red visor, or one who makes notes on a clear red clipboard. You can even buy special contact lenses to wear when using such a pack but the principle has become so well known that their use has all but died out. If you suspect such a pack is in use look at it under a red light or through a red piece of cellophane. This is the least likely of all the marked packs that you may come up against! The only reason I mention it here is the nice deck I've recently added to my collection, picked up at a Bridge Tournament. They may be rare but, like Model T Fords, there are still a few around!

Commercial Marked Decks

Your local joke and novelty or magic store will almost certainly have for sale a number of commercially marked cards. These cards, complete with instructions on how to read the marks, can be used by amateur magicians for their tricks. The cards are sold strictly '*for amusement only*'.

They can be a lot of fun. Unless you don't know they are marked! Freddy

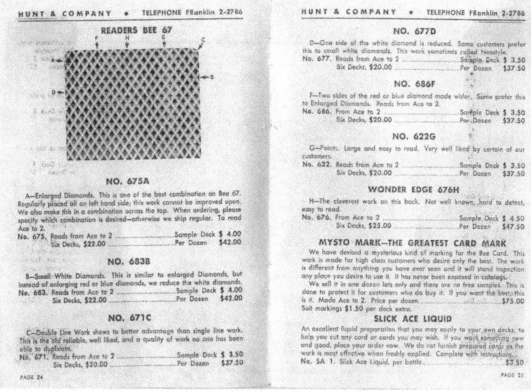

Commercially-made marked cards available mail-order. For more catalog pages turn the page.

has lost count of the number of these decks he's seen in small money games over the years. When questioned about the deck the cheat will typically respond with, *"You're joking, I found these cards in a cupboard and thought it would save me buying cards for tonight's game! I wish I'd known they were marked, I could have made a fortune!"*

Pictures

Cards are often used to advertise products. The back design will be an advert for a new drink or beer, perhaps cigarettes or even an airline company. Often these designs will be *One-Way*. This means that a card turned end for end will be noticeably upside down. The amateur cheat will exploit this by having certain cards facing one way and others the other. Often he splits high and low cards this way. For a number of hands at least, until the cards become mixed again, he will be able to tell more about your cards than he should. He can also manipulate these cards during a game to leave just a few cards reversed amongst others. Remember he only needs to know the position of one or two cards to win.

It is worth noting that if you are traveling by aeroplane and ask for cards

POPULAR READERS

No. 403 Rider

RIDER

A—All in left-hand corner in one place. Considered the best ever placed on this back. Very good for Stud.
B—Excellent blockout work on the birds. Large and easy to read.
C—Clever Work in flower at side-center of card. Good for Skin.
D—Many prefer this side combination. Also good for Skin.
E—Smart work on the left-hand corner figure.
F—Fine blockout in the flower at end.
G—Excellent combination on the grass in center circle.

No. 403. Rider A-B-C-D-E-F or G
Sample Deck ....$ 3.00
Six Decks 17.00
Per Dozen 33.50

NEW FAN

A—Easy to read and impossible to find. This is the best ever placed on Fan Back.
B—Brace work in Frame. Hard to detect, yet, large and easy to play.
C—Perfect shade work on the Fan.
D—Work is on the hook at side of card. One of the best. Good for Skin.
E—Blockout around inner border of Fan. Very hard to detect.
F—Fine blockout around outer edge. One of the smartest on this back.
G—Excellent blockout combination on the straight line near left corner.

No. 405. New Fan A-B-C-D-E-F or G
Sample Deck ....$ 3.00
Six Decks 17.00
Per Dozen 33.50

No. 405 New Fan

No. 407 Racer

RACER

A—An old reliable combination. Blockout which is very good. One of our best sellers.
B—In the circle. Well liked and good for Stud.
C—On extreme edge.
D—Clever work on the dots at end of card.
E—Fine blockout in wheel at left corner.

No. 407. Racer A-B-C-D or E
Sample Deck ....$ 3.00
Six Decks 17.00
Per Dozen 33.50

Suit marking supplied on any of the above cards at an additional charge of 75¢ per deck. When ordering specify name and letter of combination. Example: Rider A.

A deposit of ½ must be sent with all orders.

FAVORITE STANDARD READERS

No. 413 Bee 35

Clever blockout. Goes over big. A to 6 only. No suit. At left corner.

No. 414 Club

A—Fine blockout in left corner of card.

B—Another clever blockout combination, entirely new on this back.

No. 430 Aviator

A—Clever blockout work near the edge.

B—Ultra clever blockout in extreme corner.

C—A very good side combination for Skin.

No. 999 Steamboat

These are the genuine Steamboat Cards and are not to be confused with the inferior imitations widely offered.

No. 419 Angel Back

A—Our famous line work. Enough said. Very fast.

B—Well concealed line combination on shoulder.

No. 421 Circle

A—Fast blockout work in circle.

B—Neat blockout in left corner near border. Very fast but hard to detect.

All cards listed on this page are favorite standard brands. Supplied in red or blue back, marked for size only. Suit marking supplied at an additional charge of 75¢ per deck.

Sample Deck **$3.00**   Six Decks **$17.00**   Per Dozen **$33.50**

A deposit of ½ must be sent with all orders.

you will often be given a deck whose back design advertises the airline you are traveling on. These decks are invariably one-way decks.

This ruse sounds incredibly obvious but, as we've noted, it is often the obvious that is overlooked. A very wise man once said, *"If you want to hide in a crowd, paint yourself red and stand at the front"*

Edge Marks

These cards are marked on the edges. No marks are visible on the front or back of the cards but the cheat can read the deck from the edge. These cards are normally of the type with an all over back design where the edges can appear speckled because of the design bleeding through. These cards would appear to have little use to the cheat until you meet a guy who wants to cut the pack against you for a bet. He can cut high or low by *reading* the edge of the deck. Thankfully these cards are amongst the easiest to spot. Square the deck and look at the long edges. The marks will appear as a series of erratic dots.

Juice Work

This is a real dangerous deck for you. The marks are next to impossible to spot *even* if you know what to look for. The Juiced deck is marked with an application of ink heavily diluted with alcohol. If the *juice* (diluted ink) has been properly prepared it will not actually mark the card in the accepted sense. It will only produce a slight change in the sheen of the card. Juice decks are marked with large dashes and dots, which cover the entire back of the card. The marks are invisible to all unless you have learned how to read them. Even an experienced *juice worker* may take several weeks to get used to a new deck. Seeing the marks is a bit like seeing those strange 3D Pictures that were all the rage in the 90's. You have to look and focus beyond the card while looking right at it. It's by no means easy. An experienced juice worker can read the cards across a room. Such packs have fooled experienced casino personal who, even after being told the cards were marked, were unable to find a thing!

Luckily for you such cards are not readily available. Good ones are also *very* expensive.

You'd have to be really unlucky to come up against a juice deck in an average card game.

Seals

Don't think that because you are opening a brand new deck, still sealed in its box, that it can't be marked. A clever cheat can, using a razor blade, open the box at the bottom. He'll pry open the cellophane after steaming it then carefully use the blade to open the bottom of the box. Once the pack is marked he can reseal it into the box using contact adhesive. Have you ever checked the wrong end of a card case when opening it? I bet you do now.

Seals are often used as a convincer.

In a private game, where it would appear that some suspicion is starting to form, the cheat can call out, *"These cards are getting just a little unlucky, waddya say we open up a fresh deck to change the luck?"* He may even send out a shill to 'buy' new cards. The shill returns (not from the shop but from the cheat's car) with some *seals*. The player who seemed most suspicious can open the deck themselves. The game goes on. Still with marked cards.

The cheat can also buy, if he knows where to shop, resealing kits. These come with correct cellophane and stamps for the deck required.

A sealed deck is no guarantee that the cards are safe!

SPOTTING MARKED CARDS

Most marked cards can be detected by the very simple *Riffle Test.*

Hold a nicely squared deck face down and riffle through the cards by running your thumb down a short edge. Look carefully at the back design as you riffle through the cards. If there is no marking then the back design will stay still. If there is a form of visible marking the back design will seem to move. You may see tiny flecks jumping around or patches of color appear and disappear. This is the same principle used in children's *flicker books* where a series of pictures are animated by flicking through the pages. Frank Garcia, a fine New York City magician and gambling expert, dubbed this test *Going to the Movies.*

When doing the test, look carefully in the top right hand corner of the back area. This is where most cards are marked. Since the deck may only be marked at one end make sure to repeat the test at both ends. Do the test several times. First close to your eyes, then from a distance. Some cards are marked so lightly that they will pass a casual riffle test.

Finally, feel the backs of the cards with a light touch to try to detect any bumps.

During play watch the dealer. An inexperienced *paper worker* may give himself away in a number of ways. He may deal slowly to give himself time to see the cards. He may seem to study other players cards just a little too closely. He may fan out the top few cards of the deck when waiting for a decision during a game of Blackjack, Pontoon or Draw Poker. He wants to know what is coming up.

He will also make illogical or lucky bets far too often and, suspiciously, win them all. The smart semi professional will only use the marks sparingly and

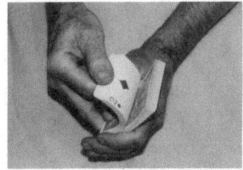

"Going to the Movies."

is *much* harder to spot. A professional juice player will kill you!

If you have *any* doubts get out of the game.

MISCONCEPTIONS ABOUT MARKED CARDS

Nearly everybody has heard about marked cards but, until now, not so many have known *how* they were marked. They just assume that every card is marked for suit and value. That's just not so.

The cheat, trying to avoid detection, will mark the cards as little as possible.

Most marked cards used in Blackjack and Pontoon for example are only marked for high and low. In other words the high cards have a tiny marking while the low ones are normal. Just knowing whether the top card of the deck is high or low can give the cheat an enormous advantage during the game. The marks, in this case, can be so small as to pass all but the most careful of riffle tests.

Also, despite the popular belief common even among experienced magicians, *any* cards can be marked whether they be plastic, linen covered or good old cardboard.

Some years ago a cheat cleaned up a huge Baccarat game using cards that had plain white backs. His secret was that he'd marked the cards with a very soft application of white ink. His marks looked like tiny dull white spots against the shinier surface of the cards.

Nobody suspected a thing!

MARKING CARDS DURING PLAY

Remember the *honest marked cards* we talked about earlier? A cheat like Freddy won't wait for such a pack to appear by chance.

He'll create one.

The following methods are used by amateurs and professionals alike to gain advantage over you.

Nailing.

Nailing

The cheat will mark the cards in his hand by digging his nail into the edge of the card. This leaves a small dent on the edge of the card that, with practice, can be *read* over a considerable distance. Freddy will try to mark the card on both long edges so that his work can be spotted whichever way up the card is. He will, generally, only mark the cards for high and low.

Waving

The cheat places a wave like bend into the card by holding it between three fingers. The two outside fingers are on top of the card, the middle one is below. With a slight pressure the *wave* is applied. These waves will be very slight. Once more high cards can be detected from low ones.

Waving.

Daubing

Daub is a pasty colored substance available to the cheat. A crude daub can be made by rubbing wax or Vaseline with cigarette ash. Some of the modern ladies blushes, from cosmetic counters, make excellent daubs and are often used by professionals.

The daub will be hidden somewhere that the cheat has easy access to. Some will keep it under a button on their jacket. Some will keep it in a small tin in their pocket. Others may simply stick a small blob of it to the underside of the playing table!

When he wants to mark up the deck the cheat will get some daub onto his finger tip. He can then leave

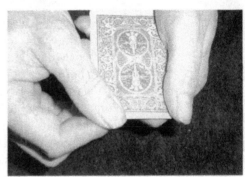

Daubing.

a tiny smear of the daub on the backs of the cards he is holding. A good *daub worker* or *smear man* will leave only the very faintest of smudges that are almost undetectable to the human eye. Your human eye that is. Not his.

In a true 'improv' situation a cheat can create a daub using cigarette ash and saliva. It doesn't last long and can be messy. But, in skilled hands, it works. Watch out for a dealer who constantly licks his fingers.

Freddy tells me of a unique form of daubing he saw many years ago. It was used by a man who had slicked his hair back with a form of greasy gel. The fellow would rub his hands through his hair to transfer grease to his fingers. He would then daub the cards using the grease. This had an effect of dulling the cards where he marked them. A few years ago I was asked to appear on a television program called *Casino Wars* to discuss cheating. It was most amusing to see this very method being described by one of the other cheat experts as something brand new!

Sanding

The cheat will have a tiny, and I mean tiny, piece of fine grade sandpaper stuck to his palm just below his first finger. The cheat will pull the edges of the cards he wishes to mark along the paper.

Sanding.

Card edges become dirty with use. The sandpaper cleans them up making their position apparent to anybody (read 'the cheat') who may be looking for them.

The cheat may conceal his little piece of sandpaper inside a Band-Aid that has had a hole cut through it to allow the sandpaper to do its work.

Pegging

Pegging is an impromptu form of *high line* or *punch* work. The cheat will leave tiny bumps in the cards by pressing his finger nail into them. This not the same as *nailing* where the edge of the card is marked. The bump here is put somewhere in the top right hand corner of the card where it can be felt during a deal. The cheat will try to *peg* both ends of the card in case it gets turned around in a shuffle. If he just manages to *peg* the four aces in an impromptu game of Blackjack or Pontoon he is going to murder you!

Some cheats will use a *pegger* or *pegging tool*. This is a small point, often a tiny drawing pin, attached to their finger with a Band-Aid. The point is on the inside and it looks just as the cheat has cut his finger and covered it with a plaster. In fact he is using the pegging tool to mark the cards. Most professionals try to avoid such toys as they, if found, provide *stone wall* evidence of cheating. But these toys are used by amateurs. Always keep a close eye on a man with a Band-Aid on his finger.

SPOTTING MARKED CARDS IN A GAME

To spot *waving, sanding* or *nailing* square up the cards and look down the long edges of the deck. The marks and bends will stand out.

To spot *pegging* feel the backs of the cards carefully. It may slow down the game but, if you discover the work, everybody but the cheat will thank you for doing so.

To stop *daub* work change the cards often. This puts off a *painter* (a daub worker) as, just when he's got a deck marked up, he has to start all over again.

Always check both ends of the deck. Although the cheat likes to mark both ends of the cards he will certainly settle for marking just one end. When his marks are the right way up he has his advantage in play. A cheat will take *any* advantage he can!

WHAT TO DO IF YOU FIND MARKS

You suspect from the play that a man is using marked cards against you. On

How to Cheat at Everything

your deal you casually give the deck a riffle and notice tiny marks jumping up and down the border of the design. What do you do?

A lot depends on whether or not you think you can win a fight against the cheat and any possible friends he may have with him. For all you know you could be sitting in a *Hot Seat Game!*

The best advice is to take the coward's way out.

Leave the game. You won't be able to get back what you've lost but at least you'll walk away with some of your money.

Raise a ruckus and you may be lucky to walk away at all. Unless you like being carried around on a stretcher just walk away. *Any* cheat caught red handed is a dangerous person. Treat them with extreme caution.

Marked cards are primarily the weapon of the amateur cheat.

There are literally hundreds of thousands of such decks sold each year. One can only guess at the number of home-made or marked-in-play decks.

You are more likely to be cheated by an acquaintance with marked cards than by any other method.

Always give the deck a good check before a game.

Always insist on a new deck after an hour or so of play.

Be constantly on the look out for bent, chipped or torn cards.

If you suspect marks are in play just leave the game.

As Freddy says, "*The man who can read them from the back is going to win.*"

A FINAL AMUSING TALE OF MARKED CARDS

Unlike the movies the cheat, in real life, rarely loses to the golden haired hero. In the real world the good guys lose. So a tale of a cheat being cheated is always a joy. The following is one of Freddy's favorite such tales when swapping stories with his friends.

A *paper* worker had a deck marked so subtly that it could pass even the most studied of *riffle tests*. He had practiced for over six months just to be able to read it. We're talking some seriously fine marking here.

He was sitting in a Poker game with some businessmen and was winning heavily. One of the businessmen, an amateur magician, was sure that marked cards were being used.

He knew a little about cheating and applied a riffle test to no avail. He scrutinized the edges of the cards but found nothing. Against any advice I would have given him he decided to put the *frighteners* on the player who was cheating.

In the course of gathering up the cards for his deal he quickly memorized five cards and made sure that they ended up on the top of the deck. His experience as an amateur magician made this a reasonably easy task for him.

"*These cards are marked!*" he suddenly announced. "*And what's more, I can prove it!*"

He pretended to read the back of the top card and called it out before turning it over. He proceeded to do this for four more cards before throwing the deck down in disgust. Of course he wasn't reading the marks but just turning his five memorized cards!

The game ended with arguments and mutual suspicion. Nothing could be proved except that *somebody* in the game had introduced marked cards.

The cheat collared the businessman in the bar. *"How much did you lose?"* he asked.

"Three hundred," replied the businessman. *"I'd like to know who put the damned deck in the game."*

"It was my deck," said the cheat, *"and I'll give you back your three hundred if you'll just answer one question."*

"What's the question?"

"Well I know how you read the values on the cards but how the hell did you know the suits?"

The deck had only been marked for value!

Freddy always collapses with laughter when he tells this story!

Twinkles

BY USING MARKED CARDS THE CHEAT CAN GAIN AN ALMOST UNBELIEVABLE advantage over you simply by knowing which types of cards you are holding.

He can gain the same advantage with unmarked cards.

By using a *Twinkle*.

A *twinkle* (also known as a *glim, light* or *shiner*) is a reflective surface that allows the cheat to see the faces of the cards, from underneath, as he deals. A tiny convex mirror hidden in the right place will reflect the entire index corner of a card during the deal. This gives the unscrupulous operator the same advantage as if he were using a see-through deck! That's the kind of advantage that can cost you big money.

It follows that cheats have spent long periods of time devising ingenious methods to position and disguise their mirrors from other players in a game and yet keep them in a position where they can be used.

Here are some of the ways that Freddy has seen used to conceal twinkles over the years.

MASKING THE GLARE

The Chip

Many card games are played with *chips* instead of money. The cheat will attach a piece of reflective tape (Mylar) to the back of one of his chips. This chip is placed on top of a pile of ordinary chips, which is then surrounded by taller stacks of chips. The taller stacks conceal the twinkle from the other players.

Since his chips are in front of him it is natural for the cheat, while dealing, to hold the deck higher than

Chip Twinkle.

Mirror Twinkle.

his chips. As each card is dealt the cheat can catch the reflection of its index corner.

At any time he can hide the fake by turning it over as he messes with his chips.

If the game is being played with real money the Mylor twinkle can be stuck to the back of a coin or onto the corner of a bank note.

The Cigar

In this case the twinkle is a highly polished drawing pin or thumb tack. Before the game the cheat will push the twinkle into the end of a cigarette or, more normally, a cigar. Because the twinkle will be smaller than the diameter of the cigar the cheat can still light and smoke it. But, by keeping it clipped between his fingers as he deals, he can not only smoke it but see the cards as he does so as well.

The Pipe

Twinkles have even been fitted into the bowls of pipes. The innocent looking pipe is left on the table angled so that the cheat can use the concealed mirror to see the cards as they are dealt.

Ordinary Twinkles

Any highly polished surface can be used as a twinkle. A cup of black coffee correctly positioned makes a great reflective surface. A metal cigarette lighter or cigarette case can also be used. Even the table surface itself can give enough information to Freddy if it is nicely polished. Always cover a playing surface with a nice cloth. If the light is in the right place even a tiny, spilled, puddle of beer or soda can give information to the well-trained eye.

Professional Twinkles

The professional cheat may well use any of the above if he thinks he can get away with them.

But most professionals will use either a piece of jewelry (a pinkie ring is very common) or a tiny, convex, mirror ranging in size from about a penny to a quarter. This mirror will be kept hidden in their dealing hand, palmed or stuck with wax to base of the little finger.

As the cheat deals he will have a habit of pulling back the top card slightly before dealing the card. This action is fairly common amongst fair players but here it gives the cheat time to see the lower index corner of the card in his twinkle.

The professionals prefer this type of twinkle to any other because it is so easy to get rid of. At any time it can be ditched in a pocket as he reaches for more money or his cigarettes. If he just wants to *flash* an empty hand it can be dropped into his lap to be retrieved moments later.

A lot of professional cheats use the small mirror from a dental inspection tool for the purposes of *inspecting* the cards. "*Saw a queen once that needed a cavity filled,*" jokes Freddy.

Gambling supply houses (yes, such stores exist) can supply twinkles in many forms. The professionals avoid such toys as, if discovered, they provide absolute evidence of cheating.

Jewelry Twinkles

Although most of this book is written as if the cheat were a man it must be noted that the trade of cheating and hustling is not a male bastion alone. There are many cold-hearted lady cheats as well. Playing against a pretty woman or nice little old lady can be just as deadly as playing against Freddy.

Both men and women commonly wear jewelry. A highly polished pinkie ring can make a fabulous twinkle. That delightful bangle the lady is wearing may have been paid for *reflectively*.

Tiny Twinkles

A tiny piece of Christmas tree decoration lodged under a fingernail can, with considerable practice, be used as a twinkle. It carries an advantage of being almost undetectable and can be lost easily, simply by dropping it onto a carpet-covered floor. Don't think that a dedicated cheat won't put in the considerable practice time required to perfect this technique. A well known gambling detective, investigating allegations of cheating in a game, was fooled for a long time by a hustler using this exact technique.

Because a twinkle can be so small it can be concealed just about anywhere. Twinkles are commonly concealed in cigarette packs or matchbooks. A twinkle has even been found set into the head of a toothpick!

Don't allow *anything* to be left on a playing surface that isn't part of the game. It won't stop a chip twinkle or, indeed, a palmed or jewelry twinkle. But it will stop some of the other toys.

HOW TO SPOT A "FOUR EYES"

A *four eyes* is a cheat who uses a twinkle to gain advantage over you in a game.

Like a *paper* worker he will often, especially if inexperienced, give clues about his work with his betting technique. If he seems to be almost psychic in his play it may be due to more than a spiritualistic training program.

Another way to spot a four eyes is to watch the dealer as he distributes the cards. His eyes will not be looking directly at the deck but just a *little* away from them. If he is new to the technique he may also be dealing slower than you would expect him to.

Because of its highly polished surface it is not uncommon for a twinkle to reflect a small path of light onto a wall or ceiling. I'm sure you've seen the reflection given off by a watch face. You may even have driven a pet cat to distraction by moving it around. Not many people look at the ceiling during a game of cards but it is wise to stay aware of your surroundings. Even if you don't see a flash of light while glancing at the ceiling it will tell a four eyes that you are aware of twinkles and may dissuade him from using one.

WHAT THE CHEAT NEEDS TO KNOW

The cheat will not use his twinkle for every hand or, indeed, every card during a particular deal. He may not even try to read the whole index corner of the card. If he knows just the value of *one* card in your hand it is enough of an advantage for him to take the money in the long run.

If he just knows if your cards are high or low in Blackjack or Pontoon it will cost you money over a period of time.

If you are starting to get *with it* you'll realize what I'm saying here. Many cheating methods are not *stone-walled* winners. They simply twist the odds dramatically in the cheats favor.

PERHAPS THE MOST OUTRAGEOUS TWINKLE OF ALL

Among Freddy's never ending supply of gambling tales is one of a player using what must be considered perhaps the most outrageous twinkle of all time! It happened back in the days of the Wild West.

A huge man sat down at a poker table in the bustling saloon of a busy mining town.

"*I hate cheats,*" he announced with a growl, "*and if I see anything wrong at this table while I'm here, there's gonna be big trouble!*"

At this point he removed a huge Bowie knife and laid it down on the table.

There may not have been any cheating from the other players but, by all reports, it was one of shiniest Bowie knifes anybody had seen in a long time.

Nobody wanted to argue with the man but one of the players was reported as saying afterwards, "*I must have been drunk. All I could see were cards a dancin' on the ceiling!*"

Belly Strippers and Others

DESPITE THE CHAPTER HEADING YOU ARE NOT ABOUT TO READ A PORNOGRAPHIC description relating to the *Dance of the Seven Veils*. Strippers are faked cards of which John Scarne, a well known magician and gambling expert, wrote *'They are one of the most highly prized secrets of the fast money winners'*. Freddy agrees with him.

The most naive of gamblers must realize that if certain cards can be controlled in a pack by a hustler then that hustler is onto a winner. If the hustler is a skilled *strip man* then he can do just that. The bad news for you is that it doesn't take that much practice to become reasonably skilled at using these cards.

WHAT ARE STRIPPERS?

Strippers or *wedges,* as they are sometimes called, are cards that have been shaved slightly out of shape. The most common type of strippers in the gambling world are *bellys.*

To see how the shaving system works let's assume that Freddy needs to control four aces in a game of cards. Freddy will remove the aces from the deck. The remainder of the cards are shaved along one edge to make the cards slightly narrower than when they started. In a professional deck the shaving will be so fine as to defy the human eye. Forget magicians *Wizard's Decks* that you may have seen. A professional deck may be shaved less than one sixty-fourth of an inch. Freddy now shaves the aces but with a curve. They end up slightly wider than the bulk of the deck in the middle but slightly narrower at the ends. Finally Freddy nicely rounds off the corners so the cards look just as they did at the start. For a very nice corner finish he will use a professional tool called a *Corner Cutter*.

If the deck is shuffled and offered to Freddy he can, during a cutting sequence, run his fingers down the long edges of the deck and *strip out* the aces. It takes a really light touch with a professional deck. Freddy has several in his collection that defy my finger tips but from which he can unerringly strip four a kind during a cut. *"It's only practice,"* he says.

The stripping action is covered by making a series of small cuts in which he pulls small packets of cards from the deck to drop them on top. The last packet cut, in this demonstration, would be the *stripped* aces.

HOW BELLY STRIPPERS CAN BE USED IN A GAME

Strippers are often used in a two-handed game. That's the kind of game that often happens at the end of a long evening. All the other players are going home but Freddy will talk you into a little session of *head to head* to end the evening off.

The deck has been in play all night. The game may have been straight but the cards weren't. The cards are Freddy's *belly*. It's been shaved so that ten cards (for Poker) are fatter in the center than the rest of the deck. It should go without saying that Freddy has memorized these cards. During the head to head Freddy strips these cards to the top of the deck. You deal. By looking at his cards Freddy knows exactly what you are holding. He knows if his hand beats yours or not. He can't always win but will never lose. If he holds the lower hand he can toss it in and call it a night. If he holds the higher hand he will go for it with a vengeance. He knows that, at the last hand of a session, many amateur card players go a little berserk.

If he *belly's* nine cards and uses the *Ten Card Poker* principle (of which more later) he can win the head to head every single time.

Belly's can also be used during games of Hi-Lo cutting. Here the deck will be set so that, if cut in the center of the long edges a low card will show. If cut nearer to one end a high card will show. Freddy offers a big bet at the end of the night. One cut, high card wins. The player will cut the deck near the center of a long edge. It's just the way 99 % of people do it. Freddy, joining the 1 % who don't, will cut nearer to one end. Because of the shaving work Freddy will win every time.

In his interesting autobiography, *The Amazing World of John Scarne,* later re-published as *The Odds Against Me*, John Scarne tells a tale of being taken during a game of *Banker and Broker*. In this game the dealer would make several piles of cards from the deck leaving them face down. Bets would be laid on the piles then, finally, the dealer would cut a pile from the remainder of the deck. All the piles were turned face up and if the card on the bottom of the pile you bet on was higher than the dealer's card you won. If it equaled or was lower than the dealer's card, you lost. The young Scarne was cheated with a deck made up of Belly Strippers. The story may or may not be fantasy but the game still exists in seedy establishments to this day. As Freddy puts it, *"That game could almost have been designed for a belly man!"*

OTHER TYPES OF STRIPPERS

Freddy has quite a collection of these types of decks. Among them you'll find examples of the following.

Side Strippers

In this case *all* the cards are shaved so they are narrower at one end. This gives the cards a slightly tapered shape. If certain cards are turned around in such a deck they can be stripped out because their 'fat' end is at the 'narrow' end of the deck. These strippers are the ones most magicians will be aware of as the *Wizard Deck* and, as such, have found their way into the tool kit of the amateur magician. The cards you see at a magic shop are nothing like the strippers Freddy uses. They are shaved so crudely as to often be visibly off shape to a naked eye. This is to make them easier to work with. A monkey could strip cards from a deck like this. To use Freddy's cards assiduous hours of practice are required. His decks are shaved so finely that you'd need a set of good measuring calipers to find the work.

Exaggerated shapes to give you the idea..

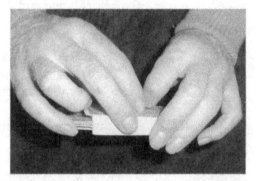

Stripping out four cards.

End Strippers

Rakes, as these cards are called, are much the same as side strippers but, here, the work has been put in on a short edge. In other words the work has been put in at the top and bottom edges of the cards as against the long edges.

These cards can defy detection from the man who knows all about the more common side strippers. He'll be looking for shaving on the *sides* of the deck!

The moral here is that, if you are checking to see if a deck is a stripper or not, you should check *all* four sides of the deck.

Professional Belly Strippers.
Can you see the work now?

Corner Strippers

Although rare and very tough to work with these can be the most dangerous strippers of all. They are almost impossible to detect.

Just one corner of the deck is shaved. The ability to use them requires very serious practice time indeed. The amateur cheat has neither the time nor patience to get the required skill. The professional would rather spend the time learning how to control normal cards. Even Freddy, who has put in quite a time to get a very light touch on his cards, considers the extra time required to learn to use this type of deck effectively just isn't worth it.

You are most unlikely to see this breed of stripper in your gambling time.

Briefs

A brief is one card that is slightly wider than the rest of the deck. The whole pack, apart from one card, has been shaved by as little as one sixty-fourth of an inch.

The cheat can easily cut this wider card to the top or bottom of the deck. This can be used to upset a fair cut or just to gain knowledge of the position of one card. In a game of head to head Stud Poker cutting a low card to the top and dealing it to your opponent as their hole card can be considered just a little more than simple *advantage* play!

HOW MUCH TO SHAVE?

The lighter the work in the cards the less reliable they become. This is especially true if using a deck of bellys to cut Hi-Lo. With very fine work the cheat may cut a low card or, conversely, his opponent may cut a high card. The harder, or more severe, the work is the more reliable the deck becomes. The harder the work though, the more likely it is to be discovered.

Freddy has a real light touch but doesn't rely on his opponent to have the same touch. He will compromise by using a deck that's shaved enough for it to give him a good edge. He says he reads the opponent and uses a deck that he feels he can get by with. I believe him. He says that, most commonly, he will use a deck that's been shaved about one thirty-second of an inch. It is, perhaps, a testament to his ability that he considers that pretty heavy work.

I've seen Freddy take a new deck and remove the four aces. He's then taken a woman's emery board and lightly sanded the side of the remainder of the deck with a couple of long strokes. He then put the aces back in and asked me to shuffle the cards. He took the deck and stripped out the aces during a cut. I didn't see a thing. I tried for a long time but couldn't get one of them to move. "*It's a feel thing,*" he says.

Decks that have been shaved heavily are called *Stubble* by Freddy in a reference to a close facial shave or a poor one. I remember once trying to fool him with a trick using a deck of side strippers. I thought they were reasonably finely shaved but, to my dismay, at the end of the effect Freddy said, "*Nice trick but your cards have got a five o'clock shadow!*"

SPOTTING STRIPPERS

Most strippers can be discovered by tapping the edges of a deck dead square against the table. Now feel along all four sides. Turn a few cards around and feel again to make sure that everything is perfectly flush. Compare a low card and a court card side by side then one atop each other. Check very carefully.

I repeat, be sure to check *very* carefully. A professional deck will only have been shaved a tiny amount and will require a very light touch to discover. As for Freddy's emery board demonstration your only hope is to believe him when he says, "*You ain't gonna see a deck like that in a game, it's too much like hard work. Anyway, there's maybe five guys in the world with a touch like that.*"

If you have doubts I'll repeat (and continue to repeat) the advice that you should get out of the game.

ORDINARY STRIPPERS

If you want to see how strippers work try this test with a normal deck of cards.

Bend all the high cards slightly lengthways. Bow all the low cards slightly across the width. Shuffle the cards together.

Cutting normally will bring up far more low cards than high cards. Cutting with your fingers and thumb on the short edges will bring up more high cards than low cards. The exercise can give you, in just a few moments, a rather fascinating insight into how strippers can work.

And, even if you don't find it fascinating, at least be grateful that you aren't the London banker who was taken for $15,000 using this *exact* set up.

It's an old cheat's joke that he checks the deck to see if the aces have been bent in any way. If they haven't then he bends them!

BATHROOM STRIPPERS

One final word of warning about the cheat and his strippers.

Just because you are playing with your own cards don't assume that he can't be using strippers. If Freddy can get away with a deck for a few moments he can turn it into a stripper deck. Not with his emery board trick but with a quick visit to the rest room.

In the toilet Freddy can make a deck into a stripper. He can shave the deck by rubbing it against the rough edge of the mirror. If the mirror has a broken edge, as so many public toilet mirrors do, then a finer shave can be made. The edge of a broken window can also be used to create a deck of strippers.

By using this technique Freddy can create a *rough* pack of side strippers. Of course, the corners aren't quite as nicely rounded as his professional packs but why should you notice that. After all, why should anybody suspect strippers when they are using their *own* cards.

Leaving nothing to chance Freddy has even been known to carry a small sliver of glass wrapped in a cloth with him. This sliver, carried in a handkerchief, so as not cut him, can be used any time he gets his hands on a deck. All he has to do is steal a deck from the pile of game cards and be alone with it for a few moments. Then he'll sneak it back onto the pile of cards and simply wait for it to come into play.

Freddy will wait a long time. He's a real patient guy when it comes to making money.

So, like his marked cards, the cheat can *create* a stripper pack if need be.

If you have a number of decks of cards for your evening's play be sure to keep them in a safe place. Make real sure that none of them go off for a walk with Freddy for a while.

Simple Partner Plays

THE AMATEUR CHEAT BY HIMSELF CAN TAKE YOUR MONEY WITH HIS GAFFED CARDS. The amateur cheat with a partner can take your money without them. Collusion cheating is, perhaps, the most common form of cheating in the gambling world today. In Contract Bridge its use is rife, with partners giving each other secret bidding signals to gain an unfair advantage.

A secret partner is often referred to as a *sidewalker*.

The sidewalker got his name from one of the crazy bets that gamblers will make when there isn't a real game around. You know the thing; "*Which raindrop will reach the bottom of a window first?*" "*How many apples do you think are in that box?*" "*How old is that man?*" And so on.

A common bet used to be to stand behind a person about to cross the road. The bet was to guess which foot they would step off with.

Hundreds of dollars have been wagered on such nutty bets.

The cheat could win every time. How? Simple. The guy he and his betting friend stood behind was a friend of the cheat. A simple signaling system told the front man which foot to step off with. The system could be as simple as a cough at the right time.

And so the sidewalker got his name.

There is an old gambler's saying, "*Some people will bet on anything, but they don't always bet alone!*"

Two amateur cheats can use a number of ploys to win the money.

SIMPLE FORCE OUTS

The simplest form of team work is to co-ordinate and control the betting of the rest of the players.

The cheats may raise a hand between them forcing an innocent mug to put more money into the pot than he wanted or needed to. They do this by constantly raising and re-raising the pot, trapping the victim in the middle. Only one of the cheats needs a good hand. The other, to keep the betting going, will stay in with nothing. What does he care? The take will be split with his partner. This trap, referring to burning somebody trapped in the middle, is sometimes called *toasting*.

The partnership, even with two bad hands, can *steal* the pot by continuing to raise the pot until the mug is forced to drop out because of a lack of funds. *"No cash, no play,"* they will say, *"That's the rules of the game."* After the hand they will roar with laughter as one of them says, *"I can't believe I was bluffing a bluffer!"*

A simple set of signals is all they need to put the ploy into motion.

Force Out teams are far more common than you may imagine.

SPOOKING

It is very common in small games for a player who has dropped out of a hand to ask if he can look at an opponent's hand. This request is often granted. The player assumes that the inquirer is no threat as they are out of the hand. They assume that the inquirer just wants to get some vicarious thrills while watching the outcome.

That may well be the case.

But if the inquirer is a *spook* he may also be just about to tell his partner, still in the hand, just what you are holding. He'll use simple signals, each team tend to work out their own making them very difficult to spot, to tell his pal exactly what cards you are holding!

A man called a *drop out* will not always ask to look at your hand. He may get up to go to the toilet or the bar. In doing so he'll look at your cards and give the signals as he leaves.

Some teams work with an *outside* man, an innocent enough chap casually watching the game. If he sees the opponent's cards he will signal them to his team member/s in the game. This charming fellow is called a *rail-bird*. The term rail-bird also applies to the lout in both casino and private games who will literally reach over and steal chips when nobody is paying attention.

It goes without saying that, from now on, *never* show your cards to anybody in a game.

Always play with your cards close to you, hence the term 'keeping things close to the vest', so they are tough to see. If you don't need to be holding them, leave them, squared up, on the table.

And finally, *never* play with your back to a mirror. Don't laugh, I've seen it!

BEST HAND FORWARDS

On each deal the cheat and his partner will signal the value of their hands to each other. Amateur cheats may even sit next to each other so that they can glimpse each other's hand.

The player with the best opening cards carries on while the player with the weaker opening cards immediately drops out of the game.

This is the equivalent of you being able to pay two antes, get two hands and carry on with the better hand. I hope you can see that this gives an advantage to the cheat that, over time, will kill you in the game.

ACCIDENTAL CHEATING

I have honestly lost count of the times in private games where, after the drinks have been flowing for a while, players have routinely shown their hands to others accidentally. Among a group of tipsy friends the advantage this gives can level out as the accidents happen to all. But if one of the players is a cheat, pretending to be as tipsy as the rest, you can be in big trouble. *"Persistence is one of my best weapons,"* says Freddy. *"The longer I wait, the better it gets in some games."*

It's bad enough to be cheated by somebody else. Cheating yourself is just plain stupid.

This might be a good time to mention that, despite its popularity, drinking and good card playing do not go together. When Freddy plays he drinks coffee or, if trying to give an impression of being tipsy, an *upside down* gin and tonic. To make this the rim of the glass has been dipped into gin and the glass filled with tonic. Anybody smelling the drink can catch the odor of gin from the rim but Freddy is just drinking tonic water. As an interesting side mention, this is one of the ways a crooked bar tender will take money from you as well! Freddy drinks them deliberately. You may be doing so without realizing it while paying for the real drink!

If you are going to play cards properly try not to party too hard until after the game!

Some Assorted Petty Hustles

THE AMATEUR AND PROFESSIONAL CHEAT BOTH HAVE ONE THING IN COMMON. They are both after your money. The amateur lacks the sleight-of-hand ability of a professional but he may well learn one or more of the following ploys to make sure that he's ahead at the end of the night. All of them require a little practice but even the laziest amateur will put *some* work in if it is going to guarantee a return.

POT SHORTING

This is one of the pettiest and most widespread forms of cheating in the world. Even players who would not count themselves as cheats have been known to do it just to gain an edge.

When it comes to the player's bet he throws in his chips or money. However he throws in less than he should. If the game is a cash one and the bet is seven dollars he may throw in five singles and a dollar fifty in small change. He may have practiced counting the coins to make it look as though he has more money than is actually there. He may also just pretend to check the amount before tossing the coins into the pot. Yes, he'll short the pot fifty cents! Petty? Sure but it can add up over time.

It is very common in cash games to take change from a pot. Here the cheat will simply take more change than he should. He may throw ten dollars into the pot and pick up a five spot with one hand while quickly scooping up six ones with the other giving him a one dollar profit. He will practice this so he can do it with hardly a glance. You can also *bet your butt* that, as he takes the change, he'll be chatting genially to distract you.

In a chip game often players put their money in a box at the start of the night and get their chips from the stash. The cheat won't short the money in the box. It's too obvious at the end of the night. But he may take an extra chip or two to get some free antes.

The above techniques rely on other players being sloppy and inattentive. They are totally safe for the cheat. If caught he can just say that he made a mistake. Are you really going to make a big scene over a dollar or two amongst friends?

Make a note to point out simple mistakes *each* and *every* time you see them. The petty thief will soon get the idea that your company is too *fast* for him to use such petty larceny.

CHECK COPPING

This, although similar to pot shorting, is more subtle. The theft is done under cover of pushing the pot to the big winner.

You've won a big hand and are basking in your glory when Freddy pushes the pot over to you. "*There you go big man,*" he says. "*You sure cleaned us out that time!*" You are so proud of your power play that you don't see Freddy palm away some of those hard earned winnings as he pushes the pot your way! He will stash that money away in a handy pocket under cover of reaching for his cigarettes.

He may, as a cover, grouse as he pushes the money your way. "*Get it out of the way,*" he'll carp. "*We'd like a chance to get some of it back!*"

The congratulations or grousing mean absolutely nothing. They are simple distractions away from the *work* going on.

Some cheats actually coat their palms with a sticky gum or bee's wax so that, as they push the pot towards you, some of the money or chips will glue themselves to their hands.

A more experienced man may use a *bean-shooter*. This is a flap of leather or cardboard which is attached to a length of elastic. The elastic runs up the cheat's sleeve. The flap, covered with gum or wax, is held in the cheat's palm as he pushes the pot towards you. A few chips or coins stick to the bean-shooter which, as soon as pressure is released, flies up the cheat's sleeve.

If you question him pushing the pot towards you he can immediately show you his hands empty and say, "*Waddya saying? You think I'm some kind of cheat?*"

Many cheats and would-be cheats will use ploys like this when they are losing. Stealing back some of the money they've lost seems all right within their twisted ideas of morality.

Never let anybody touch your winnings. Politely inform them that you are more than capable of picking them up yourself.

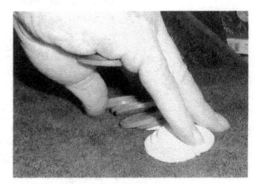

Copping a Check while pushing over a pile.

LOCATION PLAY

This is about as close to sleight-of-hand as the amateur cheat is likely to get.

He will memorize a group of cards as he gathers up the discards. These he places at the bottom of the deck. It is a pretty easy matter for him to riffle shuffle the cards and keep that group intact as he does so. He just lets a group of cards fall first before actually shuffling the rest together. Then he will offer the cards to be cut.

This sends his memorized group of cards or *slug* to the center of the pack.

During the deal in a Stud Poker game, as soon as the first memorized card appears he knows, by calculating forwards and backwards, not only some of the cards players are holding but also which cards are the next few on top of the deck. In a Stud Poker game like Five Card, where only one card is hidden and the rest are face up, this can be like an open book to the cheat if his slug falls correctly.

It is also great for Blackjack or Pontoon. The cheat knows whether to take a card or not because he knows exactly which card is coming next!

If, when the cut is offered, the player just taps the deck, *letting it ride,* meaning that they are happy with the deck as it is, the cheat still gains an advantage by knowing several cards that will not come into play.

Always shuffle between hands and make sure that the cards are shuffled properly.

Ensure that cards are discarded face down. Don't let anybody pick them up to have a *quick look* through them. The only way anybody should see any cards, other than their own, is to pay for the privilege of doing so.

The professional cheat will also use slug work but he'll add in some extra sleight-of-hand. You'll see how devastating this can be when we discuss Freddy's real work.

CHIPS WITH EVERYTHING

A lot of Friday night games are played with gambling chips. The players may feel that this gives the game more of the atmosphere of a big money or casino-style game.

Most times these chips have been purchased from a game store.

The really petty thief may well search out the shop and buy some chips of his own.

When it comes to cashing in the chips at the end of the night the banker ends up with more chips than he started with. There is no way to prove that anybody added in extra chips. It's normally blamed on the banker making a mistake. The banker, blaming that fifth scotch, has to bite the bullet and make up the loss.

Never play with cheap plastic chips unless you have marked them before the game with paint or permanent marker pen. Make sure your chips for a game you are organizing are unique in some way. Otherwise you might fall foul of a cheat who can, quite literally, buy his money *off the shelf* at a local store!

By and large, check copping and such ploys would not be used by a professional cheat. Not because he is a virtuous fellow, but because he knows that it would be stupid to raise any suspicion of cheating in a game with such *penny-ante* work. Such suspicion could put *heat* onto a more profitable play. That's not to say they won't use these ploys, they will. But only when the time is absolutely right to do so.

SHOOT PONTOON TEAMSTERS

Shoot Pontoon is a popular English pub game where the dealer puts an amount of money into a pot. Each player, in turn, playing a hand of Blackjack or Pontoon, can *shoot* (bet) against the dealer for all or part of the pot. If the player loses, their money is added to the pot. After each player has had three hands the deal moves to the next player. The dealer keeps what is left in the pot. Each player is dealt one card to start with and makes his bet before receiving a second card. All the cards are face down.

The dealer often does very well indeed but it is infuriating to build up a sizeable pot only to have somebody *shoot the pot* and take it all away.

Good team play can prevent this from happening. If the pot rises to a good size the cheat (dealer) will lose to his partner who has shot the pot. Since they are sharing the winnings he doesn't mind doing this.

Here's how it works. The dealer has set a starting pot of twenty dollars. At the start of the third dealing round the pot has risen to two hundred and thirty dollars, thirty of which is the cheat's partners. The cheat deals the cards and gives a signal to his partner. The partner *shoots the pot* for two hundred and thirty dollars. He stands on his hand. The dealer, in a 'panic', busts out his hand and the partner picks up the money. Work it out and you'll see that this has given the team a $180 profit.

Plus it's taken away the danger of anybody else getting their hands on the money.

Not bad work if you pull the scam two or three times a night.

Shoot Pontoon is not the only game of this type. In any game where the dealer holds a pot that you can bet all or part of be wary of the man who keeps shooting the pot and winning.

FLOPPING THE DECK

Another ruse used in Blackjack, Pontoon and Shoot Pontoon is a ploy called *flopping the deck*.

It is common, in friendly games, for used hands to be picked up and replaced, face up, under the deck. That way, everybody knows when the deck has been run through because face up cards will show. The pack is then shuffled and the game continues.

All the cheat has to do is to pick up the used cards in such a manner as to give himself, or his partner, a good hand.

Here's a very simple example. You and a new friend are playing a little head to head Blackjack. The used hands on the table are eighteen (a 10, 3 and 5) for you and fifteen (a 10, 4 and ace) for your friend. The cheat (your new friend) picks up the cards in an apparently random manner and pops them, face up, under the pack. What he *actually* does is pick up the cards so they are in the order he wants. In this simple case it would be 10, 10, A, 5, 4, 3. This is a very simple form of the *Pick Up Stack* you'll learn more about later on. The cheat will cover his work with idle chat and banter.

He ends up with a pre-stacked hand face up on the bottom of the deck.

The next hand is dealt normally but after you have looked at your hand and made any draw the cheat will *flop* the deck. That is, he will turn the deck over. This is literally the work of a moment and will be well covered by the misdirection of you checking your cards or reaching for the bet. He'll do it when you aren't looking!

He then hands you the deck to deal the next hand. You deal him a twenty-one!

If he is the banker in a multi-player game he will set the stack to deal himself a great hand. The deck can be flopped under cover of checking that the players are ready. "*Anybody need a drink before the next hand?*" he may ask.

In a loose bar game the cards may even go out of sight under the edge of the table as he makes the flop. The deck often goes out of sight during a loose bar game. I've even seen a dealer keep a deck in their hand that reached into a pocket for matches. I'm not saying that this fellow was cheating but he wasn't called on it. If he wasn't cheating he certainly *could* have done so very easily.

People do not recognize the repetition of the cards for two simple reasons. First the cards are mixed into different hands and, second, because people concentrate on totals not individual cards in Blackjack and Pontoon variants.

Cheating is often much easier than people imagine. Loose attention means that a petty cheat can get away with murder. The guy above, reaching for his matches, could have easily switched the deck in his pocket! Such an action would never be allowed in a professional money game and yet such things happen all the time in friendly games.

A golden rule is to play like the professionals. If there is any money in play be very vigilant. Don't allow cards to go out of sight under any circumstances. Stay sober, watch the dealer and people around the table. Play like you don't know the other players at all.

As Freddy says, "*You don't have any friends at the card table.*"

LOCAL RULES

This is going to sound silly but *always* know the local rules of any game you sit in on. These can vary dramatically from card school to card school. Before you lose a winning pot to the line, "*Oh, you didn't know that a red ace with a pair of threes beats everything before nine o'clock?*" you would be wise to read the amusing gambling legend of the Lollapalooza hand. The story is almost certainly a fable but it does make the point nicely.

This story has been around a long time. I first read it in *Poker Stories* by John Lillard, which was published in 1896!

A card cheat sat down at a poker table in Butte, Montana. He was ready to clean out the locals before moving on to another town.

After an hour or so of play the cheat decided it was time to go for the kill and stacked himself a nice Full House. He bet heavily on the hand and everybody dropped out. Everybody, that is, except for an old bearded miner with a strong poker face.

The pot was finally seen and the cheat threw down his Full House and reached for the money.

"*Not so fast,*" said the old miner, laying down three odd clubs and two diamonds, "*I think that money is mine.*"

The cheat protested but the old man explained that in this school three odd clubs and two diamonds was called a Lollapalooza and beat everything. The other players all confirmed the old man's claim. "*Thought you knew the way we played cards here,*" added the old man as he picked up the cash.

The cheat was furious. A few deals later he stacked up the fabled Lollapalooza hand for himself. He was determined to wipe the smirk off the old man's face.

He was delighted when the pot rose to astronomical proportions.

Finally the pot was seen and, throwing down his hand, he exclaimed, "*Sorry boys, it's my lucky night! I've got the Lollapalooza! Nothing can beat me!*"

"*Sorry sonny boy,*" said the old man laying down three kings and reaching for the pot, "*There's only one Lollapalooza a night allowed in this school. You lose again. Tough luck kid.*"

Freddy claims the story is true and that the old man was his great-great-grandfather. I'm not going to bet him otherwise.

The main point here is to make sure you know *all* the rules of the game if you are playing away from home.

THE SAD CASE OF THE PAW-PAW

One small time cheat that Freddy recalls was a guy they called Paw-Paw. His specialty was check copping. He even made his own 'patented' gum by burning the underside of sticky tape and collecting the glue as it bubbled off. He considered this *inside work*. He was not held in high regard by Freddy's group but they put up with him hanging around.

One night while Freddy watched him play he made the truly unforgivable error for a cheat of getting drunk while working.

During the evening he didn't win a single hand but happily stole chips every time he pushed the pot over to the lucky winner. Thanks to his condition he made two big errors.

He didn't chat or grouse as *coppers* always do to misdirect away from the work.

Neither did he steal the chips away to his pocket. He just secretly added them to his chips on the table.

Despite the fact that he wasn't winning a single hand his pile of chips was growing, almost magically, before the other player's eyes.

The Paws biggest mistake was not recognizing one of the players as a big time hoodlum. A very tough man with a real reputation. The tough guy leaned over and growled to the Paw, "*How come you've got more money than you started with? You ain't won a ****ing hand!*"

Paw-Paw thought quickly. Even sober his reply would have been amusing. Drunk it was a miracle. He smiled happily and raised his glass. "*You must be cheating me!*" he slurred. "*You're just fattening me up for a big kill later on!*"

Against anybody else it could have been laughed off. The tough guy did not see the funny side of it and the Paw, by mutual agreement, left the game.

The next time Freddy saw the Paw his hands had been smashed so badly that he couldn't pick up a glass never mind palm a chip.

It's worth pointing out that Freddy says, "*If you get caught cheating in a big money game it's unlikely that the police are going to be called to sort it out.*"

You might want to bear this tale in mind if you are ever tempted to try out a few of these easy cheat moves for yourself.

Betcha's

THE SEMI PROFESSIONAL CARD CHEAT, ALONG HIS TRAVELS, WILL USE MOST, IF not all, of the amateur's methods.

The big difference between him and the amateur is that he will foist his *skills* upon anybody rather than sticking to one group of friends or acquaintances. He'll also play in higher stake games than the petty amateur. He'll often use his position in these games to gain introductions for other cheats. For providing this service he will expect some form of *sky* or payment.

Apart from cheating during the game these guys also have quite a fund of prop, odds and NAP bets to help support their part-time business. It is worth re-reading what we've already studied about these bets. It's odds on that he knows all of them, so make sure that you do as well.

Here are a few more hustles and betchas that are particular favorites of Freddy and his group of pals.

THE CARD IN THE BICYCLE WHEEL

One of Freddy's best friends has earned the nickname of *Spokes* because of his love of this particular bet.

At the end of an evening of gambling Spokes will offer to take you along to a new club he knows of for a late drink or two. Having already had a few, and being in a good mood, you agree.

"*It's only a few minutes away,*" says Spokes. "*We may as well walk there.*"

As you walk along the road you notice a bicycle chained to an iron fence or to a lamp post. You notice that it has a slightly soiled playing card clipped to the forks so that it goes between the spokes of the wheel. Don't worry, if you don't see it then Spokes will point it out to you. "*Remember doing that as a kid?*" he'll say. "*I used to love the noise those little puppies made!*"

After walking a few more yards Spokes will pause and muse, "*Funny seeing that card. The king of spades won me a great pot tonight. Must be an omen or something!*" You may be a little tipsy and that card may have been a little dirty but you clearly remember it being a red suited one.

"*It wasn't the king of spades,*" you say.

Spokes, also in a slightly tipsy mode, argues that it was. You argue back that it wasn't.

Spokes is fabulous at manipulating people. He will cajole you into being so annoyed at his stupidity that you'll be prepared to take the bet when he offers it. Because of your temper you may well accept a bet of much higher stakes than you would if thinking coherently.

You return to the bicycle and there in the spokes is a grainy, dirty playing card.

The king of spades.

You pay up, convinced, perhaps, that you've just had one drink too many. Spokes calms down and your friendship is renewed. "*Come on pal,*" he says, "*the first beer is on me!*"

If you hadn't walked quite so far past the bicycle and hadn't be so focused about arguing your point with Spokes then you may have saved your money.

You see, you might have caught one of Spoke's associates walking up to the bicycle and switching the cards before quietly walking away.

THE GREAT POKER SORT OUT

The next couple of bets rely on poker hands. Just in case you are not an aficionado of what is, to Freddy anyway, the *greatest* money game played with cards of them all, here's a quick run down on the hands. Freddy, just for your education, has added the odds against each hand being dealt to you in a game.

1. Royal Straight Flush (A, K, Q, J, 10 all of the same suit): 649,739-1 against
2. Straight Flush (five cards, all the same suit, in order): 72,192-1 against
3. Four of a Kind (such as A, A, A, A, odd card): 4,164-1 against
4. Full House (three of one value and two of another): 639-1 against
5. Flush (five cards the same suit but not in any order): 508-1 against
6. Straight (five cards in order but not the same suit): 254-1 against
7. Three of a Kind (three cards the same value and two odd ones): 46-1 against
8. Two Pair (two pairs of cards with one odd one): 20-1 against
9. One Pair (one pair with three odd cards): 1.4-1 against
10. High Card or Buster (all odd cards): even

So now, even if you don't know how to play poker, you at least know that it is harder for a player to get a Full House than it is for them to get a Flush.

Now for Freddy's little bet.

He will ask a fellow poker player to shuffle a deck of cards and remove twenty-five cards face down. Freddy's bet is that, within three minutes, he will sort those cards into five *pat* poker hands. A pat hand is one that a player would consider to be a winning hand. Freddy says that the five hands he sorts out will be straights or higher. He'll even, if you are interested, point out the odds against such hands being dealt.

Now you've seen the odds. This would seem to be a super human task at best. Freddy never fails to get a sizeable bet down on this one.

I have *never* seen him lose the money.

There is no real cheating involved. It's just much easier to do than it sounds. First Freddy will sort the cards into suits and put down as many Flushes as he can. Then he will sort the remaining cards (if there are any) and try to make Full Houses. Finally, if he has any cards left over he will adjust the Flushes into Straights and Four of a Kinds.

Try it yourself. It may take you longer than three minutes but then you don't practice like Freddy.

If the opponent knows the game of Three Card Brag then Freddy will *double or nothing* the bet on what seems to be an even more outrageous proposition. If you don't know the game he'll be happy to teach it to you so that you can decide if you want to accept the bet or not. Since you really only need to know the order of winning hands in Brag he'll explain that each player gets three cards. The order of hands is as follows.

1. Prial (three of a kind): 424-1 against
2. Straight Flush (such as 10C, JC, QC): 459-1 against
3. Straight (such as 3H, 4C, 5D): 30-1 against
4. Flush: 19-1 against
5. Pair: 5-1 against
6. High Card: 1.33 for

An aside point both Freddy and I find it interesting that three of a kind beats a Straight Flush even though it is slightly easier to get!

Freddy follows up the first bet by offering to sort the remaining twenty-seven cards of the deck into nine *pat* Brag hands! Although this would, at first glance appear to be very difficult (especially if the poker hands sorted are very good ones), it is actually easier.

First Freddy sorts the cards into values and lays out as many Prials as he can. Then he sorts any remaining cards into suits and lays down both Straight Flushes and normal Flushes. Then, with any left over cards, he will adjust the Straight Flushes and Prials into ordinary Straights and Flushes.

Try this yourself with twenty-seven random cards. I've never seen Freddy take longer than ninety seconds for this part of the bet. It is really so easy that you should easily be able to do it within the three minutes the bet allows, even the very first time you give it a shot.

If anybody offers you this bet just smile and say, "*What do you want to bet that I can't do it?"*

FACE UP POKER

This is a real *mother* of a bet. Freddy took me for fifty dollars with it.

We'd been playing poker together one night for some very small stakes. We were playing the somewhat archaic game of Five Card Draw. In Draw Poker each player is dealt five cards and, after a round of betting, can change a number of cards to try to improve his hand. The cards they change are thrown into a discard pile and are not to be used until the next hand. The stakes were small because Freddy was using this as one of his training sessions for me. He always insists on some stake *even* when showing me how he's cheating me! Of course I lost money.

Freddy smiled and said, *"You know I wouldn't have to cheat you to beat you in a game. You really are a lousy poker player. You are so bad that,"* here he paused before continuing, *"that I could probably spread the deck face up and let you take any five cards you wanted and you still wouldn't beat me!"*

I protested that I couldn't possibly be that bad.

Freddy offered the following bet for twenty-five dollars. He would spread out the deck face up and I could remove any five cards I wanted. Then he would take five cards. I wouldn't be able to beat him. The game was to be Draw Poker.

I took the bet. I couldn't lose!

I immediately picked out a Royal Straight Flush. Freddy also picked out a Royal Straight Flush and explained that I'd lost the bet. *"I bet you, you couldn't beat me,"* he said, *"and you haven't. You've only equaled my hand, not beaten it!"*

I felt like an idiot but it was about to get worse.

Freddy offered double or nothing on the bet. He would take a hand first, then I would take one. He was prepared to bet me that he would *beat* my hand.

I considered this and decided that he just couldn't do it. Surely the best that he could hope for was another stand-off in which case he would lose. I checked the words and stressed to him that he had to beat my hand. Any tie would mean I won the bet. He could hardly stifle his giggles as he agreed.

Freddy picked four tens and a three.

Damn, I couldn't make a Royal Straight Flush. Freddy had all the tens. I picked out a nine high Straight Flush, the best hand I could get at the time.

Then came the humiliation of the draw.

Freddy discarded three of the tens and his three. He picked out four more cards to make a king high Straight Flush. He even left the aces in the deck to give me false hope! I couldn't make anything higher than a nine high Straight Flush. Freddy had one of the tens and the other three were in the discard pile! My nine high Straight Flush came a sad and lonely second to his king high Straight Flush.

He laughed like a drain as I handed over the fifty dollars.

Next time somebody offers to play you at face up poker, pick out four tens and an odd card. Then watch his face drop.

TWIN DECKS

If two decks of cards are available Freddy may pull this fast little Freeze Out bet. He will ask you to shuffle both decks and lay them side-by-side on the table. He will then ask you to turn cards simultaneously from the two decks. His bet is that at some point you will turn two matching cards. Matching both in suit and value!

To the average person the idea that a card will occupy the same position in two randomly shuffled decks seems outrageous. He will easily take an even money bet considering the odds to be well in his favor.

He's wrong. The odds on this little number, based on an old math problem about a secretary randomly putting letters into addressed envelopes without looking, are five to three in Freddy's favor. Freddy has a rather nice 26 % advantage on the bet.

Freddy may also sucker you into putting up additional stakes for every additional set of pairs that turn up through the deck. The odds now swing so heavily in his favor that you'd be insane to take the bet. He can't lose this part of the bet but he can win additional money! Take it and you may as well just hand over your money right up front and save yourself the heartache.

Any time somebody offers you a bet where the odds seem in your favor think very carefully about accepting them.

As Freddy often says, *"The money stays the same, it's only the pocket that it's in that changes!"*

TWO CARDS TOGETHER

Here's one you can try right now. Think of two card values. Not suits, just values. So you may think of K and 3 or 5 and 9 for example.

Now shuffle a pack of cards as much as you like and lay it down before you.

I'll bet you even money that in that deck, right here and right now, two cards of the values you are thinking of will be together in that deck.

The odds are heavily in my favor that they will be so. I often use this if I am asked to do a magic trick on the radio, selling it, to the listeners playing along at home as an example of how your mind can affect apparently random outcomes.

"I prefer my mind to affect their wallet," is Freddy's only comment.

CUTTING FOR CHUMPS

If the action is a little slow Freddy may 'invent on the spur of the moment' the following bet:

He'll ask you to name a card and offer you even money that you can't cut to it in a shuffled deck if he gives you twenty-six tries to do so. You argue to yourself that half of fifty-two, the number of cards in the pack, is twenty-six so it must be an even bet.

You might decide to risk a ten spot or more on the bet. After all it's a fun bet. You think you have just as much chance of winning as you do of losing.

You don't.

What you may have failed to take into consideration is that you might not be cutting a different card each time. You may, and probably will, cut to the same card/s several times.

You would actually need thirty-six cuts to stand an even chance of cutting that elusive little thought-of card.

TEN CARD POKER

This is another old timer in Freddy's armory. Ten Card Poker has been around a long time and, despite being adopted into the magical world as a neat piece of entertainment, it is still being used by cheats to take money from the suckers. Hustlers like Freddy argue that they don't need to change winning formulas. "*Why fix it when it ain't broke,*" says Freddy. So long as there are mugs around who don't know the scam he'll carry on using it. And, as Big Mike MacDonald (and not, as so often misquoted, P.T. Barnum) said, "*There's a sucker born every minute.*"

Freddy explains that there is an unusual new game of poker going around. It doesn't matter that you don't understand poker, he'll even explain the hands to you. Then he removes ten cards from a deck and lets you shuffle them as much as you like. You then deal out two hands of five cards each. Both of you turn over your hands.

I'm sure it comes as no surprise to you to learn that Freddy wins.

Freddy gives you another go. He spreads out all the ten cards face down on the table. You each take turns to take cards, surely a totally random happenstance. You turn your hands and, once more, Freddy has won the hand.

Freddy feels bad about winning twice and offers you a chance to win your money back. He gathers up the cards and explains that you will each receive a face down card. Neither of you can look at your face down cards. The rest of the cards will be dealt face up, one at a time. You can choose which cards to keep and which cards to give to Freddy. At the end he'll even give you the option to switch some of the face up cards around! He'll *even* let you choose whether he should have the first face down card or give it to you! This would seem to be as fair as it can get.

Freddy wins again.

Magicians may scoff. A lot of them know this trick. There are, however, a lot of people around who are not magicians. They don't know the trick. I've personally seen over a thousand dollars lost at this game. That game, by the way, took just a little over seven minutes from start to finish and started off with a little twenty dollar fun bet. Frightening, huh?

There are three aspects to the scam. First Freddy does not give you ten cards at the start. He won't mention a number but you'll just assume that ten cards were given to you at the start because, at the end, ten cards will be in play. Freddy gives you nine cards at the start. These cards are three fours, three sevens and three queens. Actually any three groups of three same values will do, these are just the ones Freddy commonly uses out of habit. Secondly, Freddy also ensures that the top card of the deck is an odd card (in other words, in this example, not a four, seven or queen) and, if possible, he likes it to be an eight or a nine. Third, and for the last section of the game only, Freddy needs to be able to *Second* or *Bottom* deal. You'll see how he does that in just a little while.

So how does it all come together?

You shuffle nine cards and Freddy instructs you to place them back on top of the deck as he sets up the first bet. You then deal out two hands of five cards each. Because you placed nine cards on the deck and deal to Freddy first then you must end up with the odd tenth card.

It may not be immediately apparent to you but if you have the odd card it doesn't matter how the other nine cards are distributed through the hands. You *must* have the losing hand!

For the second bet Freddy lays out all the cards face down. He knows exactly where the odd card is because he's marked it. All he has to do is try to get you to take it. This is much easier than you may suppose because he will studiously avoid it while you are picking at random. *If* Freddy has first take he is home and dry. All he has to do is avoid the odd card and you must, if you haven't taken it already, end up with the odd card. *If* you have first take Freddy will, once more, avoid picking the odd card in the hope that you will do so. If he ends up with it he has two options. He can offer to bet, without looking, that he has the losing hand or he can allow himself to lose, evening up the bets so far. He will then suggest that, since you are square, you might want to try one more variation on the game. Freddy thinks the second option has more class than the first one. He also thinks it's good to lose once in a while to show humility. He also knows that he can get the money back by upping the bet on the last *stone wall* phase.

Freddy picks up the cards ensuring that the odd card goes to the top of the packet. He explains the final variation of the game and then offers you the choice of first or second face down card. As he does this he will casually shuffle the ten cards ensuring, by one of the methods you'll read about soon, that the odd card stays on top. *If* you choose the first card he will deal you the odd card and take the next one for himself. *If* you choose the second card he will either *Second Deal* a card to himself or, alternately, *Bottom Deal* a card to himself then deal you the odd card from the top of the packet. Whatever you request, you'll end up with the odd card!

Freddy now turns the remaining cards face up one at a time. You can take them, give them to him, in fact do whatever you like with them! So long as you have that unchangeable odd card in the hole that's just where you'll end up, *in the hole!* Freddy doesn't care what you do with the face up cards. You *must* lose!

The golden rule here is to never try new variations on a game that involve money. *Especially* when the other guy seems to be trying to help you win!

As I said, this little number has become a popular effect with magicians and has spawned numerous, and most ingenious, variations. The description above is *exactly* how Freddy plays the game for money. I showed him some of the more ingenious of the magical variations and his only comment was, "*Yeah, neat tricks but my way gets the money, I'll stick with it.*"

THE HORSE RACE

This is another nice little 'impromptu' bet which can get completely out of control.

The game that Freddy *invents* on the spur of the moment (if you excuse the pun) is a horse race using playing cards. He lays out six cards face down in a line and explains that each card will represent a furlong. "*A six furlong race my friends,*" he cries out getting quite excited by this fun new way he's invented to pass the time! He may also lay out six beer coasters or any other form of measurement he can split into six.

He takes the four aces from the deck (he checked beforehand that the six he laid out didn't contain the aces) and lays them out as below.

Freddy then shuffles the deck and announces that he will turn the cards up one at a time. The first card is a club, "*That means the ace of clubs goes forward one furlong,*" he announces moving the ace of clubs one mark forward. "*It's in the lead my friends!*" The game continues until one of the aces wins. It was fun for a moment but the game is really lacking something to make it interesting. "*Ah well, it was worth a try,*" says Freddy and, putting his cards away, turns back to his drink.

It won't take somebody long to suggest that the race could be given a lot more *bite* if the players could bet on the cards just as they did on horses at the track. It won't take long because Freddy will expertly steer the conversation until they do.

The game is set up again. This time the aces are mixed around face down and four *jockeys* each choose an ace. The pack is shuffled and laid down next to the track.

Somebody is put in charge of the book of bets and Freddy will bet somebody a hundred dollars that the ace of diamonds will win. Freddy wants odds of two to one but since the real odds are three to one the man will take the bet thinking he's getting the better end of the deal.

The ace of diamonds wins the race. The race is set up again, after all this is fun now! Freddy offers the guy who lost money to him a double or nothing bet. Freddy chooses the ace of clubs. He wins again netting a tidy four hundred dollars for around twenty minutes of work.

Like some real horse races these trots are fixed.

Freddy has two packs of cards. One is quite normal. The second is stacked to first let the ace of diamonds win then the ace of clubs. Both decks are in Freddy's right hand jacket pocket. Freddy first brings out the normal pack and, as he explains the game, you may notice a girl's name and telephone number on the box. '*Lucky dog*' you may think. The first teaser game is played with everybody shuffling up cards. Freddy may even drop the deck on the floor. Those cards are seen to be thoroughly mixed. After the game the cards are put away.

When gambling is suggested Freddy brings out the second, stacked, pack. Oh yes, the box has the girl's name and number on it! It's just a ploy to convince you that it is the same deck! It's highly unlikely that you'd even consider the deck being switched but this little ruse really does take any possible doubt away.

Freddy false shuffles the pack. As you will see later he has a number of ways to do this.

Bets are laid.

Freddy wins the money.

Freddy's con is beautifully concealed by the fact that there will be lots of money changing hands. He's just one of a number of lucky winners and the guy Freddy bet with is just one of a number of unlucky losers. The only difference between Freddy and the other winners is that they bet by chance and won by luck. He didn't!

If it is only a small group then Freddy can use a very cunning version of the horse race. He becomes one of the jockeys! The aces are mixed face down, as before, and each player chooses an ace. Freddy chooses last of all. This takes all the *heat* from him. *Even if* he had stacked the deck, how could he possibly know which ace he would be left with? Since he's betting on his own card he would seem to have only as equal a chance as the others.

But Freddy's ace wins again!

You see Freddy has stacked the pack. From the top down, mixed up are six clubs, six diamonds, six hearts and six spades. Right underneath these cards are a club, a heart, a spade and a diamond.

The aces are chosen and, let's say, Freddy gets the ace of spades.

"Tell you what," says Freddy, *"let's make this more interesting!"* He quickly fans out the cards towards himself and splits the deck at the twenty-fourth card (he's memorized it). As he splits the deck he drags along the card of the same suit as his ace. He puts the lower half of the deck to one side and starts to shuffle his stack (plus the odd card of the same suit as his ace). *"Let's just use half the deck. If a horse doesn't finish with this half we'll carry on with the rest of the deck but all bets are doubled. Waddya say, just for fun? You give 'em a shuffle!"* He hands the cards in his hands to you to shuffle.

Often the players will agree to adding this extra spice into the game. If they don't agree Freddy just dumps the split off cards on top of the others saying something like, *"Men or mice, huh? squeak, squeak!"*

It doesn't matter how those split off cards are shuffled. The only horse with enough suit cards to be able to cross the line is Freddy's! The rest only have enough suit cards to get to, but not actually cross, the line. Whatever the order of those cards Freddy *must* win.

Race games are very popular among bar patrons. Many, although they might not to admit it to a stranger, will *keep book* for real horse races. Just five minutes from where I live is a bar that continually shows horse racing on a number of television screens. Watch closely and you'll see money changing hands. Racing is popular!

All Freddy has done is take a concept and turned it into a neat little money maker for himself. Should you ever be tempted to play a game that even remotely resembles this one, Freddy offers this advice to you, *"Even betting on cardboard horses is a mug's game!"*

SOME FAMOUS OUTRAGEOUS PROP BETS!

You must surely be getting the idea now that any form of bet can be dangerous. Even one from a friend. Let's finish up this chapter with three of the most outrageous prop bets of them all.

Titanic Thompson, a legendary prop better, once bet a colleague that he could drive a golf ball over five hundred yards. Once the bet was taken Thompson achieved the drive, somewhat dubiously, by hitting the ball from the edge of a thousand yard high cliff. What makes the bet even more amusing is that Thompson immediately offered to double or nothing the bet but this time on a level surface! The bet was accepted and Thompson won again, this time by driving the ball across the frozen water of a huge lake in winter. A joke going around at the time was that, *"The damned ball didn't stop rolling until the spring thaw!"*

Another Thompson bet was that he could throw a pumpkin over a house. He did this by careful pumpkin selection! He got one that was under grown and hard. It had the same size and consistency as that of a cricket ball. *"Hey,"* says Freddy, *"he did what he said he would do! It's a fair bet!"* I'm sure the loser wasn't quite so convinced.

Another bet involved the *Brain*, as he was known, who was sitting with some friends at a rural inn. A farmer pulled up and started to unload boxes of tomatos. The Brain casually mentioned that, after working on a farm for years as a kid, he could judge just how many tomatos were in box to, say, around three either way. Everybody wanted a piece of the bet that followed. The farmer, having been paid fifty dollars for his trouble, counted out the tomatos in a box. The Brain won the bet! Still, the other players didn't know that the farmer was a shill employed by the Brain so I guess they weren't too upset. It wasn't the actual cheat that was so ingenious here but the delightful way it was packaged to appear totally impromptu.

As Freddy says, *"If there isn't an edge, create one!"*

Now it's time to turn our attention back to the card tables once again and, in particular, the sleight-of-hand ability of Freddy the Fox.

This is where the ride gets kinda rough. Hold on tight!

How Freddy
Finds The Action

SURE, FREDDY HAS SPENT YEARS IN PRACTICE TO LEARN HOW TO HANDLE CARDS (and, as you'll see later, dice) adeptly. All of those years, however, add up to no money in his pocket if he can't find a big enough money game in which to use his skills.

A cheat like Freddy doesn't mind hustling for his beer or rent money but his *real* income comes from private games where a lot of cash can be on the table. The higher the stakes, the more he likes it!

A few cheats, especially those living in large, cosmopolitan cities, may be lucky enough to find action locally. They can become regular players in a number of games. In such a situation he will be careful to limit winnings so as not to *show out*. Freddy is very fond of saying, "*You can shear a sheep for wool once a year but you can only kill it for meat once.*"

Some cheats have even been known to cultivate players from smaller games to bring them into larger ones. In a thin paperback called *How To Win at Poker* the author describes exactly his process of playing in smaller games and gradually enticing more promising players (financially promising that is) into bigger games.

Some cheats will find an exclusive area to work in. There is a group, for example, who ply their trade exclusively on cruise ships. Another group consists of the *Mile High* boys who ply their trade on long aeroplane trips. On long haul flights fingers can get very twitchy as boredom soon sets in. On long haul flights games of cards, played for money, are *very* common indeed. High stake Backgammon games are also often seen. The cheat travels first class, right where the money is. A friend of Freddy's, called *Eagle*, knows every scam in the trade to get free tickets and upgrades. I'm encouraging him to write a book but he's, understandably, more than a little reluctant. In fact, he specifically requested that none of his tricks make it into this volume. It's a promise I didn't keep as you'll see later on but he's forgiven me as I've only given away a couple of his ploys! Meanwhile he carries on flying for free or as close to it that his wallet isn't hurt. It's all profit for him and the small group of friends he has told the secrets to.

On the cruise ships there are often organized games making the cheat's life an easier one. Plus he has the bonus that on most cruise liners there is a small casino or two. As casinos go these have to be the *easiest* to cheat anywhere. I remember once, on a QE2 Cruise from Southampton to New York, watching the games in play. A good casino *Pit Boss* would have cringed in horror at how loosely the games were played. The dealers were far too busy trying to make sure that everybody was having a good time than paying careful attention to the game. They also, pretty much as a rule of thumb, worked solo. Freddy has a huge added advantage of appearing to be enjoying his cruise a little more than most and will appear to be rather tipsy. It's expected on a cruise ship, after all he's on holiday! Provided that he is a *well behaved* drunk he can get away with murder! Many years ago I worked for a few weeks on a Mediterranean cruise ship. It's entire gambling facilities consisted of a few slots and two Blackjack tables. Each table was worked by a single person. No security, no pit boss, no nothing! Just one person dealing at the table. It was not uncommon for one of them to take a quick break and leave the cards loose on the table. I don't think it needs me to point out that this system was insane. A reasonable semi professional cheat could have paid for his cruise in an evening! Cheats *love* going cruising and, as we've said, a few make a career out of it.

Many professional cheats will acquire a *cover*. This is a job of some kind (real or imagined) that hides their real profession. To quote from *A Professional Gambler Tells How to Win* by Mike 'Pitcher' Barron (not his real name), "*. . . in the suburbs of Chicago, where my neighbors all believe I am an itinerant, but reasonably successful, pension planner for one of the country's largest insurance firms.*" As Mike implies, the job is to hide the main form of income. And, exactly as Mike has created, the job will nearly always be one that would involve traveling. It will also be one that, under cover of his 'trade', the cheat can set up meetings with reasonably influential businessmen in the areas he travels to. Selling things like medical insurance, expensive computer or office equipment or, of course, financial and pension planning are excellent *covers*.

The job brings the cheat easily into contact with local businessmen in an area who, after a few meetings, are happy to have some social time with this most genial of characters. They'll only be too happy to let him play a few hands in their *little* school.

The professional cheat can also be employed by other criminals as a *ringer*. Certain criminals spend a great deal of time playing and setting up card and dice games. They may set up a big private game for some businessmen. After all it is illegal in many places in the US to play cards for money. Finding a game, especially a big money game, can be tough. Whenever something has a market and it is illegal you can bet your weeks wages that the shadier side of society will be happy to provide it. Businessmen at a convention, who like to gamble, are only too happy when they befriend a local guy of their trade and find out that he knows a great game for them to play in. The local guy is happy, of course, to vouch for the other players in the game. "*Been playing with these boys for years now, they are tough players but all as straight as a die!*" Well, straight as some of Freddy's dice maybe!

The chumps are taken in by it all. The guy who knows about the game is, after all, just one of them. He's at the convention. He's got a company name tag. He *can't* be a shady character. So, by association, the friends he plays with must be just fine and honest as well. The local guy is, just in case you haven't guessed, a shill or outside man.

Cheats will take these jobs every time. There is little heat upon them and everything is organized. All they have to do is sit down and work their magic. The cheat will pay the criminals 50% of his personal take for this chance. Some top professional cheats make their living exclusively from such games. *Fast Jack,* a good friend of mine, travels worldwide to hook up with teams and earns a high six-figure income doing so. The criminals also have all the nice side rackets going on with girls, over-priced booze and even drugs available. Hey, it's a party, right!

In these heady days of the new millennium, gambling clubs are rapidly becoming more common, especially on the West Coast of the US. Here the play is a strange mix of casino and private play rules. Some would argue that, because the house takes a percentage of every hand, there is little incentive for them to cheat. Some more cynical types would also argue that this might mean that the house really doesn't have to care that much if cheating occurs or not. After all, whoever wins the money, they get their percentage. Some houses just charge a set fee per half hour or hour of play, but the argument remains the same. Security, Freddy notes, is hardly of stellar quality and these rooms have started to become nice little earners for him.

Freddy also enjoys going to large fund raising events. As gambling becomes more and more accepted, with the huge explosion of casinos, these fund raisers often feature casino style gambling. Private companies come in with Blackjack, Craps and Roulette tables to create a mini casino for the party folk to play in. The cause gets a percentage of the winnings. Since security, certainly knowledgeable security, is nil Freddy can also easily get a percentage of the money.

A traveling cheat is liable to turn up anywhere. He may be staying in a hotel where a big function or seminar is happening. He may be a guest at a golf day. He may *just happen* to be in the bar the night a big money back room game is due to start. He could be the nice man in sun glasses who offers you his deck-chair on the cruise ship. He may the genial old guy on the aeroplane who suggests a game of Gin to *pass the time.*

A good professional cheat is a little like a human chameleon. He can blend into *any* situation where a game may be starting. Or, indeed, any situation where there's a chance he might get one started himself.

He won't look like the gambler you see on films. He will look just like everybody else that is around, whoever they are and whatever the gathering is.

Having found or created a gambling situation the traveling cheat will milk it dry. Playing against him is a deadly and expensive business. He will have no morals about taking *everything* from you.

When Freddy talks about professional cheats he often quotes a puzzling line. *"Not every stranger you meet will be a cheat, but every cheat will be a stranger."* What he means by this is that, however well you think you know the person, you don't know them at all. All you get to know is the facade they wish you to see. Professional cheats are like faceless nobodies. They are men and women who are very unlikely to be remembered. The professional will drift easily into a game, take the money and drift out again. All you will remember about them is exactly what they give you to remember. Like a lucky ghost a good cheat does his work unseen and unsuspected.

All they might leave behind is a slightly sour smell.

Freddy's Sleight-Of-Hand Methods With Cards

PERHAPS THE BIGGEST DIFFERENCE BETWEEN THE PROFESSIONAL AND THE AMATEUR or semi professional is in his methods of cheating.

Although there are exceptions on both sides of the fence, the amateurs and semi professional cheats tend to rely more upon petty hustles and gaffed cards. The professional prefers to work with, but may not limit himself exclusively to, sleight-of-hand techniques.

The great advantage of using sleight-of-hand is that there is never any incriminating evidence for a suspicious mug to discover. Unless the sleight-of-hand is caught at the exact moment it occurs, and most are over in the blink of an eye, the cheat is safe. *Even* if the move is called, the professional can deny it. It will then be his word against the accuser's and, with his ever present *gift of the gab,* the cheat is real good at talking his way out of most situations.

As you are about to see there are numerous techniques the professional can use. They all rely on steady practice and, more importantly, nerves of steel at the card table.

Although there are numerous moves they fall quite neatly into just a few categories. Cheating during the shuffle and cut, cheating the deal, switching a card or cards and team plays.

Your best protection against these deadly talents is to be able to recognize the moves. You may not actually see the move but there are often one or more giveaways that it *might* be happening.

Don't overestimate a cheat. You may have seen a magician shuffle and cut a deck only to deal out several pat hands in a demonstration piece. The cheat, even if such a thing were truly worthwhile doing at a card table, needn't do anything anywhere as near spectacular as our conjurer's display. If luck favors him he may not cheat at all! He may use just one crooked move over the entire night's play at the right time. After all, one move at just the right time, can mean *big* money. If he is, however, going for the throat he will cheat assiduously all through the game. If the cards run against him he will work and work hard to kick lady luck where it hurts her most. The cheat will use his work as much as he needs to take the money.

It is interesting to note that, although the cheat puts in long hours to make the moves look perfectly fair, in an average game he doesn't even need to do the move that well! The average player doesn't suspect anything and, even if he did, he wouldn't know what to look for! If you are a player ask yourself just how often you closely watch the shuffle and deal over an evening.

Let's get one myth out of the way right up front. A lot of people will tell you that people cheat because they are bad at the game and that's the only way they can win. Most professional cheats are extremely good players of the game. They study the game more than most so how could they not be? They are superb at playing the man, *"Don't play the game, play the man!"* and at manipulating the opposition's psyches. They know the odds on the hands. They know the odds on any available draws. They are, normally, damned good players of the game! If those cards are running nicely for them they may choose not to cheat at all and enjoy the game for what it is. *"Cheating does kinda take the fun out of it at times,"* says Freddy. *"There are times when I like to give my hands a rest and just enjoy the game!"* A professional combines great card playing skill with cheating to make him as dangerous a man as you could ever meet at a card table.

A man like Freddy will bide his time in a game before pouncing. You may have had a few drinks, you may be being distracted, you might not know what to look for.

But when he pounces, you're dead.

Stacking Cards

S*tacking* MEANS TO SET A NUMBER OF CARDS, IN ORDER, SO THAT THEY FALL TO the cheat (or his shill) on the deal. Freddy has a number of ways he can use to achieve this.

THE PICK UP STACK

This is, perhaps, the most commonly used of all stacking techniques. Unlike some of the more skilled methods it requires very little finger skill. It does, however, require a very fast eye and a bold nerve to carry it off.

To see how it works with a simple example let's walk over to a game. Freddy is sitting in a five handed poker game and the boys are reliving old times with a few hands of five card draw. The final bets, as we join the game, have been made on a hand and three players are in. The three players lay down their hands and the winner picks up the pot. Freddy isn't interested in the winner, he's interested the hands. He notices that each of three hands contains a king. It's his deal next and he wants those three kings in his next hand.

Stacking two kings in a Pick Up.

He simply picks up the hands in such a manner as to leave those kings at the bottom of each hand! This is an almost childishly easy task for a man like Freddy. He picks up the cards above the first king in the first hand and uses those cards to scoop up the rest of the hand putting the king to the bottom. He will scoop up all three hands, often scooping up one with one hand while, in this case, scooping up the other two with his other hand. In an instant those kings are at the fifth, tenth and fifteenth positions in those cards. The cards are dumped onto the deck.

In all but the loosest of games Freddy will have to shuffle and offer the deck to be cut. You'll see, as we go along, that it is well within his ability to leave those fifteen cards in place on top of the deck. That's one of the reasons Freddy gets away with this wicked ploy while you may not do so. The hands are picked up, at blurring speed, with both hands simultaneously. The subsequent shuffle and cut put everybody totally at ease.

Freddy deals and gets, lucky him, three kings in his hand.

Really bad luck for you.

In the excellent book *Cheating at Blackjack* by Dustin D. Marks (not his real name) the Pick Up Stack, there described as the *Lay Stack*, is described as, "*. . . the backbone of all stacking methods in Blackjack.*" Trust me, he isn't joking.

THE OVERHAND STACK

This technique requires a little more finger work but has the advantage that cards can be stacked for any number of hands without working out complicated Pick Up splits.

Freddy, perhaps using a Pick Up technique, will get the cards he wants to the bottom of the deck. Then he will mix the cards using an overhand shuffle. This shuffle is very common amongst amateur card handlers and will raise no suspicion.

Except that the shuffle is not quite as fair as it would appear to be.

Freddy will *milk* his cards from the bottom into position during the shuffle. First he pulls off the top and bottom cards together. This is often called a *Haymow* action. Onto these two cards he will shuffle two cards less than the number of players in the game. So in our five hands example from above he would first take top and bottom cards together followed by three cards from the top. He then repeats the *milk/shuffle* action to put the rest of his cards into place. Often he will only stack one or two cards into place.

Having completed the stack portion of the shuffle he will then shuffle a single card on top of it but will allow this card to project from the rear of the pack slightly. This card is called a *jog* or a *brief*. He then fairly shuffles the rest of the deck on top of it all. Finally he cuts at the *jogged* card to put his stack on top of the deck.

Freddy may not start directly into the milking action. He may shuffle a third or so of the pack before starting the stacking procedure. He will then stack just as described above. It makes no difference, in end result, to him but he considers the action *cleaner* if done in the center of the shuffle as against right at the start. He may also have a shill make the cut for him to make everything look fairer still.

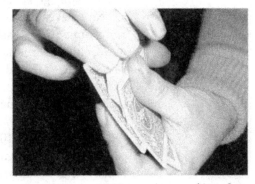

Haymowing a card into place.

The big advantage here is that the deck has already been shuffled and cut. During a Pick Up Stack the real finger work starts *after* the stack is in place.

The big give away of such an over hand stack is the unusual sound caused by so many cards being run singly. A second give away is that, unless done absolutely perfectly, the regular sound will be interrupted at regular intervals as the cheat milks in the cards from the bottom.

If you spot somebody who shuffles cards one at a time during an Overhand Shuffling action it doesn't mean that they are cheating. But it means that they *could* be cheating. Keep a real close eye on such a person and listen carefully for any interruptions in the action. Freddy says, "*A good card player watches with both his eyes and his ears!*"

Keep a good eye out for any single cards or very small groups which seem to project from a pack. They may be result of inept shuffling, they may also be jogged cards marking a cut point.

I mentioned that Freddy could use a pick up to get the cards into place but he has other ways to achieve this result. One such method is called *culling*.

The *Discard Cull* is absolutely blatant. The cheat will drop out of the hand and pass the time by glancing at the discarded hands to see if he made the right choice. In loose games this is a commonplace activity. Straight professional players (yes, there is such a beast!) call this *rabbit hunting* and, in their games, it is most frowned upon. Freddy rabbit hunts with a purpose beyond checking hands. Under cover of *simply looking* at the discards through *idle curiosity* he will arrange two or three cards at the bottom of the pile. When the discards are added back to the deck he positions them so that the hunted cards are at the bottom ready to be stacked. *Never* let anybody look through discarded hands.

With *Pick Up Culling* the cheat uses the same techniques as a Pick Up Stack but arranges the cards he needs at the bottom of the cards rather than in place. Don't expect this to look obvious. It will simply look as though he is picking up the cards in a haphazard manner. *Always* insist that hands are picked up as they lie on the table. *Don't* allow any messing around however haphazard it looks.

There are a great many magician's techniques for culling that Freddy thinks are very clever. He even complimented my own *Bucket Cull* from my book *Son of Simon Says*. I asked him what he thought of it in terms of a cheating move, culling cards as the jokers were removed from the deck for example. "*You can only take the jokers out once,*" was his only reply. Freddy likes magic tricks but this comment does cement home that, despite thinking otherwise, there are very few magician's moves that will make a difference at a card table.

To Overhand Shuffle two cards into place (more than enough to affect a game play) Freddy can use a *Fast Stack* also known as the *6, 3, 4, 1 Stack*. Freddy gets two required cards to the top of the deck. He culls them into place. The he adds a small bend or *crimp* to the bottom card of the deck. He uses his little finger to do this as he squares up the deck in preparation for a shuffle. Freddy drops a packet of about ten cards from the top of the deck then quickly shuffles six single cards on top of them. The remaining cards are dumped *behind* the shuffled off cards. This has, in effect put six cards on top of the two culled cards. Freddy then swiftly runs off three single cards and throws the rest of the deck on top. He then shuffles four single cards and throws the deck on top. He then, almost as an afterthought, shuffles a single card and throws the deck on top. With a great deal of practice this looks just like a quick and messy Overhand Shuffle. Freddy then cuts at the bent (*crimped*) card. Those two culled cards are now set to be dealt to Freddy in a four handed game.

Freddy also points out that the system can be used twice to set four cards into place. It's not something Freddy would use often *unless* he had a real mug he wanted to clean out quickly. Here Freddy would start with all four cards he wants on top of the deck. He does the 6, 3, 4, 1 Stack just as before but doesn't cut at the crimped card yet. Instead, he immediately repeats the stack and *then* cuts to the crimped card. The four required cards are now stacked for a four handed game.

You are not advised to try this in a real card game. At least not without a few years of practice to make it look as casual as it does when Freddy does the *Run Up* of the cards. There are, of course, similar numeric systems to control one, two, three or four cards to any number of hands. If you are persistent enough you can work them out. The 6, 3, 4, 1 Stack is given as an example only of how such systems work. Since it is not Freddy's wish to start up a whole new breed of cheats it is more than sufficient to make you aware that such systems exist.

As with a milk build look out for uniformity of action *even* if the shuffle looks sloppy. Look for single cards being shuffled on top of each other. Listen for a consistent *click, click* sound as the shuffle is in action. Since an Overhand Shuffle is usually used by a normal person, not particularly practiced with cards, the very ability to perform it quickly and efficiently is, in and of itself, grounds for you to start being a little bit suspicious.

If you suspect *any* kind of stacking action is taking place insist on re-shuffling the cards yourself. If that request is refused then politely leave the game.

RIFFLE STACKING

Riffle Stacking is the most difficult of all the stack methods to get down. To become perfect at it will take a cheat years of constant practice. But, when he has it pat he is capable of *fleecing* all but the most seasoned of card players.

A Riffle Shuffle is where a pack of cards is split into two halves and their inner corners riffled upwards causing the two halves to interlace. The two halves are then pushed together to complete the shuffle. Many card players have trouble just doing this action as a normal shuffle! The thought of con-

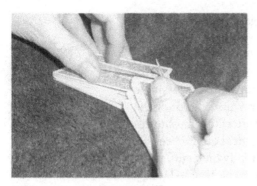
Riffle Stacking caught mid-shuffle.

trolling cards during such a shuffle is quite beyond most. Even if they have some idea that a small number of cards can be controlled on the top or the bottom of the deck (such as during *Location Plays* already discussed) the idea of actually shuffling cards into place seems impossible.

It isn't.

Freddy can have total control of several cards during the shuffle. He can count cards by feel alone, controlling their rate of fall and mix so that the cards can be stacked *exactly* where he wants them. Let's look at an example of how he does this.

Freddy has three kings on top of the deck and wants to stack them for a five handed game.

His right thumb riffles up the back of the deck in preparation for the split. Near the middle his left thumb pushes in a little harder and Freddy drops eight cards onto it before splitting the rest of the deck to the right. It looks just as though he has split the deck casually into two halves but a closer inspection will show that his left thumb is holding a tiny break on the top eight cards of its half. He starts to shuffle the two halves but, as the interlacing nears completion, he holds back the eight split cards on the left and three cards, *by feel alone,* on the right. The right thumb drops one card, the left thumb *by feel alone* drops four cards as a unit, the right thumb drops one card, the left thumb releases its final four cards and the right thumb drops its last card atop all. The deck is squared. This entire skilled work is over in a flash. The shuffle looks just like a normal one. A swift riffle and squaring of the cards. In the hands of an expert there is *nothing* to see.

The deck is split again for a second shuffle, this time the left thumb is holding a break on four cards. The deck is swiftly shuffled but Freddy controls the rate of the shuffle so that no cards from the left enter the top eleven or so cards of the right hand ones. He does this by releasing the left hand cards at a faster rate than the right hand cards. Finally he allows the broken off block of four cards on the left to land on top of all. The deck is squared.

You saw two quick Riffle Shuffles.

Freddy, using almost superhuman skill, has positioned the three kings to fifth, tenth and fifteenth in the deck. They are now ready to be dealt to Freddy. If he needs to deal to a shill he will adjust the final drop. If his shill is in the third seat for example his final shuffle will place two cards on top rather than four.

Riffle Stacking is every bit as difficult as it sounds. Not only must Freddy avoid riffling to many or too few cards he must also take great care not to disturb any important cards during the second shuffle.

A master Riffle Stacker is highly regarded in the cheating world. They have worked years to achieve an almost God like ability with the deck and deserve the respect they receive. There are few areas of card work that require more skill than this. Expertly controlled it is almost impossible to spot *but* there are a couple of things to watch for.

Watch for a shuffle that starts quickly but gradually slows with the final cards being mixed a little more carefully.

Watch for a man who studies the back edge of the deck as he shuffling. He may be visually checking his Riffle Stack.

The true master will not exhibit either of these faults. Your best chance is to catch any sign of culling which would precede the shuffle. If the cheat is that good a stacker you are unlikely to catch that either. Sounds bad, huh?

It is, but the good news for you is that, since the work effort is so high, you are most unlikely to come up against an expert riffle stacker. The small group of cheats who have this ability play in serious money games. Your pal on a Friday night, playing head to head poker for five dollars, is just not going to be cheating you this way unless you are really, really unlucky!

Riffle Stacking is ideally suited to Blackjack as only two cards need to be shuffled into place to ensure the cheat victory.

Among these most elite of cheats is another, even smaller, even more elite group. These men are known as *Double Handers* or *Double Dukers*. These men have the technical ability to shuffle not one hand but *two* into place simultaneously. This ability not only requires staggering technical ability but also no small amount of math calculations of which cards go where as well. And all done in the time it takes two Riffle Shuffles to be over!

Forget the magical demonstrations you'll see conjurors present. There are some magicians who have very fine demonstration pieces using Riffle Stacking and, without doubt, the technical skill is very high indeed. But forget them. The ability to coldly run up a hand by Riffle Stacking at a high money card table is a rare one.

If you come up against a man like Freddy who, I suspect, can Riffle Stack in his sleep it's going to cost you an awful lot of money. But, the plain truth of it is, you are most unlikely to do so.

STACKING—FACTS AND MISCONCEPTIONS

Popular films about cheating such as *The Sting* or *The Cincinnati Kid* suggest that the cheat has an esoteric ability to shuffle a deck once and be able to control every single card of the next deal.

Outside of the screenwriter's mind the cheat who can do this does not exist.

A Stacker will only ever control two or three cards at any one time. He may have the ability to stack four cards but he knows that he doesn't need to use it. By guaranteeing two or three good cards in his or his shill's hand he knows that he is going to take the money over an evening. He just twists the odds dramatically in his favor.

It is a popular fallacy that the cheat will stack a Straight Flush or four aces to come to him on the deal. These are rare hands, so rare that if he dealt himself one it would be sure to attract *hot* suspicion upon him. If dealing to himself he would rather stack a lower ranking hand that has a good chance of winning than stack a stone walled monster hand. Even when Freddy deals to a shill, his preferred technique, three of a kind is the tops he'll deal.

Your chances of meeting a Riffle Stacker are, to say the least, low.

If you play in reasonable money games your chances of meeting a man who *picks up* or *overhand* stacks are much greater than you may imagine.

Always watch and listen to the shuffle.

False Shuffles

ANY CARD CHEAT WORTH HIS SALT WILL KNOW SOME FORM OF FALSE SHUFFLE and cut techniques. There is no point in controlling or stacking cards only to lose them during a subsequent shuffle and cut. In many games the cards are shuffled and cut after each hand to try to stop cheating from happening!

It follows that if Freddy can control all or part of a deck during a shuffle and cut then he has a very powerful weapon indeed up his sleeve. The good news for Freddy is that, using Overhand or Riffle stacking, that's exactly what he can do. Using those techniques the deck is stacked *during* the shuffle.

There are lots of other ways for him to negate all or some of the shuffle and cut.

TOP STOCK CONTROL

Let's say, for example, that Freddy has twelve cards set on top of the deck from a pick up style stack. Now he has to shuffle the cards yet, somehow, keep that *stock* or *slug* of cards intact.

Overhand Stock Controls

At the most simple level Freddy will simply shuffle cards *around* his stock but not actually mix the stock in. He'll hold the deck face out in his right hand in preparation for an Overhand Shuffle. He'll shuffle about three quarters of the cards, quite normally, into his left hand. The remaining cards (his stock plus a few more) are then dropped *behind* the left hand cards. The result is that his stock stays in place on top of the deck.

Freddy can also use a *jog* or *brief* to keep his stock in place. This time he'll hold the deck back outwards in his right hand. He'll drop about a quarter of

Injog or brief.

the pack (his stock and a few more) into his left hand. With his left thumb he will pull the top card of his stock back slightly causing it to project back a little from the rest. This kind of jog is often called an *injog* or *skim*. He then genuinely shuffles the remainder of the deck on top of this set up. Finally he cuts at the skim to bring his original stock back to the top of the deck.

Some amateur players use a variation of an Overhand Shuffle called the *Chop Shuffle*. The cards are held in the right hand as if the player were about to do an ordinary Overhand Shuffle. A small block of cards is allowed to fall into the left hand. Tilting this packet backwards and forwards groups of cards are allowed to fall alternately behind and in front of it until the whole pack rests *shuffled* in the left hand. The action will often be repeated several times. This action is open to massive abuse.

Freddy can easily control a bottom stock during a chop shuffle. All he has to do is make sure that the last packet dropped goes behind the left hand cards. This leaves the stock just where it started.

Freddy can also leave a stock in place on top of the deck in two ways. First he can start with cards face out in the right hand and, as with controlling the bottom stock, put the last packet behind the left hand cards. He can also start with the cards back out. Here the first packet dropped consists of his stock (plus a few more for safety). The next group is dropped on top of his stock *but* injogged slightly. This is similar to a single card injog except that here a group of cards marks the spot. Freddy then completes the Chop shuffle normally. Finally, as he squares up the cards he can take a break at his jogged cards and cut his stock back to the top.

As you'll see in a moment Freddy can also use the Chop Shuffle to control the order of the entire pack!

Riffle Stock Controls

Freddy can also keep his top stock in place during a Riffle Shuffle. Actually it's almost childishly simple and is based on the observation that few normal people can evenly shuffle a deck by riffling. Freddy does an uneven, quite common looking, shuffle but exploits the unevenness quite deliberately.

He cuts the cards in preparation for a shuffle but takes more cards from the top of the deck in his right hand. He then shuffles the two packets together but lets the left hand cards fall slightly faster than the right hand cards. The result of both these actions is that the left hand runs out of cards before the right and that the top cards of the right hand pile (Freddy's stock) fall without being shuffled into the rest. The cards are quickly squared up.

How to Cheat at Everything

Freddy will help to conceal the action by curling his fingers over the cards to hide the block of unshuffled cards going on top. He will also keep the shuffle kinda messy for the same reason.

Of course all of these stock controls can be used to keep a block of cards together at the *bottom* of the deck as well.

Insist, during a game, that *all* the cards get shuffled properly!

FULL DECK FALSE SHUFFLES

But what if Freddy's stock is too big for a stock control? What if he needs to keep an entire deck in order? Well, he'll shuffle and cut the deck without disturbing the order of the *entire* pack. It sounds impossible but it can, with considerable practice, be done. In fact he has a whole slew of techniques to do just this feat!

A full deck false shuffle can often be compared to a monkey tapping away at a typewriter. You see a lot happening but there's no end result.

Overhand False Shuffles

Freddy can use a Chop Shuffle action to keep an entire pack in order. The move is as blatant as it is cunning and is concealed by the very sloppiness of the shuffling action. Freddy drops a packet of cards into his left hand. He then *appears* to Chop Shuffle the deck dropping cards in front of and behind the cards in the left hand. What actually happens is that he only *pretends* to drop cards in front of the left hand ones! He *only* drops packets of cards behind the left hand ones. At the end of the shuffle the entire deck is still in order. Freddy's mime work here has been practiced to perfection. Even watching closely it is impossible to see a thing during the lazy, sloppy shuffling action. When he does it chatting away to you, you haven't got a hope of catching it.

In some games players shuffle *very* lazily indeed. It's almost as though they want the shuffle over as quickly as possible so as to get on with the next hand as fast as they can. They just mix up huge blocks of cards so as to move on. In these situations Freddy can use a similar action to maintain the deck order. One such technique is called a *Three Block False Shuffle*. The cards start, held in the right hand, in preparation for an Overhand Shuffle. About a third of the pack is dropped to the left hand. Another third is dropped on top *but* injogged slightly from the first. The last third of the deck is dropped on top of all but allowed to settle

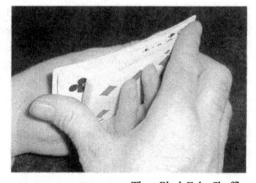

Three Block False Shuffle.

The Wedge, front view.

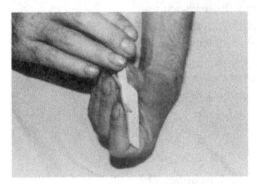

The Wedge, side view.

a little further forwards, *outjogged,* from the first two. Freddy retakes just the first two dropped packets into his right hand leaving the third, outjogged, packet behind. As he takes these two packets, because of the injog, it is easy for his right thumb to take a break between them. The cards above the break are dropped on to the right hand cards followed by the rest. A simple, rough, shuffling action that leaves the deck in order. Freddy also uses this after a more sophisticated false shuffle to confirm that the cards are really shuffled. As he is saying, *"Everybody in?"* he lazily executes this action really cementing into the player's minds that the cards are 'mixed'.

Freddy can add a little extra convincer into the Three Block shuffle by using a technique called *Block Plus Four*. He drops a third of the deck into his left hand. On top of this block he runs four cards one at a time. Then, as during the Three Block Shuffle, he drops another third of the pack leaving it injogged, followed by the final third leaving it outjogged. Leaving the outjogged cards behind he takes the rest of the pack back into the right hand (taking his thumb break at the injog just as before). The cards above his break are dropped down. Freddy then runs four cards singly and finishes by dropping the remainder of the deck. The entire deck is still in order. Freddy can choose, of course to run five, six or even seven cards during this shuffle. The whole thing looks like a lazy, sloppy shuffle and, in the right hands, is extremely deceptive.

Some amateur players will use a kind of combination Riffle/Overhand Shuffle called a *Block and Wedge.* The cards are held in the left hand. The right hand takes about half the cards from behind the deck and forces them against the top of the left hand cards. This action causes the cards to roughly interweave. It is often accompanied by a 'sawing' action to help the cards weave together. Freddy can use what appears to be a Block and Wedge to keep the deck in order. To start Freddy puts a small bend or crimp into the bottom card of the deck as he lifts up the bottom half of the deck to begin the shuffle. He appears to mix the cards but what *actually* happens is that his left thumb pushes up the top card of its half slightly and the right hand cards are *sawn* in behind it. From the front it looks just as though the right hand cards are being mixed into the left hand ones. In fact the entire block of right hand cards is going behind the top card of the left hand ones! Freddy now cuts at his crimp and repeats the entire action to leave the deck back where it started. He can also eliminate having to use the crimp by, during the first half of the shuffle, letting the right hand cards end up slightly injogged from the left hand cards.

False Riffle Shuffles

Among all the false Riffle Shuffle techniques available to the cheat, perhaps the most convincing of all, in Freddy's opinion anyway, is one called the *Push Through Riffle Shuffle*. Freddy cuts the deck into two halves. The top half of the deck is in his right hand. The two halves are genuinely riffled together. The only tiny control Freddy uses here is to allow a card or two to fall from the right hand pile last of all. It is in the squaring action that the cheating takes place. Freddy starts to push the two halves together but at a *slight* angle to each other.

Start of a Push Through.

As the cards are, apparently, squared the original bottom half of the pack (the left hand cards) are pushed a little further than they need be. Freddy uses the third finger of his left hand to do this. The result is that the bottom half is pushed *through* the top half so that, as the long edges of the cards are squared, it protrudes from the right hand end of the cards. The pack appears to have been shuffled and squared. The protruding bottom half is hidden behind the right fingers.

Push Through nearing completion.

Without pausing Freddy then strips out the bottom cards and puts them down. The rest of the cards are placed on top simulating a cutting action. The cards, although apparently shuffled and cut, are in the same order. Sounds tough? It is, but after years of practice it looks, in Freddy's hands, exactly like a shuffle and cut.

After the strip out Freddy can also put the original bottom cards on top of the deck but keep a break between them and the original top cards with his left thumb. He can then cut about half the cards from below the break to the top followed by the rest of the cards below the break. This way the deck seems to have been shuffled and given a series of cuts.

Pop Over Shuffle.

If Freddy, after the strip out, puts the bottom cards on top offset to the left he can go directly into a *Greek* cut which you'll read about in a while.

A cruder version of the shuffle, often called the *Pull Out* or *Strip Out Riffle Shuffle,* involves cutting the top portion of the deck to the left. The cards are genuinely riffled together with Freddy, once more, allowing a few cards from the right hand pile to fall last. The cards are, apparently, fully squared up but, this time the left hand (original top) cards are not pushed in all the way. They are left protruding on the left side, hidden by the left hand fingers. The right hand strips the original bottom cards away and puts them down. The remaining cards are placed on top to simulate a cut.

Keep an eye out for the man who goes into a cut sequence straight after squaring the cards without pause and without you seeing that the cards are fully squared first.

Another action used by less skilled workers is called the *Pop Over Shuffle*. Once more Freddy will start the shuffle normally but with two differences. First his hands will be curled around the cards more than normal hiding them from sight. Secondly the interlacing will be very slight. The cards will only interlace enough to make the shuffle *sound* genuine.

As Freddy begins to square the cards he will quickly lift the original top portion of cards slightly. This is a lightning fast action and is just enough to strip those cards free of the shuffle. As Freddy squares the cards the original top cards simply ride over the bottom cards and the pack is squared.

Because of the high hand cover or *shade* required this shuffle is considered to be rather crude compared to others but that doesn't mean that it doesn't work. It also doesn't mean that it isn't used by the guys who can't do a more sophisticated action.

When the gambling game of Faro was popular a specific shuffle was used to split up winning pairs of cards. It consisted of the cards being split into two halves and having the ends butted against each other. With a slight pressure the cards can be made to interweave perfectly with every single card from one half separated by a card from the other half. A perfect shuffle if you like. Because of its association with the game this shuffle has become known as the *Faro Shuffle*. Although it may sound tough to split a deck into two identical halves of twenty-six cards each and interweave them perfectly it actually isn't as hard as it sounds. Sure it's tough but it's not that tough that it can't be perfected. In fact some sleight-of-hand magicians use the shuffle for some very clever magic tricks.

There are two kinds of Faro Shuffle. One where the top card of the deck stays on top (an *Out Faro*) and one where the top card goes second from top during the shuffle (an *In Faro*).

Freddy can use the shuffle to stack a deck certain ways. At its simplest level Freddy can have three or four cards on top of the deck. One In Faro will stack the cards for a two handed game. Two In Faros will stack the cards for a four handed game. At this level, of course, the entire shuffle need not be perfect, *only* the top cards that Freddy needs to interweave perfectly. In the magician's world such a shuffle would be referred to as an *Imperfect* or *Incomplete Faro*. If Freddy can cull a large proportion of one suit to the top of the deck (not so hard in Bridge where the tricks tend to fall into suit blocks) then two perfect shuffles can stack a superb Bridge or Solo hand for him.

With astonishing cheek Freddy sometimes points out how *perfect* the shuffle is! He tells the mugs that it is called a *casino* shuffle. I am amazed that they

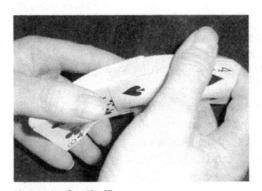

Faro or Perfect Shuffle..

believe him when he says that such a *perfect* shuffle makes cheating impossible! Ah well!

Some cheats can perform the Faro Shuffle on a table, duplicating the actions of a normal Riffle Shuffle. The group of men who can perform a perfect *Tabled Faro Shuffle* is a small one. The group who can do it and make it look just like a normal shuffle is even smaller. You are most unlikely to run up against one of these guys.

Combination Shuffles

Freddy may well combine several minor shuffles together to give a dazzling display of actually mixing up the cards. He may start with a Three Block Shuffle, followed by a Block and Wedge followed by another Three Block Shuffle for example. Smoothly done you'd swear the cards were mixed but the deck has stayed in order.

More Techniques

Even in a book of this size it is impossible to give you every shuffling technique of the cheat. There are, quite simply, enough to fill several volumes this size using playing cards alone! Indeed, moves like Riffle Stacking have filled several books by themselves! The cheat can also use variations of other false shuffling techniques such as, borrowed from the sleight-of-hand magician's world, the *Zarrow* and *Shank Shuffles*.

It is not so important for you to know *every* variation of false shuffling but it is most important for you to be aware that it can happen and do your utmost to try to prevent the cheat from being able to do so. So my advice is rather than watch an expert and being able to say, "*Hey, that's cheating!*" it is far better to set conditions where the cheat will be loath to try his skills. Shutting the door after the horse has bolted is never too wise.

Insist that cards are openly shuffled.

Watch carefully for the man who shuffles very quickly while distracting attention by chatting away about something.

Be wary of the man who follows a quick shuffle with a series of cuts.

Be Wary of the man who shuffles without looking at the deck. He knows that by looking at them it can draw attention to them. By keeping your attention away from the cards he is making his work easier.

Don't think you can't be fooled by these techniques. Performed by an expert like Freddy they look absolutely natural in action.

If you have *any* doubts at all ask, as is your right, for the cards to be shuffled again. If that request is refused calmly excuse yourself and leave the game.

Cheating The Cut

So far you've seen how Freddy can stack and cull cards. You've seen how he can shuffle the deck and keep everything in place. But, then comes the real *bette noire* of the cheat, the cut. In all proper card games it is expected that the deck will, after the shuffle, be offered to the player on the dealer's right to be cut. This simple rule can upset all of the hard work that the cheat has put in so far. Unless Freddy can beat the cut his skills are all but useless.

Freddy has *lots* of ways to beat the cut!

He can offer the pack to a shill who can help a false cut along. In looser company Freddy will be allowed to get away with cutting the cards himself. If he's working solo, and a straight player gets to cut, then he just has to beat the cut himself.

Here are some examples of all of the above.

LET IT RIDE

Freddy can get away with this once or twice over an evening and it is, perhaps, the simplest way to beat the cut. In many schools it is quite common for a gambler to refuse to cut the cards, saying, *"Deal 'em as they are."* Among professionals this is known as *Letting it Ride*. The player will often just tap the top of the deck to indicate that they are happy with the cards as they are.

Freddy can offer the cards to a shill who, knowing that this is the correct time to do so from a signal, will tap the top of the deck and say, *"Just deal 'em!"*

THE JOG

After the shuffle Freddy will throw in a cut and, as he completes the cut, jog back the original top card of the deck a little. Once again he offers the deck

to his shill who cuts the deck at the jogged card to
negate the original cut.

THE TRUE CUT

It's common for a player to cut the pack in his hands.
He grips the edges of the cards and pulls off the top
half of the pack to place it to the bottom. The adept
cheat does the same action but with one *big* difference. He pulls off the *bottom* half of the pack and puts
the original top half back on top of it! Done with a
careless, quick confidence it looks identical to a normal cutting action. It's also really fast so there's no
point calling the cheat on it. Like a great many sleight-
of-hand card moves it's over before you can get your
mouth open.

True Cut.

MULTIPLE PACKET CUTS

Some players make a specialty of complicated cuts
where a number of packets are cut in a random
sequence. They think that these cuts make them look
like *real* card men. Freddy also uses multiple packet cuts but for an altogether
different reason. To leave the order undisturbed.

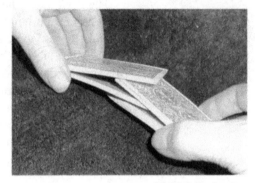

Multiple Packet Cut.

A good multiple false cut is a little like a jigsaw puzzle. All the bits just
have to go back together correctly.

Freddy's favorite is called the *Greek Cut.* It's not too flashy but it looks good.
It is also very similar to a casino style cut in action and so, for players who've
been to Vegas and watched a dealer shuffle and cut, it is particularly convincing. Freddy cuts about two thirds of the deck from bottom to top but
leaves them overlapping at the left end of the deck. With a continuing action
he pulls out the lower section of the overlapped cards with his left hand while
the right hand cuts the lower packet and the top half of the overlapped cards
as one unit to the top. He then finally, once again with a continuing flowing
action, cuts the packet of cards that are now outjogged to the right in the
center of the deck to the top. In action it looks like a smooth flowing sequence
of cuts. It looks almost like a little mini-shuffle has gone on. It looks like the
cards have been mixed.

The entire deck is in the same order it started in.

Here's another, altogether more complicated, cutting action. Freddy cuts about
a quarter of the pack from the bottom to the top but holds a break between it
and the rest of the deck with his right thumb. Now, using his left thumb, Freddy
lifts up about a third of the cards under his right thumb break (about a third of

the bottom packet of cards in other words). He splits the remaining cards into two with his right third finger. His right third finger holds the upper portion of these cards while his left third finger grips the very bottom packet.

If you are trying this with a deck of cards in hand yourself you'll have, assuming you haven't given up in total frustration, two packets of cards (top and third packet) gripped by the right hand and two packets of cards (second and bottom) gripped by the left hand.

Freddy strips his hands apart and drops the packets in the following order. First the upper right hand packet followed by the bottom left hand packet. Then he drops the remaining right hand packet and, finally, drops the last left hand packet on top of it all.

The deck has remained in order. To an average player, controlling two packets in each hand simultaneously, is impressive. To cheat under these circumstances would seem to be impossible. They are right in one case. It is impressive and takes a lot of practice to get it to look nice and smooth. Sadly they are wrong, as we've seen, to assume that cheating is impossible. Freddy can do this entire sequence in a little under four seconds.

There are *numerous* multiple cut sequences that will do Freddy's job for him. All look very flashy. It is worth bearing in mind that Freddy says that the more *complicated* a cut looks, often the *easier* it is to fake.

Insist on simple straight cuts when you play cards for money.

THE CRIMP OR BRIDGE

If Freddy is working without a shill he can often make another player into an unwitting one by forcing the player to cut just where he wants him to. He will do this by using a *Crimp* or *Bridge.*

After his false shuffle Freddy will give the cards a quick cut. As he drops his cut cards onto the remainder he will bend or bridge the bottom few cards of the cut off packet. He does this by pulling on them with his little finger or by butting his thumb against them as the deck is squared up. A single bent card is called a crimp, a bent block of cards is referred to as a bridge. Freddy prefers to use a bridge, others prefer a crimp. Both work.

These bent (and it's only a *tiny* bend at one end of the deck) cards not only mark the original top of the deck but also create a tiny air pocket in the center of the deck. Just as an old magazine tends to fall open at the same page every time these cards will tend to *split* at this point every time.

A casual cut from another player will, nine times out of ten, split the pack at the crimp or bridge point.

Most players tend to cut at about the same place every time the deck is offered to them. Freddy will,

Bridge work (highly exaggerated).

therefore, place his work as near to that general area as possible. If a player always makes a deep cut for example the work will be lower down in the deck.

Once the cut is completed Freddy will swiftly and invisibly remove the crimp or bridge work as he squares up the cards ready for the deal.

This ploy does not work every single time but that doesn't really worry Freddy. If the unsuspecting shill misses the cut then Freddy will play out the hand normally. His normal action is to drop out of the hand pretty quickly unless he gets a great hand by accident. After all, depending on where the cut hit, somebody else may have gotten his carefully stacked cards! Freddy only needs the crimp or bridge work to come home to roost a percentage of times to make him a really big winner. Freddy can also use crimp or bridge work in place of a jog when working with a shill.

Avoid cutting in a regular manner. Vary the depth of your cut each time the deck is offered to you.

To really irritate Freddy cut in the following manner. First pull a section of cards from the *middle* of the deck and put them on top. Then perform a straight cut. This action, commonly known as a *Scarne Cut*, is almost certain to destroy some of, if not all of, Freddy's stack work.

THE HOP

Like Riffle Stacking this move requires serious time investment in practice. Performed by a professional like Freddy it is incredibly difficult to even suspect, never mind spot.

Freddy offers the cards to be cut. As is standard practice, the player lifts off half the pack and places them by the side of the remainder. Freddy puts the lower portion on top of the cut off cards. As he does this he off sets the upper cards slightly to leave a small step between the halves. He picks up the whole pack ready to deal but keeps the step in place with his left little finger.

His right hand comes over the deck to apparently square up the cards. At the *very instant* the right hand grips the deck the left little finger pulls down on the step allowing Freddy's first and little fingers to enter in between the two halves. His left second and third fingers wrap over the top of the deck. Freddy's right hand grips the bottom half of the deck and, with a blinding speed, the left fingers whip the top half of the deck back to the bottom to negate the cut. The speed with which this can be done is astonishing and, in an expert's hands, can be measured in tenths of a second.

Freddy can cover or shade the Hop in a number of ways. He may use the squaring action described above. He may do it as he taps the ends of the cards against the table to square them up. He may do it using the edge of the table as a cover as he pulls the

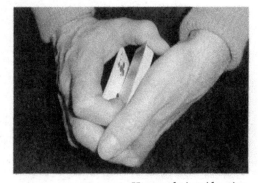

Hop caught in mid-action.

cards back towards himself. A shill may question you or create a minor distraction at the point of the Hop. Sometimes Freddy sharply riffles his right thumb up the back of the cards at the point of the Hop. This not only provides a nice visual misdirection for him but also covers any tiny noise that may be made as the packets change places.

It can't be stressed enough how devastating this is in the hands of a professional. Thankfully the man who does it under fire is rare and you are much more likely to be in a game where the cut is cheated using one of the other methods described here. Sleight-of-hand magicians call this move *The Pass*.

Always watch the dealer's hands from the time the cut is started to the time they start to deal. This is one of the most critical moments in a game both for you and the cheat.

Watch for the right hand coming over to cover the pack. It's your only real visual give away that a Hop may be about to happen. You won't see the Hop itself because of its speed (Freddy can do it one hundred and ten times in a minute without breaking a sweat) but you'll know that it *may* have happened.

Never let the deck go even partially out of sight. Some cheats use the edge of the table as a cover.

Watch for the dealer squaring the cards very carefully. This all-around squaring action may be being used as a cover for a Hop.

One Handed Hops

The Hop, also known as *Shifting the Cut* can be done using just one hand. The disadvantages of one handed Shifts are that they tend to be slower than two handed ones. However, a one handed Shift does carry the advantage that the cheats free hand can provide powerful shade and misdirection.

There are two main types of one handed Shifts.

For the *Back Cut*, also known as a *Charlier,* Freddy cuts the deck and holds it high in his left hand. He maintains a minute break between the two portions with his thumb. He now leans forward to place his ante into the pot. This action naturally drops his left hand down and behind his right arm. The edge of the table will also provide shade for the action. The lower portion of the deck is allowed to drop toward the left palm. It is pushed back by the left first finger and allowed to ride around the upper portion. The deck is then squared. The pack is back in its original order. An expert like Freddy can do the Shift in around one second.

The *Front Cut* is much harder to learn but carries several advantages. First the packets use up less space going around each other so it is much easier to cover. Secondly, it is faster. The pack is cut and held with the thumb curled over the top short edge of the pack.

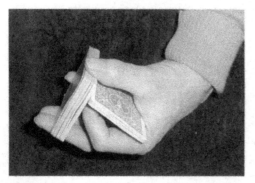

Charlier Cut.

How to Cheat at Everything

A tiny break is held between the two halves with pressure from the left fingers. The right hand approaches to square up the cards and the moment that it is close enough to provide cover the left little finger scoots around to grip the deck at the inner short edge. In a continuing action the left first and second fingers enter into the break and the left third finger curls underneath the deck. The lower portion is levered forward and around the upper portion of cards. The upper portion is held between the thumb and left little finger. The lower portion is held by the left first and second fingers on top and third finger underneath. By

Erdnase or Front Cut.

the time the right hand reaches the deck the Shift is over. The right hand only provides cover for the Shift and does no actual work in its execution. The shift can also be covered by placing a bet or reaching across for a cigarette. It can be covered by *anything* that puts the deck out of sight for a moment. And I mean a moment. This Shift is *very* fast in the hands of a professional.

The Poor Man's Hop

For the cheat who has neither the time nor inclination to learn a Hop properly there is a small time hustle that he can use to leave a small block of cards on top of the deck during a cutting action. The pack with its desired cards on top lies on the table. The cheat cuts off a little more than half the pack to the right. He keeps hold of the top six or seven cards as his hand returns to pick up the remainder of the deck to complete the cut. These cards are dumped on top of the remainder as it is picked up to be placed on top of the cut off cards. It sounds as though this must be instantly obvious but, covered with strong verbal misdirection, is extraordinarily deceptive. Having just seven known cards on top during a game of Stud Poker can be a heady advantage for cheat!

Another Poor Man's Hop

If the cheat needs to keep a bigger stack in place the Hop described above could get a little obvious but there is another that he can use. The deck is on the table in front of him and he will cut the top half (containing his stack) into his left hand. He will now reach down and pick up the rest of the cards to complete the cut. However, *as if by accident,* he will leave several cards behind and place the cards he has picked on top of his stack but he will over lap them to the left. At this exact moment the hands come together he will 'notice' the cards left behind and say, "*Oops!*" His right hand drags out the original top half of the deck and dumps it on top of the left behind cards. He then lifts all the cards up and replaces them on top of the cards in his left hand. The stack is now on top. The whole cut, oops, pick up action is remarkably disarming. It is also very common for a few cards to be left behind during the cut, especially after a few drinks, so there is nothing to tip off that this is a cheat in action.

The "No Hop" Hop

The brazen amateur in loose company may try out a version of the Hop that requires absolutely no sleight-of-hand at all. Once more the tabled cards are ready to be cut. The cheat cuts half the pack to the left. He asks a question to somebody at the table such as, "*Are you in the pot?*" As all attention goes from the cards he picks up the original bottom half of the deck and then scoops the original top half back on top!

Don't think that a cheat won't try a move like this. He will. If called on it he can always claim that it was an error and nothing more. What's sad is that in a lot of situations he just won't be called on it.

Always watch the shuffle and cut closely. Don't allow yourself to be distracted.

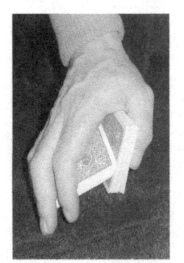

Table Shift, mid-action.

THE TABLE SHIFT

This is a very deceptive action indeed. Even if you are watching closely its lightning-like action is very tough to catch.

The deck is offered to the player on the right for a cut. The player cuts off the top half of the deck. The cheat then picks up the bottom half of the deck as if to place it on top of the cut off cards. However the cards are being primarily gripped in the crotch of the thumb. The right hand comes over the cut off cards as the left hand comes in to help square up the cards. The left hand provides vital shade for the action that follows.

Behind the moving left hand the right fingers drag the cut off cards back on top of the cards it is holding. The pack in a continuing action is twisted upright and squared between the hands.

Don't ever allow the cards to go out of sight, even for an instant.

Insist that all cuts are done slowly and openly.

Spinging the deck.

SPINGING THE DECK

Freddy has a nice little stack of twelve cards or so on top of the deck that he'd really like to keep there. He

How to Cheat at Everything

Riffle Shuffles the deck maintaining the stack but allowing one extra card to fall on top of it. He now has, after the deck is squared, one extra card on top of his stack. He now rests the deck on the table. His hands come around the deck and his right first finger rests on the top card. With a fluid motion his right hand moves to the right taking the *bottom* half of the deck *plus* the top card of the deck. The left hand cards (on top of which is Freddy's stack) are placed on top to complete the 'cut'. Because there is a visual movement of the top card this cut looks very realistic indeed. Of course all that is actually happening is that the unwanted top card is being slipped off onto the bottom half of the deck. For this reason this is also often called *Slip Cutting*.

Here you've seen a collection of fake cuts that cover Freddy cutting for himself, shill cuts (and a good false cut is often all a shill needs to learn) and even solo play cuts. There are lots more but this is a pretty good set and more than enough for you to realize that a good cheat like Freddy can beat that most irritating of moments for him in a card game. The moment the deck has to be cut!

With regard to the shuffle and cut I asked Freddy to put together his top tips to avoid being cheated. The list came out at seven points you should learn and apply.

When hands are discarded make sure that they are placed face down without anybody being able to see them.

Beware the rabbit hunter who, ever so casually, messes about with the discard pile.

Be very alert for crimp and bridge work. A *heavy* piece of work may be visible to the naked eye. Don't accuse anybody but just point out that, since some of the cards are showing a little wear and tear, it may be time to bring in a new deck. The cheat, realizing that you are more knowledgeable than you at first appeared to be, will be loath to use that work again.

Vary your cutting technique. Sometimes high, sometimes low but *never* just tap the deck to let it ride.

Be *very* alert during the time the deck is cut and right on up to the deal. This is one of the most dangerous times for you.

When you are dealing make sure that each and every card is shuffled. By not doing so you are leaving yourself open to the talents of the *memory man* who, having memorized a few discard hands will be waiting for groups to appear thanks to your sloppy shuffling. He may even be practiced enough to track small blocks through the shuffle and know just where they are. Such a player, most commonly seen at Blackjack tables, is called a *Shuffle Tracker*.

Don't just watch a shuffle, *listen* as well!

I once asked Freddy what he would do if he saw somebody else in a game of cards who was cheating and taking money from other players.

"Back them of course," was his reply. *"I may be a reformed character but I ain't stupid!"*

Peeking And Dealing

FREDDY'S MAIN ALTERNATIVE TO CHEATING BY STACKING IS TO CHEAT ON THE DEAL itself. Rather than dealing the cards in the proper order from the top of the deck Freddy can use his techniques to give himself a better hand by dealing his cards from other places!

His two big dealing weapons are the *Second Deal* and the *Bottom Deal*.

To use either, but especially Second Dealing, Freddy will need knowledge of certain cards. For example, to use a Second Deal it's really useful if he knows what the top card of the deck is! He could use *paper* but would prefer not to. Marked cards can be a hassle to get into play and can prove to be damning evidence should they be discovered. A good *mechanic* like Freddy will *peek,* or secretly look at the cards he needs knowledge of, before or even *during* the deal.

Before we look at his dealing techniques let's look at a few of his peek techniques.

PEEKS

Freddy has a number of methods to secretly gain knowledge of the top or bottom cards of the deck. Some are incredibly simple, others use more subtle techniques. Here's a few of both.

The Shuffle Peek

It is very common for a player, after a Riffle Shuffle to put the cards on their edge, faces towards them, to square them up. The average player does this because it makes the squaring process easier. The petty cheat, in the process of squaring up the roughly shuffled cards, can use his fingers to push up the top one or two cards of the deck so that, as the cards are squared, he can see them. In one simple moment the cheat gains knowledge of the top one or two cards.

As a bonus he also, of course, sees the bottom card. This is a very crude technique and not considered very highly by guys like Freddy. Just because it isn't highly considered by experts doesn't mean that your pal won't try to use it against you at the next Friday night game. If he's using this peek he's unlikely to be using dealing techniques against you but, instead, using it simply to gain knowledge of several cards positions to give him an edge even with a fair deal.

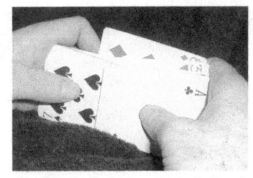

Shuffle Peek.

The cheat can also square the cards on the table but then tap the deck against the table to square it up thoroughly. He immediately sees the bottom card and, if his fingers lift at the back slightly, he'll also swiftly gain knowledge of the top one or two cards.

Freddy's mother used to play a lot of Gin and, after watching her beat another elderly lady out of thirty dollars, I mentioned to Freddy that Lizzie always squared the cards after the shuffle so that she could see the bottom card. "*That's all you saw?*" he laughed. "*She may be getting on but she's still got it!*"

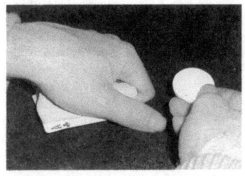

Heel Peek.

The Heel Peek

This is one of the more common peeks used by a professional cheat. Done quickly it is almost impossible to catch.

The pack is held in a normal dealing position but tilted down slightly. With the base of his thumb Freddy very slightly lifts up the inner corner of the top card. Using the hand holding the pack he will now point something out on the table. He may ask about the pot or ask somebody to move their drink. He may just toss in his own ante chip. What is important is that the action allows his hand to turn allowing him to glimpse the index corner of the top card of the deck. A good

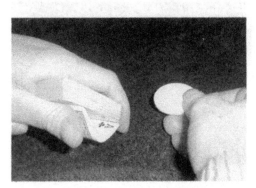

Bubble Peek, also known as a Blister Peek.

worker can even leave out the pointing action and get his glimpse directly by just relaxing his hand slightly allowing the deck to dip. At this level the peek becomes deadly in such games as Blackjack or Pontoon. The slight pauses between player's decisions mean that Freddy can peek nearly *every* card!

The Bubble Peek

This peek also works with a hand turn cover. Freddy will use an excuse to turn the deck nearly face up. Once more he may be throwing in a chip or, perhaps, he may be appearing to check his hole card/s in a game of Stud Poker. When the deck is nearly face up Freddy's thumb will push against the top left hand corner of the top card of the deck. Normally such an action, similar to pushing a card off to deal it, would result in the card moving sideways off the deck. But when using this peek Freddy's fingers stop the card from moving. This results in the top card bending away from the deck allowing Freddy to see the top right index corner of the card.

This Bubble peek, also known as *pushing a blister*, will always take place under cover of strong misdirection. Freddy *may* be looking at his hole card in a game of poker. He *may* also be looking at the top card of the deck!

Insist that the pack is held flat at all times. It won't stop peeking but it does, at least, make it harder.

The Pontoon or Blackjack Peek

It is common for the banker (dealer) in private Pontoon and Blackjack games to deal out cards by lifting them from the back of the deck before flipping them over. Straight players I've asked say it is because it's kinda cool to know the card the player is going to get before they get to see it. Almost a legal and open peek if you like. All well and good but the joy that allows that little look is wide open to abuse by people like Freddy. He'll take it a stage further.

Pontoon Peek.

Freddy will lift up the back edge of the top card as he pulls it back prior to flipping it over. As he does this his thumb lifts up the second card under cover of the first card. This momentary action is completely covered by the card he is about to flip over. The card is flipped over and, once more, Freddy knows the top card of the deck. When dealing to his own hand this makes his decision on whether to take a card or not a pretty easy one.

The Bottom Bubble

If Freddy is going to use that most famous of gambler's moves, the *Bottom Deal*, knowing the bottom card is essential. In very loose company he may just use one of his, throw in a chip, check the hole card ploys he used when peeking the top card. Here he'll just actually see the bottom card of the deck!

Freddy prefers to use the far more subtle *Bottom Bubble*. The cards are held face down in the left hand. The right hand comes over the cards, fingers in front,

Bottom Bubble.

How to Cheat at Everything

thumb at the back, as if to square the cards. During this process Freddy drags the bottom card back a little with his left fingers. The right thumb stops the card physically moving and so, like a blister peek, the card bends away from the deck. With a simple glance Freddy gains knowledge of the bottom card. The action is over in less than a second and looks, for all the world, as if Freddy just squared the cards and nothing more.

Watch for a man who squares up a pack with his right hand curled over the cards.

Insist that cards are squared, face down, flat against the table.

Don't allow the deck to turn. Insist that it is kept flat. If the dealer needs to see his hole card ask him to put the deck down before he looks.

FALSE DEAL WORK

As mentioned, the big genres of fake dealing are Second and Bottom dealing. A second dealer or *number two man* is a man who, while seemingly dealing the top card of the deck, actually deals the card underneath it. A bottom dealer (also known as a *cellar man* or *subway dealer*) deals the bottom card of the deck while appearing to deal from the top. Fake dealers are highly respected in the cheat's world. Just to learn the deals takes an inordinate amount of practice. To do the move under fire when there's a huge pile of money on a table is considered an acme of achievement.

Second Dealing

The advantage of a second deal should be apparent to even the most novice card player. If Freddy peeks the top card of the deck and notes that it would be a good card for you he can second deal and keep that card out of your hand. He can also hold a good card for himself by second dealing to other players before taking it.

There are two main types of second deal. The most commonly used is the *Strike Second*. It is the easier of the two to learn. Not easy to learn, just the easier of the two.

When dealing fairly Freddy deals the cards by pulling them from the deck with his right thumb. His right thumb hits, or strikes, the outer right corner of the deck and pulls the top card off to deal it. This is a very common dealing action.

When Freddy wants to second deal he will combine sleight-of-hand skill with perfect timing to deal the second card down. At the exact moment his right thumb is striking the outer right corner of the deck his left thumb pulls the top card of the deck down

Strike Second.

Push-Off Second.

slightly so that a small portion of the top right corner of the second card is exposed. Freddy's thumb contacts that exposed portion and drags out the second card from under the top one. As the second card is clearing the deck the left thumb moves the top card back into perfect alignment.

Some gambling books will tell you that the exposed area will be very tiny indeed. They'll tell you that the exposed area may be less than the width of the white border of the card. Freddy disagrees. It's not the size of the exposed area that is important, he claims, it's the timing on the deal.

A perfect strike second is almost uncanny to watch. When Freddy does it with the deck face up to show his pals, it looks like the second card is somehow melting through the top one. With the cards face down there is nothing to see. It looks *exactly* as though Freddy is dealing the top card.

The other type of second deal is the *Two Card Push-Off.* When dealing fairly Freddy, using his left thumb, pushes over the top card. He takes this card with his right hand to deal it. Again, this is a very common dealing action among straight players.

When he wishes to second deal Freddy will push not one but two cards from the deck in almost perfect alignment. As he apparently takes the top card to deal it, he *actually* takes the second card as the left thumb whips the top card back into place.

If you think that sounds tough to do then you are right. The push-off action is generally considered to be amongst the toughest of moves to perfect.

Entire books have been written on the exacting techniques required to learn a good second deal, including my own *Second to None*. If you decide to try to learn a deal make sure that you have four or five years free time first.

There are, quite literally, only a handful of people in the world who can do perfect second deals under fire. It takes, I'll repeat, an almost unbelievable amount of time to get to that level. You are much more likely to come up against a dealer who will be getting away with mediocre technique simply because the other players don't know what to watch for. If the technique is less than perfect there are a number of giveaways that a second deal may be being used.

Watch for the way the deck is held. The cards will commonly be gripped with the forefinger curled over the outer short edge with the other three fingers down the right long edge. The thumb will rest on the top of the deck pointing towards the outer right corner. The cards will almost certainly be beveled slightly. Although a lot of straight players hold a deck this way it is a sign that the dealer is comfortable with a deck of cards. It is also the grip used by most fake dealers. Dubbed the *mechanics grip* by John Scarne, he considered it proof that the dealer was a cheater. It isn't proof at all but, if you see it being used, you should be very wary.

How to Cheat at Everything

Watch for the action of the left thumb on top of the deck. While second dealing it will have a definite flicking action. It will also not lift from the deck at the point of the deal.

Watch for the dealer who distinctly tilts the front end of the deck up whilst dealing. He may be trying to conceal poor technique by hiding the top card from your viewpoint. This habit, much frowned upon by professionals like Freddy, is called *neck-tying*.

Listen to the deal. Unless the deal technique is perfect there will be a discernible difference in sound between a normal deal and a second deal. There will be a slight *scraping* or *swooshing* sound as the second is dealt because the second card is sliding out between the deck and the top card. You may also hear a faint *tick* sound as the card clears. Making the second sound like a normal deal is one of the prized secrets of the top professionals (and, in fact, consists much more of making a normal deal sound like a second deal so all the deals are alike audibly) but the ability to do so is known only to a few top men.

Bottom Dealing

The *subway man* is just about as dangerous as a human being can get with a deck of cards. He will cull or palm cards to the bottom of the deck (or peek the cards in place) and begin to deal. He deals the other players cards normally. On his, or his shill's, hand he will deal from the *bottom* of the deck. A good time is had by all, except for the other players of course. The bottom deal is a very demanding move to master. The cheat must duplicate the actions of a normal deal to perfection.

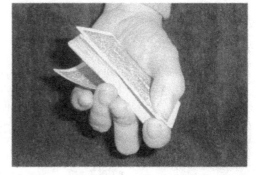

Start of a Bottom Deal.

Most bottom dealers have a unique way of doing the move that fits their hands. However all bottom deals tend to fall into one of two types.

The action of a *Push Out Bottom* is, in a way, similar to that of a push off second technique. Freddy pushes the top card of the deck over to the right with his left thumb. Under the deck his second, third and little fingers, as a unit, buckle back and push out the bottom card underneath the top card. The right fingers start to grip both cards, but, at the exact moment the fingers start to close on the thumb to take the card, the left thumb whips the top card back and the bottom card is dealt.

Freddy has to do this at dealing speed with no break in the rhythm as he deals the cards. He must make the action look and *sound* as if the top card were

Bottom Deal.

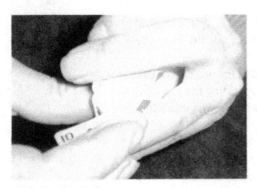

Strike Bottom Deal.

Erdnase Grip.

being dealt. He must overcome the visual discrepancy of a card being dealt from about half an inch lower than it should be. It is little wonder that it can take a dedicated mechanic five or six years to perfect a good bottom like this.

Some bottom dealers do not push over the top card preferring, instead, to just time the take perfectly. As the hands come together they just take the bottom card as it is buckled out without relying on any cover from the top card. In the right hands the illusion is perfect. If using this technique (often called *missing the deck*) the deal will often be accompanied by a dipping action of the left hand at the moment of the deal.

The other type of bottom deal is the *Pull Out* or *Strike Bottom*. The dealing action is identical to that of a push out deal but the take is different. When Freddy wants the bottom card his right first finger goes below the deck, between his left second and third fingers, to make contact with the bottom card. As Freddy's right thumb contacts the top pushed over card the left thumb whips that card back onto the top of the deck. At the same time the right first finger drags out the bottom card to deal that instead. As with all fake deals the illusion that the top card has been dealt will, in the hands of an expert, be optically perfect.

A lot of dealers who use this technique modify their grip on the cards by moving both the first and second fingers to the outer short edge of the deck. This grip, described in the early cheater's bible (and still a bible to many) *Artifice, Ruse and Subterfuge at the Card Table* (more commonly known to magicians as *The Expert at the Card Table* by *S.W. Erdnase,* has, in the magician's world, become known as the *Erdnase Grip.* All it does it give more space between the second and third fingers. This is an awkward way to hold a deck and if you see it you should be *very* wary of continuing to play in a private game.

Most professional bottom dealers prefer a push out action to a strike because it is more certain. Using a strike can lead to one of two big problems. The first is called *grabbing air.* If the pack is being held a little tightly or has become a little sticky the bottom card just may not come free. When this happens it will look for all the world as if the dealer has dealt an invisible card. The second problem is called *dragging a hanger.* When this occurs, as the bottom card is being dealt it drags out one or more with it to leave them sticking out on the right hand side of the pack. If you see either an 'invisible' card deal or the bottom cards moving around get out of the game. Don't accept any excuses. You may not have seen the bottom deal action but you've seen the result of a mistake during it.

Like second dealers, good bottom dealers are rare. You are much more likely to see a cheat foisting more mediocre technique upon the table. Freddy offers these extra tips to watch for during a game.

Watch for a slight hesitation at the point of the deal. The dealer may be a little slow in setting up his take position.

Listen to the deal. A less than perfect bottom deal will sound different than a normal deal. Instead of a sliding sound (made by the top card moving off the deck) you will hear more of a *swoosh* sound as the bottom card comes free.

Watch for movement of the left hand fingers. They need to get out of the way to allow the bottom card to clear the hand. A poor dealer may suffer from *finger flutter*.

Always insist that the cards are dealt from a full deck. It is quite common among card players to, after the cut, pick up just half the deck to deal with. Don't let them do it. Your friends may be playing fairly but it is worth noting that a bottom deal becomes easier as the left hand cards get less in number. It is to your advantage to insist that the dealer always hold the entire deck.

Of course in the hands of a real expert you won't spot any of the above tells for seconds or bottoms. The deal will both look and sound normal. Your chances of catching the fake deal are about the same as winning the lottery. Thankfully, your chances of running into such a man carry similar odds. You are much more likely to run up against a man whose technique is less than perfect. Be on your guard at all times and if you have *any* doubt walk away from the game.

Some More Seconds and Bottoms

In the esoteric world of the fake dealer there are numerous variations of both second and bottom deals. Just because a dealer doesn't deal the cards as already described doesn't mean that he can't be second or bottom dealing. It is impossible to give examples of each and every deal as each mechanic will have his own touches to make the deal unique to himself. I can, however, describe a few that I've seen used in action.

This bottom deal I first saw being used in a pub in Glasgow, Scotland. It had a blatant action that caused me to dub it the *Poor Mans Bottom*. In games such as Stud Poker or Pontoon it is common for the dealer to turn a card face up to deal it to a player. A common technique to do this is for the right fingers to drag the top card of the deck backwards before turning it up end for end onto the deck before dealing it out. To deal a bottom the cheat rested his fingers on

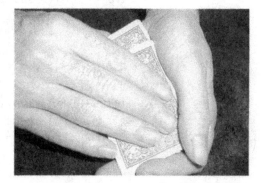

Poor Man's Bottom.

top of the deck but his thumb went underneath the deck. With startling speed his thumb dragged out the bottom card and, with a continuing action, turned the card face up on top of the deck. This easy action was very deceptive at speed.

Some cheats can also, in a most disarming manner, deal both bottoms and seconds using one hand only. They can give tremendous shade to the move by picking up a drink or cigarette while continuing to deal the cards. If a player calls for a card in Blackjack or Pontoon the dealer can casually toss one to them with just one hand.

To deal seconds with one hand the cheat will use a push off action. To deal normally the top card is pushed over and, with a tossing action, dealt to the player. To deal a second the top two cards are pushed across in near perfect alignment and, during the tossing action, the left thumb whips the top card back into place. Because the second card is free of any friction it sails across the table to the player. If Freddy turns the deck face up during the tossing action he can deal a card face up to a stud hand. Dealing in this manner (fairly) is very common in loose bar and pub games. In Freddy's hands the fake deals are identical to the real ones.

Freddy can also deal bottoms one handed using a push out action. His hand holding the deck will twist in towards him as he buckles the bottom card. As his wrist twists out with a snap his fingers push out and release pressure on the bottom card. The force of the snapping action causes the bottom card to fly out and across the table to the player. Freddy can also deal a stud or face up card by a slight variation of the tossing action. His wrist twists in, the card is buckled and the hand *rotates* outwards to end fingers up as the card is released. The card flies out face up. This particular deal has become popular with magicians and is often used to force a card on a spectator watching their tricks. Cards are dealt one at a time from the top of the deck (face down) and a spectator asked to call out, "*Stop.*" When they do so the bottom, force, card of the deck is stud bottom dealt to one side face up. It certainly isn't the first and probably won't be the last gambler's move to be adapted to the work of the sleight-of-hand magician.

Always insist that cards are dealt in a normal manner. Don't allow any type of fancy or one handed dealing. Don't allow cards to be dealt at a blurring speed.

The Center Deal

In the 1930s it was rumored that a cheat named Alan Kennedy had perfected a fake deal where the cards were dealt from the *center* of the deck of cards. The cheat could control his cards to top or bottom of the deck and allow the deck to be cut. Then, rather than having to negate or upset the cut, he could deal the cards directly from the center of the deck.

How to Cheat at Everything

The chances of you coming up against a cheat who can do this move under fire are so slim that you have more chance of being hit by lightning and a meteor simultaneously. There are only a tiny handful of men who can do the move. I have never yet met a man who would use it under fire in a game.

Two Tales of Woe

Two of Freddy's after dinner tales concern fake dealing. Here they are to add to your collection.

In a big money game the cards were being dealt by a true expert. None of the players had any suspicion of the bottom dealing that was taking place. However, an old casino boss watching the game was sure something was going on. "*Anybody got a handkerchief?*" he asked. "*Got a cold?*" asked one of the players. "*No,*" he replied. "*I just thought I'd wipe the cards. The top one is getting a little dusty!*"

Freddy's second tale originates with Philip Quinn, a notorious nineteenth century gambler. He met a man who had fallen on hard times and who wanted to earn his living as a bottom dealer. He had come to Quinn offering to work for him. Quinn offered him an audition and watched as the man went through his paces. Afterwards Quinn is reported to have said, "*I have a horse pistol right here in my pocket. I've watched your skill as a bottom dealer, and I believe that if you will only give me a signal when you intend to draw a card from the bottom of the pack, I'll fire off my gun at the same time, fully attracting the attention of every man in the room. That way nobody will see what you are doing. At all events, nobody will hear that horrible little noise you make in practicing your move!*" Needless to say Quinn did not give the man a job!

Mucking

A *Hand Mucker* IS A MECHANIC WHO SPECIALIZES IN STEALING CARDS FROM A deck in order to switch them into a game at a later time. If Freddy can *palm* away an ace during a friendly game of Blackjack then he has a deadly weapon, sometimes, as you will see, quite literally, up his sleeve. Assume he is dealt a ten and a four. By *mucking* the ace and stealing away the four he has turned a poor hand into a winning twenty-one!

In order to muck cards Freddy must first steal a card or cards from the deck.

Full Palm.

PALMING

Palming involves hiding a card or cards in the hand. Don't think that you'd see Freddy palming a card. Most people would think that it would have to be obvious, surely the hand holding such a large object would have to look cramped and awkward? Not when you've been doing it as long as Freddy has. He has several ways to palm a card and his hands look so natural and relaxed when using any of them that you'd find it hard to believe that he was concealing a card even if you were told!

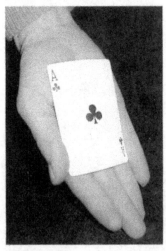

Flat Palm.

Standard palms include the *Full Palm* (where the card is gripped between the tip of the little finger and the base of the thumb), the *Flat Palm* (where the card is gripped between the edge of the little finger and the side of the thumb), the *Cop* (where the card is held crosswise in the palm with the hand tilted back to conceal it) and the *Back Cop* (where the card is gripped well back in the palm between the base of the little finger and the edge of the thumb).

STEALING CARDS USING PALMING

Four For Five Discard

One of the ways Freddy can steal cards is to discard fewer cards than he has in his hand. Freddy will just palm one of the cards he wants from his hand and, when it comes to his bet, he will throw in his losing cards. No attention is on him at the point of the palm, everybody is watching whoever's turn it is to bet next. Nobody pays attention to a guy dropping out, his cards are no longer of any interest. Freddy's stolen card will be put to use later on in the game.

Cop.

Capping The Deck

At the end of his deal Freddy will take the cards and place them on the table. As he lifts the cards from his dealing hand, his right hand will cover the deck for just an *instant*. It is at this moment that he will steal two or three cards from the top of the deck. He will add shade to the move with misdirectional chat, "*Everybody in? Let's play!*"

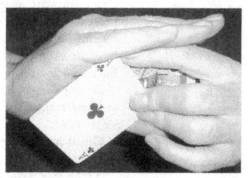

Skinning the Hand.

Skinning the Hand

Freddy, as is very common with card players, will hold his face down hand from above in his right hand. His cards will be held sideways to him with his fingers and thumb on opposite long edges. Like many players Freddy will move cards from the bottom of the hand to the top. All quite legal and normal. He can also use his left fingers to push the bottom card of the hand back into a right hand Flat Palm. Not legal! If Freddy has added extra cards to his hand he may use a skinning action to get rid of unwanted extra cards.

Stealing From the Bottom

At the end of the deal Freddy will lift the deck away from his dealing hand to place it aside. As he lifts the deck he will first move it back slightly deeper into his hand. He leaves two or three cards behind in a Cop Palm as the deck is placed aside. Once more this will be covered by a disarming line. Freddy can also reverse this action to add cards to the bottom of the deck in preparation for a bottom deal.

HIDING THE CARDS

Freddy won't want to keep that card or cards in his palm for long (called *holding out* in the trade). He will hide it in one of several places. He may hide the cards in his armpit (under his jacket) as he reaches for a pack of cigarettes in his inside pocket. This gives him pretty free movement and, after several hours of hot and sweaty play, is an area unlikely to be quickly searched. He may pull his chair forward and store the cards between his leg and the chair. He may, in loose company, simply store the cards on his lap.

He may also use a device to hold the cards in an easy to reach place. A very common device consists of a folded piece of plastic or card held on his upper arm with an elastic band. The device is covered by the sleeve of his short sleeved shirt. He can store cards by crossing his arms so that hand holding the palmed cards comes just under the device. With a rubbing action he can load the cards into it. He can retrieve the cards by reversing the action. Such devices are generically termed *Hold-Outs*.

Be very wary of a man in a short-sleeved shirt who consistently rubs his arms *especially* if the rubbing hand seems to go too near to or even under the sleeve edge.

Cheats have also been known to stick cards, using wax, to the underside of the table.

A true expert can palm or unload cards with ease every time he is within spitting distance of the deck.

Having stolen cards Freddy now needs to switch them in at the right time. Switching, or mucking, cards offers Freddy some big advantages over other cheating methods. He doesn't have to cheat on the deal when attention is strong. He can muck when somebody else is betting and the attention, on him, is low. Second he can wait for a good pot to develop. A good stacked hand may fall at the fence if everybody drops out quickly. The mucker has more of a chance to pick his moment.

SINGLE CARD MUCKS

Simply by switching one of his cards Freddy can give himself a huge edge on a game. In poker he can turn a pair into three of a kind and in Blackjack turn a nothing hand into a devastating winner for example.

Single Card Table Draw

In games like Pontoon or Stud Poker Freddy will leave his cards face down on the table. The card to be switched is Flat Palmed in the right hand. In the action of looking at one of his cards Freddy's right hand covers the card to be switched and draws it towards himself. As the hand comes to the edge of the table this card is allowed to drop in his lap and the palmed card is brought into view as he lifts it up to 'look' at it. The switched-in card is replaced on the hand of cards on the table. Remember he will do this as another man is putting money into the pot. All eyes will be on the bettor, not on Freddy checking his cards.

Multiple Card Draw

Freddy leaves his hand in a loose pile in front of him. Once more the card to be switched in is Flat Palmed in the right hand. He pulls the whole hand back towards himself, adding the palmed card as he does so. He takes a quick 'glance' at his hand and apparently just replaces it on the table. Actually what he does is cop the bottom, unwanted, card of the hand carrying it away as the rest of the hand is dropped down onto the table. He may also wait and *skin* the unwanted card later on in the round.

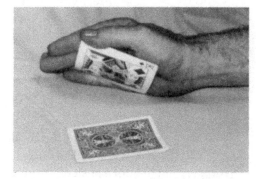
Start of The Slide.

The Slide

This is a switch requiring a great deal of practice and is often used by a mechanic like Freddy to switch a *hole* (face down) card in a Stud Poker game. What you'll see is Freddy glimpsing his hole card. What you won't see is him switching the hole card.

It is very common for a player peeking a hole card to curl the fingers of both hands around it as he does so. He does this to stop other players catching a glimpse of it. Freddy uses the same actions to cover the switch.

Freddy has the card to be switched in Flat Palmed in his right hand. Freddy's left hand curls around the hole card covering it from view. The right hand curls in and, as it does so, the right thumb releases the edge of the palmed card. The palmed card slides neatly beneath the hole card. Freddy then pretends to look at his hole card but actually lifts the back edge of it to allow the right hand to grip it into a Flat Palm. The original card is palmed away leaving the switched in card in the hole.

This move can, by an expert, be performed without the left hand cover. The actions are the same.

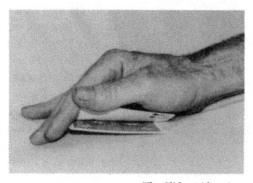
The Slide, *mid-action.*

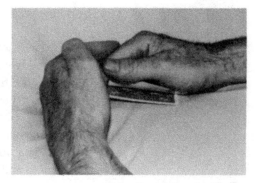
Using the right hand as Shade..

MULTIPLE CARD MUCKS

Freddy can use the Multiple Card Draw to switch more than one card into a game. By using the same motions described for a single card he could add two or three cards and, afterward, cop out the unwanted cards. I've even seen entire hands switched this way. Daring and bold but, in the loose game I saw it done, it passed muster. I awarded that cheat the *Balls of Steel* prize for that night.

Freddy can also use the Slide to switch two cards instead of one. The actions are identical with each pair of cards being treated as a single card.

Freddy is unlikely to steal out more than two cards from a deck. It's not that he wouldn't want to but an experienced eye might think that the deck was starting to look a little short if he stole more. Freddy, especially with the incriminating evidence of loose cards on him, doesn't want to risk it.

The Double Deal Muck

Freddy can, on the deal, overload his hand using half a push off second deal! He will deal fairly to the other players but on his hand will start the action of a push off by pushing two cards in near perfect alignment from the deck. Rather than doing the second deal he will just deal the pair down onto his hand. He may do this two or three times to give himself two or three extra cards. When he checks his hand he will keep it very covered. The other players may think he's a very careful player. He is, careful that they don't see the extra cards! He chooses the best hand from his block and cops the unwanted ones away. He can keep these for another time or, more commonly, add them to the discards as he pushes them to one side. He may also add them back under the pack before passing it to the next dealer. Playing with more cards than anybody else is, to say the least, deadly. The term *Double Dealer* has drifted into common language to describe a less than honest person. Now you know the origin of the term!

The Drop Muck

Another way Freddy can add extra cards to his hand is with the *drop*. During the deal Freddy will hold a break between the deck and the bottom two cards with his little finger. At the end of the deal his right hand takes the deck from above to place it to one side. His right thumb takes over the break. As the pack is placed to one side it passes momentarily over Freddy's hand. The *instant* that it does so he will drop the broken off cards onto it. Performed with skill this is absolutely invisible. It is covered, as are so many muck moves, by timing and misdirection. The move here happens as other players are picking up, and looking at, their own cards. The attention on Freddy is very low at that moment.

Freddy can use a very similar action to switch a hand during a game of Pontoon or Three Card Brag. Instead of dropping the broken off cards onto the hand he will drop them right next to the hand. He will then put the deck onto his dealt cards. Bold? Yep, it is and will often be given extra shade as Freddy throws in his ante. I demonstrated this switch on my set of video tapes (along with a lot of the other moves here) *How to Swim With the Card Sharks.* When magicians tell me that this switch can't work I show them the tape. Trust me, it works!

DOUBLE PLAY MUCKS

If Freddy is playing with another cheat or competent shill the deadly art of mucking becomes even more deadly.

Four Flushing

Freddy says this isn't really used these days except perhaps in very small games. If nothing else it's wise to be aware of its existence, just in case!

Many people have heard the term *four flusher* used to describe a man who is not totally honest but few know where the term comes from. Well it comes from this cheating move used, most often, in the archaic game of five card draw. Don't get me wrong here folks, five card draw is still a popular game in private schools. I simply call it archaic because you are unlikely to see it in fast big money schools where Texas Hold-em and other faster games seem to be more popular.

The origins of this cheat come from a very petty hustle. A cheat with four cards to a flush and an odd card of the color but opposite suit to the others would throw it down, with the odd card hidden, and call it as a flush. If the other players were not alert he could take the pot. If it were discovered he could pass off the incident as a mistake made in the heat of the moment.

Team work can turn the hand into a real flush. Freddy is holding four hearts and an odd card. Using

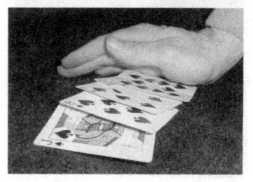

Four Flushing.

Adding card under cut off pile.

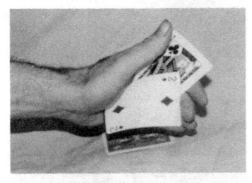

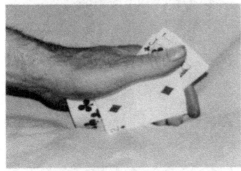

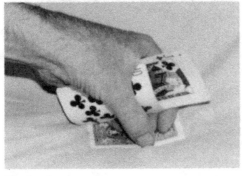

The Brush.

a simple signaling system (of which more later) he tells Sam, his partner in crime, that he needs a heart. Sam signals back that he holds one and tells Freddy to go ahead. Freddy bets his hand as a flush. During the betting two things happen. Freddy cops away his odd card leaving him just four cards. Sam Flat Palms his heart and throws in the rest of his hand. Sam just watches the rest of the hand go along.

At the end of the hand Freddy throws his four cards, in a loose pile, face up on the table and calls a flush. Sam, acting like a suspicious player, says, *"Let's see those cards properly,"* and spreads out Freddy's cards. In the process of spreading the cards Sam adds his palmed card *underneath* Freddy's cards. He can't just drop it on top or it would be obvious that a card had appeared from nowhere. Freddy's hand now shows a heart flush.

The psychology of the move is very powerful. Nobody suspects Sam because he has simply been a player checking for cheating!

It would be rare to see this bold action these days but the same action is commonly used to cheat during a cut for high card. Freddy will hold out a high card (ace or king) from the deck in a flat palm. He'll allow you to shuffle and cut the deck before squaring it on the table. You take the first cut and then Freddy cuts off a section and puts it down in front of himself. As you turn your cut off cards to see your card Freddy will pick up his cut of section and, using the *slide* action used in the original *four flusher* scam, load his high card underneath. He then turns the cards in a continuing action to show that he has 'cut' to a high card to win the bet. This is a very useful ability to have if cutting for *double or quits* at the end of an evening's play!

The Brush

Rather than Double Deal Freddy may rely on Sam to give him extra cards. If they are sitting next to each other they will use the *Brush*. Freddy signals to Sam that he has three of a kind. Sam signals back that he has a pair. Between them they have a *Boat* or Full House. That's considered the kind of hand

How to Cheat at Everything

you'd bet your wife on but unfortunately the hand is split between the two of them.

At a very simple level Freddy can palm away the two cards he doesn't want and put the rest of the cards onto the table a little too close to Sam. Sam, with the pair palmed, can push Freddy's cards back towards him (adding the palmed cards) with a line like, *"Hey, look after your cards, I'm not a baby sitter!"* Sam will discard what's left of his hand at the earliest opportunity.

At a more skillful level the brush can be taken to an art form. Freddy and Sam will pretend not to like each other much. Sam will make a habit of dropping some of his cards, perhaps for a change, during a friendly game of five card draw, down the table. This, apparently, irritates Freddy who keeps telling him to pick them up. At one point Freddy will push or *brush* the cards back to him saying, *"Can't you keep your damned cards in your hand!"* No switch will have taken place here, just the actions of the switch. Freddy is testing the waters by *Splashing* the action to see if it will pass muster. When it's time to do the move for real, the cards Sam drops will be the ones Freddy needs. Freddy has adjusted his hand so that the cards he wants to switch are in his palm with the rest, closest to the palm, sticking upwards.

In the action of brushing Sam's cards back to him he allows his cards to slide under Sam's. As he does this his left thumb pushes the palmed cards to the left. As the brushing action is completed his original palmed cards end up in front of Sam while Freddy is holding the pat hand. Under fire by an expert the switch of cards is absolutely invisible.

In a loose game Freddy can also do the move solo. Freddy drops the cards he wishes to *keep* down in front of him as if to discard them. He then draws his cards and picks anything good from them to help his potential hand. He then *notices* his discarded cards and *brushes* them over to the discard pile collating his finished hand in the process.

Just because two players seem antagonistic to each other does not mean they aren't in cahoots with each other!

Never allow one player to touch another player's cards.

Insist that discards are on the discard pile before handing out cards.

Capping the Draw

Freddy and Sam can achieve the same result as a brush but more easily if one of them is the dealer. Sam, as the dealer, will palm the cards Freddy needs and, at the point Freddy is calling for his cards, Sam will add them to the top of the deck. Sam deals Freddy the cards he needs to complete his killer hand.

Palming and Mucking, especially in team play, is very hard to spot. Freddy offers the following sage advice.

If you suspect anything, immediately insist on counting the cards. The cheat will often drop the palmed card onto the floor when nobody is looking (and, it's safe to assume that *all* attention will be on the deck being counted). When the deck is found to be short, a card or cards will be discovered on the floor. This has happened in numerous games by mistake and nobody, except perhaps you, will think anything of it. *But* it will show the cheat that you are wise to his action.

Watch for any covering of cards or the deck no matter how momentary it may be. Insist that cards are left in view.

Never let a player touch another player's cards for *any* reason.

To repeat, *never* let anybody rabbit hunt through the discards.

Watch for a nervous player or one who is constantly going to his pockets for cigarettes, money or whatever.

It is worth noting that just by taking one known card out of play Freddy gains a large advantage in a game of poker. If he knows the deck is short the four of hearts for example he knows heart flushes will be harder to make, he knows straights with a four are harder to make and so on. This, in a five handed game, has been calculated to give the cheat a ten percent edge on the game.

Ever discovered a card was accidentally left behind in a card case? Still think it was an accident?

As ever Freddy has a couple of tales of woe to close out the chapter with. He claims they are both true. But, remember, this is also a guy who claims to be reformed!

The Knife

Freddy claims to have been watching a game one night and suddenly came to the realization that one of the players was *holding out* a card. The cheat was not experienced and was, by Freddy's idea anyway, holding that palmed card for far too long.

He was right.

In a flash the player beside the cheat pulled out a switchblade and stabbed it straight through the cheat's hand, impaling it to the table. His only comment, amid the chaos that ensued, was to say, "*If the queen of hearts isn't under your hand, sonny, then I owe you an apology!*"

The Sandwich

During a game a cheat had a card ready to be mucked into his hand. A waiter appeared to hand out sandwiches and drinks. One suspicious player, thinking that the waiter may have been helping a player to cheat, insisted on the cards being counted. The cheat, in blind panic, mucked his card into a sandwich and ate it! "*I guess cardboard can be good for your health,*" laughs Freddy!

Dropping A Cooler

Perhaps the ultimate *muck* move is to switch the entire deck in play. By switching the deck for a pre-stacked monster hand Freddy and his pals can really clean up. Some of these hands are so subtly structured that even a penny ante game can turn into serious money. We'll look at one of the best at the end of this chapter. The other reason for mucking the entire pack is to switch in a deck of marked cards.

Switching in a deck (known as *dropping a cooler* or *the iron man*) is one of the strongest of all the ploys Freddy can pull at the table.

It will normally be used just once, often toward the end of an evening. At this time a few drinks will have gone down and players may well be betting at a higher rate (either chasing losses or to ride a winning streak) and attention will be looser than at the evening's start.

The advantage of knowing the position of each and every card is obvious. The advantages of continuing any further hands with a professionally marked deck are also obvious.

What might not be so obvious is just how Freddy switches an entire deck! He has several methods and, like quite a few of the cheat's moves, they rely more on bold nerve than digital skill.

All *coolers* will be done with misdirection either from Freddy or from a shill. Although some of the switches are visually deceptive there is always a chance of somebody catching something even if it is only a suspicion. Freddy realized long ago in his career that, *"If they ain't lookin', they can't see it!"*

Some books tell lurid tales of a shill spilling a drink at the point of the switch. There is no doubt that this would provide powerful misdirection but it would also be far too memorable. The kind of misdirection Freddy uses is brief and subtle. It does the job but is not enough to be remembered as important later on. It will appear to be a casual, normal action.

He may, earlier in the game, drop a chip on the floor. Later, at the point of the switch, he may 'notice' the chip and say, *"Hey, who's so rich they're throw-*

ing money away?" All eyes to move their money and/or the floor. Freddy is just helping out somebody who has dropped a chip. The cover is perfect.

A large distraction, like a spilled drink, followed by a large winning hand would give rise to immediate suspicion amongst big money players. A small, but sufficient, distraction will not.

METHODS

The actual switch of the decks will be the work of just a few seconds. It requires a bold, ice-cold nerve that few have. However, once the move is over the money is certain. To the professional cheat those few seconds of extreme tension are well worth the result.

The Coat

Freddy will have the cooler in his jacket pocket. He will hang his jacket over the back of his chair as he plays.

At some point he will decide to leave the game for a rest. He will get up and start to put on his jacket. Sam will talk him into, "*Just one or two more for the road,*" and order Freddy a fresh drink before he can refuse. Reluctantly Freddy agrees and sits down again with his jacket draped over his arm. The cooler, hidden under his jacket, now rests in his hand. He has got it into place under cover of Sam's distraction.

On his deal the cards will be cut and he picks them up to deal. Noticing *for the first time* that his jacket is still over his arm he will put it back over the chair. As he does this the jacket will momentarily cover his hands and the cards. Under cover of this *move* the packs will be switched with the cooler coming into play and the other deck ditched in a jacket pocket.

Sam will be chatting away to add extra misdirection. He may ask who is short in the pot causing attention to go the pile of chips or money on the table.

Every action is totally natural. Attention will be lax. Players may watch for cheating during a hand but rarely *before* one. Sam's patter about the pot being short simply puts the icing on the cake. It's all over so quickly that you haven't got a chance.

The Lap

One of the more cunning cooler techniques is to switch in the deck on another player's deal. Even the most suspicious player is unlikely to think that he has been cheated if he is dealing the cards himself!

The cheat will move the cooler from its hiding place into his lap. As the dealer is shuffling he gets the cooler into a loose *cop* in his hand.

When the pack is offered to him he will sweep the real deck into his lap and then false cut the cooler before handing it back. The cooler will be set with a bridge so that the cut can be nice and clean.

The switch is covered by his hands curling around the packs. The left hand, with the copped cooler, is at the table edge. The right hand sweeps the deck back towards the left hand. For just an instant the left hand holds two decks before tipping back slightly to allow the real deck to fall into the lap. The cooler immediately comes into sight. Visually the move is perfect but will also be covered by an inevitable distraction from a shill.

Pressure Moment of Dropping a Cooler!

The dealer then starts the hand without realizing that he is using a switched deck and, as such, is now a part of the cheat!

Whenever a deck ends up in Freddy's lap you can be sure it won't stay there for long. He'll move it to a safer hiding place, such as a pocket, as soon as he can safely do so.

The Waiter

Drinking is common during card games. A waiter or friend will bring drinks to the table from time to time. Under cover of this powerful misdirection a cooler is almost child's play.

A shill will have the cooler hidden under a tray of drinks. He arrives at the table just as the cheat has finished shuffling and cutting the cards. He rests the tray against the edge of the table for players to take their drinks.

As he does this, the deck is covered by the tray for just a moment. It is a moment of perfect misdirection. The other players are eager for their drinks and they will relax their guard. Under the tray, with a well-practiced action, the cheat will take the cooler and hand the shill the deck to be switched out.

Trays have been found with clips attached to hold the cooler and even a little bag to dump the cards to be switched out. The speed of this switch is uncanny to watch in the hands of a practiced duo like Freddy and Sam.

The shill walks away with the other deck and dumps it as soon as possible. This switch, above all others, carries the supreme advantage that the *evidence* vanishes leaving nothing to be found!

The Drop

Freddy often wears a jacket when he plays cards. It's not to look smart, it's to cover this switch.

The cooler is in a pocket sewn to his shirt, just below and to the left of his right arm pit. The pocket is just deep enough to hold a deck with about three quarters of its length sticking out. Sometimes these pockets are elasticized so that the deck can be held sticking out downwards.

Another bag-like pocket is positioned, on the same side, lower down and pinned between the jacket and shirt. Often called a *poacher's pocket*, magicians sometimes refer to this kind of bag as a *Toppit*. Freddy calls it the *ditch* or *ditch bag*.

On his deal Freddy takes the deck, after the cut, into his left hand dealing position. Just before the deal he reaches across to his left side to drop a cigarette into an ashtray. He may also pick up a chip a little to the left of his stash to throw in his ante. This action, just for a second, covers the pack in his left hand as the right side of his jacket naturally swings across. It is a totally disarming and natural action.

As the cover happens Freddy drops the shuffled deck into the ditch bag and grips the cooler in his left hand.

By the time he has dropped the cigarette into the ashtray or thrown in his chip, the switch will be over. It takes a little under two seconds and is, in Freddy's hands, undetectable.

Often times the cooler will not be stacked for the hand about to be dealt but for the one *after*. The switch takes place and an ordinary hand dealt. By the time the next hand is dealt time has been put between the moment of the switch and the big stacked hand.

And don't forget the cards switched in are nearly always marked as well!

HOW THE COOLER GOT ITS NAME

A switched in deck is often referred to as a cooler for an obvious reason.

A pack that has been in play all night is said to get warmer from players handling the cards. A new, switched in deck, is supposed to be colder because it hasn't been handled.

I have yet to meet a player who can tell the difference.

The reason it is also often referred to as an *iron man* is simple as well. It is *impossible* to beat.

Be more alert when other players are relaxing.

Never allow the deck to go out of sight, even for a moment.

If you have *any* suspicions insist on shuffling the cards yourself *just for luck*. If this is denied, leave the game. This won't stop any marks being used against you (I'd advise asking for a new deck or leaving anyway) but will at least break an iron man stack getting you or, indeed another, player.

The cold deck takes three seconds of work and will kill you. It is, among professionals, considered one of the top moves.

A SAMPLE GAME

This is a real hand taken from a real game. In the world of poker it has become legendary as one of the most sneaky of all iron men set ups. It is a great example of how a tiny amount of money can be raised and re-raised to become a significant amount.

The game was dealer's choice, which means that the man with the deal can call any variation of poker they wish. Five players are in the game, Freddy has dropped the cooler and is ready to deal. All the players have plenty of cash and like to bet big when the right time comes along.

He calls Seven Card High-Lo Poker. Ace plays high or low. He also calls, as is common, Pot Limit.

In this game three cards, two down and one up, are dealt to each player. With betting rounds between each, three more face up cards are dealt and finally one last face down card. Each player left in the game then uses five of their seven cards to make up either a high or low hand. A player may also call 'high' and 'low'. A player calling this way must have both the highest *and* lowest hand at the end. Calling is done by putting a hand under the table and coming up with either an empty hand (calling 'low'), one chip (calling 'high') or two chips (to call both 'high' and 'low'). The highest high call takes half the pot, the lowest low call takes half and a high, low takes all.

Pot limit means that the maximum bet is whatever is in the pot at any one time. Since pots can grow (as you'll see here) quite swiftly the ante is often low.

Get the idea? Okay, now the game.

Freddy deals the cards and it looks like this.

Bill	X	X	JH
Jim	X	X	3D
John	X	X	2H
Freddy	X	X	4H
Sam	X	X	10S

(X = Face down card)

Bill opens for twenty-five cents and both Jim and John call (cover the bet). The Fox raises half the pot (all of fifty cents at this point since the pot consists of a quarter ante and three quarter bets). Sam calls and everybody calmly follows suit. What a pot, all of four dollars and fifty cents!

Since Bill, Jim and John are the suckers in this game let's turn their cards face up so that you can more easily follow their thinking as they are suckered in. The next card is dealt and the hands show as follows.

Bill	(JS	JD)	JH	4D
Jim	(AS	5C)	3D	4C

John	(QH	QC)	2H	QD
Freddy	X	X	4H	AC
Sam	X	X	10S	9S

Freddy bets half the pot. Sam calls. Bill, feeling a little hot, raises. Jim, playing tight, calls but John re-raises and why not? He's got a strong, strong hand. Freddy raises ten dollars. Bill, thinking he's suckering everybody in, merely calls the re-raise as do the others. This tiny pot is now starting to grow. It stands at ninety dollars! The fifth card is where it's going to start getting a little crazy. After the deal the hands lie as follows.

Bill	(JS	JD)	JH	4D	8D
Jim	(AS	5C)	3D	4C	7C
John	(QH	QC)	2H	QD	AH
Freddy	X	X	4H	AC	8H
Sam	X	X	10S	9S	6S

Bill's jacks are still looking pretty good to him especially with two concealed. Jim is looking good with a seven low call and John's ace is, he calculates, neatly disguising his hidden pair of queens. Freddy is only showing a moderate eight low but Sam is looking very dangerous indeed.

John bets half the pot and is called round to Jim who, with a pretty safe seven low, raises. Next, after Freddy calls, Sam throws in two hundred dollars. The other players feel a panic attack, has he caught a straight flush or just going for one? But, their hands are strong and they've invested heavily into the pot by now. They aren't going to be bluffed out of this one by Sam who has been heavily bluffing all night long. They call the bet. Right now, from a quarter ante, the pot is standing at $1,460! Are your knees starting to tremble yet?

What happens next is a superb psychological ploy from Freddy and Sam. Having got everybody at a mild fever pitch of panic about his hand Sam, right after the next card, folds his hand and drops out. Whew, suddenly the game is hot again! The cards now lie as follows.

Bill	(JS	JD)	JH	4D	8D	2D
Jim	(AS	5C)	3D	4C	7C	6D
John	(QH	QC)	2H	QD	AH	2C
Freddy	X	X	4H	AC	8H	7H

John *feeds* in a small bet hoping to drag the others in against his powerful full house. Jim, now with a staggering six low, decides it's time to strike. He raises five hundred dollars. Freddy, not looking too good with an eight low showing, calls and Bill, who really should fold those three jacks, decides to come along for the ride. He's put too much in now to drop out. Amazingly, the money is rising outrageously and, in the heat of the moment, the players are flying with it. High money pots are common to these players but this is obviously going to be the big one of the night. How big? Currently it stands at $4,500.

The last card is dealt face down. Bill is in heaven as he gets the last jack to make up four of a kind, what a killer moment for him! The hands now lie as follows for the final bets.

Bill	(JS	JD)	JH	4D	8D	2D	(JC)
Jim	(AS	5C)	3D	4C	7C	6D	(KC)
John	(QH	QC)	2H	QD	AH	2C	(10D)
Freddy	X	X	4H	AC	8H	7H	X

Bill checks (passes the bet) as do the others. Freddy weighs in with a big one thousand dollar bet. It's getting out of control now, even by these boy's standards, but they've just *got* to finish.

Bill and John call high. Jim calls low. The Fox calls high and low. The cards are turned. Freddy's incredible hand consists of the 6H, 5H, 4H, AC, 8H, 7H and the 2S. His 6, 5, 4, 2, A takes the low bet from Jim's 6, 5, 4, 3, A and his straight flush in hearts wipes out the four jacks. Freddy picks up $8,500. Actually he picked up a lot of cash and a set of car keys. One player had to walk home.

It must be stressed that, although an extreme example, this is a true story.

A read back will show how the hands fell perfectly to build the betting. The killer moment when Sam folded was a strong, strong incentive to the others to carry on.

You could say that was just one of those hands. They happen. Couldn't it have been a freak hand? Well apart from you knowing that Freddy and Sam are partners in crime, the word freak is quite apt when describing this hand. The odds against it falling in this exact manner are over 2.2 quadrillion to one against. A quadrillion, by the way, is a thousand, million, million! That's what I'd call a freak hand!

PROBLEMS

The above example shows an iron man hand played out to perfection. The players, with the possible exception of Bill holding onto his three jacks, played the cards well. They just didn't know that they were up against Freddy in the lead and Sam in a minor, but critical, role.

If Bill had tossed the jacks Freddy could have used a second deal to adjust for him falling out.

Perhaps the biggest problem with a cooler is that, once set, the players may change. One could fall out of the game or another could sit in before the switch occurs. Freddy can overcome this by having several decks set for varying numbers of players. There are also iron man stacks carefully calculated to adapt to varying numbers of players. Although the hands may vary the same stack will give the cheat a winning hand against lesser strong hands *even* if a man leaves or, indeed, joins the game.

And, at the very worst, Freddy will be playing with marked cards. Even if, by some freak his iron man stack is destroyed or just doesn't hit, he'll take the money eventually with the marks!

Hidden Language

As you've seen, when Freddy and Sam communicate with each other their conversation must sometimes, by its very nature, be secret. Signals between cheats who know each other will often be unique to them, although they tend to fall into two categories. They will either signal in coded speech or use signals with hands and/or cards. The pre-arranged signals can be very subtle indeed and are *very* difficult to spot. It is little wonder that collusion is considered the most dangerous of all cheating techniques and it is rife in the world of Contract Bridge.

There are also some universal signals that will be recognized by just about any cheat worth his salt.

LANGUAGE

Let's get the most stupidly obvious example out of the way right up front. *Never* allow conversation between players in a language you don't understand. *Insist* that all the players speak with a language that everybody can understand. If you think this is too obvious to mention go to a Spanish resort and watch a game where English and American tourists play cards against the Spanish locals who continually chatter away in their native tongue!

It should be noted here that Freddy speaks seven languages fluently and is currently learning Japanese. He never points this ability out to foreign players, pretending, instead, that he has no idea of what they are talking about. He lets them chatter away as much as they like and exploits any information he receives. A true case of the professional cheat cheating the amateur one!

Unless you share Freddy's ability insist on a language you can understand. If the other players persist just leave the game and be grateful that you won't understand the insults they will hurl after you.

UNIVERSAL SIGNALS

There are a very few true universal signals in the hustler's world. Study and remember them.

Hand against chest, thumb spread out—When a stranger uses this gesture, almost as if he were about to do an old fashioned bow, he may well be saying, *"I'm a cheat, is this table taken?"*

Right hand palm down on the table, thumb spread out—As an opening gesture in reply to the above, it simply means, *"I'm with you, we'll split it afterwards."*

Closed fist against chest—The cheat, already at the table is saying, *"I understand you but I don't need help. The table is taken."*

Closed fist resting on the table—The same refusal to co-operate with another cheat.

If agreement is made they will meet during a break in the game to set strategy.

BASIC POKER SIGNALS

The following, although not universal, are very common as described here. There may be slight variations but both Freddy and I have seen over a dozen teams use just this system to signal hands to each other.

Fist on table with first finger out—*"I'm holding a pair"*
First finger and third finger pointing—*"I'm holding two pair"*
Three fingers extended—*"I've got trips"*
Four fingers extended—*"Four of a kind here buddy!"*
Hand flat on the table with fingers spread—*"Full house for me!"*

These signals are made with the right hand resting casually on the table. The left hand, holding the cards, will not be idle. The *way* the cards are held can give supplementary information to a partner.

If the left forefinger overlaps the cards to rest on top of them the cheat may be signaling aces. The right hand tells how many he has.

If the left forefinger is a little lower he is indicating kings. If his finger rests across the center of the card he is indicating queens and if the cards are held high in the hand with the forefinger near the bottom he is telling his partner he has jacks.

If the first *and* second finger overlap the hand to rest on top he is signaling tens. In the king position two fingers indicate nines, in the queen position they show eights, in the jack position they show sevens and the ten position they indicate sixes.

Fives are shown by upjogging the fifth card of the hand, fours by upjogging the fourth card, threes by upjogging the third card and, finally, twos by slightly upjogging the second card.

Without speaking two cheats can have quite a hidden conversation. This is just one example of how a simple signaling system can work. By using these very simple signals they can play *best hand forward* and use *force out* techniques among others.

There is no point in calling players on this *even* if you suspect signaling. It is just your word against theirs. If you suspect signaling just, once again, leave the game.

HOLE CARD SIGNALING

In stud games the cheats can use a hole card to signal their cards, or other players cards, to each other. Values of the cards are conveyed by the *clock*.

The clock consists of resting the first face up card onto the hole card in a specific manner. If it lies squarely upon the hole card it generally represents that the hole card is an ace.

Turned slightly to the right it indicates a king. A little more to the right, so about a third of the hole card is exposed, indicates a queen. A little further, exposing around two thirds of the hole card, shows a jack and, if the face up card is nearly off the right hand side of the hole card, he is indicating a ten.

For nine the card is turned slightly to the left, for eight a third to the left, for seven two thirds to the left and for six practically off the card to the left.

For five through two the face up card will be placed *under* the face down hole card. For a five about half the card will be sticking out with the exposed half forwards. Turned to the right indicates a four, to the left a three and from the back a two.

The suit of the card can be indicated by the cheat's fingers. He can also, using his fingers, indicate which players hole card he is referring to if it is not his own.

With simple card positioning and fingers Freddy can tell Sam your hole cards in a game of stud. Dangerous for you!

Again this is just an example of a system I have seen used. There are plenty of others although many would appear to be variations upon this theme.

Odd and varied ways a hole card is positioned by a player should be enough to make you a little suspicious *especially* if he moves the card deliberately into a different place each time one is dealt to him.

CONTRACT BRIDGE

Above all other games this one has more cheating than any other. Partnership play in Bridge is open but signaling is illegal. That not withstanding, partnership collusions are rife.

If Freddy fans out his cards you may notice one that is standing up slightly a little more than the others. If you counted the number of cards up to and including that upjogged card would you deem it chance that it just happens to be the exact number of cards in Freddy's strongest suit?

Freddy could help his partner along by indicating the suit type with his fingers.

In Bridge there are so many different signaling ploys, both verbal and non-verbal, that it is beyond the scope of this book to detail them. *Entire* books have been written on such systems.

Having established their system and practiced it, two cheats become among the gambling world's most invincible foes.

If you suspect that any form of signaling is going on you have no option but to leave the game. It can happen in so many ways, from an obvious kick under the table to the most subtle of voice codes, that you can't hope to ever have much more than just a vague suspicion.

Never trust obvious appearances. The caustic remarks between two players may be covering a verbal code as well as making you think that these two wouldn't be working together. Signaling is less likely to be suspected if you think they hate each other!

Learn the standard types of signals but don't relax if you don't see them or positions similar. Stay alert for any changes in voice tones, the slightly too careful placement of a cigarette pack, piles of chips being played with etc. *Anything* can be a signal!

When trying to confirm any tiny suspicion try to close out distractions. Concentrate and focus upon the man you think is doing them.

Don't be discreet about listening and looking. Even if you can't see a coding system the cheats may think that you have. At worst they will notice your suspicion and will be more wary about using it.

Two players working together can clean you out with little or no risk. You'll have absolutely no proof, only suspicion. Can you see just how dangerous these teams can be?

Get out of *any* game where you have those suspicions. I once stopped going to a friend's Friday night poker game because I suspected that two of his other friends were using signals. I wasn't invited back to his house again until after the two 'friends' were caught one night, several months later, passing cards between each other. With signals there is no point in making accusations. It's better just to walk away.

"No single player can defeat a combination of others."

———•———

S.W. Erdnase

How to Cheat at Everything

More Moves From Freddy

As you are seeing, Freddy has a whole armory of sleight-of-hand with which he can manipulate the cards. Some of the moves are more difficult than others but all require tremendous nerve and an ice-cold heart.

At the start of the sleight-of-hand chapters I did say that all the moves required hours of practice and training. Some, especially the ones in this little tidy-up chapter, may seem to be very easy to do. That may be true when you are sitting at home playing with a deck at your dining room table. But, when sitting at a table covered with money, *all* sleight-of-hand becomes very difficult indeed. If a cheat slips up badly it may not be the end of his career. In the wrong game it could be the end of his life. Freddy practices *every* move, however simple, for hour upon hour before risking it *under the cosh*.

Much of the cheat's work goes towards trying to make his visible actions look almost amateurish. He wants you to believe that he can't handle cards at all. His sloppy shuffling and handling of cards conceal his deadly talent. This is especially true in private games where, for example, the Overhand Shuffle will be acceptable.

Freddy actually says he is jealous of magicians for the simple reason that they are allowed to be skillful in performance. They can show off a One-Hand Riffle Shuffle or a fancy piece of flourish work and the audience is delighted. Freddy has had to work hard to look like he can't handle cards at all. Any sign of skill from him is unlikely to elicit a delighted response!

But all combine to give him an unbeatable advantage.

Here are a few more little *poke peckers* as he likes to call them.

THE DOUBLE DISCARD

Freddy says that this move has been designed specifically for draw poker variations. Although the game of Five Card Draw Poker has fallen out of favor in casinos and gaming clubs it is still very popular in private games. Freddy says that there is a *lot* of money in the private games he plays in!

The Double Discard, almost a precursor to The Brush, requires nothing more than an iron nerve. Let's assume that Freddy holds three tens and two odd cards during a game of draw poker. It is his turn to change some of his cards. He calls for three cards and, as he does so, drops his three tens down in front of himself on the table.

He scoops up this three draw cards and adds them to the two he is holding. He spreads these five cards and selects the best two from them. He drops these two cards on to the tens and throws the other three on to the discard pile.

At speed this is incredibly disarming. But, on closer look, instead of changing three cards Freddy has, in effect, picked the best five from eight cards. A big advantage!

Call him on the action and he'll go into his confused player act. He's so good at this that you will almost certainly give him the benefit of the doubt.

THE SLUG

If the game is the vicious poker variant known as Five Card Stud, Freddy counts it as quite advantageous to know the values of the other player's face-down hole cards! Here's how he does it.

When it's Freddy's deal he will gather all the discards and drop them on top of the pack. His cards go on top last of all. Freddy has memorized his hand and made sure that its highest card is at the bottom. So on top of the deck are five known cards with the highest of those five cards resting fifth from top.

Freddy false shuffles the cards leaving those top five cards in place. He then cuts, putting in a bridge or crimp. He then offers the deck to be cut. His known five cards end up back neatly on top of the deck.

Freddy then deals the cards. In a five player game of five card stud Freddy knows every hole card and has the extra advantage of knowing that he has the highest hole card! In other variations of the game he knows information about some of the hole cards of the other players.

This is, as Freddy puts it, a beautiful ploy. There is nothing to catch!

A RUNNING FALSE CUT SHUFFLE

In lieu of a full deck false shuffle Freddy may substitute the following running cut action which simulates the shuffling action often seen at Blackjack tables in casinos. Freddy often points out this similarity to prove that his shuffle is a *fair and honest* one.

Freddy holds the cards on the table as if he were going to go into a Greek Cut. His right hand draws out a small packet from the bottom of the deck and dumps it on top of the deck set slightly to the left. In other words leaving a small step on the right hand side of the pack.

He then pulls another small packet from the bottom and slaps that on top of the first. He repeats this action of pulling small packets from the bottom and placing them on top until the step is right near the bottom. With a final pull out he cuts the stepped packet to the top.

It looks like a casual mixing action. Actually the deck is in the same order it started. Magicians often refer to this type of cut as an *Up the Ladder Cut*.

To make this type of action simulate a casino shuffle Freddy starts in the same position but this time cuts out a large packet of cards from the bottom of the deck leaving just a small packet of cards on the table. He holds the large packet, in his right hand, above and to the right of the tabled cards. His left fingers strip a small packet from the *bottom* of the right hand cards and drops it, stepped slightly to the left, onto the tabled cards. He continues to strip packets from the bottom of the right hand cards, dropping them onto the tabled cards. When the right hand cards run out Freddy cuts the bottom, stepped cards, to the top.

Although this looks very like the way Blackjack dealers shuffle cards, the deck is in the same order that it started.

THE THREE-TWO DEAL

In many British bar poker schools the cards are not dealt singly to each player. Instead, presumably to speed up the deal, they are dealt in groups of three followed by groups of two. The players also feel that, because cards are getting clumped up in groups as the game goes on, this system will bring out better hands.

That may well be so.

It's also an invitation for Freddy to pick up real easy money.

Let's say Freddy is playing against three others. By use of his talents he has got three of a kind on to the top of the deck. It's also his turn to shuffle. Using an Overhand Shuffle he drops half the pack into his left hand and runs nine cards on to it. Then he drops a small group of cards but injogs them. Then he completes the shuffle. He cuts the pack at the injog leaving his three of a kind 10th, 11th and 12th from the top of the pack.

Freddy deals out the cards throwing three to player one, two and three. Then he gives himself the next three (the three of a kind). Then he throws out the groups of two and the betting begins.

This kind of dealing does speed up the game. It also makes Freddy's work easier.

NO SHUFFLE THREE-TWO

Some groups, especially in the south of England carry this to extreme. They will, to ensure good hands turning up, only shuffle the deck when four of a kind turns up!

Sure it guarantees that good hands will turn up. It is also suicidal if Freddy is in the game.

By means of a Pick Up Stack and a good memory Freddy can get a known Slug or *bullet* of cards into the pack. The pick up technique is also easier because of the three-two style of dealing.

All Freddy has to do is wait for his Slug to come up and he knows every player's cards.

This system of dealing, especially with no shuffles, is so open to abuse that you would be mad to play in a game that allowed it.

Always shuffle the deck between hands.

Remember dealing systems like the three-two may speed up the game but they also make the cheat's job far easier. Don't allow them.

A SIMPLE BRIDGE AND SOLO STACK

As I hope we've made clear, controlling, or knowing the position of just one or two cards, can give Freddy a huge advantage.

This simple stacking action gives Freddy two known cards during a game of Bridge or, indeed, any game where the entire deck is dealt out. Let's assume that Freddy wants the ace and king of spades during a Bridge rubber.

He gets them to the top of the deck. This is a fairly easy procedure in Bridge using a very simple pick up action.

Freddy Overhand Shuffles the deck in the following manner. He runs one card then a small block of cards. He then runs three single cards. Next a small block injogged followed by the rest of the cards shuffled on top of all.

Now Freddy takes the deck in preparation for another Overhand Shuffle but allows the deck to split at the injog so that his right thumb is holding a break at that point. Now he pulls down a small block from the top and *at the same time* pulls down the bottom card of the deck using pressure from his left fingers. Freddy then shuffles normally up to his break and finishes by throwing the remaining cards on top. This sounds a little confusing but, with cards in hand, is a very simple action indeed.

One of Freddy's cards is on the bottom, the other is fourth from the top of the deck. All he has to do now is deal out the cards and both will fall to him.

HIGH CUTS

Freddy can, with skill, cut high cards any time he wants. Freddy gets some high cards to the bottom of the deck. When you cut the deck, you do so normally and get a card by chance.

When Freddy cuts he lifts some cards from the top but, as he does so, his fingers nip under the deck and slide out the bottom card under his cut cards. This is a little like Spinging the Deck but upside down. He turns his packet to reveal the high card.

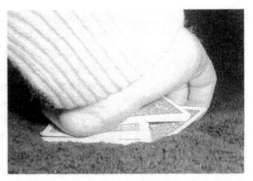

Freddy gets high cards while you rely on plain old luck.

The give away on this action is that the cut packet will not be lifted straight up but, instead, pulled forwards from the deck.

Pulling out Bottom Card on Cut.

Freddy can also use awesome psychological ploys to cheat you on a cut. I've seen him let a mug shuffle a deck. They can then choose high or low cards to win and yet Freddy still won.

Freddy had no control over the cards and so did a genuine cut. Depending on his card he acted out the scenario in various ways. If he had a middle value card he offered the bet to his mug quite normally, *"You want high or low cut to win?"* It's pretty much a fifty-fifty bet for him in this situation.

If he has a high card he will look a little crestfallen and say, *"High or low to win,"* putting a little more emphasis on the word low. This makes you think that he must have a low card and is trying to wriggle out of the bet. You call that high card wins and he's got you! If he has a low card he uses the same kind of ploy but this time looks just a little smug as he says, *"High or low to win,"* putting tiny emphasis on the word high. You assume he has a high card, call low and, once again, are buried.

The voice inflections and emotional responses are very subtle indeed. Of course Freddy can't hope to win every time but he'll take *any* advantage he can.

FRONT LOADING

Freddy is very fond of saying that, *"An accident can be a beautiful thing."*

Front Loading and its ilk require no manipulation from Freddy at all. You, quite literally, cheat *yourself!*

Many people in a bar game will toss cards to the players as they deal. To do this they often deal quite high across the table top. If they get lazy, and Freddy slumps very slightly, he can often see the faces of cards as they sail across the table. An honest person would point this out to the dealer. Freddy doesn't.

In other games if a dealt card accidentally flips up the player is given the choice of keeping the card or having another. No big shakes to most but to Freddy, regardless of the player's choice, he has knowledge of the position of one card in the deck. It's either in the player's hand or it's on the bottom of the deck. Either way it is out of play from him. As we've said, knowing the position of just one card can give Freddy a big advantage in a game.

If a card gets flipped up accidentally, re-shuffle and start the deal again.

Some Blackjack dealers can get very lazy. A player in the right seat can see the dealer's face down card because of a flash. This is most common with unseasoned dealers who are getting tired towards the end of a shift.

In a pub or bar game Freddy has sat back in a relaxed manner and casually seen several full hands of cards. It is very wise to take a look at your cards then put them face down onto the table. Keep them there unless you absolutely have to look at them.

If this all sounds rather petty bear in mind that Freddy doesn't mind how he gets the money. He just minds that he gets it.

DEALER'S CHOICE

As you've seen, some cheats are designed for specific games. Luckily for Freddy it is very common during private schools to play *Dealer's Choice*. That means that the dealer chooses which game that is to be played. Players like this type of school because it adds interest and variation to the evening.

Freddy calls it *Mug's Choice*.

A simple glimpse, a tiny stack or any one of a number of actions can give him a win. He can call any one of a number of variations that allow him to use specialized moves. Allowing Freddy to choose which game to play is simply allowing him to choose the game that gives him his best advantage.

Of course Dealer's Choice can be a lot of fun. Just bear in mind it can also be very expensive.

Indian Poker

A good example of how Dealer's Choice can murder you is the game of Indian Poker. It's a very popular game for the end of a session as not only can the betting get completely out of control but it's very silly indeed. Each player is dealt a card face down. They lick the back of the card and stick it to their forehead face outwards.

Every player can see every card *except* their own. The betting goes on until only one person is left in the pot or until all agree that the betting is over. Last man or highest card gets the pot.

The fun element for a straight player is fairly obvious. The game is full of amusing byplay, heckling and panic.

Freddy gets his fun in the game by knowing his card as well. It is childishly easy for him to do so as you've seen in this section on card cheating.

I've lost count of the times he's had a bad five stuck to his head only to win against a selection of fours, threes and twos.

Posted Indian Poker

I can't resist finishing this chapter by telling a tale of Indian Poker that is one of Freddy's favorites.

One of his many acquaintances was playing in a big money school. He was a muck man and had stolen, towards the end of the evening, the ace of diamonds from the deck. It was hidden in his pocket for use in the next couple of hands. The dealer suggested, perfectly for Freddy's pal, a game of Indian Poker.

Freddy's pal switched his dealt card for the ace leaving him in a no lose situation. At absolute worst he'd split the pot against another ace. It wouldn't be a big pot but, hey, somebody may try to bluff him out.

Unfortunately he had hidden the ace in a pocket with other stuff including some postage stamps. Somehow one of the stamps had become adhered to the face of the ace of diamonds. The card on his forehead had a postage stamp stuck right in the middle of it.

Freddy's pal looked around the table and saw a whole lot of very suspicious faces. There was a horrible silence.

The silence was finally broken by one of the players asking, "*So who posted you the winning card then?*"

Mechanical Aids

THE PROFESSIONAL CARD CHEAT WOULD ALWAYS PREFER TO USE SLEIGHT-OF-HAND over a *gimmick* or *gaff*. If he is caught with a mechanical aid there is damning evidence against him. If he's using sleight-of-hand it's really just his word against the accuser.

However there are a number of gadgets he will consider such as the sleeve hold-out device discussed in the mucking chapter. He may also use a twinkle or a well made deck of marked cards.

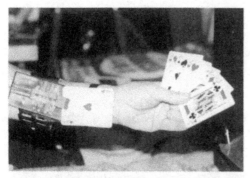

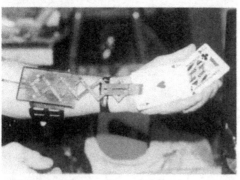

Crude holdout used to deliver or switch cards.

He may also consider, as at least one of my acquaintances does, a device first perfected by a Dutchman named P.J. Kepplinger. Kepplinger made the first mechanically perfect *Holdout* for use in games. He didn't invent the principle, which dates back to just a little after the invention of playing cards themselves, but he did perfect the device.

A Holdout is a device worn under the cheat's clothing (normally, but not always, up one of his sleeves) that will deliver a card or cards into his hand at a given moment.

The main part strapped to the arm consists, in most cases, of an expandable *Jacobs Ladder* or telescopic arm on one end of which is a clip to hold the card or cards. At the other end is an arrangement that will allow the cheat to expand or contract the device at will.

A simple Holdout may just consist of a tag that the cheat can press against his body. When he presses the tag the Holdout will expand down to his hand. An elastic connection draws the Holdout back into the sleeve when its work is done.

A more complicated arrangement may have a cord running across the cheat's chest. A deep breath expands the Holdout into the hand. Another arrangement may have a cord running down the trousers to the cheat's heel. By lowering his heel or stretching out his leg the Holdout delivers the card or cards to his hand. Again an elastic arrangement withdraws the device back into the sleeve.

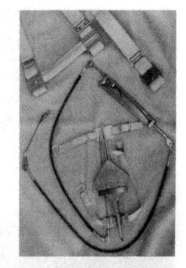

Some Holdouts are designed to come out from under the jacket and Freddy has even seen one that, most amusingly in his opinion, pops up from the front of the trousers!

A catalog in my collection from a gambling supply company lists, *Knee action Holdouts, Hip or foot action Holdout, Hip and foot action Holdout, Cold deck Holdout, Vest pocket Holdout* and an *arm pressure Holdout.*

The cheat uses a Holdout as a substitute for palming. During a game he can expand the Holdout to first steal away a good card or two. At an appropriate time he can then switch these cards into a hand and use the Holdout to steal away the unwanted cards. He never has to get cards hidden in his palm or, indeed, have to retrieve cards from a hiding place such as his pocket. All the action happens cleanly in his hands.

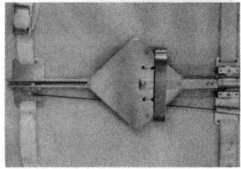

The big disadvantage of such a device is, of course, that if the device is found, the cheat is in *big* trouble. The device provides *absolute* proof that he is a cheat.

A Kepplinger Rig.

Some half smart players have a habit of gripping a player's arm and giving a good firm handshake when they meet them. If the other player has something up their sleeve they will feel it. This is called the *pump* shake. Even Freddy is unsure of any casual way to check for the Holdout that worked from the crotch of the trousers!

Many amateur cheats believe that Holdouts, being mechanical, require no skill. Nothing could be further from the truth. A good Holdout man is a highly skilled cheat indeed. He uses his mechanical device and combines it with incredible talent and timing to pull off outrageous switches under real fire. One of my friends in the cheating world uses a device in high end casino Baccarat games. I have watched him over and over again. When he switches the hand there is absolutely nothing to see. It's almost uncanny to watch. His Holdout device by the way is a twenty-five thousand dollar piece of art. He's made the cost of the device back many, many times over.

It takes a *lot* of practice to operate a Holdout with natural actions. Of Kepplinger, one of his opponents wrote, "*He sat like a statue at the table. He kept his cards away from him and did not move a muscle as far as the eye could see. We could see up his sleeves and yet he won!*" Kepplinger's device was only exposed when some very suspicious players beat him to the floor and liter-

Note the visible card in the prism concealed in the shoe.

Dealing a second from the shoe.

ally stripped him to discover if they could find anything amiss. *"Sounds like quite a guy,"* says Freddy.

You are unlikely to run into a Holdout man of this sort quite simply because there aren't many about. This rare breed of ice cold cheat make their money in high end, high money games where a single hand can mean thousands. Calling *Banko* in a big game of Baccarat can often mean over a hundred thousand dollars are being bet on the turn of just two cards. One bet, one move and a big profit. *"Nice,"* says Freddy.

Your best defense against *any* mucking technique is to occasionally count the cards in play.

If any are missing or, indeed, there are any extra ones leave the game *immediately.* Don't even bother to wait to say goodbye to another player.

Even if the deck is fine a Holdout man or muck player will know *why* you are counting the cards. Your *fast company* action may well discourage him from stealing cards. Well, at least until you leave the game.

In a number of private games I've witnessed the cards have been dealt from a Dealing Shoe of the type seen in casinos. The players think that it makes the game look a little more classy and, they argue, means that the cards cannot be cheated. These players have obviously never seen a *Prism Shoe*. Using this ingenious device the dealer gets knowledge of the card about to be dealt *before* he slides it from the shoe. A cunningly placed prism reflects the cards index so he can see it. The shoe also allows him to deal this card or, if needed, to second deal the card below it. You are unlikely to ever see one, a professional one runs around $1500.00 at the time of writing, but be aware that a shoe does not stop cheating.

But Freddy still prefers sleight-of-hand over any form of mechanical device. Often the mechanical devices sold by supply houses, in his opinion, are of little use in any game even if you do practice with them. The supply houses are cheating the wanna be cheats!

Friendly little world isn't it!

Freddy's Final Comments on Card Cheating

AS YOU'VE SEEN, FREDDY, WORKING ALONE OR WITH PARTNERS, HAS A WHOLE bag full of tricks and techniques that he can use. Even though you've seen a lot you've still only seen examples of some of the techniques. New methods and scams are appearing all the time. Nobody can hope to know them all.

A good cheat will be a patient man and wait for the right moments. It may take an hour, it might take all night but when he pounces it will be quick and deadly.

FREDDY'S ADVICE

Freddy offers these final summary tips on how to avoid being cheated in a card game.

Learn to shuffle and cut properly. Freddy is amazed at how so many players will shuffle and expose cards. Place the pack face down on the table. Cut about half the pack to one side. Lightly riffle the corners together and *push* the two halves into each other. *Don't* use any fancy waterfall type moves. *Don't* lift the cards from the table to square them. By shuffling in this tight way you'll eliminate the chances of anybody peeking cards on the top or bottom of the deck. Now cut *one third* of the pack from bottom to top and repeat the shuffle. Finally cut *one third* of the pack from the middle to the top and, once more, repeat the shuffle. This will eliminate ninety nine percent of any pre-stacking that has been done. Push, or allow another player to push, a face up joker, or marker (*cap*), card into the deck and cut the cards at that point leaving the joker sticking out slightly. This will eliminate most of the false cutting techniques. All of the above is done with the deck flat on the table.

Learn to deal properly. Lift the deck from the table, fingers at the front, thumb at the back and keep it *flat*. Make sure that you don't flash the bottom card as the deck is placed into your dealing hand. As you deal make sure that the cards are kept low to the table. Shuffling and dealing in this manner will not eliminate all cheating but will eliminate a great deal, especially most of the petty, more common, hustles.

If you suspect any form of false shuffling and/or cutting from another player or any form of marked cards, coolers or, indeed, *any* form of cheating is going on, insist on shuffling the cards again.

Learn and *remember* everything you can about the cheat's methods. You don't have to be able to do the moves but by understanding them you will know a lot about when and where to look should you suspect anything.

Count the cards occasionally to make sure they are all there.

Never allow rabbit hunting and *never* allow a player to touch any cards other than his own.

Don't drink when you are playing cards for money. Alcohol dulls the senses making the cheat's job much easier.

Never play cards for large sums of money with strangers especially in a *spur of the moment* game.

Be wary of a regular player who wins consistently *every* week. Be especially wary if his wins tend to come from one or two lucky hands.

Never let another player distract you away from the game. Ignore *all* distractions. Look at your cards and place them flat on the table.

Never let somebody stand behind you. *Never* let another person, player or not, look at your cards.

Listen and *look* for any signs of signaling.

Before and *during* the game use safety checks for marked cards and strippers.

If you have *any* doubts get out of the game. Don't accuse anybody of cheating. Don't raise an argument. Just get out as quickly and politely as you can.

Paranoid? Maybe but, then again, maybe not. I'd always rather be safe than sorry especially when it comes to my hard-earned money.

Some gambling experts go further. They will tell you, with some justification, that something like the *mechanic's grip* is a one hundred percent give away of cheating. Well, it isn't. A good many players hold the deck this way including dealers in a casino where the deck is dealt from the hand in certain games. It is, however, a sign of somebody who is comfortable with cards. To me, such a player casually joining a bar game would heighten my suspicion.

As Freddy is fond of saying, "*Show me a good loser and I'll show you a loser!*"

To repeat, if you have *any* doubts then get out of the game. It's a cruel, tough world out there, don't be a victim.

A FINAL AMUSING TALE OF CARDS

A delightful tale that Freddy tells concerns a game where two cheats at the table were completely unaware of each other.

On the final hand of the evening both were throwing money into the pot like madmen.

Both had cheated.

On the final show down one of the crooks said, *"I'll see you! What have you got?"*

"Four kings," said the second crook.

"You cheated!" accused the first.

"How do you know that?" asked the second, ready to go into defense mode.

"Because those aren't the cards I dealt you, I only gave you three kings!" yelled the first without thinking.

They agreed to split the pot.

Just because you are honest, don't expect others to live up to your high standards. And, as the above tale shows, if you are dishonest don't drop your guard. You may not be the only one!

"Phew—Let's take a break from the heavy stuff."

Simon Lovell

A Quick Break Before Moving On!

AFTER FREDDY AND I HAD FINISHED OFF THE CARD CHEATING SECTION HE decided that he needed a quick break at his favorite bar before moving on to another big section; cheating at dice games. I ordered a cup of coffee and Freddy ordered a beer with a whiskey chaser. I guess it needn't be mentioned that I paid the bill on a stupid bet.

Freddy bet me that he could prove that ten plus four was equal to two. *"That's right,"* he said, *"I'll prove to you that the following sum makes sense!"* He had even written it out on a cocktail napkin for me. 10 + 4 = 2.

I thought about this for quite some time. Enough time, in fact, for the bar tab to be up to three cups of coffee and three more drinks for Freddy. I just couldn't see the angle on it. Unless it was some incredibly complicated piece of Quantum Math, or something incredibly stupid that I just couldn't fathom, it seemed to be impossible. I gave up and took the bet just to see how the hell Freddy could do it.

He asked me what time it was. I looked at my watch and told him. He laughed and said, *"Haven't you got it yet?"* I was completely confused. He told me to look at my watch again. I did so and still didn't get it. *"Maybe I'm just not training you as well as I thought,"* mused Freddy. *"Remember, with these bar bets you've always got to think laterally, think of the weird, the obscure, think science, think sneaky!"* I thought of all of those things but still didn't get it.

Then it struck me. Of course! It was so obvious that I was amazed I hadn't got it straight away. I was also pretty irritated at the $27.00 bar tab it cost me to learn it. I was mad enough to call Freddy a complete bastard, which just made him laugh out loud.

The answer is to look at a watch face and think. What's ten o'clock plus four hours? Two o'clock of course. Proof that ten plus four is two. Ah well, at least it didn't cost you a bar tab to learn it!

To try to quell my irritation Freddy decided to show me a couple of bar bets for free. One demonstrated sneaky tactics the other showed science in action. Both were pretty good and I asked his permission to add them to the book. It cost me dinner but he finally agreed.

The first demonstrates Freddy's sneaky tactics when setting up a bar bet. He put a shot glass full of water in front me and asked me to pick it up and put it back down again. I did so with considerable ease. After all it's not a really difficult thing to do. He then bet me that he was confident I could not repeat the action without spilling the drink. He was willing to bet me that I couldn't just pick up the glass and put it back down without spilling the entire contents of the glass. He assured me that he wouldn't nudge me, wouldn't shout or try to distract me in any way. All I had to do was to lift up the glass and put it down with some liquid left in it and I would win.

I looked at my watch again. It didn't help this time!

This bet is all in the set up. Freddy sets the glass for you in a sneaky manner not likely to be thought of by anybody other than a fellow scam artist. To guarantee that you have to spill the liquid Freddy sets the glass upside down! He does this by covering the mouth of the shot glass with his driving license or a coaster. He can now carefully turn the glass mouth down on to the bar without spilling a drop. He then quickly pulls out the license or coaster from under the glass to leave it mouth down, but still full of liquid, on the bar!

The moment that you try to lift up that glass the liquid goes everywhere! Another win for Freddy!

That was the sneaky side of things for the evening. The other bet Freddy showed me relied on simple physics and was really fascinating to watch. It was well worth the few dollars he gathered from people around us before showing us he could do what seemed to be impossible.

Freddy put two shot glasses down on the bar. He filled one with water and the other with whiskey. He offered the following bet. "*I'll put all the water where the whiskey is and all the whiskey where the water is. In other words my friends I'll make the two liquids change places!*" Before any bets would be placed, the crowd that had gathered around us, made sure, to their minds anyway, that Freddy couldn't cheat. He wasn't allowed to use any extra glasses or receptacles, he couldn't use his mouth (to hold one of the liquids while he poured the other into the empty glass then spit the held liquid into the now empty glass) and a number of other caveats all of which Freddy agreed to. Freddy even offered some extra information. He said that he would use his driving license to make the exchange! It was too intriguing to resist and quite a large bet went down from the crowd who were convinced that it just couldn't be done. And, even if Freddy could do it, it was worth the money just to find out how he could achieve this miraculous feat!

Freddy points out that a key element of many bar bets is the fact that the loser learns the secret of the bet. The money lost becomes, if you like, a training fee to learn the bet so that they, in turn, can try the bet out upon their friends. Provided the training fee isn't too extravagant the loser is hardly likely to raise a beef. They are much more likely to want to leave and find some friends they can take with the bet!

To return to the whiskey and water bet I'm sure you don't need to be told that Freddy won the money. His method was fascinating to watch and relied upon the simple fact that water is heavier than whiskey!

Freddy covered the mouth of the shot glass filled with water with his driving license. He then carefully inverted this glass over the mouth of the whiskey filled glass but did not remove his driving license. So now he had a glass of whiskey (Freddy's preference is Wild Turkey but I suspect that's just for the taste!) on top of which was a mouth down glass of water, the two being separated by his driving license.

He then carefully pulled his license to one side until there was a tiny opening between the two glasses. Then he sat back to let the laws of physics take over to let him win his bet. The whiskey was slowly forced up to the top glass while the heavier water forced its way down into the lower glass. A few minutes later the two liquids had changed places and Freddy picked up the money . . . again. Nobody complained. It really was a great bet that, as I've said, they couldn't wait to try on their pals. A couple actually asked if Freddy had any more bets to show them! Amazing!

As we walked back to my home to start work on the dice cheating section I was reminded yet again of the extraordinary ability that Freddy has when dealing with people. He'd taken $27 and dinner from me, around $50 from his crowd and hadn't paid for a thing all night! Not only that but people had been sad to see him go and had said that they hoped he'd be back soon! "*It's fun to be the nice guy from time to time,*" was Freddy's only comment when I pointed this out to him. "*But you took their money and they still liked you,*" I said. "*Yeah, but my company was worth what they paid,*" he replied. And you know something? For once he was absolutely right!

From fun guy back to hardened con man and cheat, it's time now to join Freddy at a dice game or two. And, trust me, no amount of Freddy's company would be worth the sums of money we'll be talking about!

IT CAN HAPPEN IN A BAR, A CASINO, A BACK ALLEY, OR EVEN ON A TRAIN TRIP. IT CAN BE *BACKGAMMON, CRAPS,* OR A FRIENDLY OFF-THE-CUFF *WAGER.*

YOU THINK YOU'RE IN *CONTROL*... BUT IT'S ALL A *DIZZY DELUSION!*

THE STAKES START SMALL BUT BEFORE YOU KNOW IT... YOU'RE *IN* FOR A *BUNDLE!*

BETWEEN THE FLATS, THE BEVELS, THE BUTTERFLIES...

THE DROP SHOTS, THE BLANKET ROLLS, THE OLD RELIABLE SWITCHEROOS...

YOU BECOME UTTERLY, IRRETRIEVABLY *LOST!*

YOU'RE CAUGHT IN A *MAD,* MUDDLED MAELSTROM! DREAMS OF WEALTH ARE DISRUPTED BY REVELATIONS OF DISASTER...

SCRIPT/ART: LEW

...AND YOU CAN'T SEEM TO WAKE UP FROM THIS

"WHIP SHOT NIGHTMARE!"

Cheating With Dice

IF PLAYING CARDS ARE THE LOVE OF FREDDY'S LIFE THEN DICE MUST SURELY BE his mistress. We've already seen how he can use a mis-spotted die to great effect in the Tat hustle but that, as I'm sure you have guessed, really is just the tip of a rather large iceberg.

Just as cards can be faked and manipulated, so can dice.

If you play Backgammon and think that playing with a dice cup eliminates cheating then Freddy would love to play a game or two with you!

Freddy says that dice cheating can be split into three main categories.

Faked dice and the ability to switch them in and out of play.

Sleight-of-hand with normal dice.

Manipulating dice with a cup.

As Backgammon and similar dice games have become more popular in Europe the cheats there have become more interested in controlling them for profit. The American cheats have always had a fascination with dice because of the mania for the casino game of Craps. Americans, it seems to Freddy, will play Craps almost at the drop of a hat! European cheats use the same moves as their American counterparts but tend to concentrate on bar games and Backgammon.

It all goes to show, yet again, that *wherever* there is money being gambled the cheat will not be far behind.

Having dazzled you with Freddy's card work we'll now see how his nimble fingers can take your money with the cubes.

*"Excuse me officer I suspect that I've just been cheated
with a set of loaded dice. You'll find the evidence
lodged in me where the sun doesn't shine!"*

The cry of an innocent who accused his opponent.

Types Of Dice Cheat

FREDDY SPLITS DICE CHEATS INTO TWO CATEGORIES.

The first is the amateur cheat who likes to use his 'knowledge' and faked dice to win money from his friends and acquaintances. Like the amateur card cheat he will often play in the same group week in and week out. He has some knowledge of correct odds and a good collection of bar bets to take a buck or two along the way.

Then there is the professional dice mechanic or *bust out man*. He will be an experienced worker with faked dice and sleight-of-hand. He's not at all particular about his victims and his work will vary from private games right up to, if talented enough, the casino floor. Professional dice workers often work with a back-up team known, rather fancifully, as a *dice mob*.

The amateur cheat is becoming more and more common as time goes by. Crude gimmicked dice can be bought from most novelty or joke shops and, rather like the amateur card cheat, this dice man has the advantage that his friends don't expect him to be a cheat. Who cheats their friends? That was a rhetorical question by the way!

Nobody questions the motives of a pal who suggests a game of Poker Dice or whatever. The suggestion will just be seen by the others as a way of passing an hour or two amusingly. The smarter amateur cheat may just leave his faked dice on the floor of a bar. He knows that often somebody will find them and, perhaps, start up a friendly game. All he has to do then is get into the game and start betting. No suspicion falls on him because he didn't start the game!

The professional will switch dice in and out of play with such finesse that even if you suspected cheating you'd have a real tough time spotting anything. The professional will also use controlled throws to twist the odds in his favor. In Freddy's hands a pair of completely honest dice suddenly seem to act like trained monkeys every time he throws them.

Ready?

Okay, welcome to another section of Freddy's world of easy money.

Switching Dice

IN ORDER FOR FREDDY TO USE FAKED DICE HE MUST HAVE THE ABILITY TO SWITCH them in and out of a game. Before looking at the types of dice he may use let's see how he manages the switch. Actually there are quite a few ways for him to do this.

SWITCHES

The Change Over

In loose company Freddy can use an adaption of the switch used in the Tat hustle. He will have the two dice (generally for a game like Craps he will switch *both* dice) loosely palmed in his left hand. He will pick up the two dice to be switched, from the table, with his right hand. He will then, apparently, transfer the dice to his left hand to make the throw.

Actually, as his hands come together, he palms the dice in his right hand and allows the dice in his left hand to come into view. This very simple switch is done completely on the off-beat and often at a high point of misdirection. During a Backgammon game he will do it just as you are throwing your dice. Obviously, here, you are much more interested in your roll than on what Freddy is doing.

The switch can also be done by a partner. Sam picks up the dice to hand them to Freddy performing the switch along the way.

Never allow a hand-to-hand transfer of dice.

Come On Baby!

It is very common among players to hold the dice between their hands and shake them. Some will even kiss their hands for good luck before rolling the dice.

Duplicating this action makes Freddy's simple Change Over Switch even easier. He has the two faked dice palmed in his left hand. He picks up the straight dice from the table with his right hand. Then, he brings his two hands together and shakes the straight dice. The rattling sound is very fair and, indeed, the straight dice are being shaken fairly. But Freddy isn't going to throw the straight dice.

As he kisses his hands he palms the two straight dice and proceeds to throw out the fake dice.

If any player brings two hands together to kiss them you might want to point out that, although it may bring them luck, they can kiss one hand with just as much effect.

Insist that dice are picked up and thrown with one hand. It won't stop all switching but will, at least, eliminate most two handed methods.

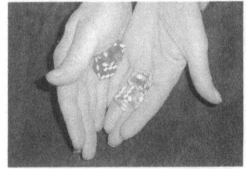

Palm to Palm Switch.

The Money Change

Here Freddy will have the faked dice under some paper money being held in his right hand. He picks up the straight dice in his left hand. Because Freddy is right handed (or at least appears to be; actually he is ambidextrous) it is natural for him to throw the dice here with his right hand. Because of this assumption the following action, even if spotted at all, will go unnoticed.

Freddy passes the money to his left hand and throws the dice with his right.

What you don't see is that he doesn't transfer the dice from hand to hand as he should have done. He boldly puts the money on top of the straight dice in his left hand and rolls out the dice (gaffed) from his right.

In some areas this is also called a *Butterfly* switch.

Never allow anything other than the dice in a player's hand.

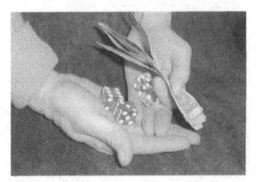

Butterfly Switch.

The Thumb Switch

As with cards, there are dice moves that take a great deal of dedicated practice to achieve. The *Thumb Switch* is one of them. Freddy considers the time required as time well spent. If he does this move perfectly (and he does) all you will see is him pick up two dice from the table and roll them out using just one hand. Yet the dice will have been switched!

Thumb Switch.

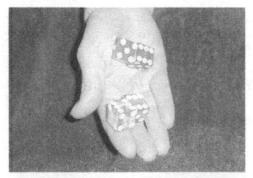

Freddy starts out with the two faked dice loosely hidden in his cupped fingers. As he picks up the two straight dice he grips them in the crotch of his thumb, holding them secure between his thumb and the edge of his hand.

With a continuing action he will shake his hand and then roll out the faked dice. When done by an expert like Freddy the Thumb Switch is a lightning like action and extremely difficult to catch.

The Palm Switch

This switch is perhaps the hardest of all the sleight-of-hand switches used by dice cheats. But, once the mechanic has the move down pat, it will fool all but the most knowledgeable of watchers. It is so good that it is the switch preferred by casino cheats where scrutiny is of the highest order.

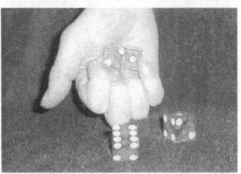

Palm Switch.

The gaffed dice are hidden in the palm of the hand gripped between the base of the thumb and the edge of the hand.

The true dice are picked up by Freddy and are trapped between the little and first finger.

Freddy's fingers curl in and his hand makes a throwing action. The gaffs are released to roll across the table and, with a continuing action, the fingers curl in the leave the straight dice in the palmed position occupied by the fakes just a milli-second before. This entire, very difficult, action looks just as though Freddy has picked up the dice and thrown them. In his hands the switch is absolutely natural and innocent in look.

It takes just a split second to perform.

If you think this sounds hard then consider John Soares, one of the greatest dice men of the twentieth century. He was reputed to be able to switch five straight dice for five gaffed dice *one handed*! That meant he had to be simultaneously controlling five fakes and five straight dice. You can read more about this extraordinary man in his autobiography *Loaded Dice*.

Thankfully for you, men like Soares are as rare, if not rarer, than a good Riffle Stacker.

EMPTY HANDS

Obviously the ideal situation for Freddy would be for him to pick up two dice, shake them, roll them out and then be able to *flash* an empty hand while still doing his switch.

Actually there are several ways he can do this!

Freddy can have the dice palmed in his left hand. He will reach for the straight dice, covering them for just a moment. Then he will change his mind and pause to light a cigarette. Picking up the dice with his right hand he will roll them out showing a clearly empty hand as he does so.

Freddy has simply split up a hand-to-hand transfer action into two separate units. The switch happened as he *changed* his mind. As he covered the dice for just a second his thumb gripped the two straight dice in a tabled version of the Thumb Switch. The two fake dice were left behind. The straight dice were ditched as Freddy got his cigarettes. Even a good watcher will forget about the moment that the dice on the table were touched. It was only for a heartbeat and, after all, it is normal to think about a switch at the time of the roll but not some time *before* the roll.

Always watch the dice at *all* times. Freddy may seem to touch them for an instant but that's time enough for him to do the 'deed'.

Freddy can also have a *Poacher's Pocket*, or, as a magician would call it, a *Topit*, hidden under his jacket, pinned between it and his shirt. He starts with the faked dice palmed in his hand. He picks up the straight dice executing a Palm Switch or Thumb Switch as he does so. He throws out the gaffed dice and, as his hand comes back, he releases the straight dice which will fly into his secret pocket. There is nothing to see. Two dice have been picked up and two dice have been rolled.

Be *very* wary of a large shaking or tossing action.

Freddy may not bother to use the secret pocket. He can just let them fly under his jacket and hold them in place with arm pressure. It takes a little more practice to get down pat but it does lose the bag which is potentially incriminating evidence.

In casino games this switch is often worked with a woman shill. She stands next to the cheat and, at the point of the switch, is looking for something in her handbag (purse). The cheat, as part of his action, dumps the straight dice into the bag as his hands come back to roll out the fakes or just after the fakes have been rolled. The woman leaves soon after taking the incriminating 'spare' dice with her. If you think that sounds crude bear in mind that it is the *exact* technique used by John Soares and his team to switch in *shapes* (of which more later) during casino Craps games.

In loose company Freddy may just dump the dice in his lap during a game of Backgammon.

SWITCH BACKS

With some gaffed dice Freddy may leave them in the game a long time. Percentage dice like *shapes* and *loads* need time to do their work. But others, like *tops and bottoms*, need to go in and get out as quickly as possible. Freddy will use a thumb or palm switch to switch the straight dice back in at the earliest opportunity. That's why it's wise to be on your guard at all times. The game may start and finish with straight dice but it doesn't mean that fakes didn't enter the picture for a roll or two along the way.

If Freddy has been using a Poacher's Pocket the faked dice can be a little awkward to retrieve. To get around any potential problems Freddy has modified his bag so that it has one end higher than the other. At the bottom of the low end of the slope is a hole. His right hand throws the dice into the bag which roll down and out of the hole at the bottom to land in his waiting left hand. Another way, in fact, in which Freddy splits up a hand to hand transfer.

I recently showed Freddy the magician's idea of a *Topit* that can be accessed from the magicians jacket pocket via a slit. This idea, published in Michael Ammar's *Topit Book,* seems to have been an idea of Bobby Baxter, a fine New York City magician. Freddy was absolutely captivated by it and predicted that if it isn't already in the cheat's world then it soon would be.

Don't expect Freddy to keep his dice palmed for a moment longer than he has to. Like a good card mucker he will have them stashed away in a safe place until he needs them. The moment any required switching is over he will ditch them at the earliest opportunity.

SPLASHING

Before making any switches Freddy may well go through all the motions of a switch *without* any palmed dice. He does this to test the observation and knowledge of other players.

If he is called on an action during a *splash* he can show empty hands and feign innocence.

If he isn't called on it then he knows that he is safe to make the switch proper next time around.

All switches will happen at a moment of misdirection. Freddy may do it, as we've mentioned, as you make your roll in a Backgammon game. He may employ a shill to misdirect you at the critical moment by asking for change, offering a side bet or asking if you need a drink. Anything that takes your eyes from Freddy's hands for just a second will give him the time he needs.

If you insist on the dice being thrown from cups bear in mind that the cup itself can be used as a cover to switch in gaffed dice. The fact that the fakes are thrown from a cup will not affect their action in the slightest. There's a lot more to be said on cups later on!

6-4 THE HARD WAY

Freddy has a large collection of gambling tales concerning dice games. Here's a rather tragic one you may want to read before considering becoming a dice cheat yourself.

Freddy it seems had met up with a gambler friend of his who had been watching a Backgammon tournament the night before.

"*I saw a guy roll 6-4 the hard way,*" the friend casually mentioned.

"*How do you mean,*" asked a rather puzzled Freddy.

"*He picked up two dice, missed the switch and rolled out four dice.*"

"*Bad luck for him,*" said Freddy. "*Where does the six come into this?*"

"*That's how many times they smashed his hand with a baseball bat,*" the friend replied. "*He won't switch dice with that hand again.*"

That's what I call 6-4 the hard way!

Freddy's Fakes

WHEN USING CARDS FREDDY WILL, AS WE'VE SEEN, USE SLEIGHT-OF-HAND ABOVE fakes as often as he can. With dice it's a different story all together. Controlling two straight dice is both difficult and unpredictable. It can be done but, as a rule of thumb, the cheat will concentrate on learning a top class switch which he will use in conjunction with gaffed dice.

Nearly everybody has heard of *loaded dice* but they are actually only one of the gaffs that Freddy can use to take your money.

Here's Freddy's run down on the main types of gaffed dice in use today.

PERCENTAGE DICE

A pair of percentage dice will not throw the same number *every* time they are rolled but are gaffed in a manner to *favor* certain numbers turning up. They are the favorite weapon of the amateur cheat because he doesn't need to switch them in and out of the game at regular intervals. He may not even bother switching them into a game at all but just start the game with them!

They are also favored by the professional cheat *especially* casino cheats or *Crossroaders*. If they can get the dice into a game they can leave and allow two 'innocent' shills (known as *horses*) to do the betting for them.

Freddy has seen a game of *Crown and Anchor* (of which more later) where the cheats managed to start a game with loaded dice. The cheats cleaned up and left the dice game behind as a gift to their new-found friends. One of the cheats returned to the area six weeks later and found the players still using the set, completely unaware of the gaffed dice they were using!

There are various kinds of percentage dice.

Shapes

Here one or more of the sides of the dice are shaved by around one sixty-fourth of an inch. This effectively reduces the area of some of the faces. Because some faces are larger than others a roll will favor the die coming to rest upon them. It may not sound like much of a deal to you but *shapes* are amongst the most common of all faked dice in use today.

Many cheap *shop bought* dice are mass produced plastic moulds. Nine out of ten are *accidental* shapes. If you take the time to measure them carefully with calipers you'll see that you can buy your *shapes* off the local store's shelf!

A die with just one shaved face is also known as a *flat*.

As little as one five-hundredth of an inch shaved off the face of a die will alter the odds over a period of time. It's little wonder that most casino managers carry calipers in their pockets.

Just as a cheat can make an impromptu Stripper deck he can also create impromptu *shapes*. By wetting one side of a die and rubbing it against newspaper he can *shave* it slightly down. *Shapes* made this way are often referred to as *prints*.

The only way to check for good *shapes* is to use a set of measuring calipers. If you go to this trouble make sure to measure all the faces of all the dice in play. Do be prepared to find, despite your suspicions, nothing wrong with them. By pulling out your calipers you are giving a lot of misdirection to the cheat to give him time to switch his fakes out.

Poor or cheap *shapes* can be detected by putting the dice together on a flat surface and rubbing a finger nail across them. Try this test with the dice in various positions. If you feel a tiny bump as your finger nail goes from one die to the other you may have found a set of *shapes*. Don't scream, they may be *accidental shapes* that have been bought from a store. But, I would advise leaving the game just in case.

Dice in casinos have to be accurate squares to within minute allowances. Anything found to be less than perfect is rejected. Casino owners realize that even the tiniest of discrepancies can affect the odds. Cheats also realize this!

Bevels

Bevels are dice that have been shaped so that one or more of the sides are slightly rounded (or humped if you like) rather than being totally flat. On a throw they will tend to roll off the rounded sides to come to rest on the flat ones.

To test for *bevels* rub each side against a hard flat surface. There will be a distinct rocking action on the gaffed sides.

Cut Edges

In private games many dice have rounded edges as against the razor sharp square edges of casino dice. With *cut work* some of the edges will be rounder than others. Once more this will effectively reduce the size of some of the

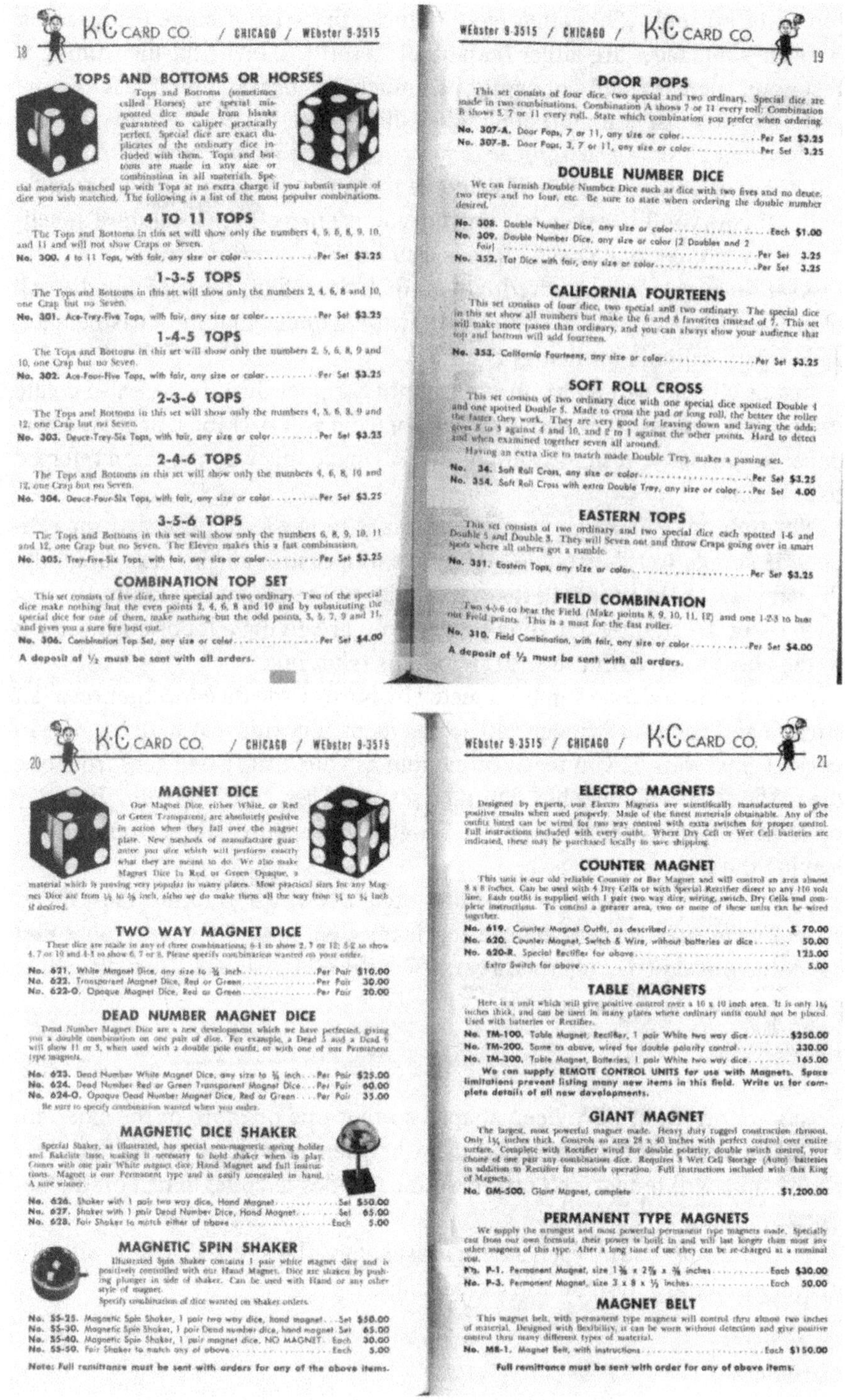

K·C CARD CO. / CHICAGO / WEbster 9-3515

18

TOPS AND BOTTOMS OR HORSES

Tops and Bottoms (sometimes called Horses) are special misspotted dice made from blanks guaranteed to caliper practically perfect. Special dice are exact duplicates of the ordinary dice included with them. Tops and bottoms are made in any size or combination in all materials. Special materials matched up with Tops at no extra charge if you submit sample of dice you wish matched. The following is a list of the most popular combinations.

4 TO 11 TOPS

The Tops and Bottoms in this set will show only the numbers 4, 5, 6, 8, 9, 10, and 11 and will not show Craps or Seven.

No. 300. 4 to 11 Tops, with fair, any size or color .... Per Set $3.25

1-3-5 TOPS

The Tops and Bottoms in this set will show only the numbers 2, 4, 6, 8 and 10, one Crap but no Seven.

No. 301. Ace-Trey-Five Tops, with fair, any size or color .... Per Set $3.25

1-4-5 TOPS

The Tops and Bottoms in this set will show only the numbers 2, 5, 6, 8, 9 and 10, one Crap but no Seven.

No. 302. Ace-Four-Five Tops, with fair, any size or color .... Per Set $3.25

2-3-6 TOPS

The Tops and Bottoms in this set will show only the numbers 4, 5, 6, 8, 9 and 12, one Crap but no Seven.

No. 303. Deuce-Trey-Six Tops, with fair, any size or color .... Per Set $3.25

2-4-6 TOPS

The Tops and Bottoms in this set will show only the numbers 4, 6, 8, 10 and 12, one Crap but no Seven.

No. 304. Deuce-Four-Six Tops, with fair, any size or color .... Per Set $3.25

3-5-6 TOPS

The Tops and Bottoms in this set will show only the numbers 6, 8, 9, 10, 11 and 12, one Crap but no Seven. The Eleven makes this a fast combination.

No. 305. Trey-Five-Six Tops, with fair, any size or color .... Per Set $3.25

COMBINATION TOP SET

This set consists of five dice, three special and two ordinary. Two of the special dice make nothing but the even points 2, 4, 6, 8 and 10 and by substituting the special dice for one of them, make nothing but the odd points, 3, 5, 7, 9 and 11, and gives you a sure fire bust out.

No. 306. Combination Top Set, any size or color .... Per Set $4.00

A deposit of ½ must be sent with all orders.

WEbster 9-3515 / CHICAGO / K·C CARD CO.

19

DOOR POPS

This set consists of four dice, two special and two ordinary. Special dice are made in two combinations. Combination A shows 7 or 11 every roll; Combination B shows 5, 7 or 11 every roll. State which combination you prefer when ordering.

No. 307-A. Door Pops, 7 or 11, any size or color .... Per Set $3.25
No. 307-B. Door Pops, 3, 7 or 11, any size or color .... Per Set 3.25

DOUBLE NUMBER DICE

We can furnish Double Number Dice such as dice with two fives and no deuce, two treys and no four, etc. Be sure to state when ordering the double number desired.

No. 308. Double Number Dice, any size or color .... Each $1.00
No. 309. Double Number Dice, any size or color (2 Doubles and 2 Fair) .... Per Set 3.25
No. 352. Tat Dice with fair, any size or color .... Per Set 3.25

CALIFORNIA FOURTEENS

This set consists of four dice, two special and two ordinary. The special dice in this set show all numbers but make the 6 and 8 favorites instead of 7. This set will make more passes than ordinary, and you can always show your audience that top and bottom will add fourteen.

No. 353. California Fourteens, any size or color .... Per Set $3.25

SOFT ROLL CROSS

This set consists of two ordinary dice with one special dice spotted Double 4 and one spotted Double 5. Made to cross the pad or long roll, the better the roller the faster they work. They are very good for leaving down and laying the odds; gives 8 to 5 against 4 and 10, and 2 to 1 against the other points. Hard to detect and when examined together seven all around.

Having an extra dice to match made Double Trey, makes a passing set.

No. 34. Soft Roll Cross, any size or color .... Per Set $3.25
No. 354. Soft Roll Cross with extra Double Trey, any size or color .... Per Set 4.00

EASTERN TOPS

This set consists of two ordinary and two special dice each spotted 1-6 and Double 5 and Double 3. They will Seven out and throw Craps going over in smart spots where all others got a rumble.

No. 351. Eastern Tops, any size or color .... Per Set $3.25

FIELD COMBINATION

Two 4-5-6 to beat the Field (Make points 8, 9, 10, 11, 12) and one 1-2-3 to bust out Field points. This is a must for the fast roller.

No. 310. Field Combination, with fair, any size or color .... Per Set $4.00

A deposit of ½ must be sent with all orders.

K·C CARD CO. / CHICAGO / WEbster 9-3515

20

MAGNET DICE

Our Magnet Dice, either White, or Red or Green Transparent, are absolutely positive in action when they fall over the magnet plate. New methods of manufacture guarantee you dice which will perform exactly what they are meant to do. We also make Magnet Dice in Red or Green Opaque, a material which is proving very popular in many places. Most practical sizes for any Magnet Dice are from ½ to ⅝ inch, altho we do make them all the way from ½ to ¾ inch if desired.

TWO WAY MAGNET DICE

These dice are made in any of three combinations; 6-1 to show 2, 7 or 12; 5-2 to show 4, 7 or 10 and 4-3 to show 6, 7 or 8. Please specify combination wanted on your order.

No. 621. White Magnet Dice, any size to ¾ inch .... Per Pair $10.00
No. 622. Transparent Magnet Dice, Red or Green .... Per Pair 30.00
No. 622-O. Opaque Magnet Dice, Red or Green .... Per Pair 20.00

DEAD NUMBER MAGNET DICE

Dead Number Magnet Dice are a new development which we have perfected, giving you a double combination on one pair of dice. For example, a Dead 5 and a Dead 6 will show 11 or 5, when used with a double pole outfit, or with one of our Permanent type magnets.

No. 623. Dead Number White Magnet Dice, any size to ¾ inch .... Per Pair $25.00
No. 624. Dead Number Red or Green Transparent Magnet Dice .... Per Pair 60.00
No. 624-O. Opaque Dead Number Magnet Dice, Red or Green .... Per Pair 35.00

Be sure to specify combination wanted when you order.

MAGNETIC DICE SHAKER

Special Shaker, as illustrated, has special non-magnetic spring holder and Bakelite base, making it necessary to hold shaker when in play. Comes with one pair White magnet dice, Hand Magnet and full instructions. Magnet is our Permanent type and is easily concealed in hand. A sure winner.

No. 626. Shaker with 1 pair two way dice, Hand Magnet .... Set $50.00
No. 627. Shaker with 1 pair Dead Number Dice, Hand Magnet .... Set 65.00
No. 628. Fair Shaker to match either of above .... Each 5.00

MAGNETIC SPIN SHAKER

Illustrated Spin Shaker contains 1 pair white magnet dice and is positively controlled with our Hand Magnet. Dice are shaken by pushing plunger in side of shaker. Can be used with Hand or any other style of magnet.

Specify combination of dice wanted on Shaker orders.

No. SS-25. Magnetic Spin Shaker, 1 pair two way dice, hand magnet .... Set $50.00
No. SS-30. Magnetic Spin Shaker, 1 pair Dead number dice, hand magnet .... Set 65.00
No. SS-40. Magnetic Spin Shaker, 1 pair magnet dice, NO MAGNET .... Each 30.00
No. SS-50. Fair Shaker to match any of above .... Each 5.00

Note: Full remittance must be sent with orders for any of the above items.

WEbster 9-3515 / CHICAGO / K·C CARD CO.

21

ELECTRO MAGNETS

Designed by experts, our Electro Magnets are scientifically manufactured to give positive results when used properly. Made of the finest materials obtainable. Any of the outfits listed can be wired for two way control with extra switches for proper control. Full instructions included with every outfit. Where Dry Cell or Wet Cell batteries are indicated, these may be purchased locally to save shipping.

COUNTER MAGNET

This unit is our old reliable Counter or Bar Magnet and will control an area almost 8 x 8 inches. Can be used with 4 Dry Cells or with Special Rectifier direct to any 110 volt line. Each outfit is supplied with 1 pair two way dice, wiring, switch, Dry Cells and complete instructions. To control a greater area, two or more of these units can be wired together.

No. 619. Counter Magnet Outfit, as described .... $ 70.00
No. 620. Counter Magnet, Switch & Wire, without batteries or dice 50.00
No. 620-R. Special Rectifier for above 125.00
Extra Switch for above 5.00

TABLE MAGNETS

Here is a unit which will give positive control over a 10 x 10 inch area. It is only 1¼ inches thick, and can be used in many places where ordinary units could not be placed. Used with batteries or Rectifier.

No. TM-100. Table Magnet, Rectifier, 1 pair White two way dice $250.00
No. TM-200. Same as above, wired for double polarity control 330.00
No. TM-300. Table Magnet, Batteries, 1 pair White two way dice 165.00

We can supply REMOTE CONTROL UNITS for use with Magnets. Space limitations prevent listing many new items in this field. Write us for complete details of all new developments.

GIANT MAGNET

The largest, most powerful magnet made. Heavy duty rugged construction thruout. Only 1¼ inches thick. Controls an area 28 x 40 inches with perfect control over entire surface. Complete with Rectifier wired for double polarity, double switch control, your choice of one pair any combination dice. Requires 3 Wet Cell Storage (Auto) batteries in addition to Rectifier for smooth operation. Full instructions included with this King of Magnets.

No. GM-500. Giant Magnet, complete $1,200.00

PERMANENT TYPE MAGNETS

We supply the strongest and most powerful permanent type magnets made. Specially cast from our own formula, their power is built in and will last longer than most any other magnets of this type. After a long time of use they can be re-charged at a nominal cost.

No. P-1. Permanent Magnet, size 1⅜ x 2⅞ x ⅜ inches .... Each $30.00
No. P-3. Permanent Magnet, size 3 x 8 x ½ inches .... Each 50.00

MAGNET BELT

This magnet belt, with permanent type magnets will control thru almost two inches of material. Designed with flexibility, it can be worn without detection and give positive control thru many different types of material.

No. MB-1. Magnet Belt, with instructions .... Each $150.00

Full remittance must be sent with order for any of above items.

Gambling catalog pages for Gaffed Dice. Straight from the shelf!

faces. Also the dice will tend to roll off the more heavily rounded sides. They work rather like a combination *shape/bevel*.

Other dice have their edges cut at an angle. You'll find this in trendy Backgammon sets where, I guess, they are thought to look rather *chic*. The cut tends to be at a forty-five degree angle. With *cut edged* dice some of these edges will have had their angle of cut increased. I have a set where the angle has been increased to sixty degrees although this is a rather extreme example.

To detect *cut work* hold two dice together and look at the gap between the angled or curved edges. If this varies when you try different positions then you may well be looking at gaffed dice.

The cheat can make impromptu *cut edged* dice by using the newspaper rubbing technique that created his *prints*.

Loaded Dice

Perhaps the most famous fakes of all! Contrary to popular belief it is very rare that a set of loaded dice will be set to throw the same number every time. Instead they are loaded to favor certain numbers on a roll.

Among the very first modern loaded dice (or *peeties* as they are sometimes called) were *tappers*. These had a central load chamber filled with mercury. If the mercury was in the center the die was said to roll normally. If the die was tapped against a surface the mercury was supposed to shift and turn the die into a loaded one. Freddy is convinced that these dice just wouldn't work. *"Anyway,"* he says, *"even if they did, by the time you'd finished bashing your load into place everybody would know something was going on!"* The only place you are likely to see a set of these dinosaurs is in a museum of gambling devices!

Modern loaded dice are weighted with non-shifting loads placed behind the spots of one or more sides of the die.

Opaque dice are loaded by drilling the spots on the face a little deeper than normal. The extra depth is filled with a small lead plug which is then painted over. They will caliper as completely square dice but will still now favor certain numbers.

Many people believe that transparent dice cannot be loaded. Nothing could be further from the truth!

The good *maker* will drill all the spots on the die a little deeper than normal. He will then fill the unloaded spots with paint. The sides he wants loaded will contain slugs of platinum, gold or tungsten. These slugs are heavier than lead and so the maker can use thinner slugs to conceal his work even further. When you look through the transparent dice all the spots appear to be recessed to the same depth but some are loaded.

The hardest dice to load are those which do not have recessed spots. Casinos these days tend to use transparent dice with the spots painted only onto the surface. Any form of slug loading would be apparent when the dice were looked through. It is rumored that some dice crews have managed to lightly load these dice by using heavier ink! This would seem to offer a tiny advantage but remember a tiny advantage is better than no advantage at all! Any *reasonable* advantage is worth having over a period of time. Perhaps the advantage offered by heavier paint is better than I first thought when you consider that many casino dice now have Bull's Eye spots made of concentric spots thus cutting down the painted areas! Artistic improvement? Maybe. Then again, the heavy paint advantage is even less, so maybe it's more than art.

A die loaded up on just one side to favor a single number is called a *dead die*. Sometimes the cheat will load up two adjoining sides of a die so that the load favors two numbers over the others. *Corners* are dice that have been loaded up at one corner so that three numbers are favored out of six.

With a good set of loaded dice you would have to make a good many rolls and check the results against probability to spot anything wrong. There are, however, two other methods that can be used to check for loads.

Hold a suspect die loosely between your finger tip and thumb at diagonally opposite corners. Hold it as lightly as you can without actually dropping it. Try this with all four combinations of diagonal corners. If the die is loaded it will tend to pivot downwards when the loads are uppermost. The feeling is quite unmistakable. Casino security use a small machine that holds the die at opposite corners. This allows the die to be loosely spun. A true die will slowly come to a stop smoothly. A load, as it stops spinning, will wobble back and forth.

Another test involves a tall glass of water. Hold the die just above the surface and drop the die gently into the water. Do this several times with a different face upwards every time. Note whether the die settles evenly or whether it turns as it descends. *If* it turns and seems to favor certain numbers then it is loaded. The water slows the die down and gives the load more time to work, making the load much easier to spot.

If a pair of dice is being used then be sure to check both of them. Cheats sometimes use one faked die in combination with a straight die. Just one loaded dice in combination with a straight one will still twist the odds in favor of the cheat.

Some rare opaque dice are not loaded but are *lightened* on one or more sides. This is done by drilling the spots deeper and hollowing out some of the interior. The spots are then refilled. Such dice are known as *floaters* and can be detected in exactly the same way as loads.

Loads are amongst the oldest of faked tools the gambling cheat uses. The University of Rome has an exhibition all about the doomed city of Pompeii. Among the pottery and coins you will see a pair of dice. One of them has a hole in it with a metal slug lying beside it. It may well be one of the earliest examples of a loaded die found to date.

Strength of Work

Some joke shop dice are so crudely made that it is amazing how anybody gets away with them in a game. The fact that they do is an indication of just how closely the average player pays attention during a game.

Freddy claims that once, during a moment of what can only be described as temporary insanity, he saw a cheat switch two red dice for two green dice. The cheat swiftly picked up the green dice and switched back in the red ones to roll again. Nobody said a thing.

At the professional end of the scale the dice can be so finely produced as to defy anything but the most careful of scrutiny.

Obviously the *lighter* the loading or the *finer* the shaving is, the less the odds will be twisted in the cheat's favor. Strong work is, however, more likely to be noticed. It is up to the cheat to decide between safety and greed.

TOPS AND BOTTOMS

Normal dice bear the numbers one to six and the opposite sides of a die will always add up to seven. Not all dice used by cheats conform to this norm however.

Tops and Bottoms are not percentage dice. They need to be switched in and out of a game quickly. But their results are, to Freddy, well worth the effort. Imagine a game of Craps where you could never *crap out* for example! With a pair of *Tees* and a switching ability, the dream can be had!

Tops and Bottoms (or Tees) work on the principle that only three sides of a die can be seen at any one time. The gaffs here have numbers repeated on opposite sides. The opposite sides of one of these dice might be three-three, four-four and one-one for example. When these dice are rolled the mis-spotting goes unnoticed because no single player can be in a position to see duplicated numbers.

Amateurs rarely use Tees because of the need to switch them in and out of a game quickly. They can't be left lying around on a playing surface as all a player has to do is pick them up and give them a quick study to see that they are not straight.

The professional will carry several number combinations to allow him to manipulate as many situations as possible in a game.

The best way to detect these dice is, of course, to grab them and examine them. However, this could lead to quite a scuffle so it's better to be just a little more subtle. Look at the three faces that can see on each cube. If all of them are low numbers or, alter-

1-3-5 Tops in a mirror. See the duplicate faces?

nately, high numbers then it may be time to *casually* pick one up to, for example, wipe a bit of dirt from it. As you wipe the imaginary dirt free take a closer look.

Check *all* sides of the dice being played with. There is a kind of Tee known as a *percentage tee*. These have five normal sides with just one number repeated on the sixth side. Another type has one number repeated several times (such as a Tat die) and is known as a *misspot*.

JUICED DICE

Juiced dice can be thrown straight all night but, at a given moment, can act like a trained pair of seals for the cheat whenever he wants.

They are very slightly loaded with tin. The loading is so fine as to not discernibly affect the odds. But, if these dice are exposed to an electro magnetic field they will hop into place rather neatly. This would be a rather obvious little hop about if it were not covered in some way. Ever played Poker Dice, Crown and Anchor or Backgammon? In games like this the dice are shaken in a cup, the cup turned mouth down and then lifted away to reveal the dice.

If the *juice* (electric current) is activated while the dice are still covered then nobody can see them hop neatly into place. The current can then be turned off and the cup lifted. On the table are dice that can be examined quite thoroughly and yet still be controlled.

If you think that this kind of set up sounds a little nutty then chat with Freddy. He knows at least three bar owners that have a little juiced section built into their bars. These bar owners love to introduce newcomers to a little game of Poker Dice. Hey, it pays for their vacations each year!

Even transparent dice can be juiced up. In much the same way as a transparent die is loaded, the maker will drill the spots a little deeper. Some will be filled with paint, others with tiny tin slugs. The drilling will be much finer than that required for a load since only a tiny slug of tin is required.

If you are getting a little paranoid about your local game put a strong magnet into a cigarette packet. Put this packet down on the bar near the dice and see if they jump!

HEAVY LOADERS

A pair of dice so heavily loaded as to give the same number each time they were rolled would be pretty obvious. But they can be used in conjunction with a cup. The cheat switches in the heavy loaders and drops them into the cup. He shakes and turns the cup mouth down on the table. Lifting the cup he reveals the total. The heavy loaders are then swiftly switched out. Such dice are also called *first floppers*.

Always insist that dice are dropped from a cup to bounce freely on the table or bar top. This won't stop percentage dice working but will make any *juice* or *first flop* work easy to spot. By insisting on this type of throw you will also eliminate many of the sleight-of-hand cup moves we'll be discussing soon.

MATCHING DICE

You may think that you are safe because your dice game uses nice monogrammed cubes.

You aren't.

If the money is big enough the cheat will make exact duplicates of your dice, except that his will be gaffed. Professionals often carry the tools required for the job with them. They also carry a case containing hundreds of dice of all shapes and sizes.

Of course if you don't have any dice Freddy can willingly supply a pair. *"I think my kid left some from a game of Trivial Pursuit in the car a while back!"*

MUG WORK

There are other kinds of faked dice available than the ones mentioned here. You may see for sale in gambling magazines or at joke shops such natty sounding items as *trips* (certain edges have a tiny lip that is supposed to stop the die rolling onto certain sides, *caps* (which have some sides made of a *softer* material than others so that these sides will bounce less) or *burrs* and *saw tooths* (which have tiny nicks cut into the sides or rough edges left where the spots have been drilled thus favoring some sides over others).

You may also see substances called *honey* or *slick* in the same adverts. These are liquids which, when applied to a face of a die, will make it stickier, so more likely to land on, or slicker, so less likely to land on, that face.

Freddy regards these gaffs as for suckers only. The dubious advantage they offer is so minute as to be almost worthless. Any advantage, as Freddy has said, is worthwhile but with these puppies you could be a very old person before any significant swing of the odds started to show up. The only people who make real money from these toys are the people who sell them to you at highly inflated prices.

Another case of the amateur being cheated by the professionals.

Be warned though. Much like marked cards, gaffed dice are *much* more common in money games than you might imagine.

Controlled Rolls

AGOOD DICE MECHANIC IS WORTH HIS WEIGHT IN GOLD. NOT ONLY CAN HE SWITCH in faked dice but also, given a good playing surface, control the actions of a pair of completely straight dice. There are a group of cheats who have put in intense hours of practice to make the cubes behave pretty much as they wish.

But, and this is a pretty big but, they can only use these talents under certain conditions. The man who can bounce two dice off a backboard or wall and bring up two desired numbers when they stop rolling has not yet been born. However, in a bar game the dice are just as likely to be thrown onto a table or floor with no bounce off a backboard needed.

Under the looser conditions of a private game the cheat can appear to roll the dice in a random and uncontrolled manner and yet still control one or both of them by skill.

ROLLS

In order for a dice roll to be completely random the cubes must do two things simultaneously. Each die must spin with a lateral motion while at the same time also rolling over like a top. A standard die thrown from the hand will do this all by itself thus saving you a study of mechanical physics.

But, if a cheat can eliminate one or both of the turning actions he can *control the shot*. This, in fact, is precisely what he does.

The Slide

One of the most primitive, but nonetheless effective, of controlled rolls involves making sure that one of the dice does not roll or spin at all. The *slide* is used to control one of a pair of dice.

How to Cheat at Everything

The die to be controlled is gripped with the little finger. The required number is uppermost. The cheat shakes the second die in his hand letting it rattle and click against the gripped one. The noise is similar to that of two dice been shaken fairly.

When he throws the dice his hand slides along the table and releases the top die. The bottom die is also released but *flat* against the surface. The result? The controlled die slides along the table without turning. The free rolling die helps to conceal the fact that the other one doesn't roll. The cheat keeps the roll very short to help conceal the action. He will also, often, put a spin on the controlled die so that it whirls around as it goes across the table but *doesn't* tumble end over end.

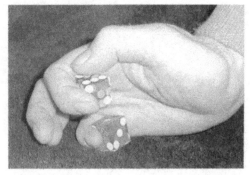

The Slide.

This may sound obvious but it's over in an instant and is very difficult to spot. The very worst that can happen to Freddy is that somebody will ask him to throw again.

Controlling one die may not sound like much to you but imagine a Backgammon game where you are allowed to throw the dice from your hand. You need a double four to win. The odds against this throw are, of course, thirty-five to one. If, on the other hand,

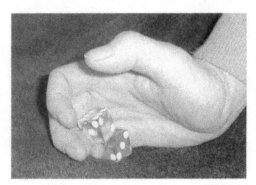

The Drop.

you can ensure one four, the odds drop dramatically down to just five to one. That's a pretty big advantage!

Note also that on a Backgammon board the rolls, because of the size of the board, are very short making this type of action very difficult to spot indeed.

The Drop

A variation on the *slide* is called the *drop*. Once again, a single die is controlled by allowing no rolling action. The die to be controlled is gripped in exactly the same manner as for a *slide* shot. Once again the hand is shaken with the loose die rattling against the gripped one.

But, instead of sliding his hand forwards, Freddy turns his hand palm down simultaneously dropping the dice down to the table surface. Timed just right, the loose, topmost, die hits the lower, controlled, die and traps it, just for an instant, against the tabletop. This momentary *trapping* action kills the motion of the lower die leaving the desired number upward. The top die falls away from the lower one and rolls freely to one side.

Once again the whole thing is over in an instant and is very hard to catch in action.

Pad or Blanket Roll.

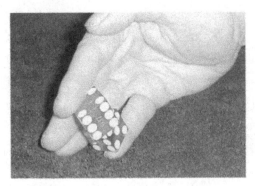

Pique or Whip Shot.

The Pad or Blanket Roll

This roll got its name because it really works best on a soft surface such as a blanket or thick tablecloth. It's popular with the tourist cheat who may start up a little game on the beach for fun. The surface of his beach towel is perfect for this little number.

Instead of eliminating the rolling action, this shot eliminates the spinning action of the dice. It's actually a percentage shot in that you can't guarantee which numbers will come up. You can however guarantee which numbers will *not* show up.

Freddy gets the dice into a *locked grip*. They are trapped in a box made by his thumb at the back, forefinger on top, little finger on the bottom and the second and third fingers curled around. They can rattle but they cannot turn. Freddy locks the dice into place so that the top and bottom numbers are the ones he doesn't want (this locks out four faces as the two face to face numbers will also be excluded). The numbers Freddy likes are round the sides of the dice.

He rattles the dice to simulate a fair shake then turns the back of his hand back up. As he does this he opens his fingers out straight allowing the dice to roll evenly out, like two little cartwheels, across the playing surface.

Since the numbers he doesn't want are, effectively, the axles of the rolling motion, they cannot come into play.

The Pique or Whip Shot

With this rather difficult piece of sleight-of-hand Freddy can throw both dice across the table and yet control *both* of them. To do this he eliminates the rolling action but keeps the spinning action.

Once again he gets the dice into the *locked grip* but this time the numbers he wants are on top of each die.

When he throws the dice he does so with a whip-like (hence the name) back and forward motion of his hand. Any snooker or pool player will tell you that this will put a lot of *side* or spin on the dice.

Like two little spinning tops they will hurtle down the table, turning round and round but *not* over and over. When they stop Freddy's numbers are on top. The dice spin so quickly that it's very difficult to tell that this is not a fair roll. Even if one of the two dice gets a little hop and loses its control the other will hold its number still giving Freddy a big advantage. In fact some

How to Cheat at Everything

cheats will only use the *whip* to control one of the two dice not only making it easier but also makes it much harder to spot.

ROLLS AND FAKES

The cheat using any form of percentage dice will also use, if he has the ability, a fake roll as well. With the sleight-of-hand and the gaff working together the *work* in the dice is much more likely to come up. A cheat learning fake rolls will often use this technique. If his work misses out he still has his percentage dice bringing in the money for him. Yet he still gets to practice the sleight-of-hand move *under fire.*

Freddy once joined a little game in a bar but before he could go to work he noticed that the game was already rigged. Two petty hustlers were using joke shop percentage dice to take the mug's money. By using controlled shots *against* the gaff Freddy taught them a lesson I suspect they will never forget. He cleaned them out leaving them thinking that the percentage dice had gone against the odds in an almost incalculable manner. The cheats had sadly invested all their money waiting for the percentages to grind in. They didn't!

Eliminating the controlled shots Freddy has told you about here is pretty easy.

Always play on a hard surface.

Insist that the dice have to bounce off a backboard or wall before coming to rest.

THE GOD SHOT

There is one controlled shot that can be used against a backboard or wall. It is, I guess, the exception that proves the above rule! Fortunately for you, the *Greek* or *God Shot* requires a practice regime that makes a *whip* shot look like child's play. You are most unlikely to come up against a man who can do it with any degree of regularity.

Even Freddy can only hit it eight out of ten times and he's been playing with the shot on and off for over fifteen years.

The throw, difficult as it is, only controls one of the dice. The master cheat considers this enough of an advantage to be worth the time spent learning the shot. If he can hit it consistently he can play just about anywhere and take money.

The dice are picked up as if for a controlled *slide* shot. The lower die has the number to be controlled uppermost. The dice are thrown so that the lower die will hit *exactly* where the backboard or wall meets the playing surface.

The upper die, in a manner similar to a *drop* shot, hits the top of the lower die and traps it momentarily on three sides; the playing surface below, the backboard or wall at the back and the upper die in top.

This kills the motion of the lower die. The upper die rolls off, randomly, helping to conceal the lack of motion of the lower one.

There are men around who can handle this move but unless you play in really *big* money games you are unlikely to run up against one.

It is interesting that casinos take this kind of shot so seriously that a great many Craps tables now have a trip wire and insist that the dice must tumble across it as well. "*Now that would be a shot,*" says Freddy, "*the trip wire would be a bitch to beat.*"

In private games a *Greek shot* can be eliminated by insisting that the dice hit the backboard or wall half way up.

A cheat in loose company may try the *poor man's Greek*. He will throw the dice with a long *slide* shot. He times the shot so that the uncontrolled die bounces off the backboard or wall but the controlled one stops just short of it.

Insist that both dice *always* hit the backboard or wall.

If you follow all the rules you've read about in this chapter you'll go a long way toward stopping the cheat using his fake rolls.

But don't get complacent. It'll only take one momentary lapse of attention from you and he'll get a pair of percentage dice into play.

Controlled Rolls From The Cup

I N *Backgammon For Blood* BY BRUCE BEEKER THE FOLLOWING SENTENCE APPEARS, *"The advantage of using a cup is that, when dice are shaken and thrown from a cup, there can be little if any question about the legitimacy of the roll."*

Freddy, after reading this quote, said that it could make the basis of a great comedy script for a gamblers only sitcom.

You'll understand why when you realize just how many ways there are to control dice thrown from a cup.

DUMPING

The theory behind the *dump* shot, of which there are several types, is that one die is stopped from being shaken in the cup. When the dice are poured from the cup the controlled die does not turn over and so reveals a desired number.

If you are playing Poker Dice with Freddy (a game using *five* dice) this may not seem like much of an advantage. But, when playing Poker Dice, the player has three goes to make his hand. If Freddy pulls a pair on his first shot he can use the *dump* to guarantee three of a kind after the second shot and, if he needs to, four of a kind after the third shot!

We've already seen how controlling just one die in a Backgammon game can twist the odds remarkably in Freddy's favor.

Clearly the *dump* is a powerful weapon.

Dumping From Inside the Cup

Let's assume that Freddy is playing Poker Dice and wishes to control an ace (remember Poker Dice have cards, not numbers, on their faces) on the first roll.

He picks up the five dice and tosses them into the cup held in his other hand. As he does this he secretly grips one of the dice between his forefinger and third finger. This die is held, if you like, in a kind of *flat palm*. The face he desires is the one facing out from his hand.

He covers the mouth of the cup with this hand. The palmed die goes inside the cup but is still gripped between the fingers. The other dice are rattled about but the palmed die is held firm.

Freddy, after the shake, releases the palmed die so that it slides *without turning* into the cup.

Transferring a die.

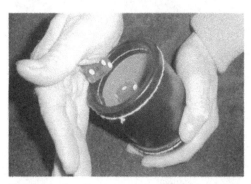

Holding back a die.

About to add a palmed die.

He then quickly turns the cup over and, rather like a *drop* shot from the hand, the other dice will fall on top of the controlled one to prevent it from turning.

If Freddy starts with the face to be controlled pointing towards his forefinger while palmed he can use an alternative *dump* technique. Here, after the release, the cup will be held parallel to the playing surface. With a quick back and forth motion the dice are slid out. Once again the controlled die doesn't turn.

Dumping From Outside the Cup

Many dice cups have a lip running just inside the rim. This is not an artistic design to make them look pretty. In fact it is to eliminate *dump* shots from inside the cup. Dice cannot be thrown from the cup without turning over so any internal control is destroyed. This addition is called a *Trip Rim*.

Freddy overcomes this problem by not bothering to put the die to be controlled in the cup at all!

He can do this in a number of ways. A simple technique involves pretending to throw the five Poker Dice into the cup but holding one back in the crotch of his thumb. The cup is picked up with the same hand and shaken. The palmed die is concealed by the thumb and the cup.

His empty hand now takes the cup to roll out the dice. As he does this, the palmed die is also taken in the following manner. His empty hand takes the cup by the base so that the base of the cup is in his palm and the fingers extend along the sides. This is a very common way to take a cup and arouses no suspicion. However, the extended forefinger and second finger can clip that palmed die between them

How to Cheat at Everything

and keep it hidden under the cup.

When the dice in the cup are rolled out the hidden die is dropped from between the fingers to join them. Performed by an expert like Freddy it is impossible to tell that the dice were not rolled fairly.

The cheat can even simply palm one die in his hand as he drops the others into the cup. This can be dropped behind the cup as the others are tipped out after the shake!

Obviously the controlled die was palmed so that a desired face would show after the roll.

Actually Freddy may not put the die to be controlled anywhere near the cup at all! As he throws the five Poker Dice into the cup he palms one away by hooking his little finger around it. The hand, hiding the stolen die (with a desired face upward), rests on the table near to where the roll will be made.

Freddy shakes the cup and rolls out the dice in the direction of his resting hand. At the last second the resting hand moves away *leaving* the controlled die behind.

This would seem to be an outrageous bluff but, timed immaculately, the illusion is perfect.

Freddy can also use this *hold out* technique in a different manner. It is common in bar games of Poker Dice for the cup to be shaken and inverted onto the playing surface. The players other hand then curls around the base of the cup. The cup is lifted away but the dice remain hidden behind the curled hand. This is the time for any bluff side bets to be offered. The player may offer, "*Even money I haven't got an ace,*" or some other nutty little fun betcha. Finally the curled hand is lifted away to reveal the dice.

Some players love the side bets. Others think it adds a little extra tension and excitement to the roll. Some even think it's lucky!

Freddy loves these players.

He will palm out a die and shake the other four fairly. He then turns the cup face down onto the table and curls the hand palming the die around the base of the cup. Slowly his other hand lifts the cup. When the curled hand moves away it is impossible to tell that the palmed die was not in the cup.

Never allow this action, however much fun it may seem to be.

During a game of Backgammon Freddy can use a *dump* very easily to control one die. He puts one die into the cup fairly. The second appears to go in but is gripped at the base of the fingers. The hand, complete with palmed die covers the mouth of the cup. The cup is shaken well. Because the loose die repeatedly hits against the palmed one the sound is a fair one. The shake also looks fair because all the other player can see is the back of Freddy's hand.

Freddy then turns the cup mouth down onto the board releasing the palmed die as he does so. The controlled die rests *between* his hand and the cup. The back of his hand still stops the other player from seeing a thing. He lifts away the cup to reveal the dice. "*Nice,*" says Freddy.

THE THUMB

Using the curled hand ploy an amateur cheat can use a very crude control known as *the thumb*.

It is especially common in Liar's Poker where, using Poker Dice, the five dice are concealed behind a hand as part of the game. The five dice are shaken fairly from the cup. The five dice remain unseen by the other players because of the players curled hand around them.

The petty thief can easily adjust one or more of the dice by turning them with his thumb.

Don't think that a friend won't do this to you. They may do it just for fun, to get an edge, or because they are an amateur cheat. Don't forget that games like Liar's Poker, played either with dice or with dollar bills, are often played for considerable sums of money.

How much money?

In his wonderful book *Liar's Poker*, regarding Wall Street traders, Michael Lewis describes a moment where John Gutfreund (then chairman of Salomon Brothers) offered a game of Liar's Poker to John Merriwether (a member of the board). His single line offer has become a Wall Street legend.

"One hand, one million dollars, no tears."

THE BACKGAMMON CUP

Traveling Backgammon sets contain all the required equipment within a folding board. Because the boards fold to a narrow case the dice cups must, by design, be a flat oval rather than circular shape. Often they are only just as wide as the dice that go in them.

If the dice supplied with the set are very small, Freddy will often replace them with larger ones.

Freddy drops the dice into the cup with the desired numbers pointing downwards. He will then shake the cup with a side-to-side motion. Because the dice are large in relation to the cup they will rattle but not turn. Then he swiftly turns the cup face down allowing the dice to drop down with his numbers up.

If the cup doesn't have a *trip rim* inside he can set the dice with required numbers on one side. After the shake he turns the cup parallel to the board (making sure his desired numbers are pointing up) and, with a quick backward pull, leave the dice on the board with his number up. *"Inertia is a beautiful thing,"* comments Freddy.

Using this shot Freddy may even let the dice hit the side of the board. This puts a slight spin into them helping the effect. The spin, however, isn't enough to cause them to roll.

THE WHIP CUP

The *whip* or *slick* cup is a dice cup, which although looking quite normal, has two differences between it and normal cups. First it has no inside lip or *trip*. Second the inside is highly polished and slippery.

Amateur cheats often use this cup in combination with heavily loaded dice (first floppers).

Shaken up and tossed the dice will tend to act normally because the toss is short and the loads, heavy as they are, don't get enough time to come into play.

When the cheat shakes the cup he does so with a very different action. He shakes the cup with a rotating action with some up and down *snaps* of his wrist. These actions cause the heavily loaded dice to line up in the cup with their loads downward. Of course, and more importantly for the cheat, they line up with the desired numbers upward.

The dice are then shot from the cup with a sharp backward pull. They slide onto the table without rolling.

The cheat will play fairly until a big money bet goes down and then he will, quite literally, *whip* that money away.

If you suspect the use of such a cup then suggest the use of a lipped cup and follow Freddy's rules for a fair throw which you'll find at the end of this chapter. If a lipped cup is not available, or your opponent seems reticent, make your excuses and leave the game.

THE BUTTERFLY CUP

This charming little number is a cup designed for the cheat with little or no sleight-of-hand ability. The *Butterfly Cup* will switch dice for the cheat!

The cup has two compartments in its base. By turning the base of the cup either compartment can be open or shut. The cheat has his gaffed dice in the closed compartment. When he needs them, he drops the straight dice into the cup and, as he goes into the shake, twists the base of the cup. The compartment holding the gaffs opens while simultaneously closing over the straight dice (see photograph).

Details of a Butterfly Cup.

The gaffed dice are then thrown from the cup.

The inside of the cup will be colored matt black to help conceal the work inside.

The professional cheat would prefer not to use a fake cup. It is *drop dead* evidence of cheating.

The petty cheat, however, *will* use it.

STOPPING CONTROLLED ROLLS

Freddy is confident in his ability to fake a roll without you spotting a thing. But by following his tips you might stand a chance of stopping him thinking about attempting one.

Although it won't stop all controlled shots use of a lipped or *trip* cup will eliminate internal *dump* shots.

Insist that the dice are dropped *openly* into the cup and that the player shows an empty hand afterwards.

Insist that the player shake the cup with one hand.

Insist that the shake is good and hard so that the dice turn and not just rattle around.

Insist that the dice are poured from the cup from at least six inches above the playing surface.

Freddy says that there isn't a *mechanic* alive who can control straight dice thrown from a cup in this manner.

Freddy Puts It All Together

I ASKED FREDDY TO TIE UP SOME OF THIS DICE STUFF INTO A WHOLE. WHERE FOR example did he hide his gaffed dice? How could their use make a big score quickly?

He lighted one of his cigars and, while relating a tale of a game of Backgammon, answered those questions and more.

First he told me a couple of tricks that hadn't been mentioned. First he spoke about how *juiced* work can come into play in a traveling game. Here the required magnetic field is not electrically controlled but comes from a small rare earth magnet strapped to the cheat's knee. The dice, for a game of Backgammon, may be loaded up to give six-six, a roll considered by most to be the best opener.

On his opening roll the cheat raises his knee up under the table by crossing his legs. This presses the magnet up underneath the board on the table. Rolling his dice gives him an ideal opening throw. By lowering his knee the dice will then behave quite normally until the magnetic knee is raised again. The cheat can literally roll double sixes to order!

Freddy also mentioned a rather odd form of impromptu *juice* work. It is arranged by getting a little puddle of spilt beer or soda near the board. In a bar situation it would often be rather hard to position a board without one already being in place! At some point the cheat can get some beer or soda onto his fingers and wet the surface of the dice on select sides. These wet sides, being a little stickier than the others, will tend to land down more often. The cheat obviously wets the sides opposite to the numbers he wants.

On a hard surface this advantage would be negligible at best. On the soft, felt-like surface of a Backgammon board it can offer a distinct advantage.

Before Freddy discussed a game plan he also decided to stress the importance of the *Doubling Cube* in Backgammon. This is a die featuring the numbers 2, 4, 8, 16, 32 and 64 on its six sides.

The two players each roll a single die at the start of the game. The highest number not only gets first go but also controls the Doubling Cube. At any point in the game the player who owns the cube can offer to double up the stakes. The Doubling Cube, if the bet is accepted, is turned to show 2 and placed on the center bar of the board. The control of the cube at this point passes to the other player. If the bet is not accepted the player has lost the game and pays the full original stake to the other. Its use is considered to be paramount among Backgammon players.

The Doubling Cube is an open invitation to the cheat to ease up the stakes.

If both players roll the same number at the start of the game the stakes, in many games, are automatically doubled. This continues until one player rolls a higher number than the other.

If Freddy can roll after you and duplicate your throw Freddy can double the stakes *before* the game begins! Then Freddy, using another controlled shot, can get first go and all-important control of the Doubling Cube. Often these opening rolls are done from the player's hands making his job even easier.

During the game Freddy, knowing he will win, will raise the stakes even more. He will allow you to get into what seems to be a winning position. He then offers a double. Thinking that you are ahead of the game you accept his offer!

Even more deviously Freddy may allow you to get control of the Doubling Cube right from the start. He will, once more, allow you to get into a strong position. So strong in fact that you offer to double him. He accepts and takes control of the cube. One or two moves later, with you still looking good, he will offer a redouble. You'll be happy to accept it. Well, happy until the end of the game that is!

Freddy also mentions that there are two ways to bet on a Backgammon game. The first is an agreed bet of, say, five dollars for the game. The second, and far more interesting for Freddy, is to play for so much a point. Each of the fifteen men on a board start out at one point so if you have ten men left at the end of the game and are playing for ten cents a man you've just lost a dollar.

Let's join Freddy now as he takes his seat opposite Albert Fisher at the start of a train journey. After a while Freddy offers to play him a little Backgammon to pass the time. He's even got a traveling board with him in case he could find anybody who liked the game.

Tragically Albert is a keen player and agrees.

To add a fun edge to the game Freddy suggests a small stake of ten cents a point. Even all fifteen men left only adds up to a dollar fifty. A freak *Backgammon* (all fifteen of Freddy's men gone with some of Albert's men in Freddy's home table), which triples the stakes, can only add up to four dollars and fifty cents so it's hardly a lethal bet.

Albert hasn't thought much about the Doubling Cube. If a game looks bad enough for a loss by a *Backgammon* he's unlikely to accept a double!

Towards the end of the journey a rather freak start to a game has them both throwing the same number three times in a row. The cube is turned to eight. Albert ends up with control of the Doubling Cube.

This early double up worries Albert a little but he calms down as the dice seem to turn against Freddy with a vengeance. Albert has lost money over the journey (remember the Monte and Razzle teams!) and sees a chance to recoup his losses. He calculates that he's ahead by more than enough to offer a double and win the game when Freddy refuses it. Much to Albert's surprise, and, to be honest, delight, Freddy accepts the cube which now stands at sixteen.

Two throws later Freddy gets a double four. It helps him but not by much. *"My luck is changing,"* he announces. *"I'm doubling you back!"* Albert thinks Freddy may have had a sip of scotch too many. He's so far ahead in the game that it would be idiotic to refuse. The cube stands at thirty-two.

The game gets closer but Albert is still ahead. He considers turning the cube again but thinks that Freddy may accept it. The game is getting just a little too close to risk it.

Suddenly Freddy hits a run of luck the like of which Albert has never witnessed before. He is throwing everything he needs. Freddy's men are scooting around the board while his are getting bogged down and unable to move. His men are being hit and sent onto the bar. It rapidly turns into a game from hell for Albert.

The incredible happens. Freddy *Backgammons* Albert!

This triples the stake and so, starting off at ten cents a man, Albert ended up playing for nine dollars and sixty cents a man! With all fifteen men on the board that's a whopping one hundred and forty-four dollars!

Freddy, embarrassed about such a large and lucky victory, will tear up Albert's check. He'll refuse to let a friendly game end in such a way. Albert's check will, of course, be cashed the next day. Freddy performed the *Tear Up*.

"Hey, it could have been worse for him," notes Freddy. *"He could have doubled it up to sixty-four!"*

If you think the above example sounds like fantasy then think again. It wasn't Albert Fisher in the game that I watched but the rest of the tale is true.

Freddy used a combination of controlled shots and gaffed dice to win the game. A magnificent double six finish was achieved with his little magnetic knee. Instead of the two dice that Freddy appeared to be using he actually used eight in various combinations. Of course, Albert only ever saw two.

During this game Freddy used *Thumb Switches* performing the move as the dice were dropped into the cup. The cup provided extra cover for the move.

SO WHERE DOES FREDDY HIDE THE DICE?

Freddy has a number of options in a dice game of where to conceal the gaffed dice.

He can use a dice *hold out*. This is a small box concealed under the edge of his jacket which neatly holds two dice in place. They are easily obtained by the fingers of one hand resting under the edge of the jacket for just a fraction of a second.

There are also dice *hold outs* that, like a card *hold out*, will deliver the dice right into his hand.

At Backgammon Freddy can have a small slot like pocket built into his side of the board. The fakes are stored there but are easily accessible.

For traveling games Freddy just likes to have the *gaffs* stashed in his pockets. By reaching for a piece of gum or a pencil they are easily obtained. In a one-on-one situation across a table (as during this train game) the dice can be temporarily stored on his lap.

Freddy does have a very safe place for the fakes should he think he'll be accused of cheating. You can search him but you are most unlikely to find anything.

He has a *sneak pocket*.

A *sneak pocket* is made by cutting the top of the narrow strip of lining which lies around the zipper of a pair of trousers. The inside top of his side pocket is also cut and connected on. This creates an extra tube like pocket that can be accessed from the side pocket.

If trouble seems to be brewing, or if Freddy has finished with the dice, he will palm them into his side pocket. Then he will pop them into the *sneak pocket.*

He can pull out his pockets to show them empty but the dice stay hidden in the tubular *sneak pocket*. And it's pretty rare, even during a body search, to grope somebody right in the crotch area.

Freddy says, *"I'll always hide them where nobody is going to want to look!"*

Crown and Anchor

CROWN AND ANCHOR IS A POPULAR DICE GAME PLAYED THROUGHOUT THE world. The fact that it is an illegal game in casinos and most fairgrounds in many countries does not seem to have stemmed its popularity in private games.

Go to somewhere like the Channel Islands for your vacation and, on festival or race days, you'll be able to see the game worked publicly. The speed of the money changing hands will take your breath away.

Freddy adores the game of Crown and Anchor because, although he may cheat at it, he doesn't need to do anything to get the money. The game itself is as close to a magic money printer as you are ever likely to run into.

At a friend's stag party a few years ago I set up a little game of Crown and Anchor in the party gambling section. My tiny little table made more money than the rest of the games (two Blackjack tables and a Wheel of Fortune) put together. The groom was a very happy camper when I handed the evening's profit to him.

It'll take you about four seconds to learn how to play the game and not much longer to lose everything you have in your wallet if you choose to play.

THE GAME

Freddy suggests a little dice game at his local bar. To pass the time some of the drinkers, gleefully unaware of his chosen profession, agree to take a look.

Freddy lays out a cardboard rectangle. It is divided into six sections and in each section is a different shape. The various shapes are the four suits of a pack of playing cards (a club, a heart, a spade and a diamond) along with two others (a picture of a crown and a picture of an anchor).

Freddy also has three dice. Instead of numbers the six faces of each die will correspond to the pictures on his cardboard rectangle.

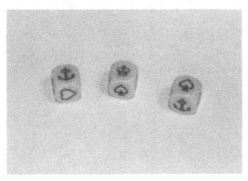

Crown and Anchor Dice.

Finally Freddy has a dice cup to *eliminate any cheating.*

Freddy says that he'll take on the job of banker and proceeds to explain the childishly simple rules. Players can bet on any shape by putting their money down on the corresponding space in the rectangle. As many players as they like can lay bets. More than one bet per space can be placed.

When all bets are down the three dice are shaken in the cup and the cup turned mouth down, The cup will then be lifted to expose the dice.

Freddy will pay even money if one of the dice shows a betted symbol. He will pay out two to one if a pair of dice show a betted symbol. Finally he'll pay three to one if all three dice show the betted symbol. So a showing of a crown, an anchor and a spade will pay even money to any bets on those three symbols. Three hearts will pay three to one to the bets on the heart shape.

Easy rules. Easy money.

Well, easy money for Freddy anyway.

THE TRUE ODDS

Crown and Anchor seems to be a game that's fair and above board. A harmless piece of fun to pass away the time. It's harmless enough *until* you analyze the true odds. To test the game out for this chapter I played it by myself for five minutes betting in one dollar units. At the end of the five minutes, if I had been betting in a real game, I would have been sixty-five dollars down.

The odds, even with multiple bets, are staggeringly against the player.

Freddy pays even money on one die showing your chosen symbol. The true odds are a shade under two to one against you.

Freddy pays two to one on a pair matching your chosen symbol. The true odds are just under thirteen to one against you.

Finally, astonishingly, Freddy pays three to one on all three dice turning up to match your chosen symbol. The true odds against this are two hundred and fifteen to one against!

Little wonder that Freddy cleans up very quickly indeed.

THE COVER

With a number of players it is likely that, between them, all the symbols will be covered. In this case there will always be money going out as well as money coming in. Of course there will be a lot more coming in than there is going out.

Watch the game at a Fairground and you'll see it with five or six layouts being played simultaneously by three or four operators. The big commercial units often increase the payouts to lure the money in. Even paying out a hundred to one on three of a kind would hardly be generous. The commercial operators don't even go that far. The biggest payout I've seen offered is thirty-five to one.

The commercial units will play all day and there is unlikely to be a betting limit.

"Almost as profitable as owning your own mint to print money," says Freddy.

CHEATING AT CROWN AND ANCHOR

It should really be redundant to cheat at this game but a really unscrupulous operator will use dump shots and the *thumb* to stop certain heavily bet combinations from coming in.

If he does this the odds against you rise from the unbelievable to absolutely ridiculous.

Freddy says that he has only one piece of advice to anybody who feels tempted to play a few goes at the Crown and Anchor game.

The advice can be encapsulated in a single word.

Don't.

A VARIATION IN BUENOS AIRES

It was a long flight to Buenos Aires to do a magic show but it was all made very worthwhile when I witnessed the following little game being played in a hotel bar.

A friendly game of cards was in play with low stakes. It seemed like everybody was having quite a bit of fun.

As the evening wore on odd little variations of games were suggested and played to much amusement. Then one of the chaps, an older follow, suggested a new little game. He sorted out six cards and laid them face up on the table. They were, in order, the ace, two, three, four, five and six of spades. He then took three dice from a Backgammon set in the bar and explained the rules.

Six people at a time could bet so there will be, he explained, three winning bets and three losing bets. The game, he continued, was a fifty-fifty piece of fun. He didn't need any money as a fee for running it. It was all just a piece of fun.

So each of the six players bet on a number each. All bets were to be equal amounts of money. The numbers that come up are paid out. The numbers that don't appear are losing ones. If two of a number come up then the player on that number gets two to one. If three of a kind come up then that lucky player gets three to one. All payouts come from the losing bets. There are always three winning pay out bets to six bets in total. It *must* be a fifty-fifty chance, right?

Wrong.

This game would appear to be a great grandfather of Crown and Anchor and, just like its frisky young relative, takes money for the operator rather nicely.

There are three options that can happen.

First the dice can roll three separate numbers (such as 1, 2 and 5 for example). The three losing bets (3, 4 and 6) are placed onto the three winning bets for the payout. This option actually is a true fifty-fifty bet for the players.

Option number two is that a pair of dice show the same number (1, 1 and 5 for example). The bettor on number one gets two to one (paid from numbers two and three) and the bettor on number four gets paid at evens (from number five) leaving number six as profit for the operator.

The final option is that all three dice show the same number (1, 1 and 1 for example). The bettor on number one gets paid at three to one (from numbers two, three and four) leaving a nice operator profit of two bets (from five and six).

Try getting three dice (raid some of your kid's games), some cards and some bits of paper to represent money. Now play the game with six imaginary players and see how long it takes you to win all the bits of paper. Then imagine if those bits of paper were twenty dollar bills. Almost tempting isn't it?

The nice man in Argentina left with quite a sum of money after the game.

"But wait," you cry, *"didn't he tell them he couldn't make a profit and yet obviously did?"* You know, the people playing the game couldn't care less. The action began fast and got more and more frenetic as the game went on. Payouts were happening fast and the money ran faster. Everybody was carried away on a roll and there was even a small group of people waiting to join the game when a player dropped out.

Just because a hustler tells you he can't make money when you are betting won't necessarily stop you doing so when he obviously does make money!

"A beautiful thing to be admired," says Freddy, *"from a very safe distance."*

More Unfair Odds

CROWN AND ANCHOR CAN BE DESCRIBED AS THE KING OF THE UNFAIR ODDS games. But it also has plenty of underlings and friends where the odds are heavily stacked against the player.

Should the mugs ever get tired of Crown and Anchor then Freddy has a few more games to suggest. In fact you've already seen one of them, *Under and Over Seven*.

Here's a few more.

HIGH DICE

In this game, also known as *Beat the Dealer*, Freddy lays out a cloth upon which is printed *Beat the Dealer*. Below this are printed several boxes containing the numbers 2, 3, 4, 5, 6, 7, 8, 9, 10, 11 and 12. Underneath the boxes is another legend, *Banker Takes All Ties*. Finally, right at the bottom, there are eight or nine empty boxes.

Freddy also uses a poker chip, a pair of dice and a cup.

The rules are, if anything, easier than Crown and Anchor.

The players each place their bets into one of the empty boxes.

Freddy rolls the dice and puts the poker chip onto the equivalent numbered box. This serves as a reminder of his score. Each player, in turn, then rolls the two dice. Those who score higher than Freddy are paid off at evens. Those who tie, or score lower, lose their bet.

The game would be even *except* for the ties. By taking those Freddy is giving himself an advantage adding up to a shade over eleven percent (11.3%).

Played with one die (and boxes numbered one to six) Freddy's advantage rises to just under seventeen percent. Freddy often draws out an impromptu layout on a cocktail napkin while 'inventing' this little game 'on the spur of the moment'.

Even an incredibly lucky run for you will be eaten away by odds like that. Perhaps this game should be renamed *Just Give the Dealer Your Money*!

KLONDIKE

A nifty little variation on *High Dice* this game is played with five Poker Dice.

In the game the dealer will throw the five dice. He explains that the other players have to roll and beat him to win. He explains that winning rolls get paid off at even money and, of course, losing rolls don't!

The kill for you is that he, once more, takes those all important ties.

If the hustler really wants your money quickly he will exclude Straights (runs) from counting as a hand. The odds against you rise so dramatically that it is little wonder that, played this way, the game is often called *Killer Klondike*.

Freddy's advice if you see such a game being played is simple, *"Don't walk away. Run away!"*

HAZARD

If you get caught up in this game it will certainly be hazardous for you. At first glance it is a little like Crown and Anchor but there are more betting possibilities. Here, you can bet on a number of combinations being thrown with three dice. For a little more to add to your hustling education here's what Freddy offers you on the bets along with the all important correct odds. These figures have been taken from an actual Hazard game I was witness to.

The Raffle—A player bets that any *specific* three of a kind (such as three fours) will be rolled. Freddy will offer one hundred to one on this bet. He can afford to; the true odds are two hundred and fifteen to one against. Freddy has a nice safe advantage of over *fifty three* percent on this bet. Even a Nevada layout, which offers 180 for 1 on this bet, has a 16.7% advantage!

Any Raffle—The player bets that any three of a kind will be thrown. Freddy pays this bet off at twenty-five to one. Unfortunately for the player the true odds are thirty-five to one with Freddy's ever present advantage running at around twenty-six percent.

Lows—The player bets that all three dice will total less than ten. The true odds here, with a stipulation that any three of a kind loses, are 111-105 so, by offering even money, Freddy gains a two point eight advantage. By insisting that all three dice show *different* numbers the advantage rises considerably.

Highs—The player bets that the total of the three dice will be eleven or more. See *Lows* for the odds and payouts.

Odds and Evens—The player bets on a total being either odd or even in total. See *Lows* for the odds and payouts.

Numbers—Here the player bets on a specific total turning up. Freddy's payouts along with the correct odds are as follows:

4 or 17—Freddy's payout is 59-1. True odds are 71-1 giving Freddy a 16.7% advantage.

5 or 16—Freddy's payout is 29-1. True odds are 35-1 giving Freddy a 16.7% advantage.

6 or 15—Freddy's payout is 17-1. True odds are 20.6-1 giving Freddy a 16.7% advantage.

7 or 14—Freddy's payout is 11-1. True odds are 13.4-1 giving Freddy another 16.7% advantage.

8 or 13—Freddy's payout is 7-1. True odds are 9.3-1 giving Freddy a 22.2% advantage.

9 or 12—Freddy's payout is 5-1. True odds are 7.6-1 giving Freddy a 30.6% advantage.

10 or 11—Freddy's payout is 5-1. True odds are 7-1 giving Freddy a 25% advantage.

Combines—Here the player bets as if the game were Crown and Anchor. He bets on any number from one to six. If one of his number turns up he is paid at evens, if two turn up he is paid at two to one and for the big three turning up he gets a paltry three to one. You've already seen how expensive this can get!

Remember when I warned you right at the start about knowing odds? Now, I hope, you can see why.

Hazard comes in many forms and is known by a few different names like *Hazard, Grand Hazard, Chuck-a-luck, Chuckluck,* and *Birdcage* amongst others. The dice are usually spun around in a wire hourglass shaped device called a *Chuck Cage.*

Hazard is a game for idiots. Don't waste either your time or your money trying to beat it. In Mitchell Beazley's wonderful little publication *The Gambler's Pocket Book* he writes of this genre of game that it will "*offer a variety of bets nearly all of which are heavily, some scandalously, in favor of the operator.*"

Freddy thinks that's a rather delightful understatement.

THIRTY-ONE WITH A DIE

Early on in your tour through Freddy's world you saw the game of *Thirty-*

One and learned how swiftly it can take your money. I mentioned that it could also be played with a die.

Here's how.

The game involves rolling the die to determine a start number. Whatever number turns up is the first count. Each player then takes turns to give the die a quarter turn in any direction bringing up a new number to add on each time. A running total is kept and the first player to reach thirty-one is the winner. If a player is forced to go over thirty-one he loses.

The game seems to defy a system and yet, although Freddy can't *absolutely* guarantee a win, he can do so over ninety percent of the time. He uses two basic principles to do this,

He tries to hit key numbers of 4, 13 and 22.

He stops the opponent from hitting key numbers. He does this by subtracting the running total from the next key number and turning the die to prevent the opponent from hitting it. Remember the numbers at the top and bottom of the die are out of play for each turn. By *having* to give the die a quarter turn the player loses the top number and cannot bring the bottom number to the top.

If Freddy can hit four on the first turn he will *always* win the game.

In most cases Freddy can turn a three or four to prevent the opponent hitting a key number on the next play. There are only two situations in which he can't do this.

If Freddy is seven away from a key number and can't play a three or four then he will play a two. An example would be if the die was rolled at the start to show a two and the opponent turned the die to bring four up (giving a running total of six). Freddy can't play a three or four as both are out of play. He turns up a two, which puts five at the bottom. This prevents the opponent from turning a five up to make the key number of thirteen. If this sounds a little complicated try it with a die in front of you to follow it along.

If Freddy is one away from a key number but can't turn a one he will, instead, turn a five. An example would be if the die was rolled at the start to show a two and the opponent turned it to show one (giving a running total of three). Freddy has to turn the die so his opponent cannot hit his key of four. Instead he turns up a five making a total of eight. The opponent can't use the five to make the next key number of thirteen as the five is effectively out of play for him on that turn.

There are a couple of slightly tricky situations for Freddy. If he is two away from a key number and cannot play a two he will, instead, play a three. This gives the opponent more chance to make a mistake. If the opponent hits the key number of four on the first roll Freddy will play low numbers such as one or two to, once more, give the opponent plenty of space to make a mistake.

Trying this out with a die will show you that the game is much easier to master than you may imagine. If you don't master it and decide to take on

Freddy he will wipe you dry in a very short time indeed. Your only chance of winning is to accidentally hit the key numbers without giving Freddy a chance to hit them. Pretty long odds my friend!

If Freddy plays for fun he may let you win a few games until the money goes down on the table. Fall for his honey-baited trap and it will snap shut around your wallet.

CRAPS

Forget the plush casino game you've seen. It's time to introduce you to Freddy's private game. With just a pair of dice he'll introduce you to one of America's most popular gambling pastimes, the game of *Craps*.

Actually Craps goes back to an old English version of Hazard that used two dice. During this game a total of two or three was referred to as *crabs* and was a losing throw. When the game moved to New Orleans, the center of American gambling in the early 1800s, it became known, with a minor name change, as Craps. It became a popular casino game over a century later when a New York banker invented Bank Craps which charged the players 5% of their wagers.

The rules are fairly simple.

Two dice are rolled and their faces added together to get a total. The first roll and also each roll that happens after a result has been effected is called the *come out*. If the *shooter* (the player throwing the dice) throws a *natural* (a total of seven or eleven) this is a winning throw known as a *pass*. A total of two, three or twelve is a losing throw known as a *miss out* or *crapping out*.

Any other total becomes the shooter's *point* and he continues to roll the dice until he either throws his point again (which is a winning *pass*) or he throws seven (which is a losing *miss out*). When the shooter misses his point by *crapping out* the dice pass to the next player.

Players worldwide love the game for a number of reasons. First they adore the 'gangster' like language of the game, "*Geez, Mikey, ya blew me four big ones on that snake eyes crap out!*" It makes them feel like real gamblers. Second the game is popular because players get to bet not just on their own throws but also on the outcome of other player's throws. Side bets between players make up a considerable amount of a Craps hustler's income.

Craps has been called the world's fastest gambling game.

Okay, now you know the basics let's join a little private Craps game being run by a fellow called Freddy the Fox.

On each *come out* throw the shooter places the amount he wishes to bet down in front of himself and calls that amount out. If he is betting a hundred dollars he'll call, "*I'll shoot a hundred.*"

The other bettors can then accept all or part of that bet. By covering the bet in whole or in part they are said to be *fading* the shooter.

If the shooter passes (wins) then he picks up his bet plus the faded money. If he craps out the faders get back their money plus an equal amount. In other words they are paid off at even money.

Once the shooter has been totally faded (covered) the other players cannot add to the pile unless, of course, the shooter adds more money. But they can make quite a number of side bets between themselves.

A *Right Bet* is one that says that the shooter will make his point before crapping out. A *Wrong Bet* is one that says that the shooter will crap out before making the point.

A *Come Bet* is one that says that the shooter will pass (win) treating the next roll of the dice as if it were his first. For example if a player has a point of four. He accepts a come bet on his next roll and throws seven. He craps out but *wins* the come bet because the seven counts as a *natural*. If he rolls a two, three or twelve the come bet is lost but he carries on rolling for his point of four. If he throws any other number then that number becomes an additional point to his four as regards the come bet. With the faders he is betting on a point of four. With the come bettor he is gambling on this new point. If he throws his four point the come bet can be carried on to his next roll. Read the above again. It's really quite easy to understand!

A *Don't Come* bet is similar but bets against the shooter passing on the next roll.

Hard way Bets are gambles that the player will roll a particular number the *hard* way. The hard way is to roll an even number with a double (two-two, three-three and four-four for totals of four, six and eight for example). The right bettor loses if seven is thrown or the number is thrown any other way (one-three making up four for example).

There are other bets on a casino Craps table but Freddy feels that the above are more than enough to give most players a good taste of the game. In fact, just by understanding the bets, you are ahead of most of the amateur mugs who play the game.

But Freddy's big advantage over the average player is that he knows the correct odds on each and every shot. The new player having fun will not know, and be unlikely to be able to calculate, the correct payout odds on the bets. They will simply take Freddy's offered bets.

Once a game is going the action is fast and furious with money changing hands at an almost alarming speed. It's very easy to get lost in it all and, in the excitement, accept bets that only an idiot would be stupid enough to take. After the game you'll feel like it was a lot of fun to act like a big time gambler. Freddy will be too busy counting money to feel any fun.

Let me give you an example of why you should burn correct odds into your memory banks. It comes from *A Professional Gambler Tells How to Win* by Mike Barron (not his real name). Mike writes, *"If you saw what followed you wouldn't say the poor patsy was any unluckier than the next player; it was just that in the white heat at the peak of the game you could always depend on him losing his head."* He then describes the moment of his proposition bet, *"I'd wait till he was sweating over a point, say an easy six with one hundred dollars or so riding on the outcome. When he began to bite his lip I knew I had him. I'd pounce on him with something like, "Twelve to one you don't shoot a three on the next roll!" I baited him with a wad of ten spots amounting to sixty or one hundred and twenty dollars on the board. I doubt if he ever knew what the real odds were for a bet like that. Actually they figure out to seventeen to one. But Lamb wouldn't think twice about it. All he could see was that stack of bills staring up at him from the table, and he gobbled up my bet every time. He usually walked away from the big payday games with empty pockets, and most often it was because of the bets he'd dropped to me."* To put the money into perspective, the game described was one taking place in 1943 during World War Two.

Freddy may offer you even money that the shooter will make a point of six or eight. The correct odds are six to five. These side bets can kill you very quickly if you don't know the correct odds.

So here they are.

Number	Ways	Single Roll	Before a Seven
12	1	35-1	6-1
11	2	17-1	3-1
10	3	11-1	2-1
9	4	8-1	3-2
8	5	31-5	6-5
7	6	5-1	-
6	5	31-5	6-5
5	4	8-1	3-2
4	3	11-1	2-1
3	2	17-1	3-1
2	1	35-1	6-1

So now you know that if Freddy offers you four to one that you'll roll twelve before rolling a seven he is not giving you a fair break for your money. Now don't get twitchy when you look at the next table. All it shows are the correct odds on the hard way bets. Freddy will adjust those odds accordingly to give him a significant edge.

Bet	Ways	Other Ways	Losing Throws	Odds Against
4	1	2	8	8-1
6	1	4	10	10-1
8	1	4	10	10-1
10	1	2	8	8-1

So next time a guy like Freddy offers you five to one against you rolling a hard six you know you'd be a complete mug to accept the bet. If you want to

Cheating with Dice

play Craps for money then ingrain these figures into your head. That way you'll at least know if you are being offered a fair side bet.

If you want to play in a casino then a careful study of their odds would be useful for you as well. The bets offered on a casino table vary from a paltry 0.832 % edge right up to a pretty crippling 16.667 %. It's wise to know which ones you are actually betting on! Although this book isn't covering casino play I'll break the rule for once and include the table odds for Craps here. Hardened Craps players read on while the rest of us can skip past this table and move on. The true odds have been averaged out in a number of cases.

Type of Bet	Payout Odds	True Odds	House Edge
Pass	evens	251-244	1.414 %
Pass with odds			0.848 %
Come	evens	251-244	1.414 %
Come with odds			0.848 %
Don't Pass bar 12 (or 2)	evens	976-949	1.403 %
Don't Pass with odds			0.832 %
Don't Come bar 12 (or 2)	evens	976-949	1.403 %
Don't Come with odds			0.832 %
6 and 8 to win	7-6	6-5	1.515 %
5 and 9 to win	7-5	3-2	4 %
4 and 10 to win	9-5	2-1	6.667 %
6 and 8 to lose	4-5	5-6	1.818 %
5 and 9 to lose	5-8	2-3	2.5 %
4 and 10 to lose	5-11	1-2	3.03 %
6 and 8 Buy Bet*	6-5	6-5	4.761 %
5 and 9 Buy Bet*	3-2	3-2	4.761 %
4 and 10 Buy Bet*	2-1	2-1	4.761 %
6 and 8 Lay Bet*	5-6	5-6	4 %
5 and 9 Lay Bet*	2-3	2-3	3.225 %
4 and 10 Lay Bet*	1-2	1-2	2.439 %
Big 6 and Big 8 Field	1-1	6-5	9.091 %
(2, 3, 4, 9, 10, 11, 12)	1-1	5-4	11.111 %
Hard 4 or 10	7-1	8-1	11.111 %
Hard 6 or 8	9-1	10-1	9.091 %
Any 7	4-1	5-1	16.667 %
Any Craps	7-1	8-1	11.111 %
2 and 12	29-1	35-1	16.667 %
3 and 11	14-1	17-1	16.667 %
4 and 10	9-1	11-1	16.667 %
5 and 9	7-1	8-1	11.111 %
6 and 8	31-5	5-1	16.667 %

*5 % Commission

How to Cheat at Everything

These odds are for an American Craps table. In some other countries, such as the United Kingdom, some of the odds may vary slightly. Even if the above looks a little daunting a quick glance should be able to tell you which are the silly bets. Next time you visit Las Vegas or Atlantic City you still may not win but at least you should lose your money a little more slowly!

Now Freddy won't just make money on his profitable side bets. He'll also have his little collection of gaffed dice with him.

He can use percentage dice such as six-ace *shapes* which will cause the shooter to crap out more often. When these dice are in play Freddy will bet against the shooter. Freddy can also switch in loads to do the same work.

He can also, on his throw, switch in a pair of 2-3-6 or 1-3-5 *Tops* where the numbers are repeated twice on the dice. Since neither set can throw a seven Freddy cannot crap out when going for a point. Since he can't crap out he will gleefully accept all bets against him making his point.

Freddy can also use all of the controlled shots from his hand or from a cup that we've discussed.

Entire books have been written about Craps but I think you are getting the idea. In private games it is strictly for the big boys and should be avoided at all cost unless you know exactly what you are doing. By combining his proposition bets with gaffed dice Freddy can fleece you so quickly you'll be in a daze.

A COUPLE MORE SUCKER PROPOSITIONS

Freddy, as I'm sure you've guessed, won't just offer wrong odds on Craps bets. You may be playing a friendly game of Backgammon or any other game involving dice when, during a break, he'll *invent* a betcha or two.

Six or Eight

Here's a bet that Freddy will pull on an experienced Craps player. He'll bet them even money that he'll roll a six and an eight *before* rolling two sevens. The Craps player figures (and you can check the odds for yourself from Freddy's tables) that the odds against throwing a six before a seven are six to five against. So are the odds for throwing an eight before a seven. The mug figures he has an advantage and accepts the bet.

He doesn't have an advantage.

You see Freddy doesn't specify which number has to turn up first. There are ten ways to make a six or eight roll and only six ways to make a seven. The odds are five to three that Freddy will roll a six *or eight* before a seven. Having rolled one of those numbers the odds revert to being six to five against him rolling the second number *but* the five to three odds will beat out the six to five over a run.

Freddy puts a lot of thought into working out the odds on these little bets.

You don't have to understand the calculations. You just have to be aware that any bets offering you what seem to be favorable odds probably aren't.

Seven for Three

Freddy will bet you even money that you can't roll a seven with three rolls of the dice. You figure that with seven being the easiest total to get this could be easy money.

Seven *is* the easiest total to roll but the odds are still four to three against you doing it within those three rolls.

Another mug's bet from Freddy.

Five Dice Special

Freddy rolls out six dice and explains to you that there is an even chance of any one of the dice showing a specified number such as two. This because each dice has six faces so it's an even chance that one of them will show two after a roll.

Freddy now removes one of the dice and offers to bet you even money that a two (or, indeed, any number you care to specify) will turn up on one of the dice after a roll. The explanation seems to make sense and now, with one die removed, the game appears to be a little in your favor.

Right?

Wrong, if you accept the bet you are bucking horrendous odds of three to one against you!

Hard life isn't it? Especially when you realize that Freddy, using controlled rolls and gaffed dice, can twist those odds even further against you. Freddy will even let you offer him one of these bets and accept it. He turns those percentages around with controlled shots. You'll think lady luck has let you down but it's just Freddy kicking her hard.

Odd bets can look very complicated and somewhat frightening, math-wise, in print. The simple advice is to avoid them. Of course this may not be quite as easy to do as you may think. You've never seen Freddy put one forward to a mug. By the time he's finished his sell on it you'll not only think you understand it perfectly but you'll be reaching for your money to take a go or two. It's not just his sleight-of-hand ability and knowledge that make Freddy so successful. It's his gift of the gab as well.

I often tease him by saying that he didn't kiss the Blarney Stone.

He swallowed it!

Finding The Action

N OW FREDDY DOESN'T OFTEN HAVE PEOPLE LINING UP TO PLAY DICE WITH HIM. He either has to join a game in play or create his own action.

He can *hook* you into a game in a number of different ways.

Freddy often travels to a hotel or convention center where a meeting or trade show is in progress. These are very common throughout the year with the sales teams and managers all rather conveniently staying in one place. Once checked in and armed with a fake name tag Freddy will drop some dice where they are likely to be found. He may put them on the floor or on a chair seat.

Freddy then waits around until somebody finds the dice. With drinks flowing freely and a good time being had by all it doesn't take much coaxing to get a little game started up.

All Freddy has to do is gradually build the ante to make the game worthwhile for him.

In these *spontaneous* games Freddy will use his percentage dice. Since the gaffs are the discovered dice he doesn't need to go to the trouble of switching any dice in. Since he joined the game after it started he can't be thought of in a suspicious way.

Freddy can also start up a game himself. He will just happen to have a set of Poker Dice with him. "*Me and the boys found em a while ago,*" he'll chat. "*Hell of a lot of fun!*" Maybe he'll have a pair of dice with him that he picked up from the floor of his car. "*My kids are always playing some board game on a journey. This is the third set I've found under my seat!*" Then he'll start a few fun bets leading to a game of Craps. He may explain the rules of Craps to you during a break in a Backgammon session. Of course you'll only be able to play if you have any money left after playing him at Backgammon!

Freddy says that often all he has to do is sit at the bar idly rolling a set of dice. Somebody will ask him what he's doing and he'll reply, "*Oh nothing, I was just a bit bored and found these in my pocket. I'm just playing around with them!*" From there it's a short hop to a Craps game being played in a hotel room.

Games with dice are very common indeed. The next time you or a friend find some, be very wary of a stranger wanting to join in your little friendly game. If you find dice while away at a seminar or convention the best bet for you is to throw them away.

They may have been dropped from a Monopoly game.

Or they may be Freddy's.

Freddy's Final Advice On Dice

IF YOU INSIST ON PLAYING DICE FOR MONEY DO YOURSELF A FAVOR AND FOLLOW Freddy's top tips for a fair shake.

Insist that the dice are thrown from a *trip* cup and that they drop at least five or six inches onto the playing surface.

Insist that the dice are dropped into the cup with the player showing an empty hand afterwards.

Insist that the cup is shaken and the dice thrown with *one* hand only.

Before, during and after the game watch for any tips that fakes have been switched in. Be vigilant at all times. If you have any suspicions just leave the game.

If it is at all possible *insist* that the dice be thrown against some form of backboard or wall. A cheat will start a private game at a table well away from the wall to avoid this. If you really want to join the game ask that the game be moved. Yes, it's a hassle but it is in your interest to do so. If the request is refused just curb your playing desires and walk away.

Never accept odds on a bet that you don't understand. Don't take a stranger's word for it that he is explaining them correctly to you.

Never play with strangers for large sums of money *even* if it looks like a good bet for you.

Never gamble when drinking.

Look back through this section to know as much as you possibly can about both the cheats and hustles that will take your money if you give them a chance.

Never grouse or shout about suspicions of cheating in a game. It must be stressed over and over that people like Freddy are not nice folks. If you have any doubts about a game just quietly make your excuses and leave. You may think you are tough and mean but, trust me, Freddy employs *minders* who are tougher and meaner.

Your friends may think you are a little paranoid about insisting on all these precautions but your wallet will thank you for having done so.

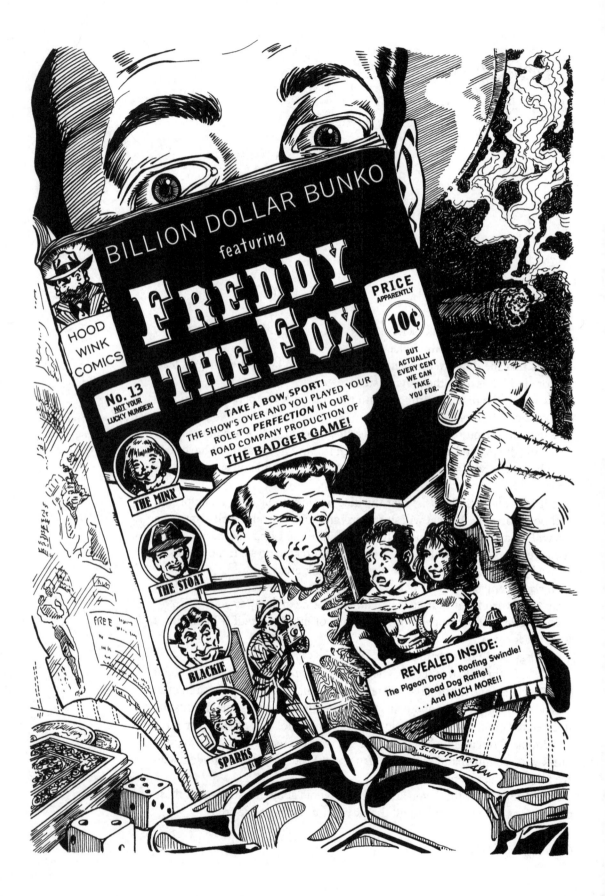

Sneaky Ways To Beat The System!

P EOPLE LIKE FREDDY DON'T LIKE TO PAY FOR ANYTHING IF THEY CAN GET AWAY with scamming it. Just for a break between bigger hustles here are a few ways that Freddy and his ilk manage to beat the system. None require any skill other than an innocent face and a bold nerve to pull off. You are not, however, encouraged to try any of them for yourself.

HOW FREDDY GETS OUT OF PAYING HIS SPEEDING TICKETS

As you can imagine Freddy is often in quite a hurry to leave town. As a result he's managed to acquire quite a few speeding tickets over the years but has yet to have to pay a single one of them. His system for beating them is both devious and almost foolproof.

Freddy always pleads not guilty to the offense and, as such, is given a court date to plead his case against the policeman who stopped him. The hub of Freddy's swindle pivots on the fact that the officer must appear in court for the hearing or the ticket and charges are dropped. Since officers are paid for their court appearances Freddy can't rely on them not to bother doing so. Instead he almost guarantees it by writing a letter.

The letter to the officer informs them that they have been left some money in a will. The will was handwritten so doesn't hold much legal weight and unless the officer can turn up in person with photo ID his portion will be turned over to the State. The letter stresses that it would be in the officer's best interest to show up to the meeting. He is invited to a breakfast meeting with the attorney in charge to settle the matter. The money mentioned is quite a tidy sum.

Freddy has an out of state pal post the letter for him with no return address or phone number on it. It is simply addressed to Highway Patrol, attention officer _____.

The date of the meeting just happens to coincide with Freddy's court appearance!

Freddy reports that he has never had to plead his case for the simple reason that the officer never showed up! Big surprise! Should you be crazy enough to want to try this then at least check your local laws first. For example, in some states, at the time of writing, the police officer may be asked to return at another time. It can take three no-shows for the case to be dropped!

It is worth noting that, the same system can be used by crooks to get a person away from their house for a time. I'm sure you can guess why!

FREDDY'S FREE POSTAGE SCAM

Freddy has a very simple and incredibly devious way to get a letter delivered for free. He simply switches the position of the addresses on the envelope. In other words he addresses the envelope to himself and puts the address of the person he wants the letter sent to in the upper left corner of the envelope as a return address.

He then posts the letter without a stamp on it.

The letter will be returned to the 'sender' for postage. Another freebie for Freddy!

There is also the well known ploy of just putting a one-cent stamp on an envelope when paying a bill. The post office will deliver the letter with a postage due notice which the company will, albeit reluctantly, pay because they know their bill payment is in the envelope. If using this somewhat tacky method of saving a few cents be sure to send the envelope without a return address upon it so that the Post Office can't send it back to you.

FREDDY FLIES FIRST CLASS

Sometimes Freddy's boldness amazes me but it is this very boldness that allows him to fly first class for a coach fare every time he gets on board a plane. He learned the following tricks from a pal of his they call Eagle.

He waits until the final boarding call of a busy flight. He walks on board and calmly takes a seat in first class. Because he's one of the last on board he's most unlikely to be in anybody else's seat. Because he's in first class and looks as though he should be (Freddy always stresses that you have to look like a first class passenger to pull this off) the flight attendants do not want to run the risk of offending a high fare paying passenger by requesting to look at his ticket. They'd much rather run a risk of letting a con man get away with a swindle than have high level complaints looming over them. Freddy fastens his seat belt and relaxes for a comfortable flight.

If, and he stresses that it is a small if, he is questioned Freddy has a number of back-up stories depending on the attendant. He may tell them that he booked a first class seat but that the ticket people made a mistake and gave him a coach ticket. He carries several (fake) gold/platinum frequent flier cards and can be most convincing. Seeing the cards carries a lot of weight and once more, rather than risk upsetting a frequent customer, the issue will be dropped. Freddy may also offer to pay the price difference and ask that he be billed by the airline. This is often accepted and, once more, Freddy enjoys the flight. When the bill arrives he refuses to pay it citing the rudeness of the crew when he was asked to leave first class. Freddy has been so convincingly horrified on these rare occasions that not only has the fee been dropped, but he's often earned free tickets for more flights on the same airline!

Freddy claims that only once have they insisted that he move back to coach and then only with a promise to sort everything out nicely for him.

Freddy says that this con is hard to pull of on a smaller plane when, often, the crew knows exactly who should be where but that it is almost childishly easy to get away with on larger busy flights. Even though the passengers are listed and meant to be checked, it's often chaotic right before take-off on a full flight and the cabin crew are bustling around with no time to discuss a passenger's seat. Especially if the passenger looks as though they are where they are meant to be!

The big secret, Freddy tells me, is to be very polite but firm with the crew, acting as if you were the injured party. It's also very important to look the part.

Freddy can also use a very cunning ploy to get upgraded if the coach section of the flight is full. After take-off he asks, very politely, to speak to the head of the cabin crew. He asks to speak to them in private. Once he has their full attention he explains, almost as if he is embarrassed to do so, that the person he is sitting next to has some form of body odor or cologne that is making him feel very ill. He knows that the cabin crew is very busy but would very much appreciate being reseated. He doesn't want to cause any problems but this situation is really causing him problems.

Problem? Coach is full!

The cabin crew member will note how nice Freddy has been. He hasn't made a scene, he's been polite, and, more to the point, looks, to use an airline buzz word, upgradeable. It's 5 to 1 on that Freddy will find himself seated in business or even first class to enjoy the flight. At absolute worst he will be given good attention and great service on the flight to repay his polite manners.

The Eagle has hundreds of scams that could cause an airline official to faint. Some require tremendous nerve, others just require specialized knowledge of the industry and how it works. Nobody, but nobody, is safe when people like Freddy and the Eagle are around!

NEW TIRES FOR FREDDY'S CAR . . . FOR FREE!

A good friend of Freddy's once pointed out to him that his tires were getting a little old on his car. Freddy agreed but thought that there was a bit of wear left in them. His friend thought that, that could be the case but went on to ask Freddy if he'd get newer tires if they were free!

Freddy liked the price and his friend went on to explain his diabolically simple (though totally illegal) plan. He and his friend went out and hired a car of the same make as Freddy's (although one with the same size tires is fine) and drove to his garage. Once in the safety of Freddy's garage they swapped the tires on Freddy's car and the rental car. Freddy claims that he made up the rental cost (thus getting the tires for free) by changing over a few other items as well!

When the rental car was returned the rental company employee didn't notice anything because there was still some wear left on Freddy's tires. It just looked as though it could be normal wear and tear on their car! Even Freddy says he wouldn't return a rental car with bald tires! Nice to know he has some standards, however low!

FREDDY'S FREE BIRTHDAY CAKE!

Freddy is no mean cook and on his birthday he likes to make a giant cake for his friends. As you can imagine he doesn't like to pay for the cake ingredients though! He uses a simple ploy to ensure that he never has to.

He buys all the ingredients and makes his cake. He then shares the cake with all his friends to much enjoyment by all. Freddy can be a most gracious host when he is among friends!

The next day Freddy gathers up all the boxes for the ingredients along with the remains of the carton of milk used in the process. Before returning to the store he adds a little lemon juice to the milk. Although the milk is fresh this juice gives the milk a slightly rotten smell and causes it to curdle up.

He takes this delightful package to the store manager where he bought the items along with, of course, the receipt for the items. He has the store manager smell the milk often inducing a mild coughing session in him and so Freddy waits for his recovery. He then tells a sad tale of making his birthday cake and sharing it with his friends all of whom became sick. Freddy seems close to tears as he tells of his wrecked birthday party and of his friend's distress.

Often the manager is so saddened by this distressing tale that not only is Freddy's money returned but they often throw in gift certificates for further purchases as well!

A happy birthday indeed for Freddy!

Just a few more examples of Freddy's attitude that *everything* in life should be either free or make him a profit!

A Collection of Odd Cons

There are so many ways a con man can take your money that it would be insane of Freddy and me to tell you that this book contains all of them. Hopefully though you are going to be a lot more astute about spotting the build up to a con or hustle and so be able to be better equipped to avoid them. Just to keep your education rocking along here are a few cons that Freddy hasn't pulled but that his close friends and associates have.

ROOF AND DRIVE FIXING

If you have a tiled or slate roof you had better watch out for this. If you have a nice tarred driveway be aware of cheap fixes.

You'll get a knock on your door one day and meet a workman. He'll tell you that he's been doing a job in the area and just *happened to notice* that some tiles on your roof were loose and looking a little unsafe. He'll tell you that this might conceal deeper trouble underneath. Alternatively he may tell you that your driveway is looking a little shabby.

His hook is that he overestimated on the job he's doing and has left over materials. He can offer you an unbelievable price to redo your roof or driveway. Looking over his shoulder you can see a truck filled with building supplies and looking rather professional.

If you take the job he and his workmen will turn up and start a very noisy job. You may decide to go out for the day or, at least, just watch TV in the den with the volume turned up. At the end of the day he'll ask you to inspect his team's work.

Wow, a beautiful new shiny roof or fabulous new drive covering. Happily you pay up and the team moves on. You'll probably stay pretty happy until the next time it rains.

All they've done on the roof is make a lot of noise and painted over the original tiles or slate with machine oil (often heavy number nine weight motor oil). If you are lucky they may have also hammered down any actual loose tiles. For the driveway they've dumped machine oil on top and spread it out to look like a nice new one drying away. When it rains the oil on the roof will drip everywhere costing you a lot more than a new roof in repainting. The oil on the driveway will spread everywhere ruining your lawn and flower beds.

These teams spend the summer traveling from town to town. A lot of them spend the winter relaxing in Florida spending their ill gotten gains.

> *"'Caveat emptor.' Let the buyer beware."*
>
> Old but wise saying

BROADWAY SHOW TIME

It's your lucky day! In the mail you discover that you've won a night out at a big show. Everything will be paid for, the show, dinner beforehand and even a limo to and from the city. Being a little skeptical you phone the contact number on the winning ticket but discover that there is no catch. Your name was entered automatically from a mailing list and you've really won. There is no catch at all, all you have to do is name the date and show you'd like to see and the trip is on!

Just for once you've joined the list of lucky winners my friend.

On the night a limo turns up. Being a little cautious you check that it has all been paid for. The driver assures you that even the tip for the journey has been covered by the prize winning!

You and your spouse go off and have the night of your lives. A fabulous dinner, wine and, of course, that show you've been dying to see. You cuddle up on the way home thinking that, just for once, life has been really kind to you. Life is good!

Well, life is really good until you open your front door and discover the empty house that used to be full of stuff.

The thieves literally bought themselves a guaranteed time with which to empty your house.

The house will have been looked at before hand to make sure that the investment required is going to be worth it. If you have a visitor asking questions for a survey or some such followed a week or so later by a competition win you might want to be a little more suspicious than normal.

BLUE WATER

A fast version of this scam works when a pair of men dressed in very official looking overalls turn up at your door. After showing some ID they explain that the state has been having problems with the water in the area. It is thought to be something to do with the way cleansing processes of the water are reacting with the pipes. It all sounds very scientific to you and you are happy to let them check your pipes, especially when they mention that if the reaction occurs it could cause long term health problems.

They explain that it is a simple test. One of them will go into the upstairs bathroom and pour in some chemicals. You'll wait downstairs in the basement with a tap running. As soon as the water turns a different color you are to inform them. You are warned that it may take a few minutes for the chemicals to work.

You wait by the tap hoping that the water will turn a light blue, the color, you have been assured, that means all is well.

After a while you may decide to check with the men to see if it should have reacted yet.

The good news is that your pipes are fine.

The bad news is that you are going to need a shopping trip for a new TV, stereo and computer or whatever else is missing from your house.

Another example of moving the mug out of the way for a while so that the theft can occur.

THE BADGER GAME

An age-old area of crime is that of using lust and love for profit. A good hooker can turn a nice high six figure income in the oldest profession of all.

But there are others who'll use just the promise of lust to turn a few dollars. The Badger game often just employs the 'poor female being mistreated' syndrome to bring out the best in the mug.

You are away from home on a business trip and sitting alone in the bar enjoying a drink or two after a successful day. A charming young lady sits beside you and a conversation starts. You learn that's she's not very happy. She's just had an argument with her husband. "*He's just paranoid about me talking to anybody,*" she tells you.

At that moment the husband walks in and comes straight over. "*There you are, talking to a stranger again*" he says to his wife. He turns to you and says quite coldly, "*She's married, leave her alone!*" Obviously you make your excuses and, perhaps feeling a little sorry for her, move away.

Later in your room you hear a knock on the door. You open it and find the young lady there. She looks very distressed and has blood running from her nose. "*I'm sorry,*" she says. "*I just didn't know where to go. He hit me. Help me please!*"

You bring her into your room and sit her down. She is crying her eyes out. You do your best to console her, perhaps giving her a stiff drink for her nerves.

She starts to calm down and stands up. "*I guess I'll have to go and face the music. Thank you for being so kind.*" She throws her arms around you to give you a big hug.

It is at that *exact* moment that your door bursts open and in leaps the husband. "*I knew I'd need this,*" he shouts taking a picture with his camera. "*That'll screw you in the divorce court!*" She tries to protest that it's not what it seems like but he won't listen. The husband notices your wedding ring and says, "*Bonus for me you dog,*" he shouts. "*Cheating on your wife! Huh, let's see what she says when I drag you into court at my divorce as the other man!*"

It won't take long before you are buying the film in the camera.

But it wasn't just your photograph that was taken.

You were as well.

You have just been an actor in a beautifully acted piece from start to finish.

The girl in this piece used the bleeding nose as a special extra emotional hook on you. This kind of *Roper* or *Mack* (a girl who lures a man into a con) is called, for obvious reasons, a *Bleeder*.

SELLING GREEN

Everybody is short of cash sometimes. Even the ultra rich, with all their assets tied up in investments, can always use an extra dollar or two.

Freddy's pal, a kindly fellow known as *Printer,* can supply them with forged money at the right price. His problem is that good *Queer* (forged money) is pretty tough to come by and he wants to be able to sell them poorly made, cheap forgeries at a top price.

His method for doing so is so simple that it's almost criminal. Well actually it *is* criminal!

Printer will get to know somebody pretty well. He picks his friends carefully by checking out businesses and befriending those who might need money. After a few chats and social affairs he lets lose his secret of always having lots of cash. "*Don't tell anybody,*" he'll say, "*but I can get the best forged money around. It's not cheap but it's cheaper than the real thing! Check this one out.*" He'll give them a twenty dollar bill that looks real and tell them to keep it. "*I use them just to keep ahead of the game,*" he says. "*Anybody will take them so it's not like anybody is losing!*"

When the mug starts getting interested he'll waive away any thoughts of being caught by taking them with him on a visit to the bank. "*Gotta top up my account. There's a few bills due.*" The forged money goes through the cashier without any problems whatsoever. Now the mug, a little short of cash himself, is really interested. He may ask Printer the cost of the bills. The Printer will tell them that it's about a third of the face value but warns them not to get involved. "*After all,*" he'll remind them, "*it is a bit naughty you know!*"

His friend sees the Printer passing off his forged money everywhere without ever being questioned and pushes to be able to buy some. The Printer finally relents and tells him that there is a minimum order of five thousand dollars which will give his pal fifteen thousand dollars of forged money. The friend bites and somehow, the Printer doesn't care how, comes up with the money.

The friend receives a case of pretty shoddy forged money in exchange. In the darkness of the parking lot where the exchange took place it looked fine but in the cold light of the next day the stuff looks pretty crude even to the friend's untrained eye.

The Printer tells him it's fine and to leave him alone. If the friend persists the Printer will tell him to get lost. What's the friend going to do? Can you really see him trying to complain to the police that he tried to buy forged money that just wasn't quite what he expected?

The Printer, of course, at the start of the con had just been using real money all along. He just told his pal that the money was forged. He convinced his friend that passing these bills was easy and it was. Passing real money is very easy indeed! The friend was allowed to talk himself into a criminal buy and, quite literally, the friend paid the price of trying to be part of a world he just didn't belong in.

Ah well.

A QUICK WORD ABOUT SYSTEMS

Read the classified ads of any tabloid or magazine and, in among the numerous offers of 'psychic advice', you'll find offers for gambling systems covering everything from Lotto to Roulette. They may have exotic titles like the *Martingale* and *Anti-Martingale*, the *Labouchere* or the *d'Alembert*. They may claim to have uncovered secret patterns of numbers that turn up more often than others. All will have glowing endorsements from past winners and *all* will claim to have found *the* way to beat the system.

Here's the quick word on them.

None of them work.

Well, okay, there are a few well written and superbly thought out Blackjack counting systems such as the *Omega II* (Bryce Carlson), *Card Counting for the Casino Executive* (Bill Zender), *Professional Blackjack* (Stanford Wong) and the daddy of them all *Beat the Dealer* (Edward O. Thorpe) among others. If you put in the requisite hours of self training and are dedicated enough to apply the systems correctly you will, at least at times, be playing with an advantage. This is not as easy to do as you may at first think thus explaining the small number of very successful professional Blackjack players. Still, careful study of these books may stop you playing like a complete idiot. These Blackjack systems are, if you like, the exception that proves the rule about systems. Even so they will only give you an edge on the game at certain times. There is still, to my knowledge anyway, no such thing as a 'can't lose' system for *any* game.

"Even the Devil can quote Scripture."
————•————

American Proverb

THE AGE OLD PIGEON DROP

This is one of the oldest of the street cons and is known by many names, *Dropping the Poke, The Drag, Pigeon Drop* and the *Spanish Handkerchief Switch* for a few. It is also played out in a number of forms but the root of the game is always the same.

It still survives today and is a specialty of two of Freddy's pals called *Leather* and *Pigskin.*

The two con men pretend to find a wallet in the street. They 'find' it just as the mug has seen it and so three sets of hands reach for the wallet. The mug is always chosen very carefully. *"They have to be somebody who'll be carrying a few dollars,"* says Leather. I asked him how he knew if somebody would be carrying money or not and his reply was quite interesting. *"You can try to peek their poke beforehand,"* he replied. *"Or you can look at their shoes. Good shoes are always a giveaway of somebody with money."*

An argument breaks out as to who has legitimately found the wallet. They all look inside. The wallet contains some cash and a money order for around six hundred dollars. *"Hey,"* says Pigskin, *"we could stick the money order in a bank account and get the cash. Then we could split it!"* Both con men are from 'out of town' and so can't cash the money order. After some discussion the mug offers to cash it at his bank. Pigskin seems very wary. *"What if you don't come back?"* he asks, *"it's not like I could complain to the cops or anything."*

The mug is set for what street con men refer to as the *Hurrah.* He is now so committed to the easy money that he'll do anything to avoid losing it. What follows sounds logical but is going to cost him money.

Leather offers a solution. The mug can give them half the money to ensure his return. He's got to give them three hundred dollars as a surety while he cashes the money order, then they can all split the money like lucky friends.

The deal is done and so is the mug.

When he tries to cash the money order it is, of course, a useless forgery. The wallet may have been switched for one with newspaper. Whatever, when he returns to confront his friends they are long gone.

A version of the Drop can be seen at the start of the movie *The Sting.* Here the mug runs into a man trying to escape with some money. The mug is asked to hold on to the money for the runner. The man's money and the mug's (for safety from the chasers) is wrapped into a handkerchief and hidden down the front of his trousers. The con man even shows him how to position it. It is during the demonstration that the handkerchief full of money is swapped for one full of newspaper. The con man 'hears' the chasers coming and runs off. It's all over in moments to leave the mug with a crotch full of newspaper wrapped in a cheap handkerchief.

A large money version of the Drop can also be seen in the movie *House of Games* where the stakes run into tens of thousands of dollars.

In cold print it seems incredible that people would fall for such nonsense but they do so each and every day. The words *Silver Tongued* don't even begin to describe how persuasive a good con man can be. They twist the truth and play with emotions with a skill that leaves the mug no chance at all.

"Some lies are more believable than the truth."

An old Gypsy saying

GUESS YOUR WEIGHT?

You know, Freddy has just reminded me of another friend of his from the carnival. He's nicknamed *Jenny* after a famous diet system. His scam is very cool indeed. He will, for a dollar, guess your weight. If he's more than three pounds off either way you win five dollars. If business is a little slow he'll up the prize. He can offer you whatever he wants as a prize, he's *never* more than three pounds off unless he's guessing the weight of a shill.

He brings out a pad and pencil. He asks you your name. Let's say it's Albert. He writes down 'Albert weighs' then turns the pad towards himself so that you can't see what he's writing. "*After all,*" he says, "*you might tell a white lie about your weight just to win the prize!*" He puts the pencil away.

He then gets you to announce your weight. You do so and he turns the pad to show that he is either exactly right or just one or two pounds off. For your dollar you get the piece of paper and move on marveling at his observational skill.

Well, he is using a skill but it's not an observational one.

When he turns the pad to himself he only pretends to write in a weight before putting away the pencil. When you announce your weight he quickly writes it in on the pad using a tiny piece of pencil lead either jammed under his thumb nail or clipped there in a tiny holder called a *Swami Gimmick* by magicians. It is not an easy writing skill to pick up but Jenny has been doing it for forty years and is an expert. He can write entire sentences on a pad very quickly indeed so adding a weight to his note is child's play to him. Actually both Freddy and me think it's worth the dollar just to see his skill in action!

THE BANK EXAMINER SWINDLE

This is commonly played on old people who fall for the con artist's glib line of patter more easily than a younger person. It all starts with a phone call to the victim. The victim is told that the caller is a bank examiner and that several large withdrawals, including some from the victim's account, have been made at a local bank in the last few days. They suspect a dishonest employee and would like the victim's help in trapping them. The victim is told to go to the bank and make a withdrawal from a certain window. They are then asked to put the money in an envelope and give it to a bank examiner who will identify themselves outside the bank. The money, it is explained, will be marked and redeposited the next day. The victim is thanked for their help in assisting the apprehension of a criminal.

Actually all they've assisted in is a crime. Any inquiries about their account will show no irregularities apart from one large withdrawal made by them!

Despite you thinking that nobody could fall for this, it is considered one of the top ten cons being played today. A lot of senior citizens have been taken for their life savings using just this very technique.

Check *all* so-called official phone calls by phoning the institution and asking for the caller by name and title. This way you can verify, or not, the original telephone call. *Don't* call on a number given to you by the caller. *Always* check in the directory for the correct number. Report the phone call to them.

Remember no legitimate institution ever makes a practice of asking clients to engage in detective work for them.

CHEATS PLAYING STRAIGHT!

Freddy has told me that one of the problems with cheating at cards is that it takes all the fun out of the game. It simply becomes work.

For this reason, once a month, he gets together with some fellow cheats to play straight poker. All of them are skillful cheats at some move or another but, in this game, absolutely no cheating occurs. They play just for the sheer fun of running a bluff without knowing if it will succeed, pushing a good hand and feeling the adrenaline rush of another player bucking up against it, and the sheer good thrill of picking up a pot that they've earned rather than stolen.

It's not a big money game. They all put in five hundred dollars at the start of the night and play till their money is gone. The winners treat the losers to drinks and dinner. There are no big money winners here, just a group of guys having fun.

"Kinda makes us feel like kids again," smiles Freddy.

I do find it interesting to note the delineation between work and play here. It is perhaps best summed up by a poem written by one of the greatest gamblers of them all, Nicholas Andrea Dandolos or Nick the Greek, when he penned the following.

> *There's no road back to childhood, but*
> *What fool would care to go?*
> *There is no joy in playing games*
> *Whose final score we know*

LET'S BE SAFE OUT THERE

Here are the top ten rules to avoid being scammed by one of these cons or, indeed, any other of their ilk. The advice is given in the NYPD brochure that is distributed to senior citizens. Put in my words it goes as follows:

Always be very skeptical of unsolicited calls.

Be *very* wary of door-to-door sales.

Never fall for any high-pressure sales technique. *Always* take time to think things through.

Take as *much time* as you need when thinking about any home improvement offer.

Remember you are entitled by law to cancel *any* transactions you have agreed to within three business days. This is the law in NY, you may want to check your own local and state laws for where you live.

Never sign a contract or make a purchase without *fully* understanding the terms of the agreement. In the summer of 2001 a huge scandal erupted over a health club chain and their dubious, but legal, contracts. This scandal proved that it is wise to read the small print even if you have to squint!

Never give out any credit card or bank information over the phone to a company not known to you.

Never, never, never be taken in by any "You have won" notifications over the phone or on-line and be *very* wary of any that arrive in your mail.

Never assume that a charity request is legitimate just because their cause seems so heartwarming.

Don't do business with a company you know little or nothing about.

And, as the police suggest, if you suspect a fraud or scam do not be embarrassed to call the police immediately. By following the above advice you'll be way ahead of the game in avoiding these types of scams.

THE DEAD DOG RAFFLE

Finally here's an outrageous tale of con men at work!

Blackie (you read about him in the Horse and Dog racing chapter) swears the following story is absolutely true. Even Freddy has trouble believing it but that doesn't stop it being one of his favorite after dinner stories!

It seems that one of Blackie's friends, a dog owner who shall remain nameless, had a big problem. One of his best dogs had hurt its hind quarters and was never going to be able to race again. It couldn't even be used as a stud dog because of the nature of the injuries. This famous dog, thanks to an unlucky accident, had become worth next to nothing. Even worse, the owner had no insurance on it. Disaster!

Blackie suggested a cunning plan. They would advertise that, for a promotional event, they would raffle the dog off to a lucky winner. A portion of the proceeds would be sent to charity and the publicity would be phenomenal! The owner pointed out that the injuries would be obvious to the winner. Blackie said that they could say that the dog had been injured in transit to the winner! A cunning plan indeed and one that was quickly put into action.

Adverts were taken out in the trade papers and soon, thanks to the dog's famous name, the money was rolling in.

The day of the draw arrived, and amid much hoopla, was made. The winner, thanks to a rigged draw, lived some considerable distance away and so, the owner announced, the dog would be sent, at his stable's expense, to him straight away.

It was all going smoothly until they went to get the dog to put it into its traveling crate. It seems that the injuries were worse than they thought. They found that the dog had died in the interim.

Thinking quickly Blackie had them crate the dead dog and send it off to the winner. "*We'll claim that it must have died in transit,*" he told the owner.

And that's exactly what they did.

I'm sure that, like me, the first time I heard this tale, you are dying to ask what happened when the winner phoned up to inform them of the dead dog's arrival.

"*We refunded the cost of his tickets!*" laughs Blackie every time he is asked. "*But we kept the rest of the money!*"

In Freddy's arcane world even a worthless dead dog can be sold to make a profit!

"It's morally wrong to allow suckers to keep the money."

Canada Bill Jones

Letter From A Cheat!

FROM THE MOVIES AND TELEVISION SHOWS YOU MIGHT GET THE IDEA THAT CHEATS are always white, well-dressed, gentlemen. Of course this is absolutely wrong. The art forms of cheating are not limited to any race, color, sex or creed. Cheats literally infest every level of society.

I was delighted then when an African American friend of mine called simply 'J' decided to write me a letter giving his side of some of the cons. He works in the ghetto and lower income black areas of large cities. His style of writing reflects his life and education but you'll read about what works for him. It is particularly fascinating to me that he specializes in some very old cons such as the *Pigeon Drop* and *Selling Bricks*. If nothing else his letter proves that such cons are still being played every day on the streets. It is also interesting to note how carefully he has researched the possible penalties for his work should he be caught and prosecuted! Of course, during his letter, he claims to be reformed these days!

So here is the letter which he titled, *"The Con Game from a Black Man's Experience."* He has assumed some knowledge on the reader's behalf but I think you'll find this most educating!

Simon,

I hope this will be interesting enough for you to include in your new book. Just some notes on my games to give you my side of the fence.

1. The best games (hustles)—HK Gold Jewelry, Watches, Electronics (all fake of course). Then you have the 'note' and 'stuff'

2. Breakdown—Electronics—Ex taking a television or VCR found discard at first in electronic store or for someone's home, cleaning it up, then carefully wrapping it up with brown wrapping paper so the masking tape won't show. Then cut out pictures of a TV, remote control and any wording from a brochure. Tape onto TV or VCR. Then take clear plastic. The kind from a cleaner or storm window plastic and seal the item nice and neat. Leave the screen exposed. The Vic (sucker) must be with a vehicle or access to immediate ride like a cab.

Total cost in expenses $8 for equipment—min return $100. The same can be done with Camcorders. Chances of charges being brought—2 out of 100. Jail time 1 to 3 months.

3. The Note—To whites known as shortchanging. A trick based on lack of math abilities most Americans have. Involves making a purchase with a large bill, ask for change with another bill, confusion sets in and the player (hustler) comes out ahead on purpose. The score, min $9, max unlimited. The charge—theft by deception—max 3 years. Profit min 25k a year. Best Vic, young white girls are primary targets, under 25 years old, because the black male will almost fight you if they wake up to what you are doing.

4. Stuff—also known as the pigeon drop or handkerchief switch. The handkerchief switch is more predominant in the black community than the pigeon. They are basically the same with one exception, the time it takes to separate the Vic from his money, planning and the amount you are going after. In the pigeon drop the player usually (may) have to stalk a Vic for weeks and con him to draw his life savings. In the handkerchief switch they usually con him for what he has on him. The player approaches the Vic with a tale of distress and in need of their help and advice. They are joined by a second player. The tale is strengthened and larceny produced in the Vic to separate him from his money. Min take $500, max unlimited. Jail time up to 10 years. The charge can be robbery. These stuff players MUST travel to keep from being caught.

This is from J, a former black player himself.

Footnote—Blacks do not have the resources to do it as big as our white counterparts so they must do it with whatever resources are available. Most black players do not go into the white communities because they may not be used to dealing with them, so they can be uneducated and scared. The amount of money I mention is small but in the course of a days work, 6 days a week it adds up to 'grand theft' money (min $25K a year). These days I like all people until I discover that they have evil or larceny in their hearts. Remember the best con players are lawyers and advertising men!

With much respect to you Simon,

J

This letter reads like the class notes of a student attending a college for cheating. I found his description of the perfect victim to be very educating indeed. Yep, these guys really are master studiers of mankind!

Did you notice one thing missing from the letter? Not once is any remorse or care for the victim mentioned.

Thanks J for a most interesting look at life from your side of the fence!

The NYPD Pictures

WHEN I DESCRIBE VARIOUS CONS AND HUSTLES TO PEOPLE DURING MY SHOW, *Confessions of a Cheat,* people are often incredulous that anybody would ever fall for such scams. *"Surely,"* they say, *"nobody but an idiot would go for a story like that!"* Tragically of course, they are wrong. These dark operations are a multi-billion dollar a year industry and are taken very seriously indeed by law enforcement agencies.

Thanks to my friends at the NYPD I have in my collection a set of the training videos used to teach their officers about such big money games. These videos are also distributed to senior's clubs and homes to try to protect our elderly citizens who are often the target of such insidious criminals.

If you are questioning whether some of the con games described here are fanciful inventions let's take a walk through the training tapes to lay those questions to rest. You'll recognize the scenarios as variations on cons described elsewhere in these pages and you can rest assured that not only are these games for real, but that they are far more common than you could possibly imagine!

The videos are made in Chicago as part of the Confidence Crimes Prevention and Education Program. They are very well produced and each section is based on actual crimes reported by victims. They are a chilling example of the absolute lack of any compassion or conscience shown by con men and women when pulling their scams.

The videos start with an introduction by Dr. Russell Levy, PhD, chairman of the Crime Justice Program at Lewis University, IL. He stresses that the tapes will not only show the con games but also give good advice on how to avoid the crimes and what to do if you think that you have been taken. It is the advice sections of the tapes that make them such wonderful viewing for the seniors they are shown to.

A short piece by the Superintendent of the Chicago Police stresses that a great many confidence games are played upon the elderly with no compassion being shown for them. There are no punches pulled on these tapes. The con men and women illustrated are not loveable rogues but simple criminals with smooth tongues and ice-cold hearts.

SCENARIO NUMBER ONE

Now we go to scenario number one. Here it is called *The Ruse Entry* but you will recognize it as a variation of the *Roof and Drive Fixing* and *Blue Water Scam's* described a few chapters back.

A senior officer points out that these scams are often pulled on the elderly who can be more trusting, have poor eyesight and who lead quite shut-in lifestyles. The con team has targeted such a lady and noted that her house looks as though it is need of minor repairs.

As they drive up to her house remember, this is not a story, this is a *real* case.

The lady answers her door and sees two workmen scraping away at her steps. A third tells her that they've noticed they need some repair and, since he'd done some work for her son, he'd offered to do the job for free. The woman says that it doesn't look too bad to her but the workman insists that it's okay and that they are happy to do it for her.

A little later there is another knock at the door and the workman is there with two large buckets. He tells the lady that he needs some hot water for the concrete mix. She lets him through to the kitchen and follows along as he keeps up a constant line of chat and questions to her. He turns on the taps to fill his first bucket and comments on her curtains. "*Nice drapes,*" he comments as he feels them.

A short while later a car horn is heard outside but seems not to be noticed by either the workman or the old lady. Having filled his buckets the workman goes outside to continue his work.

Net loss to the old lady: more than $7000.

The whole thing was a set-up from start to finish. When the workman fingered the drapes he was signaling to his two partners that the coast was clear and the noise of the running water covered any noises they made when entering and searching around. Once they had finished their looting (done as quickly as possible) they sounded the horn to let the inside man know that it was time to leave. As simple and as fast as that! They had learned the lady's name from looking at her mail and guessed at her having a son. Had they been wrong they would have apologized and either moved on elsewhere or offered to do the job for free anyway since they had already started.

Older people often keep large sums of cash in their houses and the crooks know that the most common hiding places are under furniture or inside books. They will take anything that strikes their fancy though. In this case the thieves stole a locket that had been given to the lady by her late husband. They have absolutely no respect for money or memories.

The advice given may seem obvious with 20/20 hindsight but is well worth burning into your brain. It's not just the elderly at danger from these schemes! Look at the truck. In this example it was too clean to be used for concrete work. Likewise the 'workmen' were not dressed appropriately for the work. The sign on the van was a magnetic one and thus easily removed. Be very wary of out of state plates (this truck had Florida plates on it). Watch for all of these small things, they add up. If you are told they've been working for a relative (a very common ruse) then phone and check with your family members. Always ask for, and check, ID's. Ask for references and check them. Do not be side-tracked by smooth talk, always check everything you can. Never allow strangers into your home however logical the reason. In this case the poor lady was obviously unaware that hot water is not needed for a concrete mix but it was a huge mistake by the con man. Look and listen for such mistakes.

Perhaps the wisest advice given is not to be embarrassed. Report any suspicions immediately to the police. They won't laugh at you for being silly. It's not, as this poor lady found out, a laughing matter.

The *Ruse Entry*, also known as *Entry by Deception*, for the purpose of burglary (also called *Burning the Victim*) is a Federal Offense and is taken very seriously indeed. Methods of entry are limited only by the criminals' fertile imagination and have varied from city employees to workmen to being charity collectors. Don't think you couldn't fall for such a ruse; instead just be real careful whenever anybody knocks at your door.

SCENARIO NUMBER TWO

A charming young lady introduces this tape by warning us all to expect the unexpected in life. She warns us that con men and women prey on the fact that there is a little greed in all of us. We all love to think that we are either getting something for nothing or, at the very least, getting a great deal on something.

We cut to the Mall where we see a lady leaving a jewelry store. She's just got a great bargain! A fine bracelet in a sale where she's saved 60% from the retail price. This happy lady sits down in a rest area before moving on to more shopping and bargain hunting. She's just about to be offered a bargain she could not possibly have anticipated. Let's call this lady the victim from now on.

A lady sits down beside and asks for help. She claims to have found a great deal of money. Forty thousand dollars!

The victim moves to walk away saying that she wants no part of it. The lady follows saying, as she does so, "*Please, I just need help. How do I find out whose money it is? What should I do if I can't find the rightful owner?*"

At this point another lady joins the scene. "*That's an awful lot of money!*" she exclaims as she sees the bundle of notes. "*Have you robbed a bank or something?*" The first lady explains that she's just found the money and doesn't

Simon lecturing the NYPD.

How to Cheat at Everything

know what to do. *"Turn it in to the police,"* says the victim. *"Take the money and run,"* says the second lady.

The first lady says she is very tempted to keep it. She really needs the money. Her husband has left her and she has three kids to support. She is behind on her mortgage payments and the money would be a godsend to her. Our second lady tells the first that if she hands it in and the money is not claimed then she can legally get to keep it after thirty days. She even knows a lawyer who would be happy to help sort it all out for her. The first lady is thrilled to be getting all this help. *"You two are so kind,"* she says. *"I'd like to share the money with you both. I'm a very spiritual person and this would feel so right to me. We can all share in this wonderful stroke of luck!"*

The second is delighted and says, *"My, my! So in thirty days we'll all have a big windfall. I tell you what I'll do for you. I've just been to the bank to get money and I'm going to give you four thousand dollars as good-will money to help you with those mortgage payments. I was going to get new furniture but, what the hell, since you are being so kind it's the very least I could do. I can get my furniture on the big payday!"*

This leaves our victim in a sticky situation. If the money can be legally theirs to share she is interested but she doesn't have four thousand dollars on her. It doesn't take long though before she decides that she could go to the bank and put in four thousand dollars of good-will money of her own. *"The money can be used to get your kids some school supplies and new clothes,"* she says. Our first lady is overcome with all this kindness and says that this must be her luckiest day ever.

The second lady offers to drive them all, first to the victim's house to pick up her bankbook then to the bank and finally to the lawyer's office. When they get to the victim's house the second lady uses the phone to set up the lawyer's appointment and then the three happy ladies go off to the bank. Along the way our victim asks if it is really all right to share the money. *"Sure,"* says the second lady. *"It's probably just dirty money anyway. We'll all put it to much better use! Anyway, it's fun to be greedy sometimes!"*

Our victim picks up her money and, back in the car, the forty thousand dollars along with the four thousand dollars of 'good-will' money from the second lady and the four thousand dollars from the victim are put into a pouch-like purse. *"We'll keep all the money together,"* says the second lady. *"We'll call this our good-will pouch!"*

The dynamic trio arrives at the building where the lawyer's office is located. The first lady asks the other two to go ahead. She feels too embarrassed to go up with them and wants them to go ahead first. She gives our victim the pouch with the money and says, *"I know it sounds stupid but I feel a bit like a criminal here and I'm just too shy to do this. Please can you do this for me?"* The second lady thinks this is a bit silly but agrees to go on up to see her lawyer with the victim.

At the elevator the second lady says she needs to use the bathroom. *"Here, you take this up to Mr. Berns,"* she says to our victim. Then she continues,

"I'll be right on up. Don't worry he's expecting us, I told him all about it on the phone!"

The victim enters the elevator and pushes button number thirteen, the floor Mr. Berns office is located on.

Net loss to the victim: $4000.

Astute readers will have recognized this as an elaborate version of the *Pigeon Drop*. The pouch, somewhere along the way, has been switched for one full of cut up newspaper and by the time the victim realizes that Mr. Berns does not exist the two partners will be long gone.

The victim was carefully picked out because of her nice clothes and the expensive jewelry purchase she made. She was a lady with money and an eye for a bargain.

The roll of money was a fake. It contained just two $100 bills one on the outside and one sticking out of the middle of a bunch of $1 bills. This type of fake roll is known as a *Michigan Bankroll*.

The second lady is the key element to the working of the con here. It is her job to become friends with the victim and to lure or *steer* her along during the playing of the game. She will be highly skilled at answering any questions and very persuasive about the legitimacy of the events unfolding.

The tips given on the tape may, again, seem obvious but are well worth reading and thinking about. This game comes in many forms with the most common being a found wallet. Whenever anybody approaches you with a 'find' suggest they turn it in to the police and walk away. The police have noted that shopping malls, banking areas and bus stations are the most common areas for this crime and advise special care there. Perhaps the most important advice given is to *never* get into a car with a stranger and *never* take them to your house and invite them in. This could have been much more serious than simple money loss. It could have turned into a kidnapping or, at worst, a murder.

Finally the viewer is reminded to report the crime. So many crimes of this type are not reported to the police because the victim feels that they will look foolish. The only foolish thing is in not reporting it!

I should remind you that, once more, the above was based on an actual case.

SCENARIO NUMBER THREE

There may be good news for our victim in the previous case after all. Two weeks after reporting her theft she gets a call from the local police. They need her to come to the police station along with her bankbook to show the money withdrawal and also to identify two potential suspects. Since she doesn't drive they are happy to pick her up.

The police arrive and, after locking her door, the victim drives down to the local police station with them. The two detectives with her are very helpful on the journey and assure her that they will do their best to make it as easy as possible for her. At the station one even goes inside to see how things are going along. He returns and informs them that it's a madhouse inside. *"We'll do the check out here."* He shows the victim two photographs and asks her if these are the two ladies. The victim is delighted, they've got the right two and she'll do everything she can to see them put in jail!

"That's good," says the first detective. *"But to put them away we need their partner. He's a guy that works at the _____ bank."*

"But that's the bank I use!" exclaims the victim. This doesn't surprise the detectives who tell the victim that it's very common for a team to pick a victim that they can control at every step. Now, would the lady be willing to help catch the third member of the team? She agrees to do whatever she can.

They ask her how much money she has in her account and she replies a little over $15,000. They nod to each other; this is enough to get him on bank fraud charges. They want her to withdraw $15,000 from her account in cash, She will, of course, be given a police registered check for the amount. The victim is told not to worry because Mr. Robbins, the bank president, is fully aware of the sting operation. The victim is happy to help, she really wants to see these criminals put away for a long time.

After the withdrawal and much careful note taking the victim is dropped off at home. She is given her check but told not to deposit it until the next afternoon after the third man is arrested. She is also told not to mention this to any other officers as this is a major undercover operation that could be blown by the slightest leak.

Net loss to the victim: $15,000.

Total loss to the victim: $19,000.

This scam, known as *The Badge Play* or *Come Back*, is very common after a con game and particularly so after a *Pigeon Drop*. The police estimate that you have a better than 50-50 chance of this being played on you if you have fallen foul of a *Pigeon Drop*!

The two 'detectives' were partners of the original two women. They got her phone number during the first part of the con (remember lady number two's call to her lawyer?) and also the amount of money in her accounts (the ladies 'peeked the poke' at some stage of the first con).

It is essential to check IDs carefully. Real police IDs are quite complex and involve names, SS#'s and/or work numbers and often a holographic image. Check these carefully along with a badge. If in any doubt call the police station to check. Even after the very first call we are told to take the 'officer's' number and to call the station back just to be absolutely sure.

The police would never conduct business of this type in a car park. It would always be done in an office at the station. Also they would never show just photographs of the criminals. The legal system dictates that a number of potential criminals are shown for the victim to pick from.

Last, and most critical of all, the police would *never* ask you to supply personal funds in order to catch a criminal as part of any sting operation.

Knowledge of these simple rules would have helped this lady keep her money more or less intact.

The tape then shows a summary of how a real follow up would be done including the use of a codeword between the lady and the police so that she'll know when she is dealing with the real thing or not.

These tapes are currently being used to educate the police and the elderly about the actions of criminals. They do a pretty good job of doing so. Sadly, there is very little that can prepare anybody for the real thing. You can just hope to be as careful as you possibly can be at all times.

Don't ask, "*Who would fall for this idiocy?*" Instead just realize that people do, each and every day. Don't be one of them!

Conned them again!

How to Cheat at Everything

Some Specialty Cheats

THERE ARE SOME PEOPLE WHO WILL TELL YOU THAT SOME GAMES JUST CAN'T BE cheated at. But Freddy says, "*If a game is played for money then it will have been cheated at.*"

That means everything from *Tiddlywinks* to *Scrabble*.

Here are some of Freddy's little specialty hustles along with some more amusing betchas.

SCRABBLE

Freddy and his associates went through a big phase of playing Scrabble for money. Instead of counting points for fun they counted them as five dollar bills. A score of forty on a word would be worth two hundred dollars for example! There was too much at stake for Freddy to leave it down to lady luck and intellectual ability.

Freddy used a version of the Seven Card Poker Deal to help himself along.

When he reached into the bag containing the tiles, he wouldn't take the number of tiles that he needed. He'd take one or two more.

These extra tiles would be palmed and hidden on his lap.

By using very simple *mucking* techniques, Freddy was now able to play with nine or ten tiles instead of seven. This gave him a huge edge over the opponents and he, as is his want, took the money.

He just had to be *real* careful not to lay down an eight letter word!

CHESS

Freddy doesn't play Chess at all. It is rarely played for the kind of money he likes to play for and, as he says, "*It takes two or three hours to play just one game!*"

So it came as a shock to me to learn that, a few years ago, Freddy had taken on a challenge bet with a Chess Master who had been needling him about skill versus games of chance.

Freddy had offered to play *ten* of the Chess Master's top students simultaneously. All games to be played to the finish so that there could be no arguments. Freddy had to get at least a draw to take the one thousand dollar bet. I pointed out to him that with the club's high standards it would be unlikely that he'd get a draw in one game, never mind draw or win over the ten games. He shrugged and said, *"Don't worry, I'm going to cheat."* I couldn't see any way he could do so and went along to watch the Master Cheat take on the Master Chess Player.

Freddy won his bet. He drew four games, won three and lost three making the match a draw.

Back at his house Freddy was so pleased by how simple it had been that he couldn't resist telling us how it had been done.

It was little short of genius! He didn't even have to know how to play the game to win the bet!

Freddy knew that he couldn't win the match himself and so he engineered a draw by playing a kind of postal Chess. He arranged the boards at the match so that players 1-5 were playing white and that players 6-10 were playing black. When player one made his move Freddy repeated that move on board number six. When player six made his reply Freddy did the same on board one.

Using this system all along the line meant that Freddy wasn't actually playing at all. Player one was playing player six, player two was playing player seven and so on.

Actually Freddy could neither win or lose the match. He *had* to draw.

GOLF

Like a lot of hustlers Freddy is a very good golfer and often plays for high stakes.

But, as ever, he does like to have an edge. Would you like to add ten or twelve yards onto your eight iron shot? Would you like help straightening out a slice or hook? Try rubbing a thin smear of Vaseline onto the club face before taking your shot but don't let your opponents see you do it. In the PGA it's illegal and your friends may consider it rather bad form. Freddy hides his Vaseline in his cleaning cloth.

Freddy also has a habit of complimenting all of his opponent's bad shots. He'll always have a reason for an awful shot being a great one. *"If you've got a reasonable lie in the woods you've cut a hundred yards off the hole, what a shot!"* Any time they play a good shot he will say, *"Bad luck,"* and have a reason why your beautifully played shot is placed badly. *"Yeah it looks good there in the fairway but the locals will tell you that it brings the Death Trap Bunker too close to play. Sorry, I thought you knew or I would have told you!"*

This can slowly drive them to dementia and Freddy says that, often, they are lucky to break a hundred!

THE SOCCER BET

In Europe, Soccer is a game that inspires everything from absolute passion to rioting. The game has also become very popular in the US and was given a huge boost when the ladies team won the World Championship in 1999.

When Freddy finds a team fan he will tell them that, much as he admires their team, his team is so much better.

He will then, quite deliberately, name the weakest team in the league.

His comment will be met with much derision and Freddy, in the heat of anger, offers the following bet on points scored over a season. All of his team's points will be added together to make a season's total. His opponent's team's points will be *multiplied* together for a season's total. His opponent, thinking that he is insane will often accept the bet.

When the good team wins, their total will rise rapidly making the opponent very happy indeed. But, they only need one game where they lose. That means no points. And any total multiplied by zero is zero!

Unless his team wins *every* week the unlucky opponent has to end up with a total of nothing! On the other hand Freddy simply needs his team to win just *one* game over the entire season. This bet can be adapted to just about any sport where team positions are decided by points awarded.

"*I'm just a sporting fellow!*" laughs Freddy.

AN EASY POOL SHOT

Nobody in their right mind would bet on a trick shot set up on a Pool table. Even the most petty of hustlers knows that impossible looking shots can be made by a good player combining skill and sneakiness.

Freddy has a whole arsenal of trick shots but keeps them for nights when the boys want to see a little show.

But he does have one neat little bet you might consider taking. He will set up an easy shot on the table and bet you that you can't close your eyes, turn around three times with your hands on your head and then make the shot.

He suggests that you'll be too dizzy to do so.

A great many people, thinking otherwise, have taken on the bet but only a handful have beaten him.

You see while you are busy turning around, Freddy will kindly be holding your cue set for you. Rather unkindly he'll also have liberally wet the tip of the cue with beer.

You'll be lucky to hit the object ball never mind make the shot.

ONE HUNDRED DOLLAR DARTS

This killer bar bet has made Freddy enough money to have several great vacations and a brand new car or two. He doesn't have to cheat to win at the bet, he just has to hustle you into playing it.

He puts a one hundred dollar bill in the center of a dartboard. He fixes it into place by tucking the corners of the bill under the wire section dividers on the board. He can also use thumbtacks or gum on the back to stick the bill horizontally across the center of the board.

All you have to do is, from the throwing line or *Ockey*, throw a dart into the bill. Then take one step forward and throw the second dart into the bill. Finally you have to take two steps back and throw a third dart into the bill. If all three darts hit the bill you've won it. It's as simple as that.

The bill looks like a huge target and you are a pretty good darts player. Sure you'll put up a ten spot of your money for a go at winning Freddy's hundred.

Make sure you have plenty of ten spots ready for extra goes. This shot is so difficult that professional darts players find it next to impossible to hit. The first dart is easy, the second almost always goes high and, should it hit, the third dart is lucky to hit the board at all. Over the years I've seen this bet used I've only ever seen the bill taken once out of hundreds of times.

Try it and see. It looks like it should be an easy win but it's ludicrously difficult.

THREE WHISKEYS FOR A DOLLAR

Freddy is very fond of good Scotch Whiskey but, as a cheat at heart, just hates to pay the full price for it. He will often take a mug for three large measures of the amber nectar with a classic hook, line and sinker bet.

The mug orders a large scotch for the bet. The loser is to pay for it. Freddy covers the scotch with his hat and claims that he will drink it *without* lifting or touching the hat. The mug accepts this fascinating little wager. Freddy bends down under the table and makes some loud slurping noises. Straightening up he claims that he's drunk the whiskey. The mug doesn't believe him and lifts up the hat to check. At that point Freddy grabs the whiskey and drinks it to win the bet. You see, he didn't touch the hat, the mug did!

Freddy offers to teach the mug the bet properly so that he can use it to take his friends. The mug gets another large whiskey and Freddy covers it with the hat. He teaches the mug the opening chat line but, when the mug dips under the table to *practice* his slurping noises, Freddy lifts up the hat, and drinks the whiskey. He replaces the glass and covers it with the hat before the mug straightens up. "*I've drunk it,*" says the mug using his newly learned patter. Freddy lifts the hat to reveal the empty glass and cries out, "*My God, you have drunk it! How did you do that?*"

Freddy now explains the second stage of the bet to the mug. Now Freddy offers one more go at it. The mug knows both ways the bet can be done but Freddy is still prepared to bet him a dollar that he can still do it. For a dollar bet he'll drink a large whiskey without touching the hat. The mug willingly agrees. There is no way that Freddy can beat him here. The mug gets the large whiskey and covers it with the hat.

He was right. There is no way it can be done. Freddy lifts up the hat and drinks the whiskey.

"*But, but, but you touched the hat,*" the mug protests.

"*So I did,*" says Freddy, "*There's your dollar.*"

Freddy pays the dollar.

And that's how you get three large whiskeys for a dollar. You can see this betcha, along with others, on my video *The Party Animal*. It was also featured on the popular television sitcom *Cheers* performed by Harry Anderson in his role of Harry the Hat.

HEADS OR TAILS

A great many games are started by tossing a coin. A player calls heads or tails and the winner gets the choice of who starts the game.

In a game of Pool or Darts this decision can be crucial. Freddy will therefore cheat the toss.

He doesn't need a faked coin for this, just an ordinary quarter and a modicum of skill.

Freddy has practiced a *perfect* toss. By this I mean that when he tosses a coin he can throw it to the same height every single time. This is much easier to do than it sounds. Freddy keeps his eyes straight in front of himself. Then he tosses the coin to the height of his eyes. He can repeat this toss over and over again. When I questioned his ability to do so he immediately threw twenty-three heads on the trot for me. The odds on doing that by chance are one in ten million or, to put it another way, nine million, nine hundred and ninety nine thousand, nine hundred and ninety nine to one against. I never doubted Freddy again.

Freddy sets his perfect toss with a dry run, noting how the coin falls. From then on he can throw heads or tails to order.

If the opponent tosses the coin Freddy always calls heads. The tail side of most coins has a stronger design on it than the head side. This gives it a tiny bit of extra weight. Freddy calls heads because the tails side will have a tendency to fall down because of this extra weight. It really is a minute advantage but, as we've seen, Freddy will take any advantage he can.

FREE CHRISTMAS POSTAGE

Freddy's pal the Minx loves to send Christmas cards but hates the high cost of postage. With the help of her son and his nice new computer system she's worked out a way of getting all of her stamps for free. She gets her son to print up some garish looking copies of stamps on his computer. She likes them to be of brightly colored cartoon characters, as wild as possible. Her son takes time to do a great job for her. She gives him extra TV time for each passable sheet.

The Minx then walks into an office or business looking for all the world as if she belonged there. She is carrying a stack of envelopes and her 'stamps'. She asks the person in the office to exchange the stamps because she needs to send some very important quotes off and doesn't want to use the silly looking stamps for them. The office clerk might think she's a bit of a grouch but exchanges the stamps. After all, the Minx looks pretty important.

The Minx walks out with lots of nice free, legal stamps. The Minx has also exchanged the sheets of fake stamps for cash.

"Gotta pay for that computer somehow," she says. I reminded her that she got the computer for free. *"Whatever,"* she replied.

FIFTY DOLLARS MINUS A BEER

This little number dropped out of favor for a while but is making a big come back with the variation I'll tell you about after you've seen the original version.

Freddy, holding court at the bar, offers to show the bartender a great magic trick. Now Freddy has already shown a couple of great card and coin tricks so the bartender is happy to see one more. Freddy asks him for a fifty dollar bill. *"Don't panic,"* he'll say, *"I'm a magician, not a thief. You'll get the bill back!"*

He gets the bartender to sign his name across the bill and then, Freddy folds up the bill. Slowly he opens his hand and the bill has vanished! Freddy then goes into a comedy routine of not being able to find the bill. He checks his wallet, not there. He looks in the card case, there's a bill there but it's a twenty. *"Whoops! Must have forgotten to give that one back!"* he says to much hilarity. Freddy has a lot of jokes here but finally, as all great magicians do, he sets up the climax of the effect.

"Since I can't find your bill here, I'll have to make it appear somewhere impossible!" he cries, *"Presto, Malagoolo, MacKorkan! My friends, you are not going to believe this but his signed bill is in the cash register!"* The bartender checks the cash register and there, to everybody's absolute astonishment is the signed bill! They all agree that it's one hell of a trick.

It is a good trick. It's also just made Freddy around forty-five dollars.

You see when Freddy vanished the bill he actually sneakily handed it to Sam. While Freddy was going through his jokes Sam went to the other end of the bar and bought a beer from one of the other bartenders. He paid for it using the fifty dollar bill. The fifty dollar bill ends up in the till just where Freddy needs it to complete his effect and Sam gets the beer plus the change!

"*Now that's magic!*" says Freddy.

These days the stunt has come back in a slightly different form. Sam goes to the bar and buys a beer. He gives the bartender a fifty dollar bill and gets his beer and change.

Enter Freddy who goes to the bar and, from a different bartender, orders a beer and pays for it with a five dollar bill. When his change of a dollar or so comes back Freddy says, "*I gave you a fifty!*" The bartender protests that it was a five but Freddy checks his money and says, "*No, it was a fifty. I remember writing a phone number down on it. I'd been chatting to my friend Sam and he gave me a contact number I needed. I just jotted it down on the bill and I don't have it now. Can you please check your till?*"

The bartender opens the till and there is a fifty dollar bill with, thanks to Sam in more ways than one, a phone number scribbled on it. Freddy can even tell the bartender the name by the number if he has to. What can the bartender say? You're right, he can say nothing and hands over the change thinking that he must have just made a very silly mistake. At the end of the night, when the till is found to be short the money will probably have to be made up by the bar staff. But, as you've learned, that doesn't bother Freddy at all.

THE EXPLODING BEER BOTTLE

Freddy loves this betcha for its amusement. It isn't a big money maker being played, at best, for a dollar or two but it does make a very satisfying mess.

Freddy sets an open bottle of beer on the bar. He bets you that he can empty that bottle of most of its beer without moving it. He won't, he tells you, use something sneaky like a straw. The bottle won't be moved, tilted or altered in any way but most of the beer will come out.

The secret of the bet is that Freddy hits the bottle with a thick glass right on top of the opening. This compresses the gas in the bottle and the beer, or most of it anyway, will shoot out everywhere. Certain beers work better than others with Guinness creating a particularly gruesome mess. The stunt also works very well with fizzy sodas like Coca-Cola and Pepsi.

If you try this do be very careful not to clout the bottle too hard. Freddy and I saw one of his pals try to duplicate the stunt after seeing it. He got a little over confident and really whacked the bottle hard. The result was a smashed glass, smashed bottle and a gash in his thumb requiring eleven stitches. He also lost the bet because although the beer left the bottle, the bottle had been altered! He was not a happy camper!

TIDDLYWINKS

Freddy has never met anybody who will play Tiddlywinks for money.

But his five year old niece plays for candy with her friends.

Thanks to Freddy she is in grave danger of needing false teeth by the time she reaches her early teens. You see Freddy made up a special set of Tiddlywinks for her. She plays with the ordinary ones and is getting pretty good at the game. Her friends play with ones that have been loaded on one side. Those little plastic disks just won't fly straight for them.

Freddy says that he is not training her to be a hustler. He says that he just loves seeing the smile on her face when she shows him all the candy bars that she's won.

Freddy is also delighted that she knows the rules of his world.

She *always* gives him ten percent of the take.

"Never give a sucker an even break"

Edward Francis Albee

*"When that hatless, barefooted, one gallus thing
called luck frowns, a man sins against good gambling
if he don't quit"*

Frontier gambler, Ben Thompson

Playing Life To Win

Y OU HAVE NOW HOPEFULLY LEARNED A GREAT DEAL ABOUT THE METHODS OF cheats and hustlers. You've seen how even a friend can take your money with a bewildering variety of games, cons and outrageous bets.

But if you are playing a game and are playing badly you'll lose whether you are being cheated or not. Playing badly means that you'll lose to any other player with any level of experience or honest skill. You can spot a cheat but can you play the game?

Follow Freddy's guidelines to win, and keep on winning, in a fair game.

Do learn everything you can about cheating methods that could be used in your game. Learn how to spot them and how to nullify them being used as much as possible. This book is good starting point for you to be able to do so.

Whatever the game be sure that you know *all* the rules. If you are playing away from home be absolutely sure of any local rules before starting to play for money.

Always be in tiptop condition, both mentally and physically. If you have worries on your mind or feel tired then don't play for money. To win you need to be able to concentrate and feel good.

Play with a professional attitude. If you feel bad about picking up a big pot then you have no right to be playing for money. There are no friends at the gaming table. It's strictly business, however low the stakes.

Never try to bet bigger to get back early losses. Keep to a conservative stake play throughout the game.

Watch other players closely. They may give themselves away with particular reactions or habits. Jim, for example, may always scratch his nose when he is about to bluff. These reactions and habits are called *tells*. Learn to read your opponent's tells and use this knowledge to go for the throat. For the same reason don't talk at a gambling table except where necessary and try to vary your actions. You don't want to give any information to others that can be used against you. Poker is often said to be a game where, "*You don't play the cards, you play the man.*" Now you know why.

Never drink while gambling. It dulls the senses.

Always vary your style of play through a game to keep your opponents guessing. Work hard not to get into the rut of playing the game the same way each time.

Never let another person look at what you have hidden in the hole. He may be a shill for another player. Even if they aren't a shill *their* emotional response may give something away about the hand you've so skillfully given nothing away about. When playing cards look at your hand and put it down on the table. If you keep checking the cards you are giving others a chance to see them as well.

Always keep your eyes open. Look at the cards in a Stud Poker game and use the exposed ones to adjust your play. So few players pay attention that they make very stupid bets indeed. Don't be one of them.

Do develop willpower. Set a time for playing and stick to it regardless of winnings or losses. To play in a game you need to be starting out with about forty times the betting limit at least. If your game is a little fifty cent maximum Friday night game then you need at least twenty dollars in your stash to prevent you being killed off early in the game with a run of bad luck. Be prepared to lose that money without any worry. This will help you to avoid developing the crassly stupid habit some players have of plunging in to try to win back money they can't afford to have lost. If you lose your stake it's time to get out of the game. Never borrow money in order to play on. If you reach your time limit it's also time to leave the game, however much you are ahead or behind. Ignore any carping from others about, "*Just one more hand.*" Playing this way you will limit losses to what you can afford and, hopefully, allow you to hold on to some of those winnings.

If you are nervous about pushing a good hand to the limit then don't play for money. A good gambler requires ice-cold nerve to maximize his winnings.

Never play to a system. Systems have been, and are still being sold promising to *guarantee* winnings in every game from Blackjack to Roulette. They don't work. Look at it this way: if you had an infallible system what's the last thing you would do with it? That's right, the last thing you'd do is advertise it! The only people who make money from these systems are those who sell them. Avoid them at all costs. If you need convincing a little further let me tell you about a conversation I had with a casino owner. I asked him what he would do if a player phoned him up and said that they had an unbeatable roulette system and were willing to bet up to a million dollars on it at the casino. The player would gleefully guarantee to clean out the casino and bankrupt it. The casino manager, without a pause, replied, "*I would charter an aeroplane of his choice to get him to my casino before anybody else found out about this nut.*"

Spend time learning the odds. It may be a little less exciting to play a mathematically based game but it will pay you in the long run. One of the greatest Poker players of all time, Pug Wilson, was renowned for both his dead-pan face and ability to calculate complex odds in his head with the speed of a computer. *"Just remember,"* he was so fond of saying, *"nobody, but nobody, can beat the law of averages over the long run."*

If you are playing cards break the above rule a few times to bluff on one or two hands. If you only ever push a solid hand then other players will take it as a tell that you do so. One or two bluffs will pay big dividends later on. If you win on a bluff *don't* show your cards. Wait till you lose a bluff and are forced to do so. That way nobody can be sure if you have a good or bad hand. *"To put it another way,"* says Freddy, *"never show your cards unless they pay to see them."*

Remember that nobody (except perhaps a cheat like Freddy) wins all the time. Accept the fact that, despite your fine playing tactics, you are going to be down at the end of the night on some occasions. Learn to minimize losses and maximize your winnings. A professional gambler will never stay in a Stud Poker hand to chase a last card if the odds are against it turning up, especially if it will cost him a big bet to do so. Some players chase cards with a lemming like stupidity. Everybody gets lucky once in a while but all the losses can be very costly to your stake.

Never play out of your league. If you can't afford the game then leave it. Perhaps the best advice given on how to win was given by gambling expert, John Scarne, when he said, *"Always play with others who aren't as good at the game as you are."* Avoid no-limit games. If you have a limited stake then a richer man can take your money by buying the pot. In no-limit games the player who starts with the most money is more often than not the player with the most at the end.

Don't play cards with strangers for money.

Never call a man a cheat. Just leave quietly if you suspect that all is not as it should be.

Never play one last hand at the end of the night. As we've seen these, at best, can be insane with players betting more than normal. They are also a prime time to bring in a big hustle.

Do read through this book again to reacquaint yourself with the tips and tactics it contains. Learn to think like a professional each and every time you play.

If you think that the advice given here, and, indeed, throughout the book, sounds too ruthless and nasty think again. If you think that you shouldn't be so suspicious and untrusting of people, if you think that nobody could be so callous and vicious as Freddy and his associates, if you believe in lady luck, then there is one last piece of advice just for you:

Never, never, never play anything for money.

Get out there and be a winner! When you do pick up a big pot tell them Freddy sent you!

A Tale For The Wise

YOUR TREK THROUGH FREDDY'S WORLD IS VERY NEARLY OVER FOR NOW. AFTER careful study and revision a cheat will find it much tougher to take your money than before in a rigged game of cards or dice. He'll be frustrated by the way you constantly turn down his simple propositions and proceed to carefully explain odds to him. He'll be amazed at how easily you turn down his *easy money* ideas or games. You are well on your way to holding onto your hard-earned money.

But just in case you are ever tempted to buck the odds of life again, here's one last tale from Freddy to put the icing on the cake for you.

Albert Fisher was a sad man. It was the last day of the worst holiday he'd ever had. Not only had he lost money at the little game with three cards but he'd also dropped a bundle on a game of Backgammon on a train trip. A game he'd learned was called Razzle had taken just about every penny he had and now his wife had screamed bloody murder at him for being such an idiot. Just before he'd stormed out of their hotel she had been threatening divorce. Now Albert was wandering the streets of London with just a crumpled five pound note in his pocket.

In a dejected mood he was wondering how he was going to calm his wife down. He really didn't want to go through the rest of his life with her thinking he was a complete jerk.

He paused outside the brightly lit entrance to what looked like a nightclub.

"*Go in,*" said a voice in his ear. "*Go in!*"

Albert looked around. There was nobody there.

"*I am the god of luck,*" the voice whispered. "*I've been sent here to help you. Go inside.*"

It was then that Albert noticed that he wasn't standing outside a nightclub. It was a rather nice-looking casino. In a daze he walked into the club and paid the three pound membership fee. He paid another pound for a watered down glass of beer. With his final pound he bought a single chip.

"*Go to the Roulette table and put it on number thirty-one,*" the voice whispered.

Albert did as he was commanded. The wheel circled around. The ball rattled and bounced. It finally settled in number thirty-one.

"*Whoopee,*" said Albert.

"*Whoopee,*" said the voice. "*Now put it all on number seven!*"

The wheel was spun again. The ball landed in number seven.

"*Hooray,*" said Albert looking down at over twelve hundred pounds worth of chips.

"*Hooray,*" said the voice. "*Stick it all on number one!*"

"*Bloody hell,*" whispered the pit boss with an impending feeling of gloom. He phoned up to his boss as Albert placed his chips on number one.

The wheel was spun again. The ball seemed to take forever to settle. When it finally did Albert saw it neatly sitting in number one.

"*Yeah!*" shouted Albert.

"*Yeah,*" shouted the voice. "*Get it all on zero!*"

"*Jesus,*" whispered the casino owner who had just arrived on the floor after the frantic phone call. Albert's pile of chips was now worth over forty-six thousand pounds. The pit boss closed his eyes and prayed. All to no avail. The ball popped, like a trained seal, into the zero. Albert had won again.

"*Yeah, yeah, yeah!*" he screamed.

"*Yeah, yeah, yeah!*" said the voice. "*One last bet Albert. Put it all on thirty!*"

The casino boss watched Albert place a bet of over one million five hundred thousand pounds onto thirty. He couldn't believe that he'd been so short sighted as to allow a few no limit tables at his casino. With a sigh he watched the action unfold. The dealer, with sweating palms, spun the wheel. "*No more bets,*" he said somewhat redundantly. Nobody but Albert was betting anywhere in the casino. Every single bettor was looking at Albert and the biggest bet any of them had seen in their lives.

The ball circled the wheel. It bounced and leapt.

And landed in number eight.

"*Thank God for that,*" whispered the casino owner, his belief in the odds renewed.

"*What a shame,*" cried the bettors as they turned back to the games.

"*Oh @#%&,*" said the voice in Albert's ear as it faded away forever.

Albert smiled the smile of a man who has just lost a fortune and slowly walked from the casino. At least he'd made his mark. Nobody would ever forget the man who had bet a fortune on number thirty.

The moral of this tale?

Not even a god can beat the odds.

Freddy often adds an extra ending onto this tale. He says that Albert went back to his hotel and, amid much tearful apology, made up with his wife. He promised her that after this particular evening he would never gamble again. She had asked him what had happened.

"*I lost a pound,*" Albert had replied with a wry smile.

Let's Talk Freddy

IF YOU EVER HAD THE DUBIOUS PLEASURE OF TALKING WITH FREDDY YOU'LL NOTICE that his language is peppered with odd sounding words. These words are the language of the professional cheat. You've seen a lot of the language throughout the pages of this book already. Here's a compilation of some of the ones you've read already, some of the older terms and a lot of newer ones. It's by no means all of the language of Freddy's specialized world but it will at least give you some idea of how to talk like a person considered to be *Fast Company*.

Some of the words come from Europe, some from America. Hang out around cheats long enough and there's a good chance that you'll hear a lot of them being used. After reading this you'll know what they mean!

Ace	One English pound.
Action	Gambling activity (often dishonest).
Advance Man	Man who travels ahead of a carnival to arrange for licenses, advertising etc. May also put in the *Patch*.
Against the Wall	Running a con game.
Agent	The operator of a fairground or carnival game.
Alibi Store	Game where the operator always has reasons and excuses for why the player is failing to win.
Apron	Money made from a hustle.
Army Odds	An old expression meaning to quote the correct odds.
Badger Game	A con where a mug is discovered with a woman and forced to pay money to buy silence.
Bale the Kale	To put down a big bet.
Base Dealer	A man who deals cards from the bottom of the pack. Also known as a *cellar man* or *subway dealer*.
Beanshooter	A device used to steal chips or coins in a game.

Beard	A person who lays down bets for a cheat to keep the *heat* from them. Also called a *horse.*
Beef	Any complaint about a game in action.
Berries	Money to bet with.
Belly Strippers	Shaved cards where some are wider in the center than others.
Bevels	Dice which have one or more faces slightly rounded.
Bindle Stiff	An amateur player.
Bird Dog	An informant (often a semi professional cheat) who will guide professionals to a good money game for a fee.
Blanket Roll	A controlled percentage dice shot.
Blister	A method for peeking the top card of a deck. Also used to denote a small bump put into a card.
Blockout Work	A method for marking cards by covering a tiny portion of the back design with matching ink.
Blow	Lose a bet.
Blow Off	To get rid of a mark after they've lost their money.
Bones	Dice.
Bread	Money.
Bricks	Gaffed dice.
Broads	The game of *Find the Lady.*
Broad Tosser	The operator of the above game.
Brush	A partnership move in a card game to get the best hand from two.
Bug	An inveterate gambler who'll lay money on just about anything.
Bull	The police.
Bum Steer	False or bad information.
Bumble	Any dice hustle.
Bundle	A large sum of money.
Bust In	To switch faked dice into a game.
Butterfly	A mechanical dice cup used to switch dice. Used mainly by amateurs.
Cabbage	Money.
Cackle	To rattle dice in the hand so that they make the noise of a fair shake but do not turn get mixed up.
Capping	Adding palmed cards to a deck.
Carny	Carnival worker.
Cart Wheels	Silver dollars.
Case Note	Your very last bet.
Center Deal	A legendary technique for apparently dealing cards from the top while actually dealing them from the center of the deck.

Check Copping	Stealing money from the pot. Also known as Chit Copping.
Clean	Any form of cheating move which can be performed under high pressure.
Clock	To keep track of who is betting the money.
Close the Gates	To move an unwanted person away from the action.
C-Note	One hundred dollars.
Come Through	When a victim realizes they've been conned.
Cool Out	To calm somebody down when they suspect that they've been cheated.
Cooler	A deck of pre-stacked cards which will be switched into the game. The cards are often also marked.
Count Store	A game where the player has to get a number of points to win.
Cowboy	A wild or unpredictable player.
Crimp	A tiny bend in a card or cards.
Cross	Where a mug believes he is in league with a cheat only to get ripped off.
Crossroader	A cheat who works against casino games.
Cull	To sort various cards into position.
Cutout Work	Cards marked by scratching the back design. Also known as *Dandruff*.
Daub	A pasty mixture used to mark cards.
Deadhead	A bettor unlikely to bet much money.
Dime	One thousand dollars. Also called a *G*.
Dip	A pickpocket.
Dizzy-Iizzy	A system player.
Double Deal	Where a cheat deals two cards as one to his hand. Also known as *Dealing the Deuce*.
Double Discard	A bold move where a cheat, in a game of Draw Poker, makes his discard after checking all the cards drawn as well as his hand.
Double Saw	A twenty dollar bill.
Dropping a Cooler	Switching a Cold Deck into a game. Also known as the *Iron Man*.
Drop Shot	A controlled dice shot.
Drubbing	To lose heavily.
Drunken Paw	A high stake bar hustle.
Dumping	Controlling dice thrown from a cup.
Dunsky	An old term for the victim of a con.
Earnest Money	A street gambler's ploy to make you bet.
Easy Pigeon	An naive bettor.
Edge Work	Cards marked on the edges.

Fairbank	To cheat in favor of the player to entice them into playing more.
Fast Company	Sophisticated players aware of at least some cheating techniques.
Fin	A five spot note.
Fix	Bribe or protection money paid to the police or local officials. Also called *Ice*.
First Floppers	Heavily loaded dice.
Fish	A mug with a big bankroll.
Flash	Expensive looking prizes to attract players to a carnival game.
Flat Joint	A fairground game where the player has no chance at all.
Flatty	Operator of a *Flat Joint*.
Floating Game	A regular game without a permanent base of operation.
Flop	A throw of the dice.
Flopping the Deck	A secret reversal of the deck.
Fly Bets	Unorthodox bets.
Four Eyes	A cheat who uses a *Twinkle*.
Frenchy	A gambler who only cheats when they are behind.
Frog	British one pound. Also called a *funt*.
Front Loader	A dealer who accidentally exposes the face or top card of the deck.
Fuzz	The police.
Gaff	A cheating device.
Glim	A tiny mirror also known as a *Twinkle* or *Glim*.
Gorilla	A thousand British pounds.
Go South	To steal money from a table. Also to steal cards or dice.
Goulash	A restaurant or bar that regularly holds dice or card games.
Greek Shot	A highly skilled shot to control a single die from a pair against a backboard.
Half Smart	A mug who knows just a little about cheating and is convinced that he can't be taken.
Hanky Panks	Fairground or carnival games that offer very cheap prizes.
Heat	Pressure on the cheat or con. Also used to denote the police.
Heart	To cheat under real pressure.
Heavy Hand	A hand of cards containing more cards than it should.
Heel Peek	A way of glimpsing the top card of the deck.
High Line Work	Cards marked in a manner that can be felt.

Hip	Has Knowledge.
Hook	A ploy used to make you think that you have a better chance of winning.
Hop	A false cutting technique.
Hot Seat	Every player at the table except you is part of the cheating team.
Hustler	A gambling cheat.
Inside Man	A person who performs the con on a mug.
Jog	A card sticking from the deck used as a marker.
Joint	A carnival concession run by a professional.
Juice Die	Magnetic dice.
Juice Work	Highly sophisticated marking system for cards.
Kick Back	To *cool out* a mug by letting them win some money back (rare).
King Dime	Ten thousand dollars.
Komapa	Forged Money. Also called *Green*.
Lamb	A victim.
Layman	Somebody with no knowledge (commonly used by magicians to describe audience members).
Lettuce	Money.
Live One	A mug with a big bankroll who is ready to be taken.
Location Play	To keep track of a group of cards.
Mack	A woman specializing in love for money cons such as the *Badger Game*.
Maggaret	Fifty British pounds.
Mark	A victim.
Match Up	To make gaffed cards or dice to look identical to those used in big money games where cards or dice are uniquely identified.
Martingale	A system where bets are doubled after each loss. Only for idiots.
Mechanic	A cheat who uses sleight-of-hand.
Mitt	Hand.
Money Store	A carnival game that pays cash rather than prizes.
Monkey	Five hundred British pounds.
Mooch	Whining loser.
Moxie	Guts or courage.
Mouthpiece	A smooth talker who hustles you into a game. Also called a *yapper*.
Muscleman	The heavy of the team. Also known as a *Fourteen*

Week Freddy.

NAP	Not a prayer.
Nut	The cost of setting up a hustle.
Office Work	Secret signals between cheats.
Off the Board	A bookie's term for not taking bets on an event.
Outside Man	A team member who helps set up a con or who stays behind to help *cool out* a mug.
Painter	A man who makes and uses marked cards.
Patch	To bribe.
Patsy	A victim.
Paper	Marked cards.
Peanuts	A tight money player.
Peek the Poke	Find out how much a potential victim can afford to lose.
Peg	To put small dents into certain cards.
Percentage Dice	Dice which favor certain number combinations over a period of time.
Pick Up Stack	A simple method of stacking cards.
Pig	A wallet or purse.
Pigeon	A victim.
Pigeon Drop	An old street con where the victim finds a wallet at the same time as the con man. The victim keeps the wallet (full of paper) after paying the con man a surety. Also called *The Drag* and *The Spanish Switch*.
Plush	Prizes of large stuffed animals, etc.
Poke	The amount of money a victim has.
Pony	Twenty-five British pounds.
Prop	A bet with odds that, while seeming otherwise, favor the cheat.
Push Off	A method of dealing the second card of the deck.
Queer	Forged money.
Queer Pusher	A man who uses or sells forged money.
Rabbit	A victim.
Rabbit Trade	A game full of mugs.
Razzle	A big time fairground or carnival scam.
Rip	To cheat without fear of any comeback.
Roper	A woman who lures a mug into a con.
Sandbagger	A player caught in the middle of two cheats constantly raising. Also known as *Toasting.*
Sanding	Marking cards in play by cleaning the edges.

Sawbuck	Ten dollars.
Shade	A distraction or cover for a move.
Sign on his Back	A known cheat.
Shill	An accomplice of a cheat. Often the only player to win any money.
Skin Game	A game where the cheating is performed as quickly as possible.
Slick Cup	A faked dice cup used with loaded dice.
Slide	A call to a cheat to let the cheat know the police are nearby. Also a way to add a card to a hand by a partner.
Slug	A group of memorized cards.
Slum	Cheap prizes.
Smack	A coin matching game.
Sneak Pocket	A hidden secret pocket for concealing gaffed dice.
Snide	Forged.
Soft Action	A game where it is easy to cheat because the players are complete mugs or are drunk . . . or both.
Splash	To try out the actions of a cheating move without actually doing it. Also called *ghosting the move*.
Spinging	A method of false cutting the deck.
Spoof	A gambling game with coins.
Spooking	Secretly peeking another player's cards.
Strike	A form of second dealing.
String Game	A carnival or fairground game where players try to win prizes by pulling on a piece of string.
Sucker	A victim.
Sucker Work	Ineffectual fakes sold to amateurs as the real thing.
Swinger	A fairground or carnival game where an object has to be knocked over by a bowling ball.
Table Stakes	An agreed amount as a maximum bet.
Tapped Out	No money left.
Tat	Small time bar hustle.
Tear Up	A way to apparently destroy a check while keeping it intact for later cashing.
Tees	Tops and Bottoms. Mis-spotted dice.
Thimbles	The *Three Shell Game*.
Tipp the Mitt	Accidentally show your cards to another player or otherwise give away secret information.
Ton	One hundred British pounds.
Touch	To push somebody for a loan.
Trim	To take a victim's money.
True Cubes	Casino dice milled to one five thousandth of an inch.

Also called *Perfects.*

Veal Cutlet	Old term for a victim.
Vic	Carnival term for a victim.
Victoria	Twenty British pounds.
Vig	A cut of the take. Also the interest on money from a *loanshark.*

Wallman	A lookout for a cheat.
Whip Shot	A controlled dice shot. Also called the *Pique Shot.*
With It	With the carnival.

Yak	A con man who sets up a victim over the phone.
Yuck	A victim.

There are many more examples of Freddy's specialized chat to be found in the pages of this book. Learn them all and you could be well on the way to sounding like a knowledgeable person.

And, if all of this hasn't put you off gambling, then Freddy and I can only wish you the very best of luck.

As Freddy says, "*If you have a hundred thousand dollars in your pocket and go out looking for a big time game then the odds are around three to two.*"

That's not your odds on winning or losing.

That's your odds on living.

A Final Admission

FREDDY THE FOX DOES NOT ACTUALLY EXIST AS WRITTEN HERE. HE IS A COMPOSite of various characters I've met and worked with during my forays into the gambling world.

No one man could hope to be an expert at *every* form of cheating. The professional cheat will often spend years devoted to perfecting a *single* move.

The fact that Freddy does not exist as a single entity is the *only* fiction within these pages. The methods, techniques and hustles are all fact with a capital 'F'.

They are all being used *every* day to take hard-earned money away from the gullible.

Hopefully, now that your study course is over, they won't be being used to take your money.

As a final piece of advice I'd like to offer the following piece from the work of Damon Runyon. It is, perhaps, the most often used quote in books of this type but is still worthy of repetition. From *The Idyll of Miss Sarah Brown*, the quote may well be the wisest words ever written on the subject of gambling with strangers. Sit down with Sky Masterson (to whom the advice is given in the play) and listen carefully.

"Son, no matter how far you travel, or how smart you get, always remember this: some day, somewhere, a guy is going to come to you and show you a nice brand new deck of cards on which the seal is never broken, and this guy is going to bet you that the Jack of Spades will jump out of the deck and squirt cider in your ear. But son, do not bet with him, for as sure as you do you are going to get an ear full of cider."

*"Remember kid . . . I've taught you everything you know . . .
but not everything I know!"*

James Coburn in *The Baltimore Bullet*

Locked up, but not for long, alas Pinard is still in jail.

CPSIA information can be obtained
at www.ICGtesting.com
Printed in the USA
LVHW100958141120
671478LV00009B/87